BEWARE
OF DOG

# THE BIG
## NEW YORKER
### — BOOK OF —
# DOGS

RANDOM HOUSE | NEW YORK

# THE BIG
## NEW YORKER
### — BOOK OF —
# DOGS

Foreword by Malcolm Gladwell

Published in the United States by Random House, an imprint of
The Random House Publishing Group, a division of Random House, Inc., New York.

RANDOM HOUSE and colophon are registered trademarks of Random House, Inc.

All pieces in this collection, except as noted, were originally published in *The New Yorker*.
The publication dates are given at the end of each piece.

Excerpt from "Metamorphoses" by John Cheever, copyright © 1983 by John Cheever (The Wylie Agency LLC).

Grateful acknowledgment is made to the following for permission to print previously published material:

*Doubleday, a division of Random House, Inc., and Faber & Faber:* "Ava's Apartment" from *Chronic City* by
Jonathan Lethem, copyright © 2010 by Jonathan Lethem. All rights reserved. Reprinted by permission of
Doubleday, a division of Random House, Inc., and Faber & Faber.

*The Estate of E. B. White:* "Dog Around the Block" by E. B. White, reprinted courtesy of
the Estate of E. B. White.

*Farrar, Straus and Giroux, LLC, and Sterling Lord Literistic, Inc.:* "Tapka" from *Natasha: And Other Stories* by
David Bezmozgis, copyright © 2004 by Nada Films, Inc. Reprinted by permission of Farrar, Straus and
Giroux, LLC, and Sterling Lord Literistic, Inc.

*Simon & Schuster, Inc.:* "The Dog Star" from *Rin Tin Tin: The Life and the Legend* by Susan Orlean.
Copyright © 2011 by Susan Orlean. Published in the UK by Atlantic Books Ltd. All rights reserved.
Reprinted with the permission of Simon & Schuster, Inc.

Credits for illustrations appear on pages 393–395

Library of Congress Cataloging-in-Publication Data

The big New Yorker book of dogs / foreword by Malcolm Gladwell.
p. cm.
ISBN 978-0-679-64475-0
eBook ISBN 978-0-679-64476-7
1. Dogs—Anecdotes.   I. New Yorker (New York, N.Y.: 1925)
II. Title: New Yorker book of dogs.   III. Title: Book of dogs.
SF426.2.B56  2012
636.7—dc23   2012033699

Printed in the United States of America on acid-free paper

www.atrandom.com

2  4  6  8  9  7  5  3  1

First Edition

*Book design by Susan Turner*

*"Did you woof?"*

# CONTENTS

## TOP DOGS

# UNDERDOGS

*"O. K., I'm sitting. What is it?"*

# FOREWORD

## MALCOLM GLADWELL

Like all emotionally fraught relationships in New York City, the interactions between New Yorkers and their dogs—and *The New Yorker* and the subject of dogs (since we are dealing with a notably intricate Venn diagram here)—are marked by guilt. Those of us who live in tiny, expensive apartments in this crowded, noisy city— who choose to live a life not fit for a dog—suspect that our lives are not fit to share with dogs. We like the fact that we can find fifteen kinds of ethnic food within three blocks of our house, and that the girl across the subway car from us was almost *certainly* on *Law & Order*. But these, we worry, are distinctively human pleasures. A dog is supposed to have a backyard to run around in. A dog needs a good bone and a brisk daily walk through verdant pastureland. So we get a dog—or, at least, we think about getting a dog—and we feel bad about it.

A case in point. In my apartment building, I had to sign a notarized document pledging never to bring a dog into my apartment. Yet every morning I am awoken by the barking of my neighbor's dog. My neighbor signed the same anti-dog pledge I did. But then she went out and got a dog, anyway—smuggling it in and out of the lobby in an Hermès bag, all the while worrying about what the dog thinks of being treated like a piece of contraband.

All three positions in this triad are emotionally equivalent. The co-op board feels guilty about bringing dogs into our building's cramped and sunless apartments, and so bans them. My neighbor defies the ban, and feels guilty about how her dog feels, zipped up in the bowels of her Hermès bag. And how do I feel about being woken up

XIII

at six every morning? Guilty, of course. Me and my selfish desire for the dog to be quiet. Who am I to judge an animal with no other meaningful outlet of self-expression? When the barking stops, I picture the dog retreating to the couch, paws in the air, to talk sorrowfully about its lost puppyhood—and my heart breaks.

You will notice that I have two pieces in this collection. I am proud of each. But I would be remiss if I did not tell you about the most important dog story I have ever written. I wrote it when I was a reporter at *The Washington Post*, and I am convinced that it was why—after I'd spent ten long, lonely years in the newspaper business—*The New Yorker*'s editors finally noticed me.

It was about Taro, an Akita in Bergen County, in northern New Jersey, who had been convicted of biting a young girl—the niece, as it turned out, of the dog's owner. Since canine attacks in New Jersey are a capital offense, Taro was on doggy death row in Hackensack as his owner's frantic last-minute appeals wound their way through the courts. I spent hours with his attorney, a prominent member of the canine bar by the name of Isabelle Strauss. I consulted with Taro's psychiatrist. I painstakingly reconstructed the events that led to Taro's criminal charges, until I was convinced that what the prosecution had claimed was a malicious bite was, in fact, an inadvertent swipe by one of Taro's considerable front paws. It was all a gross miscarriage of justice.

During Taro's trial, a woman named Helen Doody testified that Taro had attacked and killed her Welsh terrier some three years previously. The relevant parts of the transcript still dwell in my mind. Under what possible principle of justice was this evidence admissible?

DOODY: The dog was looking at me. The Akita was looking at me like he had accom-

plished something. He had just a look on his face . . .

STRAUSS: Objection, Your Honor—

DOODY: . . . all blood.

STRAUSS: —to her characterization of what was in the dog's mind.

DOODY: He had a very pleased look on his face and he was covered in blood.

JUDGE: Just describe what you saw. I know this is upsetting. But don't try to tell us what was in the Akita's mind, because I don't know whether you—

DOODY: I can just see his face. I saw his face for weeks in my dreams.

From the courtroom, I drove to Taro's bleak, high-security dog run, and listened as his anguished howl rolled across the surrounding countryside: *whoof, whoof, whoof, whoof, whoof.*

But what is the lesson of the Taro story? As the result of my effort, Taro was pardoned by the governor of New Jersey, Christine Todd Whitman. And upon releasing him from death row, she made a single stipulation: that he leave the state and live out his days on the other side of the Hudson. Governor Whitman looked at what had been done to an innocent Akita by the legal authorities within her jurisdiction and realized that New Jersey was not fit for a dog. And where did she decide *was* fit for a dog? New York! Oh, the irony. We beat ourselves up here in the big city over our cramped and sunless apartments, and we forget that it could be worse. Across the river, in the verdant pastures of New Jersey, a dog is every day denied justice.

A few words about you. You bought this book: several hundred pages on dogs. You are, in other words, as unhealthily involved in the emotional life of dogs as the rest of us are. Have you wondered why you bought it? One possible answer is that you see the subject of man's affection for dogs as a way of examining all sorts of broader issues. Is it the case of a simple thing revealing a great many complex truths? We do a lot of this at *The New Yorker*. To be honest: *I* do a lot of this at *The New Yorker*—always going on and on about how A is just a metaphor for B, and blah, blah, blah. But let's be clear. You didn't really buy this book because of some grand metaphor. Dogs are not about something else. Dogs are about dogs.

Another case in point. One of the first articles in this collection is "Dog Story" by Adam Gopnik. Adam is a friend of mine. He is a brilliant man who lives with his family in an apartment uptown. Adam doesn't just write about how A is actually about B. He specializes in pieces that argue that A is actually about B, and B is an outgrowth of C, and C has a surprising connection to D, and so on, like a elaborate version of a Russian nesting doll, except that every time you open the doll you see a smaller doll inside that is tweaked in a subtle and counterintuitive way. Adam's Russian dolls *mutate*. Except when the subject is dogs. "Dog Story" is about Butterscotch, the dog that Adam's daughter, Olivia, insisted on getting. So what is "Dog Story" really about? What is the doll inside the doll inside the doll inside Butterscotch? Why, it's Butterscotch!

To this day, people ask me the same thing about my efforts on behalf of Taro, the death row dog. What was that *about*, Malcolm? My answer is always the same. It was not *about* anything, except the plight of this brave, incarcerated Akita. Isn't that enough? In a world where one New Jersey dog is not safe from overzealous prosecution, no New Jersey dog is safe from overzealous prosecution. Let us leave the grand gestures and the metaphors to the cat people.

I know what you are thinking right now.

You're thinking that there's a twist about to happen—that I'm going to reveal, dramatically, that "Butterscotch" is, in fact, Taro, exiled from the moral wilderness of Bergen County to a junior six on the Upper East Side. In the Hollywood version of this introduction, that would indeed happen. But this is not Hollywood. This is *The Big New Yorker Book of Dogs*. Taro is Taro. Butterscotch is Butterscotch. Besides, how on earth would Adam find an Hermès bag big enough to sneak an Akita past his doorman?

I have a favorite in this collection. It is Ben McGrath's "Man Blames Dog." It begins, "Pity the poor dog. In this time of heightened fear—of drugs, of bombs, of the things we humans might do to one another—man increasingly asks so much of him." It turns out that a Hell's Kitchen nightclub called Sound Factory had been required by authorities to employ a drug-sniffing dog—in this case, a seven-year-old black Labrador named Fanta. But when the police raided Sound Factory they found Fanta fast asleep. McGrath ever so briefly entertains the notion that Fanta might have been derelict in her duties before he rushes to her defense. Fanta was commuting into the city, we are told, from eastern Pennsylvania, an hour and a half away. The raid happened at six in the morning, at which point Fanta had already been at work for five hours. "So yeah, she was sleeping," her handler told McGrath, and here we have it all: the injured tones, the defensiveness, the guilt over subjecting man's best friend to five hours of electronic music every night. Who among us has not stood in her shoes? "There's nothing for her to do," she went on. "Am I supposed to tell her to stand at attention? I can't explain to her that she must stay awake for no reason."

You will stay awake, dear reader. And with good reason. *Whoof, whoof, whoof, whoof, whoof.*

GOOD DOGS

# SNAPSHOT OF A DOG

## JAMES THURBER

I ran across a dim photograph of him the other day, going through some old things. He's been dead twenty-five years. His name was Rex (my two brothers and I named him when we were in our early teens) and he was a bull terrier. "An American bull terrier," we used to say, proudly; none of your English bulls. He had one brindle eye that sometimes made him look like a clown and sometimes reminded you of a politician with derby hat and cigar. The rest of him was white except for a brindle saddle that always seemed to be slipping off and a brindle stocking on a hind leg. Nevertheless, there was a nobility about him. He was big and muscular and beautifully made. He never lost his dignity even when trying to accomplish the extravagant tasks my brothers and myself used to set for him. One of these was the bringing of a ten-foot wooden rail into the yard through the back gate. We would throw it out into the alley and tell him to go get it. Rex was as powerful as a wrestler, and there were not many things that he couldn't manage somehow to get hold of with his great jaws and lift or drag to wherever he wanted to put them, or wherever we wanted them put. He would catch the rail at the balance and lift it clear of the ground and trot with great confidence toward the gate. Of course, since the gate was only four feet wide or so, he couldn't bring the rail in broadside. He found that out when he got a few terrific jolts, but he wouldn't give up. He finally figured out how to do it, by dragging the rail, holding onto one end, growling. He got a great, wagging satisfaction out of his work. We used to bet kids who had never seen Rex in action that he could catch a baseball thrown as high as they could throw it. He almost never let us down. Rex could hold a baseball with ease in his mouth, in one cheek, as if it were a chew of tobacco.

He was a tremendous fighter, but he never started fights. I don't believe he liked to get into them, despite the fact that he came from a line of fighters. He never went for another dog's throat but for one of its ears (that teaches a dog a lesson), and he would get his grip, close his eyes, and hold on. He could hold on for hours. His longest fight lasted from dusk until almost pitch-dark, one Sunday. It was fought in East Main Street in Columbus with a large, snarly, nondescript that belonged to a big colored man. When Rex finally got his ear grip, the brief whirlwind of snarling turned to screeching. It was frightening to listen to and to watch. The Negro boldly picked the dogs up somehow and began swinging them around his head, and finally let them fly like a hammer in a hammer throw, but although they landed ten feet away with a great plump, Rex still held on.

The two dogs eventually worked their way to the middle of the car tracks, and after a while two or three streetcars were held up by the fight. A motorman tried to pry Rex's jaws open with a switch rod; somebody lighted a fire and made a torch of a stick and held that to Rex's tail, but he paid no attention. In the end, all the residents and storekeepers in the neighborhood were on hand, shouting this, suggesting that. Rex's joy of battle, when battle was joined, was almost tranquil. He had a kind of pleasant expression during fights, not a vicious one, his eyes closed in what would have seemed to be sleep had it not been for the turmoil of the struggle. The Oak Street Fire Department finally had to be sent for—I don't know why nobody thought of it sooner. Five or six pieces of apparatus arrived, followed by a battalion chief. A hose was attached and a powerful stream of water was turned on the dogs. Rex held on for several moments more while the torrent buffeted him about like a log in a freshet. He was a hundred yards away from where the fight started when he finally let go.

The story of that Homeric fight got all around town, and some of our relatives looked upon the incident as a blot on the family name. They insisted that we get rid of Rex, but we were very happy with him, and nobody could have made us give him up. We would have left town with him first, along any road there was to go. It would have been different, perhaps, if he had ever started fights, or looked for trouble. But he had a gentle disposition. He never bit a person in the ten strenuous years that he lived, nor ever growled at anyone except prowlers. He killed cats, that is true, but quickly and neatly and without especial malice, the way men kill certain animals. It was the only thing he did that we could never cure him of doing. He never killed, or even chased, a squirrel. I don't know why. He had his own philosophy about such things. He never ran barking after wagons or automobiles. He didn't seem to see the idea in pursuing something you couldn't catch, or something you couldn't do anything with, even if you did catch it. A wagon was one of the things he couldn't tug along with his mighty jaws, and he knew it. Wagons, therefore, were not a part of his world.

Swimming was his favorite recreation. The first time he ever saw a body of water (Alum Creek), he trotted nervously along the steep bank for a while, fell to barking wildly, and finally plunged in from a height of eight feet or more. I shall always remember that shining, virgin dive. Then he swam upstream and back just for the pleasure of it, like a man. It was fun to see him battle upstream against a stiff current, struggling and growling every foot of the way. He had as much fun in the water as any person I have known. You didn't have to throw a stick in the water to get him to go in. Of course, he would bring back a stick to you if you did throw one in.

ment when, deep in the night, we heard him trying to get the chest up onto the porch. It sounded as if two or three people were trying to tear the house down. We came downstairs and turned on the porch light. Rex was on the top step trying to pull the thing up, but it had caught somehow and he was just holding his own. I suppose he would have held his own till dawn if we hadn't helped him. The next day we carted the chest miles away and threw it out. If we had thrown it

He would even have brought back a piano if you had thrown one in.

That reminds me of the night, way after midnight, when he went a-roving in the light of the moon and brought back a small chest of drawers that he found somewhere—how far from the house nobody ever knew; since it was Rex, it could easily have been half a mile. There were no drawers in the chest when he got it home, and it wasn't a good one—he hadn't taken it out of anybody's house; it was just an old cheap piece that somebody had abandoned on a trash heap. Still, it was something he wanted, probably because it presented a nice problem in transportation. It tested his mettle. We first knew about his achieve-

out in a nearby alley, he would have brought it home again, as a small token of his integrity in such matters. After all, he had been taught to carry heavy wooden objects about, and he was proud of his prowess.

I am glad Rex never saw a trained police dog jump. He was just an amateur jumper himself, but the most daring and tenacious I have ever seen. He would take on any fence we pointed out to him. Six feet was easy for him, and he could do eight by making a tremendous leap and hauling himself over finally by his paws, grunting and straining; but he lived and died without knowing that twelve- and sixteen-foot walls were too much for him. Frequently, after letting him try to go over one for a while, we would have to carry him home. He would never have given up trying.

There was in his world no such thing as the impossible. Even death couldn't beat him down. He died, it is true, but only, as one of his admirers said, after "straight-arming the death angel" for more than an hour. Late one afternoon he wandered home, too slowly and too uncertainly to be the Rex that had trotted briskly homeward up our avenue for ten years. I think we all knew when he came through the gate that he was dying. He had apparently taken a terrible beating, probably from the owner of some dog that he had got into a fight with. His head and body were scarred. His heavy collar with the teeth marks of many a battle on it was awry; some of the big brass studs in it were sprung loose from the leather. He licked at our hands and, staggering, fell, but got up again. We could see that he was looking for someone. One of his three masters was not home. He did not get home for an hour. During that hour the bull terrier fought against death as he had fought against the cold, strong current of Alum Creek, as he had fought to climb twelve-foot walls. When the person he was waiting for did come through the gate, whistling, ceasing to whistle, Rex walked a few wabbly paces toward him, touched his hand with his muzzle, and fell down again. This time he didn't get up.

| 1935 |

*Katharine and E. B. White (and Minnie) in the early 1950s*

## DOG AROUND THE BLOCK

Dog around the block, sniff,
Hydrant sniffing, corner, grating,
Sniffing, always, starting forward,
Backward, dragging, sniffing backward,
Leash at taut, leash at dangle,
Leash in people's feet entangle—
Sniffing dog, apprised of smellings,
Meeting enemies,
Loving old acquaintances, sniff,
Sniffing hydrant for reminders,
Leg against the wall, raise,
Leaving grating, corner greeting,
Chance for meeting, sniff, meeting,
Meeting, telling, news of smelling,
Nose to tail, tail to nose,
Rigid, careful, pose,
Liking, partly liking, hating,
Then another hydrant, grating,
Leash at taut, leash at dangle,
Tangle, sniff, untangle,
Dog around the block, sniff.

—E. B. WHITE    | 1930 |

# DOG STORY

## ADAM GOPNIK

A year ago, my wife and I bought a dog for our ten-year-old daughter, Olivia. We had tried to fob her off with fish, which died, and with a singing blue parakeet, which she named Skyler, but a Havanese puppy was what she wanted, and all she wanted. With the diligence of a renegade candidate pushing for a political post, she set about organizing a campaign: quietly mustering pro-dog friends as a pressure group; introducing persuasive literature (John Grogan's *Marley & Me*); demonstrating reliability with bird care.

I was so ignorant about dogs that I thought what she wanted must be a Javanese, a little Indonesian dog, not a Havanese, named for the city in Cuba. When we discovered, with a pang, the long Google histories that she left on my wife's computer—*havanese puppies/havanese care/how to find a havanese/havanese, convincing your parints*—I assumed she was misspelling the name. But in fact it was a Havanese she wanted, a small, sturdy breed that, in the past decade, has become a mainstay of New York apartment life. (It was recognized as a breed by the American Kennel Club only in the mid-nineties.) Shrewd enough to know that she would never get us out of the city to an approved breeder, she quietly decided that she could live with a Manhattan pet-store "puppy mill" dog if she could check its eyes for signs of illness and its temperament for symptoms of sweetness. Finally, she backed us into a nice pet store on Lexington Avenue and showed us a tiny bundle of caramel-colored fur with a comical black mask. "That's my dog," she said simply.

My wife and I looked at each other with a wild surmise: the moment parents become parints, creatures beyond convincing who exist to be convinced. When it came to dogs, we shared a distaste that touched the fringe of disgust and flirted with the edge of phobia. I was bitten by a nasty German-shepherd guard dog when I was about eight—not a terrible bite but traumatic all the same—and it led me ever after to cross streets and jump nervously at the sight of any of its kind. My wife's objections were narrowly aesthetic: the smells, the slobber, the shit. We both disliked dog owners in their dog-owning character: the empty laughter as the dog jumped up on you; the relentless apologies for the dog's bad behavior, along with the smiling assurance that it was all actually rather cute. Though I could read, and even blurb, friends' books on dogs, I felt about them as if the same friends had written books on polar exploration: I could grasp it as a subject worthy of extended poetic description, but it was not a thing I had any plans to pursue myself. "Dogs are failed humans," a witty friend said, and I agreed.

We were, however, doomed, and knew it. The constitution of parents and children may, like the British one, be unwritten, but, as the Brits point out, that doesn't make it less enforceable or authoritative. The unwritten compact that governs family life says somewhere that children who have waited long enough for a dog and want one badly enough have a right to have one. I felt as the Queen must at meeting an unpleasant Socialist Prime Minister: it isn't what you wanted, but it's your constitutional duty to welcome, and pretend.

The pet-store people packed up the dog, a female, in a little crate and Olivia excitedly considered names. Willow? Daisy? Or maybe Honey? "Why not call her Butterscotch?" I suggested, prompted by a dim memory of one of those Dan Jenkins football novels from the seventies, where the running-back hero always uses that word when referring to the hair color of his leggy Texas girlfriends. Olivia nodded violently. Yes! That was her name. Butterscotch.

We took her home and put her in the back storage room to sleep. Tiny thing, we thought. Enormous eyes. My wife and I were terrified that it would be a repeat of the first year with a baby, up all night. But she was good. She slept right through the first night, and all subsequent nights, waiting in the morning for you past the point that a dog could decently be expected to wait, greeting you with a worried look, then racing across the apartment to her "papers"—the pads that you put out for a dog to pee and shit on. Her front legs were shorter than her rear ones, putting a distinctive hop in her stride. ("Breed trait," Olivia said, knowingly.)

All the creature wanted was to please. Unlike a child, who pleases in spite of herself, Butterscotch wanted to know what she could do to make you happy, if only you kept her fed and let her play. She had none of the imperiousness of a human infant. A child starts walking away as soon as she starts to walk—on the way out, from the very first day. What makes kids so lovable is the tension between their helplessness and their drive to deny it. Butterscotch, though, was a born courtesan. She learned the tricks Olivia taught her with startling ease: sitting and rolling over and lying down and standing and shaking hands (or paws) and jumping over stacks of unsold books. The terms of the tricks were apparent: she did them for treats. But, if it was a basic bargain, she employed it with an avidity that made it the most touching thing I have seen. When a plate of steak appeared at the end of dinner, she would race through her repertory of stunts and then offer a paw to shake. Just tell me what you want, and I'll do it!

She was a bit like one of Al Capp's Shmoos, in *Li'l Abner,* designed to please people at any cost. (People who don't like Havanese find them too eager to please, and lacking in proper doggie dignity and reserve.) The key to dogginess, I saw, is that, though dogs are pure creatures of sensation, they are also capable of shrewd short-term plans. Dogs don't live, like mystics, in the moment; dogs live in the *minute.* They live in and for the immediate short-term exchange: tricks for food, kisses for a walk. When Butterscotch saw me come home with bags from the grocery store, she would leap with joy as her memory told her that *something* good was about to happen, just as she had learned that a cloud-nexus of making phone calls and getting the leash and taking elevators produced a chance to play with Lily and Cuba, the two Havanese who live upstairs. But she couldn't grasp exactly how these chains of events work: some days when she heard the name "Lily" she rushed to the door, sometimes to her leash, sometimes to the elevator, and sometimes to the door on our floor that corresponds to the door on the eighth floor where Lily lives.

But she had another side, too. At the end of a long walk, or a prance around the block, she would come in with her usual happy hop, and then, let off her leash, she would growl and hiss and make Ewok-like noises that we never otherwise heard from her; it was a little scary at first, like the moment in *Gremlins* when the cute thing becomes a wild, toothy one. Then she would race madly from one end of the hall to the other, bang her head, and turn around and race back, still spitting and snorting and mumbling guttural consonants to herself, like a mad German monarch. Sometimes she would climax this rampage by pulling up hard and showing her canines and directing two sharp angry barks at Olivia, her owner, daring her to do something about it. Then, just as abruptly, Butterscotch would stop, sink to the floor, and once again become a sweet, smiling companion, trotting loyally behind whoever got up first. The wolf was out; and then was tucked away in a heart-drawer of prudence. This behavior, Olivia assured us, is a Havanese breed trait, called "run-like-hell," though "Call of the Wild" might be a better name. (Olivia spent hours on the Havanese forum, a worldwide chat board composed mostly of older women who call themselves the small dogs' "mommies," and share a tone of slightly addled coziness, which Olivia expertly imitated. Being a dog owner pleased her almost more than owning a dog.)

But what could account for that odd double nature, that compelling sweetness and implicit wildness? I began to read as widely as I could about this strange, dear thing that I had so long been frightened of.

Darwinism begins with dogs. In the opening pages of *On the Origin of Species,* Darwin describes the way breeders can turn big dogs into small ones, through selective breeding, and he insists that all dogs descend from wolves. This was proof of the immense amount of inherited variation, and of the ability of inheritance, blended and directed, to take new directions.

"Who will believe that animals closely resembling the Italian greyhound, the bloodhound, the bull-dog or Blenheim spaniel, etc.—so unlike all wild Canidae—ever existed freely in a state of nature?" Darwin wrote. Out of one, many.

Ever since, what we think Darwinism says has been structured in part by what we think it says about dogs. Darwin's instinct was, as usual, right. Dogs do descend directly from wolves; the two species can still breed with one another (producing many scary-looking new back breeds). The vexed issue is how long ago they parted ways, and why. The biological evidence and the archeological evidence are at war: DNA analysis points to a very remote break between wolves and dogs, certainly no later than a hundred thousand years ago, while the earliest unequivocal archeological evidence for domesticated dogs dates to just fifteen thousand years ago or so.

One haunting scrap of evidence is a grave site in Israel, twelve thousand years old, where what is undoubtedly a dog is embraced in death by what is undoubtedly a woman. It suggests that the dog, completely doglike—smaller cuspids and shorter muzzle—was already the object of human affection at the dawn of the age of agriculture. The fullness of this early relation suggests the classic story of domestication, that of the master man and the willing dog. The historian of science Edmund Russell summarizes this story in his new book, *Evolutionary History:* "Some brave soul burrowed into a wolf den, captured cubs, brought the cubs back to camp, and trained them to hunt by command." Before long, "people realized that tame wolves (dogs) could perform other tasks too. . . . Breeders manufactured each variety by imagining the traits required, picking males and females with those traits, and mating them." If you needed to rid your camp of badgers, you bred one long, thin dog to another until you had a dachshund, which could go down a badger hole. The problem with this view, Russell explains, is that it implies a level of far-sightedness on the part of the first breeders that defies all evolutionary experience: "Wolves do not obey human commands, and it is hard to imagine that people persisted in raising dangerous animals for uncertain benefits far in the future." To see a Butterscotch in a wolf would have required magical foresight, as if our Paleolithic fathers had started breeding leaping mice in the hope that they would someday fly.

And so countering this view comes a new view of dog history, more in keeping with our own ostentatiously less man-centered world view. Dogs, we are now told, by a sequence of scientists and speculators—beginning with the biologists Raymond and Lorna Coppinger, in their 2001 masterwork, *Dogs*—domesticated themselves. They chose us. A marginally calmer canid came close to the circle of human warmth—and, more important, human refuse—and was tolerated by the humans inside: let him eat the garbage. Then this scavenging wolf mated with another calm

*"Speak."*

*"Roll over."*

wolf, and soon a family of calmer wolves proliferated just outside the firelight. It wasn't cub-snatching on the part of humans, but breaking and entering on the part of wolves, that gave us dogs. "Hey, you be ferocious and eat them when you can catch them," the proto-dogs said, in evolutionary effect, to their wolf siblings. "We'll just do what they like and have them feed us. Dignity? It's a small price to pay for free food. Check with you in ten thousand years and we'll see who's had more kids." (Estimated planetary dog population: one billion. Estimated planetary wild wolf population: three hundred thousand.)

The dog maven Mark Derr, in his forthcoming book *How the Dog Became the Dog*, offers a particularly ambitious and detailed version of how the wandering wolf became the drifting dog. He adds to the Coppingers' story many epics and epicycles, including a central role for Neanderthal dog-lovers. Though Derr's book, given the fragmentary nature of the evidence, is sometimes a little fantastical, his motive, only half-disclosed, is touching: Derr isn't just a dog fancier, one realizes, but a kind of dog nationalist, a dog jingoist. He believes that what was an alliance of equals has, in very recent centuries, been debased to produce Stepin Fetchit dogs, like Butterscotch, conscripted into cuteness. Dogs began as allies, not pets, and friends, not dependents.

At a minimum, the theory of the drifting dog can point to some living proof, though not of a kind likely to bring joy to the dog-dignifiers. As the British anthrozoologist John Bradshaw points out in his new book, *Dog Sense*, even now most dogs drift—not as equals or allies but as waifs. In Third World towns, "village dogs" hang around, ownerless, eating garbage, fending for themselves, and getting beaten off only when they become nuisances. (There's a reason that it's called a dog's life.) The usual condition of a dog is to be a pigeon.

The catch is that, from an evolutionary point of view, these village dogs are already dogs. They illuminate the problem. Since the domestication of the dog predates agriculture, dogs couldn't have wandered into settlements; there were no settlements. They couldn't have wandered with hunter-gatherers, because other wolf packs would have marked and owned the next territory. There just doesn't seem to have been enough time for the slow development from wandering wolf to drifting proto-dog without the single decisive intervention of someone to nudge the wolf toward dogdom. "The scenario of self-domestication is very hard to envision if people were still wandering seminomadically, and the evidence says they were," the anthropologist Pat Shipman says firmly in her book *The Animal Connection: A New Perspective on What Makes Us Human*. Anyway, why didn't hyenas and foxes, which have been around for just as long, discover the same advantage in hanging close to people as wolves did?

One explanation, favored by Bradshaw, supposes a classic Darwinian mutation, a full-fledged

*"Heel."*

*"Stay."*

"sport" of nature. At some point, a mutant wolf appeared, by chance, which was not just marginally tamer but far more biddable than any other creature. This sounds odd, but, as Bradshaw points out, dogs *are* odd, essentially unique—the only animal on earth that needs no taming to live with people while still happily breeding with its own. The ability of dogs to make a life with us isn't a product of their being man-bred; it was the change that let men breed them.

More is at stake here than a speculation about the history of one pet species. If the new story is

---

## CIVILIZED

An acquaintance of ours was hailing a taxi at the corner of Park and Sixtieth one recent afternoon when a large English bulldog, promenading in the custody of a chauffeur, and a French poodle, held in check by a uniformed maid, suddenly went for each other, tugging at their leashes and raising an unearthly racket of barks and snarls. According to our man, an apartment-house doorman hurried up to them and called out, "Gentlemen, please!," whereupon the two dogs fell silent and went off in opposite directions without so much as a backward glance.   | 1947 |

---

more or less right, and dogs chose to become dogs (meaning only that the tamer, man-friendly wolves produced more cubs than their wilder, man-hating cousins), then the line between artificial and natural selection seems far less solid, and the role of man at the center less fixed. Indeed, Russell suggests that even our distinct breeds may be more drifts than decisions: "Unconscious selection probably played a more important role than methodical selection because it was simpler and brought benefits in the present. . . . Keeping the dogs best at a certain task in each generation would have steadily enhanced the desired traits." There may be a providence in

the fall of a sparrow; but there is Darwinian contingency even in the hop of the Havanese.

What a dog owner, with the full authority of fourteen months of dog, suggests might be missing from these accounts is something simple: people love pets. Bradshaw, though he likes the drifting dog theory, observes that we needn't justify the existence of pet dogs in our early history by arguments about their value as food or tools. The norm even in the most "primitive" hunter-gatherer societies is to take a pet even though—as with the dingo pups that the Aborigines take in Australia—it always goes "bad" as an adult, and is of no help in any task at all. (The dingoes are feral descendants of domesticated Asian dogs, with their social genes somehow wrenched awry.) For that matter people do live with modern wolves—presumably made more paranoid by millennia of persecution—even now. As Bradshaw writes, "Humans will keep puppies purely for their cuteness." The most useful role a pet may play is to be there for the petting. The way dogs are used now might be the way we use dogs.

Another strange and haunting scrap of evidence about early dog and man is in the Chauvet cave, in southern France: a set of twinned footprints, twenty-six thousand years old, of an eight-year-old child walking side by side, deep into the cave, with what is evidently some kind of hound—a small wolf or a large dog. It may turn out that the tracks come from different times (though their paired strides seem well matched). But for the moment the evidence seems to show that the first dog in all the record was there as the companion of a small boy.

Or girl? Olivias have always wanted Butterscotches. The willing wolf may have wandered into the circle beyond the firelight, but the dog may well have first emerged on the safer side of the fire as the dream companion of a child.

The range of evolutionary just-so stories and speculations is itself proof of the way dogs have burrowed into our imaginations. Half the pleasure of having a dog, I could see, was storytelling *about* the dog: she was a screen on which we could all project a private preoccupation. In addition to the real dog, each child had a pretend version, a daemon dog, to speak to and about. Luke, our sixteen-year-old, imagined Butterscotch as an elderly, wise woman from the Deep South. "Lez not point the finger, childun," he would have her say when she did something naughty. Olivia had her as a hyper-intense three-year-old, full of beans and naïveté. "Oh, and then they took me to the Park, and then we had little scraps of steak, and, oh, Skyler—it was the best day ever," she would report the dog saying to the bird, with the breathlessness of a small child. Even the grownups had a fictive dog who lived alongside the real one: my wife's dog was a year-old baby she had loved and missed (she especially loved the early-morning off-leash hours in Central Park, when the dawn belongs to charging dogs and coffee-sipping owners); mine was a genial companion who enjoyed long walks and listening to extended stretches of tentatively composed prose. Once, I was playing recordings of Erroll Garner on piano, that bright, bouncing, syncopated plaintive jazz sound, and Olivia said, "That's the music Butterscotch hears in her head all day."

What music *does* a dog hear in her head all day? Our dog was so much part of the family that we took human feelings and thoughts for granted and then would suddenly be reminded that she experienced the world very differently. Once, we saw her standing at the top of the steps leading to the sunken living room of our apartment. She began to whine and, as she rarely did, to bark—stepping forward to intimidate some creature we couldn't see, then fearfully stepping back. We were sure from the intensity of her barking that there must be a rodent down by the baseboard that the brave little dog had spotted. Finally, one of us noticed that I had thrown a dark shirt over the back of the white sofa; I picked it up and came toward her with it. She whimpered and then began to staunchly defy her fear by barking again. That was it! She was terrified of a piece of empty brown material. When we tried the experiment again, she reacted again—not so strongly, but still.

So, what music? There is a new literature of dog psychology, to go along with and complement that on dog history. There are accounts of bad dogs cured, like *Bad Dog: A Love Story,* by Martin Kihn; of good dogs loved, as in Jill Abramson's *The Puppy Diaries;* of strange dogs made whole and wild dogs made docile; of love lives altered by loving dogs, as in Justine van der Leun's *Marcus of Umbria: What an Italian Dog Taught an American Girl About Love.* The most scientific-minded of the new crop is Alexandra Horowitz's well-received *Inside of a Dog: What Dogs See, Smell and Know.* (The title comes, winningly, from a fine Groucho joke.) Horowitz, a former fact checker in these halls, has gone on to become a professor of psychology at Barnard, and she's written a terrifically intelligent and readable book, a study of the cognition of those who don't quite have it. She details the dog's sensorium. Dogs have a wildly fine nose for scent: we can detect molecules in parts in the million, dogs in parts in the billion. She explains why they sniff each other's rear—there's an anal gland peculiar to dogs, its secretions as different each from each as a voice—and why that behavior remains mysterious: dogs don't seem to recognize the distinct smell of other dogs and always return to sniff again; yet no dog likes having it done to him.

On either side of the scientific dog writer, Horowitz or Bradshaw, one senses the phantoms of two alpha writers: Cesar Millan, television's "dog whisperer," and John Grogan, the *Marley & Me* memoirist—the pseudo-science of the dog as pack animal, on the one hand, and the sentimental fiction of the all-sympathetic dog, on the other. Horowitz tries to disabuse us dog owners of the Millanesque notion that dogs are really pack creatures looking for an alpha hound to submit to. Dogs, she explains, are domesticated animals, and to treat them as though they were still in a pack rather than long adapted to a subservient role in a human family is as absurd as treating a child as though it were "really" still a primate living in a tree.

Above all, Horowitz details the dog's special kind of intelligence. When other intelligent animals are presented with a deduction or "object permanence" problem—a ball vanishes into one of two boxes; which box did it go into?—most of them solve the problem by watching where the ball goes. The dog solves the problem by watching where his owner looks. Dogs are hypersensitive to even the slightest favoring actions of the owner, and will cheerily search for the treat in the box the owner seems to favor, even if they have seen the treat go into the other. This was the ancestral bet that dogs made thousands of years ago: give up trying to prey on the prey; try pleasing the people and let them get the prey. Dogs are the only creatures that have learned to gaze directly at people as people gaze at one another, and their connection with us is an essential and enduring one.

Yet Horowitz recognizes, too, the threat of the overly humanized view of the dog. She loves dogs in general—and her own mongrel hound, Finnegan, in particular—but throughout the book are rueful hints, perhaps partly inadvertent, that what the science shows is that the entire dog-man relation is essentially a scam, run by the dogs. Certainly, the qualities inherent in breeds—nobility, haughtiness, solidity, even the smiling happiness of the Havanese—are tricks of our mind, where we project primate expressions of inner mood into canine masks. The Havanese isn't happy and the Shih Tzu isn't angry and the bulldog isn't especially stolid or stubborn; they are just stuck with the faces, smiling or snarling, we've pinned on them through breeding. And the virtues we credit them with—whether the big ones of bravery, loyalty, and love or the smaller ones of happiness, honesty, and guilt—are just as illusory. "Maxie looked so guilty when I found her chewing the treat box that it was just hilarious," a "mom" will write on the Havanese forum—but these are illusions, projected onto creatures whose repertory of consciousness is very much smaller. Loyalty, longing, and even grief are, the evidence suggests, mere mimic emotions projected into two far simpler ones that dogs actually possess: adherence to the food-giver and anxiety about the unfamiliar.

We've all heard the accounts of dogs leaping to the rescue, pulling children from the water when the ice cracks, and so on, but Horowitz points out that, in staged situations of crisis, dogs don't leap to the rescue or even try to get help. If a bookcase is made to fall (harmlessly, but they don't know that) on their owner, they mostly just stand there, helpless and confused. The dog may bark when it sees its owner in distress, and the barking may summon help; the dog stays near its family, even when frightened, and that may be useful. But the dog has no particular plan or purpose, much less resolution or courage. This doesn't mean that the recorded rescues haven't happened; it's just that the many more moments when the dog watches its owner slip beneath the ice don't get recorded. The dog will bark at a burglar; but the dog will also bark at a shirt.

Maybe, though, Horowitz and Bradshaw are too quick to accept the notion that the dog is merely a creature of limited appetite and reinforced instinct. Not so many years ago, after all, people in white lab coats were saying exactly the same things about human babies—that they were half blind, creatures of mere reflex and associative training, on whom their dottle-brained moms were projecting all kinds of cognition that they couldn't actually process. Now psychologists tell us that babies are intellectually rich and curious and hypothesis-forming and goal-directed. One wonders if something similar isn't about to happen with pets. The experts, Bradshaw especially, tell us that Butterscotch sits by the door all afternoon because she has been unconsciously trained to associate Olivia's after-school homecoming with the delivery of treats: But what would be so different if we said that she sits by the door because she is waiting patiently for Olivia, has a keen inner sense of what time she'll be home, and misses her because they play together and enjoy each other's company, which, of course, includes

the pleasures of good food? This is the same description, covering exactly the same behavior, only the first account puts the act in terms of mechanical reflexes and the other in terms of desires and hopes and affections. Our preference for the former kind of language may look as strange to our descendants, and to Butterscotch's, as it would if we applied it to a child. (The language of behaviorism and instinct can be applied to anything, after all: we're not really falling in love; we're just anticipating sexual pleasure leading to a prudent genetic mix.)

But, if the reductive argument seems to cheat dogs of their true feelings, the opposite tendency, which credits dogs with feelings almost identical to those of humans and with making the same claims on our moral conscience, is equally unconvincing. In the forthcoming *Loving Animals: Toward a New Animal Advocacy*, Kathy Rudy, who teaches ethics at Duke, makes the case for dog equality just as strongly as Derr does in his more narrowly evolution-minded book. Rudy believes that dogs have been as oppressed and colonized as Third World peoples have, and that what they need is not empathy but liberation. She has a confused notion of something that she calls "capitalism," and which is somehow held uniquely responsible for the oppression of animals, including dogs. Of course, only advanced capitalist societies have started movements for animal rights; precapitalist societies were far crueller to animals, as are non-capitalist modern ones. (Consider the state of zoos and animals in the Eastern bloc or in China.) But her love for dogs is evident throughout. She tells us that "it would not be an overstatement to say that most of the important and successful relationships I've had in my life have been with nonhuman animals," and she makes a passionate case for treating animals as equals in rights, not as commodities to be cynically exploited for research or even, I suppose, for family bonding.

The trouble with arguments for treating animals as equals is that the language of rights and responsibility implies, above all, reciprocity. We believe it to be wrong for whites to take blacks as slaves, and wrong for blacks to enslave whites. Yet animals themselves are generally far crueller to other animals in the wild than we are to them in civilization; though we may believe it to be unethical for us to torment a lion, few would say it is unethical for the lion to torment the gazelle. To use the language of oppression on behalf of creatures that in their natures must be free to oppress others is surely to be using the wrong moral language. A language of compassion is the right one: we should not be cruel to lions because they suffer pain. We don't prevent the lion from eating the gazelle because we recognize that he is, in the fine old-fashioned term, a dumb animal—not one capable of reasoning about effects, or really altering his behavior on ethical grounds, and therefore not rightly covered by the language of rights. Dogs, similarly, deserve protection from sadists, but not deference to their need for, say, sex. We can neuter them with a clear conscience, because abstinence is not one of their options.

This is why we feel uneasy with too much single-minded love directed toward dogs—with going canine, like Rudy in her dog-centered love life. It isn't the misdirection so much as the inequality, the disequilibrium between the complex intensity of human love and the pragmatism of animal acceptance. Love is a two-way street. The woman who strokes and coos and holds her dog too much unnerves us, not on her behalf but on the dog's. He's just not that into you.

The deepest problem that dogs pose is what it would be like if all our virtues and emotions were experienced as instincts. The questions about what a dog is capable of doing—how it sees, smells, pees, explores—are, in principle, answerable. The question of what goes on in the mind of a dog—what it feels like to be a dog—is not. In this context, Horowitz cites a classic article by the philosopher Thomas Nagel, "What Does It Feel Like to Be a Bat?" Nagel's point was that the only way to know what it is like to be a bat is to be one. He writes:

> It will not help to try to imagine that one has webbing on one's arms, which enables one to fly around at dusk and dawn catching insects in one's mouth; that one has very poor vision, and perceives the surrounding world by a system of reflected high-frequency sound signals; and that one spends the day hanging upside down by one's feet in an attic. In so far as I can imagine this (which is not very far), it tells me only what it would be like for *me* to behave as a bat behaves. But that is not the question. I want to know what it is like for a *bat* to be a bat. Yet if I try to imagine this, I am restricted to the resources of my own mind, and those resources are inadequate to the task.

Though we can know that dogs live by smells, not by words, we can't really imagine what it would feel like to be a creature for which thoughts are smells. We, creatures of language who organize our experience in abstract concepts, can't imagine what it's like to be in the head of a being that has no language. To have the experiences while retaining our memory of humanness would make us a human in a dog suit, not a dog. We would have to become a dog, for real; then, reborn as a human, we couldn't explain to ourselves, let alone someone else, what it's like to be a dog, since the language of being-like isn't part of what being a dog is like.

Yet, for all the seemingly unbridgeable distance between us and them, dogs have found a shortcut into our minds. They live, as Horowitz and Bradshaw and Rudy, too, all see, within our circle without belonging to it: they speak our language without actually speaking any, and share our concerns without really being able to understand them. The verbs tell some of the story: the dog shares, feels, engages, without being able to speak, plan, or (in some human sense) think. We may not be able to know what it's like to be a dog; but, over all those thousands of years, Butterscotch has figured out, in some instrumental way, what it's like to be a person. Without language, concepts, long-term causal thinking, she can still enter into the large part of our mind made up of appetites, longings, and loyalties. She does a better impersonation of a person than we do an approximation of a dog. That it is, from the evolutionary and philosophical point of view, an impersonation, produced and improved on by generations of dogs, because it pays, doesn't alter its power. Dogs have little imagination about us and our inner lives but limitless intuition about them; we have false intuitions about their inner lives but limitless imagination about them. Our relationship meets in the middle.

One day, around Christmas, I got a mixed box of chocolates—milk for Olivia, darks for me—and noticed, in the evening, that some were missing, and that Butterscotch had brown around her muzzle. "She's eaten chocolate!" Olivia cried. Chocolate is very bad for dogs. She went at once to the forum. "My hand trembles as I write this," she typed, "but my baby has eaten chocolate!" Blessedly, we got an avalanche of counsel from Havanese-lovers all over the world: check her, watch her, weigh a chocolate, weigh the dog, keep an eye on her all night. Finally, I put her to bed in her back room, and promised Olivia I would monitor her. Olivia chewed her lip and went to bed, too.

It can't really be dangerous, I thought; I mean, these creatures eat out of garbage cans. At four in the morning, I went in to check on her. She stirred at once, and we looked at each other, shared that automatic enigmatic gaze that is the glue of the man-dog relation. I stayed with her until the light came, annoyed beyond words at the hold she had put on our unwilling hearts. She made it through the night a lot better than I did.

Dogs aren't the Uncle Toms of the animal world, I thought as dawn came; they're the dignified dual citizens who plead the case for all of

*"Howard, I think the dog wants to go out."*

mute creation with their human owners. We are born trapped in our own selfish skins, and we open our eyes to the rings of existence around us. The ring right around us, of lovers and spouses and then kids, is easy to encircle, but that is a form of selfishness, too, since the lovers give us love and the kids extend our lives. A handful of saints "love out to the horizon," circle after circle—but at the cost, almost always, of seeing past the circle near at hand, not really being able to love their intimates. Most of the time, we collapse the circles of compassion, don't look at the ones beyond, in order to give the people we love their proper due; we open our eyes to see the wider circles only when new creatures come in, when we realize that we really sit at the center of a Saturn's worth of circles, stretching out from our little campfire to the wolves who wait outside; and ever outward to the unknowable—toward, I don't know, deep-sea fish that live on lava and then beyond toward all existence, where each parrot and every mosquito is, if we could only see it, an individual. What's terrifying is the number of bad stories to which I was once inured, and which now claim my attention. A friend's dog had leaped from a window in a thunderstorm and only now could I feel

the horror of it: the poor terrified thing's leap. Another friend's dog had been paralyzed, and instead of a limping animal I saw a fouled friend, a small Hector. My circles of compassion have been pried open.

We can't enter a dog's mind, but, as on that dark-chocolate night, I saw that it isn't that hard to enter a dog's feelings: feelings of pain, fear, worry, need. And so the dog sits right at the edge of our circle, looking out toward all the others. She is ours, but she is other, too. A dog belongs to the world of wolves she comes from and to the circle of people she has joined. Another circle of existence, toward which we are capable of being compassionate, lies just beyond her, and her paw points toward it, even as her eyes scan ours for dinner. Cats and birds are wonderful, but they keep their own counsel and their own identity. They sit within their own circles, even in the house, and let us spy, occasionally, on what it's like out there. Only the dog sits right at the edge of the first circle of caring, and points to the great unending circles of Otherness that we can barely begin to contemplate.

The deal that the dog has made to get here, as all the dog scientists point out, is brutal. *I'll act all, you know, like, loving and loyal, if you feed me.* Yet don't we make the same deal—courtship and gentle promises of devotion in exchange for sex, sex in exchange for status? Creatures of appetites and desires, who need to eat, and have not been spayed, we run the same scam on each other that Butterscotch runs on us. And a scam that goes on long enough, and works more or less to everyone's benefit, is simply called a culture. What makes the dog deal moving is that you two, you and your dog, are less the willing renewers of it than just the living witnesses to a contract signed between man and wolf thirty thousand years ago. What's in the fine print that you don't read is that if you accept the terms it no longer feels like a deal.

Butterscotch, meanwhile, seems happy. She's here, she's there, a domestic ornament; she takes a place at the table, or under it, anyway, and remains an animal, with an animal's mute confusions and narrow routines and appetites. She jumps up on visitors, sniffs friends, chews shoes, and, even as we laughingly apologize for her misbehavior and order her "Off!," we secretly think her misbehavior is sweet. After all, where we are creatures of past and future, she lives in the minute's joy: a little wolf, racing and snorting and scaring; and the small ingratiating spirit, doing anything to please. At times, I think that I can see her turn her head and look back at the ghost of the wolf mother she parted from long ago, saying, "See, it was a good bet after all; they're nice to me, mostly." Then she waits by the door for the next member of the circle she has insinuated herself into to come back to the hearth and seal the basic social contract common to all things that breathe and feel and gaze: love given for promises kept. How does anyone live without a dog? I can't imagine.

| 2011 |

## FOR A GOOD DOG

My little dog ten years ago
Was arrogant and spry.
Her backbone was a bended bow
For arrows in her eye.
Her step was proud, her bark was loud,
Her nose was in the sky,
But she was ten years younger then,
And so, by God, was I.

Small birds on stilts along the beach
Rose up with piping cry,
And as they flashed beyond her reach,
I thought to see her fly.
If natural law refused her wings,
That law she would defy,
For she could hear unheard-of things,
And so, at times, could I.

Ten years ago she split the air
To seize what she could spy;
Tonight she bumps against a chair,
Betrayed by milky eye.
She seems to pant: Time up, time up!
My little dog must die,
And lie in dust with Hector's pup;
So, presently, must I.

—Ogden Nash    | 1949 |

# DOG HEAVEN

*Fiction*

## STEPHANIE VAUGHN

Every so often that dead dog dreams me up again.

It's twenty-five years later. I'm walking along Forty-second Street in Manhattan, the sounds of the city crashing beside me—horns and gear-shifts, insults—somebody's chewing gum holding my foot to the pavement, when that dog wakes from his long sleep and imagines me.

I'm sweet again. I'm sweet-breathed and flat-limbed. Our family is stationed at Fort Niagara, and the dog swims his red heavy fur into the black Niagara River. Across the street from the officers' quarters, down the steep shady bank, the river, even this far downstream, has been clocked at nine miles per hour. The dog swims after a stick I have thrown.

"Are you crazy?" my grandmother says, even though she is not fond of dog hair in the house, the way it sneaks into the refrigerator every time you open the door. "There's a current out there! It'll take that dog all the way to Toronto!"

"The dog knows where the backwater ends and the current begins," I say, because it is true. He comes down to the river all the time with my father, my brother MacArthur, or me. You never have to yell the dog away from the place where the river water moves like a whip.

Sparky Smith and I had a game we played called Knockout. It involved a certain way of breathing and standing up fast that caused the blood to leave the brain as if a plug had been jerked from the skull. You came

21

to again just as soon as you were on the ground, the blood sloshing back, but it always seemed as if you had left the planet, had a vacation on Mars, and maybe stopped back at Fort Niagara half a lifetime later.

There weren't many kids my age on the post, because it was a small command. Most of its real work went on at the missile batteries flung like shale along the American-Canadian border. Sparky Smith and I hadn't been at Lewiston-Porter Central School long enough to get to know many people, so we entertained ourselves by meeting in a hollow of trees and shrubs at the far edge of the parade ground and telling each other seventh-grade sex jokes that usually had to do with keyholes and doorknobs, hot dogs and hot-dog buns, nuns, priests, preachers, school-teachers, and people in blindfolds.

When we ran out of sex jokes, we went to Knockout and took turns catching each other as we fell like a cut tree toward the ground. Whenever I knocked out, I came to on the grass with the dog barking, yelping, crouching, crying for help. "Wake up! Wake up!" he seemed to say. "Do you know your name? Do you know your name? My name is Duke! My name is Duke!" I'd wake to the sky with the urgent call of the dog in the air, and I'd think, Well, here I am, back in my life again.

Sparky Smith and I spent our school time smiling too much and running for office. We wore mittens instead of gloves, because everyone else did. We made our mothers buy us ugly knit caps with balls on top—caps that in our previous schools would have identified us as weird but were part of the winter uniform in upstate New York. We wobbled onto the ice of the post rink, practicing in secret, banged our knees, scraped the palms of our hands, so that we would be in-vited to skating parties by civilian children.

"You skate?" With each other we practiced the cool look.

"Oh, yeah. I mean like I do it some—I'm not a racer or anything."

Every school morning, we boarded the Army-green bus—the slime-green, dead-swamp-algae-green bus—and rode it to the post gate, past the concrete island where the M.P.s stood in their bullet-proof booth. Across from the gate, we got off at a street corner and waited with the other Army kids, the junior-high and high-school kids, for the real bus, the yellow one with the civilian kids on it. Just as we began to board, the civilian kids—there were only six of them but eighteen of us—would begin to sing the Artillery song with obscene variations one of them had invented. In-stead of "Over hill, over dale," they sang things like "Over boob, over tit." For a few weeks, we sat in silence watching the heavy oak trees of the town give way to apple orchards and potato farms, and we pretended not to hear. Then one day Sparky Smith began to sing the real Artillery song, the booming song with caissons rolling along in it, and we all joined in and took over the bus with our voices.

When we ran out of verses, one of the civilian kids, a football player in high school, yelled, "Sparky is a *dog's* name. Here, Sparky, Sparky, Sparky." Sparky rose from his seat with a wounded look, then dropped to the aisle on his hands and knees and bit the football player in the calf. We all laughed, even the football player, and Sparky returned to his seat.

"That guy's just lucky I didn't pee on his leg," Sparky said.

Somehow Sparky got himself elected home-room president and me homeroom vice-president in January. He liked to say, "In actual percentages—I mean in actual per-capita terms —we are doing much better than the civilian kids." He kept track of how many athletes we had, how many band members, who among the older girls might become a cheerleader. Listening to him even then, I couldn't figure out how he got anyone to vote for us. When he was campaigning, he sounded dull and serious, and anyway he had a large head and looked funny in his knit cap. He put

up a homemade sign in the lunch-room, went from table to table to find students from 7-B to shake hands with, and said to me repeatedly, as I walked along a step behind him and nodded, "Just don't tell them that you're leaving in March. Under no circumstances let them know that you will not be able to finish out your term."

In January, therefore, I was elected home-room vice-president by people I still didn't know (nobody in 7-B rode our bus—that gave us an edge), and in March my family moved to Fort Sill, in Oklahoma. I surrendered my vice-presidency to a civilian girl, and that was the end for all time of my career in public office.

Two days before we left Fort Niagara, we took the dog, Duke, to Charlie Battery, fourteen miles from the post, and left him with the mess sergeant. We were leaving him for only six weeks, until we could settle in Oklahoma and send for him. He had stayed at Charlie Battery before, when we visited our relatives in Ohio at Christmastime. He knew there were big meaty bones at Charlie Battery, and scraps of chicken, steak, turkey, slices of cheese, special big-dog bowls of ice

cream. The mess at Charlie Battery was Dog Heaven, so he gave us a soft, forgiving look as we walked with him from the car to the back of the mess hall.

My mother said, as she always did at times like that, "I wish he knew more English." My father gave him a fierce manly scratch behind the ears. My brother and I scraped along behind with our pinched faces.

"Don't you worry," the sergeant said. "He'll be fine here. We like this dog, and he likes us. He'll run that fence perimeter all day long. He'll be his own early-warning defense system. Then we'll give this dog everything he ever dreamed of eating." The sergeant looked quickly at my father to see if the lighthearted reference to the defense system had been all right. My father was in command of the missile batteries. In my father's presence, no one spoke lightly of the defense of the United States of America—of the missiles that would rise from the earth like a wind and knock out (knock out!) the Soviet planes flying over the North Pole with their nuclear bombs. But Duke was my father's dog, too, and I think that my father had the same wish we all had—to tell him

that we were going to send for him, this was just going to be a wonderful dog vacation.

"Sergeant Carter has the best mess within five hundred miles," my father said to me and MacArthur.

We looked around. We had been there for Thanksgiving dinner when the grass was still green. Now, in late winter, it was a dreary place, a collection of rain-streaked metal buildings standing near huge dark mounds of earth. In summer, the mounds looked something like the large grassy mounds in southern Ohio, the famous Indian mounds, softly rounded and benignly mysterious. In March, they were black with old snow. Inside the mounds were the Nike missiles, I supposed, although I didn't know for sure where the missiles were. Perhaps they were hidden in the depressions behind the mounds.

Once during "Fact Monday" in Homeroom 7-B, our teacher, Miss Bintz, had given a lecture on nuclear weapons. First she put a slide on the wall depicting an atom and its spinning electrons.

"Do you know what this is?" she said, and everyone in the room said, "An atom," in one voice, as if we were reciting a poem. We liked "Fact Monday" sessions because we didn't have to do any work for them. We sat happily in the dim light of her slides through lectures called "Nine Chapters in the Life of a Cheese" ("First the milk is warmed, then it is soured with rennet"), "The Morning Star of English Poetry" ("As springtime suggests the beginning of new life, so Chaucer stands at the beginning of English poetry"), and "Who's Who Among the Butterflies" ("The Monarch—*Anosia plexippus*—is king"). Sparky liked to say that Miss Bintz was trying to make us into third graders again, but I liked Miss Bintz. She had high cheekbones and a passionate voice.

She believed, like the adults in my family, that a fact was something solid and useful, like a penknife you could put in your pocket in case of emergency.

That day's lecture was "What Happens to the Atom When It's Smashed." Miss Bintz put on the wall a black-and-white slide of four women who had been horribly disfigured by the atomic blast at Hiroshima. The room was half darkened for the slide show. When she surprised us with the four faces of the women, you could feel the darkness grow, the silence in the bellies of the students.

"And do you know what this is?" Miss Bintz said. No one spoke. What answer could she have wanted from us, anyway? She clicked the slide machine through ten more pictures—closeups of blistered hands, scarred heads, flattened buildings, burned trees, maimed and naked children staggering toward the camera as if the camera were food, a house, a mother, a father, a friendly dog.

"Do you know what this is?" Miss Bintz said again. Our desks were arranged around the edge of the room, creating an arena in the center. Miss Bintz entered that space and began to move along the front of our desks, looking to see who would answer her incomprehensible question.

"Do you know?" She stopped in front of my desk.

"No," I said.

"Do you know?" She stopped next at Sparky's desk.

Sparky looked down and finally said, "It's something horrible."

"That's right," she said. "It's something very horrible. This is the effect of an atom smashing. This is the effect of nuclear power." She turned to gesture at the slide, but she had stepped in front of the projector, and the smear of children's faces fell across her back. "Now let's think about how nuclear power got from the laboratory to the people of Japan." She had begun to pace again. "Let's think about where all this devastation and wreckage actually comes from. You tell me," she said to a large, crouching boy named Donald Anderson. He was hunched over his desk, and his arms lay before him like tree limbs.

"I don't know," Donald Anderson said.

"Of course you do," Miss Bintz said. "Where did all of this come from?"

None of us had realized yet that Miss Bintz's message was political. I looked beyond Donald Anderson at the drawn window shades. Behind them were plate-glass windows, a view of stiff red-oak leaves, the smell of wood smoke in the air. Across the road from the school was an orchard, beyond that a pasture, another orchard, and then the town of Lewiston, standing on the Niagara River seven miles upstream from the long row of red brick Colonial houses that were the officers' quarters at Fort Niagara. Duke was down by the river, probably, sniffing at the reedy edge, his head lifting when ducks flew low over the water. Once the dog had come back to our house with a live fish in his mouth, a carp. Nobody ever believed that story except those of us who saw it: me, my mother and father and brother, my grandmother.

Miss Bintz had clicked to a picture of a mushroom cloud and was now saying, "And where did the bomb come from?" We were all tired of "Fact Monday" by then. Miss Bintz walked back to where Sparky and I were sitting. "You military children," she said. "You know where the bomb comes from. Why don't you tell us?" she said to me.

Maybe because I was tired, or bored, or frightened—I don't know—I said to Miss Bintz, looking her in the eye, "The bomb comes from the mother bomb."

Everyone laughed. We laughed because we needed to laugh, and because Miss Bintz had all the answers and all the questions and she was pointing them at us like guns.

"Stand up," she said. She made me enter the arena in front of the desks, and then she clicked the machine back to the picture of the Japanese women. "Look at this picture and make a joke," she said. What came next was the lecture she had been aiming for all along. The bomb came from the United States of America. We in the United States were worried about whether another country might use the bomb, but in the whole history of the human species only one country had ever used the worst weapon ever invented. On she went, bombs and airplanes and bomb tests, and then she got to the missiles. They were right here, she said, not more than ten miles away. Didn't we all know that? "You know that, don't you?" she said to me. If the missiles weren't hidden among our orchards, the planes from the Soviet Union would not have any reason to drop bombs on top of Lewiston-Porter Central Junior High School.

I had stopped listening by then and realized that the pencil I still held in my hand was drumming a song against my thigh. Over hill, over dale. I looked back at the wall again, where the mushroom cloud had reappeared, and my own silhouette stood wildly in the middle of it. I looked at Sparky and dropped the pencil on the floor, stooped down to get it, looked at Sparky once more, stood up, and knocked out.

Later, people told me that I didn't fall like lumber, I fell like something soft collapsing, a fan folding in on itself, a balloon rumpling to the floor. Sparky saw what I was up to and tried to get out from behind his desk to catch me, but it was Miss Bintz I fell against, and she went down, too. When I woke up, the lights were on, the mushroom cloud was a pale ghost against the wall, voices in the room sounded like insect wings, and I was back in my life again.

"I'm so sorry," Miss Bintz said. "I didn't know you were an epileptic."

At Charlie Battery, it was drizzling as my parents stood and talked with the sergeant, rain running in dark tiny ravines along the slopes of the mounds.

MacArthur and I had M&M's in our pockets, which we were allowed to give to the dog for his farewell. When we extended our hands, though, the dog lowered himself to the gravel and looked up at us from under his tender red eyebrows. He seemed to say that if he took the candy he knew we would go, but if he didn't perhaps we would stay here at the missile battery and eat scraps with him.

We rode back to the post in silence, through the gray apple orchards, through small upstate towns, the fog rising out of the rain like a wish. MacArthur and I sat against opposite doors in the back seat, thinking of the loneliness of the dog.

We entered the kitchen, where my grandmother had already begun to clean the refrigerator. She looked at us, at our grim children's faces—the dog had been sent away a day earlier than was really necessary—and she said, "Well, God knows you can't clean the dog hair out of the house with the dog still in it."

Whenever I think of an Army post, I think of a place the weather cannot touch for long. The precise rectangles of the parade grounds, the precisely pruned trees and shrubs, the living quarters, the administration buildings, the PX and commissary, the nondenominational church, the teen club, the snack bar, the movie house, the skeet-and-trap field, the swimming pools, the runway, warehouses, the Officers' Club, the N.C.O. Club. Men marching, women marching, saluting, standing at attention, at ease. The bugle will trumpet reveille, mess call, assembly, retreat, taps through a hurricane, a tornado, flood, blizzard. Whenever I think of the clean, squared look of a military post, I think that if one were blown down today in a fierce wind, it would be standing again tomorrow in time for reveille.

The night before our last full day at Fort Niagara, an Arctic wind slipped across the lake and froze the rain where it fell, on streets, trees, power lines, rooftops. We awoke to a fabulation of ice, the sun shining like a weapon, light rocketing off every surface except the surfaces of the Army's clean streets and walks.

MacArthur and I stood on the dry, scraped walk in front of our house and watched a jeep pass by on the way to the gate. On the post, everything was operational, but in the civilian world beyond the gate power lines were down, hanging like daggers in the sun, roads were glazed with ice, cars were in ditches, highways were impassable. No yellow school buses were going to be on the roads that morning.

"This means we miss our very last day in school," MacArthur said. "No goodbyes for us."

We looked up at the high, bare branches of the hard maples, where drops of ice glimmered.

"I just want to shake your hand and say so long," Sparky said. He had come out of his house

to stand with us. "I guess you know this means you'll miss the surprise party."

"There was going to be a party?" I said.

"Just cupcakes," Sparky said. "I sure wish you could stay the school year and keep your office."

"Oh, who cares!" I said, suddenly irritated with Sparky, although he was my best friend. "Jesus," I said, sounding to myself like an adult—like Miss Bintz, maybe, when she was off duty. "Jesus," I said again. "What kind of office is home goddam room vice-president in a crummy country school?"

MacArthur said to Sparky, "What kind of cupcakes were they having?"

I looked down at MacArthur and said, "Do you know how totally ridiculous you look in that knit cap? I can't wait until we get out of this place."

"Excuse me," MacArthur said. "Excuse me for wearing the hat you gave me for my birthday."

It was then that the dog came back. We heard him calling out before we saw him, his huge woof-woof "My name is Duke! My name is Duke! I'm your dog! I'm your dog!" Then we saw him streaking through the trees, through the park space of oaks and maples between our house and the post gate. Later the M.P.s would say that he stopped and wagged his tail at them before he passed through the gate, as if he understood that he should be stopping to show his I.D. card. He ran to us, bounding across the crusted, glass-slick snow—ran into the history of our family, all the stories we would tell about him after he was dead. Years and years later, whenever we came back together at the family table, we would start the dog stories. He was the dog who caught the live fish with his mouth, the one who stole a pound of butter off the commissary loading dock and brought it to us in his soft bird dog's mouth without a tooth mark on the package. He was the dog

who broke out of Charlie Battery the morning of an ice storm, travelled fourteen miles across the needled grasses of frozen pastures, through the prickly frozen mud of orchards, across back-yard fences in small towns, and found the lost family.

The day was good again. When we looked back at the ice we saw a fairy-land. The red brick houses looked like ice castles. The ice-coated trees, with their million dreams of light, seemed to cast a spell over us.

"This is for you," Sparky said, and handed me a gold-foiled box. Inside were chocolate candies and a note that said, "I have enjoyed knowing you this year. I hope you have a good life." Then it said, "P.S. Remember this name. Someday I'm probably going to be famous."

"Famous as what?" MacArthur said.

"I haven't decided yet," Sparky said.

We had a party. We sat on the front steps of our quarters, Sparky, MacArthur, the dog, and I, and we ate all the chocolates at eight o'clock in the morning. We sat shoulder to shoulder, the four of us, and looked across the street through the trees at the river, and we talked about what we might be doing a year from then. Finally, we finished the chocolates and stopped talking and allowed the brilliant light of that morning to enter us.

Miss Bintz is the one who sent me the news about Sparky four months later. "BOY DROWNS IN SWIFT CURRENT." In the newspaper story, Sparky takes the bus to Niagara Falls with two friends from Lewiston-Porter. It's a searing July day, a hundred degrees in the city, so the boys climb down the gorge into the river and swim in a place where it's illegal to swim, two miles downstream from the Falls. The boys Sparky is visiting—they're both student-council members as well as football players, just the kind of boys Sparky himself wants to be—have sneaked down to this swimming place many times: a cove in the bank of the river, where the water is still and glassy on a hot July day, not like the water raging in the middle of the river. But the current is a wild invisible thing, unreliable, whipping out with a looping arm to pull you in. "He was only three feet in front of me," one of the boys said. "He took one more stroke and then he was gone."

We were living in civilian housing not far from the post. When we had the windows open, we could hear the bugle calls and the sound of the cannon firing retreat at sunset. A month after I got the newspaper clipping about Sparky, the dog died. He was killed, along with every other dog on our block, when a stranger drove down our street one evening and threw poisoned hamburger into our front yards.

All that week I had trouble getting to sleep at night. One night I was still awake when the re-corded bugle sounded taps, the sound drifting across the Army fences and into our bedrooms.

Day is done, gone the sun. It was the sound of my childhood in sleep. The bugler played it beautifully, mournfully, holding fast to the long, high notes. That night I listened to the cadence of it, to the yearning of it. I thought of the dog again, only this time I suddenly saw him rising like a missile into the air, the red glory of his fur flying, his nose pointed heavenward. I remem-bered the dog leaping high, prancing on his hind legs the day he came back from Charlie Battery, the dog rocking back and forth, from front legs to hind legs, dancing, sliding across the ice of the post rink later that day, as Sparky, MacArthur, and I played crack-the-whip, hold-ing tight to each other, our skates careening and singing. "You're AWOL! You're AWOL!" we cried at the dog. "No school!" the dog barked back. "No school!" We skated across the dark-ening ice into the sunset, skated faster and faster, until we seemed to rise together into the cold, bright air. It was a good day, it was a good day, it was a good day.

| 1989 |

*"I understand that in your country this thing is done quite differently."*

# BEREAVEMENT

Behind his house, my father's dogs
sleep in kennels, beautiful,
he built just for them.

They do not bark.
Do they know he is dead?
They wag their tails

& head. They beg
& are fed.
Their grief is colossal

& forgetful.
Each day they wake
seeking his voice,

their names.
By dusk they seem
to unremember everything—

to them even hunger
is a game. For that, I envy.
For that, I cannot bear to watch them

pacing their cage. I try to remember
they love best confined space
to feel safe. Each day

a saint comes by to feed the pair
& I draw closer
the shades.

I've begun to think of them
as my father's other sons,
as kin. Brothers-in-paw.

My eyes each day thaw.
One day the water cuts off.
Then back on.

They are outside dogs—
which is to say, healthy
& victorious, purposeful

& one giant muscle
like the heart. Dad taught
them not to bark, to point

out their prey. To stay.
Were they there that day?
They call me

like witnesses & will not say.
I ask for their care
& their carelessness—

wish of them forgiveness.
I must give them away.
I must find for them homes,

sleep restless in his.
All night I expect they pace
as I do, each dog like an eye

roaming with the dead
beneath an unlocked lid.

—Kevin Young    | 2009 |

# BEWARE OF THE DOGS

## BURKHARD BILGER

The weapons were housed in Long Island City, in a low-slung, prefabricated building on Northern Boulevard. I could hear them growling and yammering in the dark. I'd arrived well before dawn on a wet, chilly October morning, and still wasn't sure how to proceed. A police officer had told me to meet him there at five-forty-five, but there was no bell to ring, no intercom to buzz. The building was surrounded by a ragged chain-link fence edged with spools of razor wire and posted with warnings. When I tested the gate, it was unlocked, but the entrance lay across an empty parking lot and up a wooden ramp. I wasn't sure that I could make it to the door in time.

I've never been much good around dogs. In the town where I grew up, about an hour north of Oklahoma City, every other house seemed to be patrolled by some bawling bluetick or excitable Irish setter, and the locals liked to leave them unchained. When I'd fill in for my brother on his paper route, or ride my one-speed bike to a friend's house, I could usually count on a chase along the way, some homicidal canine at my heels. The dogs didn't seem to give my friends as much trouble. And my father had a way of puffing himself up and waving his arms that would send them scampering. But I never figured out how to show them who's boss.

One of the satisfactions of city life has been turning that relationship around. A pet here is always on probation, its instincts curbed or swiftly incarcerated. A hound that chases children around would be considered a public menace, and even the little yappers have to be kept on a leash. In the past ten years, though, that balance of power has shifted. Since the attacks on September 11th, New York's subways and train stations, parks and tourist destinations have been prowled by police dogs—large, pointy-eared, unnervingly observant beasts deeply unconvinced of our innocence. They sniff at backpacks and train their eyes on passersby, daring us to make a move. It's a little unsettling but also, under the circumstances, reassuring. There are worse things to fear than getting bitten.

The New York City subway has more than four hundred stations, eight hundred miles of track, six thousand cars, and, on any given weekday, five million passengers. It's an antiterrorism unit's nightmare. To sweep this teeming labyrinth for bombs would take an army of explosives experts equipped with chemical detectors. Instead, the city has gone to the dogs. Since 2001, the number of uniformed police has dropped by 17 percent. In that same period, the canine force has nearly doubled. It now has around a hundred dogs, divided among the narcotics, bomb, emergency-response, and transit squads.

A good dog is a natural super-soldier: strong yet acrobatic, fierce yet obedient. It can leap higher than most men, and run twice as fast. Its eyes are equipped for night vision, its ears for supersonic hearing, its mouth for subduing the most fractious prey. But its true glory is its nose. In the 1970s, researchers found that dogs could detect even a few particles per million of a substance; in the nineties, more subtle instruments lowered the threshold to particles per billion; the most recent tests have brought it down to particles per trillion. "It's a little disheartening, really," Paul Waggoner, a behavioral scientist at the Canine Detection Research Institute, at Auburn

University, in Alabama, told me. "I spent a good six years of my life chasing this idea, only to find that it was all about the limitations of my equipment."

Just as astonishing, to Waggoner, is a dog's acuity—the way it can isolate and identify compounds within a scent, like the spices in a soup. Drug smugglers often try to mask the smell of their shipments by packaging them with coffee beans, air fresheners, or sheets of fabric softener. To see if this can fool a dog, Waggoner has flooded his laboratory with different scents, then added minute quantities of heroin or cocaine to the mix. In one case, "the whole damn lab smelled like a Starbucks," he told me, but the dogs had no trouble homing in on the drug. "They're just incredible at finding the needle in the haystack."

The New York police have two kinds of canines: detection dogs and patrol dogs. The former spend most of their time chasing down imaginary threats: terrorist attacks are so rare that the police have to stage simulations, with real explosives, to keep the dogs on their toes. Patrol dogs, on the other hand, have one of the most dangerous jobs in public life. Canine police are often called when a criminal is on the loose, and they're far more likely than others to have a lethal encounter. "The crimes I get called out on are always in progress," one officer told me. "The suspects are armed. They're known to be violent. So, by the mere nature of that call, it's going to be more dangerous." He shrugged. "I guess I'm an adrenaline junkie. I got into canine to hunt men."

The dogs in Long Island City were heirs to an ancient and bloodthirsty line. Their ancestors, descended from the great mastiffs and sight hounds of Mesopotamia, were used as shock troops by the Assyrians, the Persians, the Babylonians, and the Greeks. (Alexander the Great's dog, Peritas, is said to have saved his life at Gaugamela by leaping in front of a Persian elephant and biting its lip.) They wrought havoc in the Roman Colosseum, ran with Attila's hordes, and wore battle armor beside the knights of the Middle Ages. In 1495, when Columbus sailed to what is now the Dominican Republic, he brought Spanish mastiffs almost three feet high at the withers and greyhounds that could run down an enemy and disembowel him. At the battle of Vega Real, each hound killed a hundred natives in less than an hour, according to the Dominican friar Bartolomé de las Casas. "They carry these dogs with them as companions wherever they go," he later wrote. "And kill the fettered Indians in multitudes like Hogs for their Food."

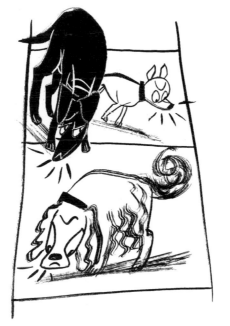

It took a while to break them of the habit. The colonists used dogs against Indians and slaves—"They should be large, strong and fierce," Benjamin Franklin recommended, "and will confound the enemy a good deal"—and the Confederates sent them after escaping Union prisoners at Andersonville. And though the U.S. Army opted for more modern weaponry abroad, attack dogs were still used at home, for crowd control. "Up until the 1970s, the police just wanted dogs that would bite everyone," Jim Matarese, the treasurer of the United States Police Canine Association, told me. "They'd go to the pound and get dogs that were fear biters— just scared to death of people. Or someone would call in and say, 'I've got a real aggressive dog. He'll bite!' Well, we saw what happened at the marches from Selma: those dogs just ate people up."

In Europe, police dogs were a more refined lot, though not always to their benefit. The German shepherd, first registered as a breed in 1889 by a former cavalry captain, Max von Stephanitz, was selected for intelligence and steadiness as well as power. The Germans fielded thirty thousand dogs in the First World War, and used them for everything from transporting medicine and wounded soldiers to shuttling messages between trenches. When the war was over, the animals were mostly killed, discarded, or consumed by the starving populace. "Dog meat has been eaten in every major German crisis at least since the time of Frederick the Great, and is commonly referred to as 'blockade mutton,'" *Time* noted, in 1940. "Dachshund is considered the most succulent."

The survivors went on to second careers in law enforcement or as guide dogs for the blind, and their breeding and training grew ever more sophisticated. In Germany, registered shepherds have to pass rigorous physical and behavioral tests, and their puppies are trained by nationwide networks of volunteers. *Schutzhund* competitions, in which dogs are tested for their ability to track, obey orders, and protect their owners, are a national passion, and the largest ones fill stadiums. "They just have a different dog culture over there," Steve White, a dog trainer and former canine officer in the Seattle area, told me. "If you look at North America, there are maybe five thousand German shepherd breeders. If you go to Germany, it's probably got fifty-five thousand."

It took the Lockerbie bombing, followed by the attacks at Columbine and Oklahoma City, to galvanize interest in police and military dogs in America. Auburn's canine program began as an attempt to build a better bomb detector. "In the eighties, we thought, Let's build a machine that can mimic the dog!" Robert Gillette, the director of the university's animal-health and performance program, told me. "But you can't mimic a dog. It's just a superior mechanical working system. So in the nineties we began to think, Hmm, let's put some of that research into the animals." The Department of Defense has apparently come to the same conclusion. Since 2006, it has spent close to twenty billion dollars searching for explosives in Iraq and Afghanistan. "The detection rate has hung stubbornly at around fifty percent," Lieutenant General Michael Oates told the magazine *National Defense* two years ago. When the same patrols use dogs, he added, the success rate leaps to 80 percent: "Dogs are the best detectors."

The American military now has some three thousand active-duty dogs in its ranks, but good animals are hard to find. The American Kennel Club requires no proof of health or intelligence to register an animal—just a pure bloodline—and breeders are often more concerned with looks than with ability. "We breed for the almighty dollar here," one trainer told me. Programs like the ones at Auburn and at Lackland Air Force Base, in San Antonio, are trying to reverse that trend. But their graduates are still the exceptions. "Some of these dogs, they couldn't find a pork chop if it was hanging around their neck," a dog broker in Minnesota told me.

The upshot is that many, if not most, American police dogs now come from Europe. Those in the New York subway were mostly born in Hungary, Slovakia, or the Czech Republic— descendants of the powerful border-patrol dogs bred during the Cold War. Other police dogs come from brokers in Holland and Germany, and still respond to Dutch and German commands: *Sitz! Bleib! Los! Apport!* "Europeans have more dogs than they can use, so they sell the excess to us," White told me. "We subsidize their hobbies."

When I'd finally summoned the nerve to sprint across the parking lot and up the ramp, that morning in Long Island City, I stumbled in on six patrolmen strapping on their gear. They were all with the transit squad, which safeguards the subway: four recruits and two trainers. A dry-erase board hung on the wall, scrawled with notes. One side listed explosives that the dogs could detect, including C-4, TNT, ammonium nitrate, and several others. The other side listed fines for canine misbehavior: five dollars for urinating in the subway, twenty-five for biting someone ("must draw blood").

Wayne Rothschild, one of the trainers, had just finished adding his weight to another list on the board—part of a contest to see who could lose the most pounds by the end of the week. (Canine police tend to be more active than others, but their dogs do most of the running.) The men in his squad averaged more than two hundred pounds, topping out at two hundred and thirty-six, for the sergeant, Randy Brenner.

"One pound?" a recruit was asked. "You've lost one pound?"

"I swallowed a lot of aggression."

"And pizzas."

Rothschild laughed. At one eighty-one, he was among the fittest men in the group. He and Brenner had first met in junior high and later played football together for the Hicksville Comets—Rothschild at quarterback and Brenner at center. Twenty years later, they still looked their parts: Rothschild square-jawed and decisive, with jet-black hair close-cropped on the sides; Brenner stolid, round, and reliable—the immovable object. Technically, Brenner was now Rothschild's boss, but their relationship hadn't changed much. "I was blocking for him then and I'm still blocking for him," Brenner said.

Like many of the men in the squad, Rothschild and Brenner had been around police dogs most of their lives. Rothschild's father, uncle, brothers, and cousins were in law enforcement, as were Brenner's father and grandfather. After high school, Rothschild spent two years at a community college and another two working construction, before joining the force. Brenner took his police-academy entrance exam at sixteen. When the transit canine unit was formed, six years ago, they each put in for it unbeknownst to the other, and found themselves back on the same team. "I'd rather be a cop in canine than a sergeant somewhere else," Brenner said. "It's all I ever wanted."

He and Rothschild led the recruits to the kennel behind the offices, to get their new partners. A week earlier, each recruit had been paired with an equally green police dog, a little over a year old. "We want the dog to make up for where the handler is weak and vice versa," Brenner said. "But I'll tell you, after a while the person's personality becomes similar to the dog's." Matthew Poletto, a rangy recruit with the jutting cheekbones and cut biceps of a bodybuilder, had been matched with Ranger, a skinny, high-strung Belgian Malinois—"like a German shepherd on steroids," as one handler put it. Horacio Maldonado, a small, soft-spoken Hispanic, had a sweet female Labrador named Ray. The others had big-boned, lordly shepherds with the contained power peculiar to the breed. The Labrador was a detection dog; the shepherds and the Malinois were patrol

dogs—though some, like Rothschild's German shepherd, Danz, did both.

For the next month and a half, the dogs and men would learn to work together, to read each other's cues and idiosyncrasies, as if in an arranged marriage: police dogs and their handlers are usually partnered for life. "He's a great dog. It's just . . . sometimes I'd like to relax a little," Poletto said, sounding like the honeymoon was already over. "You know, watch TV and not have him put the chew toy in my lap."

Inside the kennel, the dogs were in an uproar. They lunged at their cages when they saw their owners, foam flying from their muzzles. They stayed here only when not on patrol or at home with their partners, but even this much confinement was hard to bear. "A lot of them are cage chewers," the unit's other trainer, Richard Geraci, told me. He showed me a photograph on his

### RETRIEVER

We're told of a bird dog named Bob, owned by a broker who lives in Fieldston. He's an excellent retriever and is happy during the hunting season, but all the rest of the year he just sits around the yard, mooning and dreaming. One day lately, though, something stirred in him and he disappeared for half an hour. When he returned, he presented his master with a seven-pound roast of beef, rolled and tied and ready for the oven; not a tooth mark in it. The broker had it cooked.    | 1935 |

phone of a ventilation cover that his dog, Chief, had reduced to twisted scrap. "That's quarter-inch steel," he said. A German shepherd's jaw can exert upward of seven hundred and fifty pounds per square inch. "They just chew it up, tear it up. Chief's got broken teeth, but I'm surprised he doesn't have more."

And yet the moment the cages were opened

the noises stopped. The dogs trotted silently to their partners' side, then sat back on their haunches—ears erect, eyes focussed forward—and waited. "It's like you've turned on a switch," Brenner said.

Canine police tend to talk about their dogs as if they were mechanical devices. They describe them as tools or technology and say that they're "building dogs" through proper training. They say that their animals need "maintenance" to be "fully operational," and that a "dual-purpose dog"—one that has been taught to both chase down criminals and detect drugs or explosives—has "superior functionality." At home, a police dog may be like a member of the family. But once in the field it's just another piece of gear.

This is more than a manner of speaking. It's a way of thinking about dogs that goes back to the psychologist B. F. Skinner and his work on behaviorism, in the 1940s. Skinner argued that it's pointless to imagine what's going on in an animal's head. Better to treat its mind as a black box, closed and unknowable, with inputs that lead to predictable outputs. Skinner identified four ways to manipulate behavior, four buttons to push—positive reinforcement ("Good dog! Have a biscuit"), positive punishment ("Bad dog! *Whack*"), negative reinforcement ("Good dog! Now I'll stop whacking you"), and negative punishment ("Bad dog! Give me back that biscuit"). Connect an action to an outcome and almost any behavior can be trained. Skinner called this "operant conditioning," and considered it as effective for people as for their pets. "Give me a child," he once said, "and I'll shape him into anything."

By treating animals as clever machines, behaviorists managed some impressive feats: rats navigated mazes, chickens played tic-tac-toe, pigeons played Ping-Pong. During the Second World War, Skinner went so far as to design a pigeon-guided missile. The birds sat in the nose cone, each one pecking at a target on a translucent plate. The setup worked surprisingly well, but the pigeons were never enlisted—no one in the military would take them seriously, Skinner complained. Behaviorism, as a means of animal training, had a long, slow fuse.

The revolution, when it came, began with creatures beyond the reach of regular compulsion. An orca or a dolphin can't be tugged on a leash or stung with a whip. It can't hear what you're shouting most of the time. To make it do what you want, you have to break down the behavior into discrete components—swim over here, pick up that hoop, leap through the air—then offer a reward for each step. At marine parks and aquariums, in the 1960s, an orca that did something right would hear a whistle blast and get a fish. After a while, each behavior would be associated with a different hand signal, and become so rewarding, in and of itself, that the orca wouldn't always need to get a fish. One of the pioneers in this field, Karen Pryor, once taught a goldfish to swim through a tiny hoop just for the flicker of a flashlight. "It's easy," she told me. "You just have to have a healthy goldfish. And it has to be hungry."

As operant conditioning has spread from aquariums to zoos, what once would have been circus acts have come to seem like ordinary good behavior. Thirty years ago, if a lion needed a flu shot, it had to be tranquillized. These days, it will walk up to its trainer and proffer its paw. "I could give you examples all day," Ken Ramirez, the vice-president of animal training at the Shedd Aquarium, in Chicago, told me. "We have sharks that will swim from tank to tank, and a beluga whale that will present its belly for an ultrasound. Our sea otters hold their eyes open to get drops, and I've had a diabetic baboon submit to regular insulin injections." Not long ago, when a camel broke its jaw at the nearby Brookfield Zoo, it walked up to a table and laid its head on a lead plate for an X-ray. "It makes managing animals so much easier," Ramirez said. "They do things as part of a game that you've taught them."

*"They never pushed me. If I wanted to retrieve, shake hands, or roll over, it was entirely up to me."*

Dogs were made for this sort of thing. No other animal so loves a game or so diligently aims to please. No other has been shaped so specifically to our needs. Selective breeding has turned *Canis lupus familiaris* into the most physically varied animal on earth. Its genome is the Microsoft Windows of biological programming: layer upon layer of complex function and code, often accreted at cross-purposes. It can produce Great Danes big enough to kill wild boars and Chihuahuas small enough to go down rat holes, beagles that track pythons and collies that catch Frisbees. "When you get to a detection dog that wants to find ammonium nitrate just so that it can play with a rubber ball, that is a very, very complex end point," Auburn's Robert Gillette told me.

The patrol dogs in the transit squad could bark on command (Speak!) and urinate at their handler's discretion (Empty!). They could climb ladders, crawl through drainage pipes, and leap through the open window of a moving car. They were smart, disciplined, extremely capable animals. But the blood of the old war hounds still ran in them, and their most effective ability was intimidation.

"One canine team can do the work of ten or fifteen guys in a gang situation," Lieutenant John Pappas, the head of the squad, told me. "It's 'Fuck you! I'm not going anywhere.' But when you throw in some jaws and paws—holy shit! It changes the landscape." In 2010, one station on the Lexington Avenue line was hit by twenty felonies in a matter of months. Once a canine unit was sent in, the number dropped to zero. "It's like pulling up in an M1 Abrams battle tank," Pappas said.

The commuters at Union Square seemed a peaceable crowd one Wednesday morning. Yet the dogs made even the innocent nervous. When the squad filed into a subway car, I could see backs stiffen all around, eyes focussed on the floor. Each dog and its handler took position at a set of doors, overseen by Rothschild and Brenner. Between stations, the dogs watched the riders. When the doors opened, they pivoted around to study the crowd on the platform. The German shepherds soon settled into the routine, but the Malinois kept twisting about on its leash, registering each face like a laser scanner.

"Malinois just really love bite work," a canine cop from Middletown, New York, had told me. "They have this giant prey drive. Some people call them Maligators." After a while, one of the riders—a tall, spindly man in a yarn prayer cap—began to get uncomfortable. He scooted down the seat, hunching his shoulders, and glared back at the Malinois. "If you tense up, if you're feeling threatened, the dog picks that up and perceives a threat," Brenner told me. Or as my friends used to say when I was a kid, at the worst possible moments, "They can smell your fear."

Times Square is the busiest station in the city, and the main concourse was at its most cacophonous. A band of black bluegrass musicians, called the Ebony Hillbillies, was sprawled in lawn chairs playing an old fiddle tune called "Martha Campbell." The bass and banjo lines skittered from run to run while the washboard chattered underneath, mimicking the commuters around us. "New York is just different," Brenner said, looking around with satisfaction. "Our version of a crowd is different from anywhere else in the world. And these dogs are tuning in to everything. They're trained for handler protection, and they don't know when that threat is going to be upon them."

The squad had been there only a few minutes when one of the German shepherds—a huge black male named Thunder—began to bark at something nearby. I could see a man in a hoodie crouched beside a pillar. An officer was shouting at him to show his hands, but he wouldn't do it. One second, the two were frozen in a standoff, Thunder straining at the leash. Then the suspect lunged, the cop let go, and the dog leaped through the air. "Get this dog off of me!"

the man screamed, as Thunder's jaw clamped around his arm. The handler called Thunder back, but then the suspect broke away and the dog was on him again within a few steps, jerking him to the ground.

As it turned out, the suspect was a decoy—another transit cop, posing as a troublemaker. The second attack, though, had been unscripted: the decoy hadn't meant to act as if he were running away. "The dog wasn't wrong," Rothschild said. It's a police dog's job to perceive threats, and the handler's job to keep the dog in check. This is the hardest part of canine work. "You have to put emergency brakes on these creatures," one handler told me. A single loss of control could cause wrongful injury, lawsuits, or even death, but the dog doesn't know that. As Stewart Hilliard, a specialist in animal learning who works with the canine program at Lackland Air Force Base, put it, "You can't think of a reward more desirable to a dog than the opportunity to keep biting that person."

A few weeks earlier, at the National Police Dog Field Trials, in Detroit Lakes, Minnesota, I'd watched several dozen dogs wrestle with their conscience. The field trials are a kind of canine decathlon, modelled on *Schutzhund* competitions. They bring together the best-trained police dogs in the country to test their agility, obedience, and ability to track criminals and catch them. Rothschild and his German shepherd were there to represent New York, along with four other dogs and handlers from their region.

Detroit Lakes sits on a flat, glacier-scoured plain about an hour east of Fargo. Some officers had driven as far as fifteen hundred miles to get there, but were unprepared for the freezing rain and the local fare. ("It's September—I brought all shorts!" Rothschild told me the first night, at a local buffet, while his teammates eyed the brat-wurst; "I'm not eatin' those things," one of them said.) The night before, on the drive in from North Dakota, I'd received a speeding ticket on a desolate stretch of road. I later heard that the same thing had happened to two of the police officers—and they were driving their cruisers at the time.

"A lot of people are under the misapprehension that this is a dog show," one of the judges, Gary Pietropaolo, a mustachioed ex-cop from Yonkers, told me the next day. We were sitting in folding chairs on a baseball field, watching the criminal-apprehension trial. By then, I'd seen dogs search for guns in tall grass, and dogs sniff out a suspect hidden in rows of identical wooden boxes. In this case, they had to chase down a gunman, bite his arm, and waylay him until the handler caught up to make the arrest. It was a stylized routine, scored on niceties of execution—sitting slightly askew at a handler's side was enough to earn a deduction—but the dogs seemed deadly serious. At least four dogs had been killed or severely injured in the line of duty in the past year. One was thrown into traffic by an armed robber; another bit into a brick of cocaine; another was stabbed repeatedly; the last barely survived an attempted drowning. "If it's not a violent felon, you typically don't send in the dog," Pietropaolo said. "In the use-of-force scale, it's almost equal to using a nightstick."

Earlier that morning, as I was running across the field to join the judges, I'd suddenly realized that I was being watched. At the other end of the field, a half dozen German shepherds were lined up along a fence, their eyes locked on my every move. To them, I must have seemed like just another target—a man in a turkey suit, dashing through the forest on opening day of hunting season. "You got lucky," Rothschild told me later. Even with a protective sleeve on, an officer he knew was bitten so hard that his arm broke in two places, and Rothschild bore a dozen scars from trials gone awry. "It's just something you have to overcome," he said. "Most of us never got bit before going into canine. But you kind of get the feel of it. It's normal wear and tear."

Danz, Rothschild's dog, was a big, bristling male with something of his handler's swagger. When his turn came in the trial, he sat without a twitch while the decoy shot off a round and ran down the field. Then, at a murmured word from Rothschild, the dog took off—body low to the ground, feet a blur, like a shaggy brown missile. He was halfway across the field, in mid-flight, when Rothschild yelled "Stop!" The effect was immediate: Danz peeled away, circled back to his handler, and sat squarely at his side—a near-perfect routine.

Others weren't so successful. When David Causey, a patrolman from Lake County, Florida, called his animal off, you could almost see the dog weighing his options. He glanced back at Causey, slowed down for a moment, then hunched his shoulders and accelerated toward the target. "That's called 'He fucked you,'" Causey's friend David Williams told me. "Fifty points off. He's out of the competition."

For Causey, the result was made even worse by a sense of déjà vu. The year before, on the last day of the field trials, the same dog had bitten a decoy's hand and then, for good measure, his crotch. It was a case of accidental reinforcement, Causey said. A few weeks earlier, in Florida, his dog had chased a felon into a closet. A rough struggle ensued until the dog, in desperation, bit the man between the legs. Immediate surrender. The next time the dog chased down a suspect, he tried the same trick.

Success again! By the time the field trials rolled around, the behavior was locked in.

When Causey and Williams told me this story, we were having breakfast at a coffee shop with Kurt Dumond, the officer who had received the unfortunate bite. Williams, a garrulous Cajun with a life-size revolver tattooed on his hip ("I'm always packing"), pulled out his cell phone and called up some pictures he'd taken at the emergency room: Dumond in a pale-blue hospital gown, followed by several distressing closeups of his scrotum. "That's a mess right there," Dumond said. Williams nodded. "The nurse, when she sees it, she goes, 'Woo wooooo!' Then the doctor comes out and goes, 'That is going to hurt!' Kurt, he'd just told me he had a little laceration. I didn't realize it was thirteen stitches' worth." This year, Williams added, Dumond wore a cup.

How do you keep a dog in line? The answer used to be simple: you smacked it or yelled at it or yanked on its chain. It wasn't pretty, but it could get the job done. Punishment and compulsion are still common in dog training, though usually in more subtle forms—a tug on a leash, for instance, or a mild shock from an electric collar. Traditional trainers, from the monks of New Skete to *Schutzhund* champions like Friedrich Biehler, can produce very accomplished dogs. But, as behaviorism has worked its way from aquariums to kennels, more and more dogs are being taught with positive reinforcement, often using a handheld clicker. "You used to wait until the dog did something wrong, then corrected it," Michele Pouliot, the director of research and development at Guide Dogs for the Blind in Oregon, told me. "Now you're rewarding a behavior you like before it goes wrong."

Like so much else in the dog world, the change mirrors a trend in child rearing—and provokes the same heated debate. ("The only thing two dog trainers can agree about is what the third dog trainer is doing wrong," Steve White told me.) The tough love of Cesar Millan, the Dog Whisperer, and the tender manipulations of Victoria Stilwell, the host of *It's Me or the Dog,* have their exact analogues in parenting styles. Hearing Pouliot talk about headstrong, distractible puppies—the kind that usually make good police dogs—is a lot like bearing an elementary-school teacher talk about attention-deficit disorder and the trouble with boys. "If a dog loves squirrels, you have to find something that excites him so much it overpowers the squirrel instinct," Pouliot told me. "If you're constantly on top of him—punishing, punishing, punishing—that behavior is not going away. You have to get that dog to try to figure out what you want."

Canine police are conservative by nature. They have little margin for error or experiment, so they tend to play the Tiger Moms in this debate. "It goes like this," Gary Pietropaolo, the judge from Yonkers, told me. "You always want to use positive motivation first. But, if that was the only thing we used with these animals, we wouldn't have enough shelters in this country. What do you do with the dog that, if you show him the clicker, he shows you his teeth? Do you just kill him?"

It was the third day of the field trials, and Pietropaolo and the other judges were gathered in a conference room at the Holiday Inn, pooling their scores. Kurt Dumond's dog, Erek, held a thin lead over the rest of the field, with Rothschild's Danz in fifth place. (Erek would eventually drop to third, Danz to eleventh, and the championship would go to a dog from Austin, Minnesota, named Ghost—one of only a few Belgian Malinois in a sea of German shepherds.)

July 10, 1954

THE NEW YORKER

Price 20 cents

The best handlers never abuse their dogs, Pietropaolo said, but, like good parents, they make their authority clear. "If you tell your kid to sit down and be quiet at the table, and he doesn't do it, it's over. You have to make it happen. But you don't necessarily have to grab him by the hair and drag him around." The judge beside him grinned. "I still use a choke chain on the kid," he said.

"How long have you been self-employed?"

Guide-dog trainers were a lot like the police once, Michele Pouliot told me. Their methods were rooted in military dog training, brought over from Europe after the two world wars. "Everything was steeped in this tradition of very harsh treatment," she said. "Everything was 'You're wrong.'" Then, six years ago, Guide Dogs for the Blind switched over to positive reinforcement. "It was a huge undertaking," Pouliot told me. "We have sixty-five instructors who took years to get good at what they're doing. You're asking them to flip-flop a whole set of technical skills. It's like starting all over."

The benefits are already clear, Pouliot said. Less than half the dogs in her program used to complete their training successfully; now the number is close to three-quarters. "And the dogs are doing things they could never do before, unbelievable things," she said. One of Pouliot's specialties is canine musical freestyle—essentially, dancing with your dog. On YouTube, you can see her Australian shepherd, Listo, doing its best Ginger Rogers: waltzing backward, spinning pirouettes, doing double-takes, handstands, and cancan kicks, all to a medley of TV theme songs. "If you break down that routine and ask a traditional trainer, 'How do you train that?' he'd say, 'Hmm,'" Pouliot told me. "It would be impossible. If I jerk a dog on a leash, I can make him sit. I can make him cringe. But I can't make him show his natural joy."

Police dogs, though, aren't like other animals. Their work is inherently harsh and contradictory. Joy is often beside the point. "We have to have an animal that's willing to consummate its aggression on a living, breathing human, then contain it enough to come back to you," one trainer told me. "That's a lot to ask of any being, much less a dog." Positive reinforcement may be better at coaxing dogs into dancing figure eights and giving high fives, as Pouliot's partners do. But a certain amount of stress could inure an animal to the rigors of the street or the battlefield. "Dogs that are trained in a completely positive way, you deploy them in Afghanistan with the bombs going off—I think they'll crumble," a trainer at Auburn told me.

The program at Auburn is like boot camp for dogs. The Canine Detection Research Institute occupies part of an old military base in Anniston, Alabama, in the foothills of the southern Appalachians. When I visited, two weeks after the national field trials, I was taken to a low metal building across the road from the main offices. Inside, a narrow corridor was flanked by rows of steel cages, each with a small door that led to a dog run, outside. The air was edged with traces of ammonia and feces and reverberated with near-constant barking. Overhead, a loudspeaker system piped in still more noise: equipment clanking, boots stomping, engines roaring, bombs exploding.

"That's a Spook Less soundtrack," my guide explained. The system was first developed for stables, he said, and was used by police to get their horses ready for riot squads and other unsettling duties. The recordings could be swapped out to simulate thunderstorms, fireworks, screaming crowds, or construction sites. At one point, after a bombing raid—"I think that's *Saving Private Ryan*"—I heard some bagpipes playing. When I asked what they were for, I was told that police have to attend a lot of funerals.

Auburn specializes in detection dogs. It has twenty-five trainers, who supply about a hundred animals a year to Amtrak, Federal Protective Services, and police departments around the country, including the N.Y.P.D. (Rothschild and his German shepherd, Danz, both trained there.) The average canine graduate costs twenty-one thousand dollars, including ten weeks of lessons for the handler. An elite Vapor Wake dog—"They're like the Michael Jordans of dogs," one of the trainers told me. "They can pick fragments out of the air"—costs thirty-two thousand, with an extra six weeks of training.

Detection dogs tend to vary by country and by national temperament. The French like standard poodles, the English springer spaniels. The Russians, in the Moscow airport, use a strange little breed called a Sulimov dog—a mixture of wild jackal, Lapland herding dog, and other breeds—which is said to be the world's best bomb sniffer. Bloodhounds have long been used as trackers in the South. But at Auburn, as at most canine-detection programs in the country, the cages were filled with Labrador retrievers. They were good-natured, highly driven animals, and less liable to bite than pointy-eared dogs. They were in such demand, in fact, that Auburn was also experimenting with other breeds, including springer spaniels and German pointers. "The country is almost out of Labs for detection work," one broker told me. "They're gone. And they don't have any Labs in Europe, either. I had a department wait ten months for one before I found it."

Dogs have such good noses that almost any breed can detect explosives. "If there are differences among them, they're probably well within the margin of error for our ability to measure them," Paul Waggoner, the behavioral scientist at the institute, told me. "The big key is trainability." Waggoner, who is forty-five, is a bearded, bearish figure with an unnerving habit of rolling his eyes back in his head as he talks, like a psychic. Bloodhounds are usually too single-minded for detection work, he said. Once they've hit a trail, they can seem "brutally stupid" when asked to change gears. Border collies can be too smart for their own good: they follow their handlers' cues rather than their own noses. Coonhounds like to go off crittering; dachshunds are too small and stumbly underfoot; and Doberman pinschers scare the bejesus out of people. What's left are friendly working breeds like retrievers and pointers: animals both social and independent, whose bloodlines have been better maintained than those of most show dogs.

If patrol dogs are the Swiss Army knives of the canine world, detection dogs are the shivs. They don't have to chase down felons, disarm robbers, or respond to the slightest cue. They just have to find bombs. Even so, until recently, only one in four dogs made it through the program. Like *Schutzhund* and guide-dog schools, Auburn sent its puppies to families for basic training, then brought them back for detection work after a year. But the dogs had to contend with so many environments—when I visited, they ran drills in a school, a shopping mall, along a highway, and in a mega-church—that any phobia was eventually found out. Rothschild's dog, for instance, was afraid of slippery floors as a puppy, and he needed weeks of practice to get used to jumping fences.

Four years ago, Auburn decided to try a more rigorous approach. The puppies now go to prisons in Florida and Georgia, where they're trained and cared for by convicts in their cells. The compan-

---

## PROBLEM

You know those terrible arithmetic problems about how many peaches some people buy, and so forth? Well, here's one we *like*, made up by a third-grader who was asked to think up a problem similar to the ones in his book: "My father is forty-four years old. My dog is eight. If my dog was a human being, he would be fifty-six years old. How old would my father be if he was a dog? How old would my father plus my dog be if they were both human beings?   | 1957 |

---

ionship seems to have done the men good: some have been able to reduce their medications, and a few have gone on to become professional trainers. But the effect on the dogs has been even more dramatic. "You have startling noises and startling sights 24/7," one of the trainers told me. "You

have crowds, stairs, slick floors, grated floors. If a dog can get used to those, you know he's not going to be fearful." Eighty percent of Auburn's puppies now go on to become detection dogs.

I went to see the Vapor Wakes the next morning. They were being trained in an abandoned building near the woods, where the Army once taught officers to interrogate prisoners. Its dingy halls were lined with doors marked "Do Not Disturb: Interview in Progress," each one with an identical office behind it. To find a person carrying a bomb in here, an ordinary dog would have had to search the building systematically, sniffing its way from room to room. The Vapor Wakes didn't bother. They'd been taught to track explosives like living prey, following the trail of scent particles left suspended in the air.

"I'll hide in one of these rooms, then you bring her in," Tim Baird, the head trainer, told his assistant. He took a vest filled with TNT and wrapped it around his waist. Then he walked down the hall, turned the corner, and ducked into an office along the next corridor. The assistant brought in a small black Lab named Faye, her tail wagging furiously. She'd had thirty-nine days of detection training and twenty of Vapor Wake, and she knew that every drill was another chance at a reward. She scampered in a circle for a while, flaring the air, then took off in the wrong direction. Nothing there. She doubled back, sniffed at my pants—I'd stood next to Baird while he was stuffing the vest with dynamite—then shook me off and ran down the hall, catching a scent.

A dog sniffs the air like a wine taster, Waggoner had told me. It takes short, sharp breaths—as many as ten per second—drawing the scent deep into the nasal cavity to the olfactory epithelium. The receptors there are a hundred times denser than in a human, and can detect a wide array of molecules. When I followed Faye down the hall, I found her in the office, sitting on her haunches—the signal for "the bomb is here"—watching Baird with barely contained excitement. He reached into his pocket and pulled out a well-chewed tennis ball, then threw it down the hall with a whoop. Faye caught it on the first bounce.

The whole sequence had taken about thirty seconds. In one study, in Michigan in 2000, police dogs managed to track down suspects 93 percent of the time, compared with 59 percent for teams of two to four police officers. And the dogs did it five to ten times faster. Vapor Wakes focus on explosives—in an adjacent room, Baird taught the dogs to find more than a dozen kinds of chemical by hiding them in a wall fitted with small compartments—but other dogs have been taught to find everything from bedbugs to termites, lung cancer, diabetes, and the lithium in cell phones. At Auburn, a dog that can't cut it as a bomb detector could find work as a fungus hound, sniffing out growths that attack and kill the roots of pine trees in the Southeast.

Its esteem for dogs notwithstanding, the university hasn't given up on mechanizing them. When I was in Waggoner's office, later that day, he played me a video from a project called Autonomous Canine Navigation. It showed a yellow Labrador moving through a bomb site wearing an elaborate headset and a harness. The harness contained a computer, a video camera, a G.P.S., and an accelerometer, all remotely controlled. As we watched, a man on a rooftop transmitted some coordinates to the computer below, which directed the dog to the target by playing tones for "Left," "Right," and "Stop" over the headset. "The computer can get within three meters," Wag-

goner said. "That's more accurate than under human control." When the dog came to a doorway, it sniffed at the threshold and lay down. By dial, a sensor had detected its rapid-fire breathing, which meant an explosive had been found. Lying down set off a switch on its belly, confirming the discovery.

The video ended with a tennis ball flying down from the roof and the dog jumping up to snatch it. Even cyborgs, it seems, can use a little positive reinforcement.

New York City is now experimenting with a simpler version of canine navigation. In October, it acquired an infrared video camera that mounts on a dog's back and can be remotely monitored by police. "We can see what the dog is seeing," John Pappas, the head of the transit squad, told me. "So we can use it in a building search. If there's a suspicious box, instead of sending a human being down there, I'll send in the dog, then call him back if things look suspicious." The purchase was approved after the raid on Osama bin Laden, in which a Belgian Malinois named Cairo played an important role. "The real technology here is the dog," Pappas said, "and a lot of it is centered on the nose. That's the most useful tool we have."

On my last day with the squad, Rothschild and Brenner took the dogs for a sweep of Grand Central Terminal. It was nine o'clock on a Friday morning and a final wave of commuters was rushing from the trains. Police in riot gear stood guard by the tunnels to the tracks, machine guns at the ready, while voices blared overhead. When two of the squad's Vapor Wakes ambled in from the street, they stopped at the entrance and stared. The mess hall in a Georgia prison had nothing on this scene: a thousand New Yorkers late for their appointments. "It's an extreme situation," Rothschild said. "But we try to put the dogs in the hardest scenarios possible. We don't know how the next explosive is going to go through." The dogs didn't seem to mind. They just lifted their noses and sniffed the air.

Earlier that morning, Rothschild had arranged for two decoys to make runs through the subway and the train terminal. One would be carrying seven pounds of ammonium nitrate, wrapped in black panty hose and stuffed in a backpack; the other would have twenty pounds of dynamite in a baby stroller. Vapor Wakes can track a scent in the air for up to half an hour, I was told, but the trail wouldn't last long in Grand Central. "You have the trains pulling in air over here," Rothschild said. "You've got the mass of people pulling the air down under these arches. You've got vents bringing it around, and the smells from all the restaurants." He shook his head. "It's like when a boat passes. You can see the wave right afterward, but eventually it dissipates."

Horacio Maldonado, one of the new recruits, positioned himself under an arched entrance on the west side of the station. His black Lab, Ray, could smell most of the passersby from there—she had a range of about thirty feet—but a crowd like this was full of false leads. The chemicals found in explosives can also be found in drugs, cosmetics, fertilizer, construction supplies, and other mundanities. I'd heard of a police dog driven wild by a table patched with plastic wood filler, and a dog tearing down a wall with nail-gun cartridges hidden inside it. "I remember one time, we stopped a guy in Columbus Circle, he had two hundred nitrogen pills in his pocket," Maldonado told me. "Turned out he was going to Europe and had just come from his doctor. So you've got to use your common sense. The guy's sixty, seventy years old. He isn't sweating. Does he look like a suicide bomber?"

False positives are the bugbears of canine detection, but the bigger problem is miscommunication. A leash can be like a faulty phone line. The handler thinks the dog is telling him something; the dog thinks it's the handler's idea. ("Dogs are pretty easy," one trainer told me. "The problem is usually at the other end of the leash.") At Auburn one afternoon, I'd watched Waggoner put a Labrador into an fMRI scanner, to see which part of its brain lit up when detecting a scent. Some day, he said, detection dogs may carry EEGs that set off an alarm when a bomb is found. For now, though, cops and dogs have no choice but to try to talk to one another.

When the explosives went by, they were about twenty feet from Maldonado. The decoy, a young man in a blue sweat shirt with a Mets cap underneath the hood, was buried so deep in the crowd that I almost missed him. The Vapor Wake didn't. She lunged forward on her leash, Maldonado stumbling behind. The decoy walked beneath the arch and down the corridor, heading toward a set of stairs that led to the subway. Ray cut zigzags across his trail, zeroing in on the scent. Soon, she was only about ten feet away, pulling so hard on the leash that her legs were splayed like a lizard's, claws scrabbling on the tile. She was about to catch up when a middle-aged woman sauntered by with three toy dogs on a leash beside her. Ray stopped and glanced at them—a little hungrily, I thought—then shook her head and continued. But by then the trail had drifted, and the decoy was down the stairs.

It was a rare mistake. I'd seen the Vapor Wakes catch half a dozen decoys that week, and even Ray found her man eventually, when he doubled back through the subway. But would she have caught him in real life? "Yeah, she was in

## THE WATCHER

The dog who knew the winter felt no spleen
And sat indoors; the birds made tracks all day
Across the blue-white crust; he watched the
    branches sway
Like grasping fingers mirrored on the snow.
The house was warm, and long ago the grass was
    green;
And all day long bones rattled in his head,
While seven withered apples swung like time,
So quick, so short the pendulum. The tree,
Cursing with wind, prayed mercy on its knee.
He saw the snow toward evening flush to red,
Stepped on his bowl of milk, licked up his crime,
Rolled on his cozy self and smelled his skin,
And snuffed the nighttime out around the bed.

—RUTH STONE    | 1957 |

odor," Rothschild said. "She was just eliminating the possibilities. She would have gotten him."

Afterward, when Ray was chasing her tennis ball around, some commuters stopped to watch. They were standing in one of the world's prime targets for terrorism, surrounded by a bomb squad with a suspect in custody, but that didn't seem to concern them. They smiled and watched the nice dog play with its ball, then hurried on their way.

Detection-dog stories almost always have happy endings. If they don't, they aren't about dogs anymore. When the training session was over, Rothschild went to get Danz, who was waiting in a mobile kennel, nearby. His cage was brand new and luxurious by most standards—custom-built and climate-controlled, with sensors that would sound an alarm and open the windows if the air got too hot—but Danz was glad to be free of it. He leaped to the ground when the gate opened, and shook his fur as if casting off a rope. Then he ran to Rothschild's side and waited, as always, for a signal.

It was a cold, clear morning, with sunlight streaming through the treetops, and the last patches of green were aglow in Bryant Park. Rothschild waited a beat, just to remind the dog who was in charge, then quietly said "Empty." Danz jumped into the ivy and lifted his leg to a lamppost, glancing back to make sure this was O.K. A police dog's life is all about delayed gratification. *You know that ball? You can't have it. Not right now. That treat? Maybe later, if you do exactly what I say.* Danz had an alpha male's domineering drive—it wasn't hard to imagine him howling at the head of a pack—but he'd long since learned to tamp it down. And who was to say he wasn't happier this way: always cared for, always needed, always knowing exactly what was expected of him?

Some police keep their dogs in a crate at night, when the family is around. "My husband doesn't put his gun on the kitchen table," Kurt Dumond's wife, Helen, told me. "And he doesn't let his police dog loose in the house." But Rothschild, who had two young children, let his dog roam free at home. Danz was named for Vincent Danz, a New York cop and family friend, who died in the attacks on September 11th, and Rothschild never forgot that the dog was also looking after him. He let Danz wander through the park a while longer. "This is his time," he said. "His time to play. When he empties, I just let him be a dog."

| 2012 |

# DOG RUN MOON

*Fiction*

## CALLAN WINK

Sid was a nude sleeper. Had been ever since he was a little kid. To him, wearing clothes to bed seemed strangely redundant, like wearing underwear inside your underwear or something. And that was why he was now running barefoot and bare-assed across the sharp sandstone rimrock far above the lights of town. It was after two in the morning, a clear, cool, early-June night, with the wobbly gibbous moon up high and bright, so that he could see the train yard below—the crisscrossing rails, a huge haphazard pile of old ties, the incinerator stack. He was sweating, but he knew that once he could run no more the cold would start to find its way in. After that, he didn't know what would happen.

The dog was padding along tirelessly, sometimes at Sid's side, sometimes ranging out and quartering back sharply, its nose up to the wind trying to cut bird scent. Not for the first time in his life, Sid found himself envying a dog. Its fur. Its thick foot pads. A simple, untroubled existence of sleeping, eating, running, fucking occasionally if you still had the parts, not worrying about it if you didn't. Even in his current predicament, Sid couldn't help admiring the dog. A magnificent bird dog for broken country such as this, no two ways about it. Sid kept going, hobbling, feeling the rimrock make raw hamburger out of the soles of his feet. When he turned he could see smears of his blood on the flat rock glistening black under the moon. And then the shafts of headlights stabbing the jutting sandstone outcroppings. He could hear the shouts of Montana Bob and Charlie Chaplin as they piloted their A.T.V. over the rough ground.

Sid hadn't stolen the dog. He'd liberated it. He firmly believed this, and this belief was the fundamental basis of his disagreement with Montana Bob. Montana Bob thought that simple possession meant ownership. Sid thought otherwise.

He'd been in town for two months, and his path to and from work took him twice daily through the alley behind the house with the dog. The dog would follow his passing through the chain link and Sid would whistle, and the dog would raise its ears without getting up.

Sid worked at a sawmill that processed logs brought down from the mountains. The logs came in massive and rough, smelling like moss and the dark places where snow lingers into July. They entered one end of a screeching hot pole building, met the saw, and came out the other side, flat and white and bleeding pitch into the red-dirt lumberyard. The men who worked the logs and the saw were Mexicans mostly, wide, sweating men who wore dirty white tank tops, their inner arms scabbed and raw from wrestling rough barked logs. They spoke their language to each other, and Sid did not know them. He kept to himself and did his work. He was a scrap man. All day he took castoff pieces of aspen and pine and cut

and stapled them into pallets that were eventually piled with boards to be shipped out. His hands were pitch-stained and splintered. All day his mind ran laps, and after work he walked home through the alley, whistled at the dog on his way, and drank three glasses of water in quick succession, standing at the kitchen sink in the trailer that he rented by the month and hadn't bothered to furnish. Even with the windows open, the trailer smelled like a hot closet full of unwashed clothing, and Sid couldn't stand being there unless he was asleep.

In the evenings, he drove. Sometimes over to the next town, sometimes all the way back to where he'd come from, but he never drove by his old house. She still lived there and he couldn't bear the thought of her looking out the kitchen window to see his truck moving slowly down the street. He could imagine how his face would appear to her. Sun-dark. Gaunt. Too sharp down the middle, as if it were creased. Sometimes he got a milkshake at the diner and nursed it for the drive. No matter where he drove he took the same way back, a route that ran past the front of

"You can't plead cute."

the house with the dog. The east-facing windows were covered with tinfoil and Sid never saw anyone outside.

At the mill one afternoon, a full pallet of eight-inch-by-twelve-foot boards broke free of the loader and crushed the legs of one of the Mexicans who had been standing by the truck, waiting to tighten the straps. Sid, eating his lunch, saw the whole thing, heard the man's hoarse screams above the shriek of the saw until the saw was silenced and then it was just the man, pinned to the ground and writhing, his eyes bulging, with sawdust coating the sweat on his bare arms.

That evening, Sid drove the two hours to his old house, still in his work clothes. When he got there, her car was in the driveway and there was a pickup truck parked behind it. Sid pulled in sharply and got out, not bothering to shut the door behind him. He was striding fast, halfway up to her porch, before he noticed the dried smears of blood on his pant legs and boots. At the mill, he and everyone else had rushed to the man, frantically teaming up to move the heavy boards from his legs. There had been blood everywhere, making the sawdust dark, making the boards slick and red and hard to hold. Now, standing on her front lawn, he tried to clean out the rust-colored crescents under his fingernails, tried to scrub the pine pitch mixed with dried blood from the creases in his palms. He was rubbing his hands on his stained jeans when he saw movement at the curtains over the kitchen window. And then he ran, sliding into the open door of the truck, spinning gravel up onto the vehicles in front of him as he backed out at full speed.

On his way home he passed the house with the dog. As usual, there was no sign of life outside. Sid passed slowly and, after thinking about it for a minute, pulled over and let the truck idle. Then he

got out and went around back to where the dog was lying on a pile of dirty straw, chained to a sagging picnic table. The dog didn't bark, didn't even get up, just watched Sid with its muzzle resting on its front paws. Sid unhooked the chain from the dog's collar and when he walked away the dog followed him, jumped in his truck, and sat on the bench seat, leaning forward with its nose smudging the windshield. Sid drove up to the flat, windswept bench above town and let the dog run. In the hour before it got dark, they put up three coveys of Huns and two sharptails, the dog moving through clumps of sagebrush and cheatgrass, working against the wind like some beautifully engineered piece of machinery perfectly performing the one, the only, task to which it was suited.

Sid was afraid of Montana Bob. As he ran, he could feel the fear lodged somewhere up under his sternum, a sharp little stab of something like pain with each inhaled breath. It was a healthy thing, his fear of Montana Bob. You should be afraid, Sid, he thought. You should be afraid of Montana Bob, the way you should be afraid of a grizzly bear, a loose dog foaming at the mouth, anything nearsighted and sick and unpredictable. Sid stopped behind the wind-twisted limbs of a piñon pine and listened. He could hear the low growl of the A.T.V. somewhere behind him, and then the different, softer sound of the engine idling, stopped, no doubt, so that Montana Bob and Charlie Chaplin could branch out on foot to look for his sign. Sid was above them and he could see the shapes of their shadows, tall and angular, moving across the headlights, cloaked in swirling motes of red dust.

"I know who you are, Sid. I know it's you out there. We're still out here, too."

Montana Bob's voice came up to him, reverberating off the rock.

"You got the dog, and I think that is a damn stupid reason to go through all this trouble. I got Charlie Chaplin here with me. He agrees that this is a lot of stupidness just for a damn dog. Also, he has a big goddam pistol. I bet your feet hurt something fierce. You're bleeding like a stuck hog all over this lizard rock, and me and Charlie Chaplin are going to drive right up on you before long. We will. Also, you were a big damn fool to run out the back door like that. Charlie saw your naked ass. We were just coming for the dog. You can't argue my right to it. You have that what belongs to me. You catch up that dog and bring it down to me and, hell, you know what? We'll even give you a ride back down into town. We will."

Sid started out again, moving up and away from the voices and lights. He found a long piece of slickrock that stretched out farther than he could see into the darkness, and he ran. He could hear the rough whisper of the dog's pads on the rock, the click of its nails. The dog's coat shone. What was black in sunlight became purple-blue in the moonlight; what was normally white now glowed like mother of pearl.

Would Montana Bob do as he said? Let Sid go if he came down with the dog? Sid was unsure, but he thought not. The oblong little organ of fear under his sternum pulsed each time his feet slapped the rock. He kept going. The moon overhead was a lopsided and misshapen orb that at any moment could lose its tenuous position and break upon the rocks. That might be a good thing. A landscape of blackness into which he could melt.

The dog had been his for a week when Montana Bob found him out. Sid was in the Mint having a happy-hour beer before heading home and he'd left the dog in the truck. He'd taken to bringing the dog to work with him so he could let it out to run at lunch. Sid had his back to the door, but as soon as the two men came in he had a bad feeling. They sat right next to him, one on each side. Plenty of stools all up and down the bar, but they came and crowded in on him. The big one wore a sweat-stained summer Stetson with a ragged rooster-pheasant tail feather sticking out of the hatband. His hair was shaggy and flared out from the hat brim. He wore a leather vest with nothing underneath save a mangy pelt of thick black hair. His companion was considerably smaller and extremely fair-skinned, nearly bald except for a few blond strands grown long on one side and then combed over. He wore a button-up oxford shirt and corduroy pants. Sperry Top-Siders. On his belt was a large knife in a sheath, its handle made of a pale-yellow plastic that was supposed to look like bone. They ordered beers, and when the beers arrived the big man in the hat drank deeply and then leaned toward Sid, a pale scum of suds covering his upper lip.

"I don't believe in beating the bush."

Sid picked at a loose corner on the label of his bottle of beer. He thought about bolting, just getting up like he was going to make his way to the bathroom and then sliding out the back.

"I don't beat the bush, so I'm going to get right down to the tacks. I believe I recognize a familiar dog in that blue Chevy out front, and also, since you're about the only one in here, I figure that's your vehicle, so I figure that I'll need to ask you where you happened to come across that dog."

The man pushed his hat back on his head and swivelled on his stool to face Sid. He smiled.

"Also, I'm Montana Bob." He extended his hand—which Sid shook, not knowing what else

KoVarsky

to do—and nodded toward his companion, seated on Sid's other side.

"And that's Charlie Chaplin. Shake his hand."

Sid turned and shook Charlie Chaplin's pale proffered hand.

"I'm a local businessman, and Charlie Chaplin is my accountant. Also, he provides counsel to me in matters of legal concern."

Sid considered Charlie Chaplin, and when their eyes met he felt something skittering and cold move down his spine. Montana Bob was the bigger man, menacing even, with large bare arms and small pieces of pointed silver at the tips of his boots, but it was this one, small and waxen and pale, who made Sid shift uncomfortably.

Sid found himself speaking too quickly, his voice high.

"I picked up that dog at the shelter. Bought and paid for. Got him his shots—rabies, distemper, all that. I got the paperwork in the truck. They said at the shelter that he was a canine of misfortunate past. Meaning his old owner used to stomp him. Kind of a mutt, but he seems loyal. Likes to fetch the tennis ball. My kids are crazy about him."

Montana Bob nodded as Sid spoke. Charlie Chaplin nodded, too. Montana Bob motioned the bartender down to them and ordered another beer for himself and Charlie Chaplin.

"Two more. Also, a large pitcher of ice water. No ice."

The bartender went away, and Montana Bob spoke to Sid's reflection in the mirrored bar back.

"Likes to fetch the tennis ball, does he? Well, I'll be. Did you know that that dog was given to me by a Frenchman? The dog is a French Brittany spaniel and he comes from France. Born in

France of royal French Brittany stock. Also, that dog was a gift from a French count. Guy St. Vrain made me a present of that dog when it was just a pup, in payment for services rendered by yours truly. You don't know Guy St. Vrain, but that doesn't matter. That's how he likes it. He's in the movie business. Also, he's in the dog business."

The bartender came with the pitcher of water, and Montana Bob took off his hat and set it on the bar top. He poured half the pitcher into the hat and then replaced it on his head, the water streaming down his face and neck, matting the thick glossy hair on his chest.

"You stole my fucking dog." He was still looking at Sid through his reflection in the bar mirror. "Also, I had a hot and dusty day out on the trail, and I come here for a drink only to find my possessions in someone else's egg basket."

In the mirror, Sid saw his own hands go up, saw his shoulders shrug.

"Got it at the shelter. I don't know anything about any of this."

He slid from the stool and caught the bartender's eye.

"I'll take one more. Be right back. Gotta take a leak."

In the bathroom, he ran the water and splashed some on his face. He had his keys in his hand when he hit the door, and then he was out in the last evening rays of sun, firing the truck, the dog standing anxiously with its front paws on the dash. Sid drove without looking back. He drove all the way down the river road and let the dog out. He walked a path through the thickets of tamarisk and Russian olive, and when he stopped the dog perched delicately at the water's edge, standing on a rock, lapping up the muddy red water.

Before Sid had burst through the bar doors to start his truck, he'd glimpsed the barroom. Mon-tana Bob sitting astride his stool like a swayback steed. Charlie Chaplin standing in front of the jukebox, flipping the disks as if looking for a particular track, a song whose name he couldn't remember or whose tune existed solely in his head.

Sid had no clear idea where he was running. It was a strange mode of navigation, more like divination, taking the smoothest path through a shattered Martian nightscape of jumbled rock. If he turned, he could still see the shafts of light from his pursuers' A.T.V., and he thought about circling back toward town. The problem was the dog. Sid would have to cut a wide path around to keep the dog from straying close to the lights, and, if the dog was captured, then what was the point? Another thought: might the dog return to its former owner willingly? Sid was unsure. He kept running. The dog spooked a small herd of mule deer out of a ragged stand of juniper and they bounded past him, covering great lengths of ground with each leap, their forms backlit against the sky now lightening in the east. Sid had never seen desert deer this close before. At the apex of each jump they seemed to hang, suspended, vaguely avian, a group of prehistoric near-birds not quite suited to life on land, not quite comfortable with their wings' ability to keep them aloft. Just then, he had the thought that if he could keep going until the sun came up he might be O.K.

After the incident at the bar, he had broken down and called her. She hadn't answered, and he'd left a message, hating the sound of his voice. Tinny with the fear he'd wanted her to feel. *I'm not calling to try and get you to come back and be mine again. I'm just calling to tell you that if no one ever sees me around anymore it's because I ran afoul of some bad people in a matter concerning a dog. And I never meant for you to grow against me like you did. That's it.* He hung up in self-loathing. He folded an old blanket on the floor at the end of his bed for the dog, and when the knock on the door came—at two in the morning, three days after Montana Bob had called him out in the Mint—Sid couldn't exactly say that he hadn't been expecting it. For a brief moment he knew the relief of the fugitive who finally feels the handcuffs encircle his wrists.

Montana Bob spoke to him from the other side of the door, his words just barely whiskey-softened.

"You, sir, are in possession of my royal French canine. Charlie Chaplin and myself come to you as missionaries. Also, as pilgrims and crusaders."

By the time Montana Bob kicked in the flimsy trailer door, Sid had already slammed out the back, catching Charlie Chaplin off guard. The accountant was standing on the trailer's rickety back porch, and the door handle hit him in the midsection, doubling him over. Sid ran down the sloping trailer-court drive and through

## REPERCUSSION

A subscriber to the *Times* who lives up in Westchester spent a good part of last year training his Labrador retriever to bound down to the open tube beside the mailbox in front of his house and fetch the paper back to the front door. When the newspaper strike set in, the retriever kept looking for the *Times,* and in a couple of days he became morose at his failure to find it. Finally, the subscriber hit upon a scheme to cheer up his dog. Each evening, he decided, he would go down into his cellar, where he has a huge stack of *Timeses,* pick up an old copy, and sneak down to the open tube with it. The plan has worked fine. The Labrador is still busy with his retrieving.    | 1965 |

his neighbors' weed-choked yards, down the alley, across the dead main street, and through the train yard, his bare toes curling around the cold iron track as he gathered himself to hurdle over the crushed-granite rail bed. It wasn't until he reached the barren lots at the base of the rimrock's upslope that he realized the dog was running beside him, occasionally stopping to lift its leg on a rock or a clump of sagebrush. Back toward the road, Sid could see the lights of an A.T.V. coming fast. He waited until he could make out the shape of Montana Bob's hat and the pale, bare arms of Charlie Chaplin wrapped around his midsection—and then he started scrabbling his way up the slope, the dog flowing effortlessly through the rock above him.

She was a small woman, so pale that the desert hurt her in ways that Sid would never fully understand. Like Sid, she was a nude sleeper. When he found this out it became one of those happy little intersections of shared personality, the slow accumulation of which is love. With her, it was years of nights spent bare back to bare chest. Sometimes, when it was hot, they woke up and had to peel themselves apart, their tangled limbs stuck together like the fleshy segments of some strange misshapen fruit.

They were alike in other ways as well, and at one time these things had seemed natural and unaffected, important even. They both liked the river. Sid got inner tubes from the tire store, and when the heat got unbearable they would float, keeping their beer cool in a mesh bag trailing in the river behind them. And, if she never fully came to love the desert, Sid was pretty sure she came to understand why he did. Once, he took her up to see the hoodoos in Goblin Valley. It was midnight during a full moon, and they were half-drunk and a little high. They played tag and hide-and-seek around the hulking sandstone formations, laughing, hooting, and shrieking, the sounds careening, giving voice to the rocks themselves.

Things were good this way for a long time, and then one night he woke to the sound of her crying in the bathroom. The next night she came to bed in one of his T-shirts and a pair of boxer shorts. And the next night Sid slept alone.

As he ran Sid could see her, laid out on their bed, a night-blooming moonflower, her white limbs like petals unfolding, finally, in the absence of light. He remembered their house, how the door latch was broken and the wind would blow the door open if they didn't remember to throw the bolt. They'd be sitting in the little dining room, eating dinner, the table crowded with mismatched cups and plates and silverware, and all of a sudden the door would swing open. She'd flinch, as if someone were breaking in on them, uninvited. Sid used to tease her about it, but now he found himself wondering who exactly it was she thought was coming unannounced into their home. Who was the man with his hand on the doorknob, ready to push his way into their lives?

Sid ran and the rocks cut him; the piñon pines clutched and tore at him. Dried sweat crusted his bare torso and thighs, and any moment of rest brought cramps, the muscles of his legs twitching and popping of their own accord. He found himself moving his cracked lips, making strange utterances with each painful footfall, the desert a silent observer, an expressionless juror to whom he tried to make his plea. *I ran afoul of some bad people in a matter concerning a dog. Irana foul. Iranafoul. I ran, a foul?*

It sounded melodramatic and desperate, a wild call for attention. Better to leave the dog out of it. Get right to the point.

*Since we dissolved I've been a spectre running blind and naked in the desert. Is that melodramatic? Well, that's what is happening to me now.*

He imagined driving to their old house and stepping onto the porch. She'd be alone and would come out to meet him in one of the sundresses she always wore in the hot months, the fabric like gauze, like a soft bandage laid over healing flesh. She'd offer him a cool drink and they'd sit in the shade, and the words, all the right ones, would flow from him, an upwelling, an eruption of cleansing language.

*Remember when we went way up north that winter and rented the cabin and there was a hot spring not too far away? We'd go out at night and shiver down the path to the water and slip into the warmth, like pulling a hot sheet around us. My feet in the sulfur-smelling mud of the pool, your legs twined around mine like white, earth-seeking roots. Remember that? The way the deer would come down when it got really cold just to stand in the steam rising up from the water? And then the day we left for home? How cold it was? We went outside and our eyes started to freeze at the corners and you had never seen anything like it and took a picture of me standing next to a thermometer that was bottomed out at forty below. In that picture I'm standing on the cabin porch, and behind me the river is frozen solid, or so it seems.*

Here Sid imagined moving in a little closer, putting his work-roughened hand on her smooth one.

*I've been thinking about that picture and that river on the coldest day of the year. Underneath that ice, the river was still moving. Forty below, but even then the water closest to the riverbed was moving. It's like a river exists in defiance, or has a secret life. Everything above is frozen and stiff, but down below it moves along, liquid over the rocks, as though nothing happening on the surface mattered. On a day like*

*Now that the great dog I worshipped for years*
*Has become none other than myself.* Oh Joy!
*I can look within and bark.* Oh Joy!
*I am the rival of my ~~own dog~~ eyes,*

*An eye that sees through the~~s~~ dark, a mouth*
*that speaks of things impossible to probe.*

*A shadow robed in shadow. There is*
*no comfort in this happiness.*

*I can't escape. The weather sings its*
*own songs overhead or chant mercy,*

*in front thought, the moon rolls by.*
*~~The great dog is out. So what. So what.~~*

*Without mercy,*
*in front thought The weather says*
*above the bloom of trees*
*It's ~~own~~ songs. The moon rolls by.*
*The stars go out.*

## GREAT DOG POEM NO. 2

Now that the great dog I worshipped for years
Has become none other than myself, I can look within

And bark, and I can look at the mountains down the street
And bark at them as well. I am an eye that sees itself

Look back, a nose that tracks the scent of shadows
As they fall, an ear that picks up sounds

Before they are born. I am the last of the platinum
Retrievers, the end of a gorgeous line.

But there's no comfort being who I am. I roam around
And ponder fate's abolishments until my eyes

Are filled with tears and I say to myself, "Oh, Rex,
Forget. Forget. The stars are out. The marble moon slides by."

—MARK STRAND | 1996 |

*this, you could walk across the river as if you were crossing the street. But, just below that shell, the current would be flowing. That is my love for you.*

And that would be it. She'd come with him, push up next to him on the bench seat of his pickup, and he'd drive with the windows down, her hair blowing into his face and mouth and eyes. Dust and the scent of her shampoo in his nose. They'd pick up right where they'd left off.

He was moving up a dry creek bed, shuffling through the soft red sand deposited by spring floods in years past, when he got the feeling that the creek wasn't dry after all, that he was splashing through an ankle-deep current of muddy red water. He was thirsty. Christ, was he thirsty. But when he scooped a great double handful of water up to his cracked lips it turned back to sand and fell through his fingers. This seemed a particularly cruel joke, and he had thoughts of finding a dark place to curl up inside, a rock for a pillow and a soft blanket of sand. But there was the matter of the dog, the matter of Charlie Chaplin's vacuous eyes and his pistol, which, in Sid's mind, had achieved magnificent proportions. Charlie Chaplin was riding it like an evil old mare with cracked hooves and a faded brand. It was the gun itself in pursuit, half horse, half instrument of percussion and death. A spavined nag whose blued flanks were singed and smoking.

At first, running on the sand was deliriously comfortable, the soft ground like an answered prayer for the raw soles of Sid's feet. But then the farther he went the harder it became, the sand shifting and giving way under his feet, so that each stride required more effort from his already screaming calves.

When the twisting and turning of the creek bed became unbearable, Sid clambered out onto the exposed rock. From this vantage point, he watched the now greatly diminished moon drift down toward the far black horizon like a pale phosphorus match head broken off in the striking. If Montana Bob and Charlie Chaplin were still in pursuit, he had no evidence of it. In fact, some small dislodged part of him was unsure that they had ever existed. Sid couldn't see the dog most of the time. Sometimes he forgot about it altogether. It ran ahead, silent and unperturbed as the earth itself.

It was a loud dawn. Sid had never seen or heard anything quite like it, the sun breaking the horizon line with a sound like a dull knife ripping a sheet. He was walking stiffly now, moving his arms in great circles, slapping his thighs and torso to fend off the cold. He looked down and for the first time could see himself clearly, the angry red whip welts on his calves from branches, the purple cracked toenails and raised blue lines of engorged veins and capillaries, over everything a grimy patina of sweat crust and desert dust and leaking blood.

He crested a small hill where, on the back side of the slope, there was a rusted stock tank fed by a leaning windmill that rose out of a clump of acacia. He didn't believe in the stock tank. It was like that river of muddy water, a thing that would dry up and slip through his fingers. He sat on a rock and looked. The windmill was missing some slats, and he knew that there was no water in the tank. This was a definite truth, and Sid felt it like gravity. After a while the dog emerged from a tangle of sagebrush and, with no fanfare, proceeded to lap from the tank, its tail fanning slightly in a breeze that did not reach Sid.

Down the slope in jerks, his muscles and ligaments tightened like catgut tennis-racquet cord. Sid submerged his entire head, eyes wide open, into the water, metallic-tasting, gelid with the flavor of the past night. The bottom of the tank was lined with a slick layer of electric-green algae over which a single orange carp hovered, blimplike. Sid wanted to get in, to live with this carp alone in this desert within a desert. But the water was cold, and he knew that the carp did not want him. He drank for so long that points of black began to form at the edges of his vision, small black-legged forms like water striders skating the clear pool of his periphery. He broke for air and collapsed with his back against the tank, the rivets pressing into his flesh. From this position he could see into the twisted inner workings of the windmill, the busted-spring parts, the pieces held together by coils of baling wire. The dog was moving around the base of the acacia trees, its snout plowing last year's dead grass, the fur ends around its paws just slightly reddened by the touch of the desert rock. Above the dog, in the twisting acacia branches, Sid could make out two sparrows, dead and skewered on thorns.

When Sid woke he found Charlie Chaplin squatting next to him, his oxford shirt stained desert red, his corduroys dusty. His pale cheeks were streaked with twin rivulets of what looked like tears, and his eyes were leaking and red. He had his knife out and was poking Sid's bare thigh, raising bright little beads of blood, a ragged collection of blood drops like pissants gathering on his skin. From the number of them it looked as if he'd been at it awhile. Seeing that Sid was awake, Charlie Chaplin swiped at his cheeks with his sleeve. He gave Sid one more poke and then sheathed his knife and went to stand beside Montana Bob, who held a length of chain that he'd hooked to the dog's collar. The dog lay at Montana Bob's boots with its muzzle resting on its paws.

"What the hell. Why?" Montana Bob tilted his hat brim down against the sun.

Sid considered this for a moment and then put up his hands and shrugged his shoulders.

"I've always liked running." Realizing, as he said it, that it was true.

"You look like something from another planet. More dead than alive. Also, Charlie Chaplin isn't happy with you. He wears contact lenses and, seeing how you kept us out here all night in the dust, his eyes are in poor shape. He wants you to know that that's why he's tearing up. He's not actually crying. He suffers from the dust. Also, he lost his pistol. Fell out of his waistband on the ride. I know he feels badly about that."

Sid found himself nodding in agreement with Montana Bob. It was a nearly involuntary movement and he had to force himself to stop.

"You dumb bastard. I don't even know what to do to you. But I guess you done it plenty to yourself. What do you think, Charlie Chaplin?"

Sid looked up into the pale, dirt- and tear-streaked face of the accountant. He tried to read what was there but came up blank. Charlie Chaplin knelt creakily and untied his Top-Siders. He kicked them off his feet toward Sid and then turned to climb on the A.T.V., his socks star-

tlingly white from the ankle down. Silently, Montana Bob took his seat in front of Charlie Chaplin and drove away, his accountant clinging to his waist from behind, his dog padding along at the end of the chain.

It was a long time before Sid could get to his feet and walk, slowly retracing his bloody tracks. It was even longer before the pain made him slip the Top-Siders over his ruined soles, feeling, when he did, something at once like balm and betrayal. With the shoes, he was somehow more naked than before, and he faced the reality of shuffling back to town, no longer unfettered, just exposed. He thought then about going for it, turning east and just continuing on until he either evaporated or arrived, collapsing in a heap, on her porch. Begging her to wash his feet.

| 2011 |

# DOG DAYS

## MARJORIE GARBER

New York City dog owners and the Park Enforcement Patrol are periodically at odds about whether dogs should be permitted to walk (or run) free. "When you give an inch, they take a lawn," says Parks Commissioner Henry J. Stern, who keeps his golden retriever, Boomer, firmly leashed. But pressure groups like You Gotta Have Bark, in Prospect Park, and the Urban Canine Conservancy, in Central Park, have lobbied for greater access to the city's wide-open spaces. "Let Rover rove!" is their battle cry. Plans are afoot to seek permission for a spacious dog run in Central Park's Sheep Meadow, to be paid for by a dog-food company in exchange for "a tasteful bronze plaque." Meanwhile, park rangers ticket the indignant scofflaws who contend (in the words of the *Times* reporter Douglas Martin) that "canine happiness is a greater good."

The recent account in the *Times* of this controversy and a subsequent endorsement of "canine liberation" by Elizabeth Marshall Thomas unleashed a flood of responses. In a highly unusual allocation of space, the *Times* devoted its entire letters column to the topic, printing seventeen letters in all, under the urbane heading "Sunday in the Park with George, Rover and Spot." Major elections, budget battles, and acts of God have had to make do with less. Dog owners wrote to complain that they alone were being singled out by park rangers ("Have you ever seen a skater get a ticket? A litterer? A graffiti artist or a kid doing damage?"), while a bird-watcher protested that loose dogs endanger the city's "wild avifauna." "Parks and other public places were created for all Americans, be they bare of behind or covered with wool, two-footed or four-footed," one letter declared. "The latter have faithfully served our country alongside the former in war and peace, and therefore deserve to share fully in the freedom they helped to preserve." Political hyperbole was, indeed, the order of the day. "Dog lovers of New York, unite!" Elizabeth Marshall Thomas exhorted. "You have nothing to lose but choke chains."

Not content with vox populi, the paper itself weighed in with an editorial a few days later, conceding that "the dog owners do have emotion on their side" but supporting the city's "rationality" in requiring leashes on pets, at least during prime time. (The Parks Department, in what the *Times* proudly called "a very New York–style accommodation," had made it clear that it wouldn't enforce the leash law before 9 A.M. or after 9 P.M.) Nor was this the last that readers heard on the subject: an Op-Ed piece a few days later lamented the supposed exclusivity of neighborhood dog runs, the fees they demanded, and the arcana of the application process. It was like getting your child into private school, only, if possible, more difficult.

To leash or not to leash: why is this question currently testing the limits of life, liberty, and the pursuit of happiness? The answer, I think, has to do with the way the dog both does and doesn't stand in for the human being. A. R. Gurney's Off Broadway comedy *Sylvia* caught this note perfectly by casting a human actress in the part of a dog. Sylvia, "lost and abandoned" in Central Park, jumps into Greg's lap and becomes the love of his life—much to the consternation of his human spouse. When the *Times* divided the controversy between "rationality" (health, safety, control) and "emotion" ("the dog owners do have emotion on their side"), the

emotion in question was a kind of identification with the dog: "Who wants to contemplate the life of retrievers or Rottweilers condemned to go through life without ever running on their own?" The dog endures the same confinement as human city dwellers and yet remains capable of a joyful animality that human beings fear they have lost forever. It is this impossible extension of themselves that humans fight so passionately to preserve.

But why are the stakes so high in the dog wars today? How are things different from the way they were four decades ago, when Richard Nixon's "Checkers speech" established him as an ideal all-American dad? ("The kids love the dog.") Some people, of course, would like to return to the Checkers-Fala era in American family consensus-building. The Republican Bob Dole, emulating Nixon in a similarly awkward attempt at public intimacy, recently spoke out in praise of his wife and his schnauzer in an address before a group in Bakersfield, California: "I got a dog named Leader. I'm not certain they got a file on Leader. . . . We've had him checked by the vet but not by the F.B.I. or the White House. He may be suspect."

Like Dole, many Americans now live with dogs instead of children. ("Children are for people who can't have dogs," a New York friend of mine remarked recently.) Canine hip-replacement has become, like juvenile orthodontia, a household medical expense, and dogs are attending preschool and therapy sessions. A summer camp in Maryland, run by Shady Spring Boarding Kennels, features dog-paddling, Frisbee, and hiking, a Bark-and-Ride camp bus, a spa offering haircuts and pedicures, and photographs of dogs in their bunks for the proud owners to take home. "People treat their dogs like their children," the camp director, Char-

lotte Katz Shaffer, says. "They look for a kennel like they look for a pediatrician." The child-centered world of the fifties, so nostalgically recalled by the likes of William Bennett, has become the dog-centered world of *Homeward Bound, Beethoven,* and *Look Who's Talking Now.*

At a time when "universal" ideas and feelings are often compromised or undercut by group identities, the dog tale still has the power to move us. Paradoxically, the dog has become the repository of those model human properties which we have cynically ceased to find among human beings. On the evening news and in the morning paper, dog stories supply what used to be called "human interest." There was the story of Lyric, for instance—the 911 dog, who dialled emergency services to save her mistress, and wound up the toast of Disneyland. Or the saga of Sheba, the mother dog in Florida who rescued her puppies after they were buried alive by a cruel human owner. His crime and her heroic single-motherhood were reliable feature stories, edging out mass killings in Bosnia and political infighting at home. Here, after all, were the family values we'd been looking for as a society—right under our noses.

Indeed, at a time of increasing human ambivalence about human heroes and the human capacity for "unconditional love," dog heroes—and dog stories—are with us today more than ever. Near the entrance to Central Park at Fifth Avenue and Sixty-seventh Street stands the statue of Balto, the heroic sled dog who led a team bringing medicine to diphtheria-stricken Nome, Alaska, in the winter of 1925. Balto's story recently became an animated feature film, joining such other big-screen fictional heroes as Lassie, Rin Tin Tin, Benji, and Fluke.

Yet the special capacity of the dog for incarnating idealized "human" qualities like fidelity and bravery ("all the Virtues of Man without his Vices," wrote Lord Byron feelingly about his beloved Newfoundland, Boatswain) has long been the object of literary admiration. Indeed, it is as old as canonical literature itself. Homer memorably told of the loyalty of Odysseus' old dog Argus, who waited two decades for his master to return, and then died content. In the Rieus' translation:

> There, full of vermin, lay Argus the hound. But directly he became aware of Odysseus' presence, he wagged his tail and dropped his ears, though he lacked the strength now to come nearer to his master. Odysseus turned his eyes away, and . . . brushed away a tear. . . . As for Argus, the black hand of Death descended on him the moment he caught sight of Odysseus—after twenty years.

Recent collections like *Dog Music: Poetry About Dogs,* edited by Joseph Duemer and Jim Simmerman and the charming *Unleashed: Poems by Writers' Dogs,* edited by Amy Hempel and Jim Shepard, have joined the ranks of anthologies from the turn of the century: *The Dog in British Poetry* (1893), *Praise of the Dog* (1902), *To Your Dog and to My Dog* (1915), *The Dog's Book of Verse* (1916). *Dog Music* is a collection of poetry by Elizabeth Bishop, James Merrill, John Updike, Richard Wilbur, and James Wright, among others. Just to read the titles of their poems is to see how much they are about the human condition, the capacity for human emotion and consciousness: Richard Jackson's "About the Dogs of Dachau," James Seay's "My Dog and I Grow Fat," Keith Wilson's "The Dog Poisoner," Joan Murray's "The Black Dog: On

Being a Poet," and so on. "Nobody can tell me/ The old dogs don't know," James Wright says quietly in "The Old Dog in the Ruins of the Graves at Arles." In "Dog Under False Pretenses," William Dickey wonders, about the dog he adopted after her first owner returned her, "Why was she given up?"

> For the first three days I thought she was
> timorous, elderly, a quiet dog . . .
>                   After all these years
> I should recognize, when I see it, shock.

If literature is about love and loss, or loss and love, something about the world we live in today tends to make those feelings more accessible and more poignant when they center on a dog. Whether these poems are really about dogs or about people is a hard question, but that is, in a way, their point: to get to the person, go by way of the dog.

Canine tributes in prose abound, too, many of them published with the proceeds earmarked for canine charitable causes. There is the lavish and beautiful book entitled *Dog People: Writers and Artists on Canine Companionship*, edited by Michael J. Rosen, which includes contributions from Edward Albee, William Wegman, David Hockney, Susan Conant, Armistead Maupin, Jane Smiley, Daniel Pinkwater, Nancy Friday ("My Shih Tzu/My Self"), and a host of other dog-loving luminaries. Artists and writers seem to permit themselves an emotional latitude when speaking of their dogs which they might consider inappropriate, unseemly, or merely too private when referring to friends and lovers.

Identification as much as admiration seems to tie the owner to the dog. Consider *The Dogs of Our Lives: Heartwarming Reminiscences of Canine Companions*, compiled by Louise Goodyear Murray, with contributions by such dog-lovers as Steve Allen, William F. Buckley, Jr., Sally Jessy Raphael, and Norman Vincent Peale. Each writer tells a dog story to illuminate his or her own life. Thus the inspirational Dr. Peale, the author of *The Power of Positive Thinking*, tells of Barry, a German shepherd who travelled on his own from the boot of Italy back to his original family, in Bonn, Germany, and then asks, rhetorically, "If a dog will walk twelve hundred miles for one year to obtain his objective, why won't a human being keep trying again, and again, and again? . . . People who truly try are people who accomplish things!" The child-centered Fred (Mr.) Rogers describes getting his dog Mitzi when he was little "as a present for taking some terrible-tasting medicine." Roger Caras, the president of the A.S.P.C.A. and a longtime spokesman for the humane treatment of animals, tells of his adoption of Sirius, a two-year-old greyhound who was scheduled to die because he had stopped winning races. When they met, Sirius, belying his name, was smiling. ("He doesn't have a home?" Caras asked a volunteer at the greyhound-rescue network. "Well, he does now.") If those are stinging little tears you are surreptitiously wiping away, you are in good company: dog stories—especially dog-rescue (and, alas, dog-cruelty) stories—are perhaps our most reliable contemporary source of genuine, unforced altruistic emotion.

Sigmund Freud, who himself became, late in life, a devoted dog-lover, observed, "Dogs love their friends and bite their enemies, quite unlike people, who are incapable of pure love and always have to mix love and hate in their object relations." This is a view that many have held. In his epitaph for Boatswain—by whose side the poet asked to be buried—Byron declared:

> To mark a friend's remains these stones arise;
> I never knew but one—and here he lies.

Not for nothing is Fido the pet name of man's best friend—and woman's, too. Emily Dickinson found life without her beloved dog Carlo almost insupportable, writing to her friend and mentor Thomas Higginson a spare and eloquent missive:

> Carlo died—
>
> E. Dickinson
> Would you instruct me now?

But if dogs are mourned they are also famous mourners. Emily Brontë's mastiff, Keeper, followed her body to the grave, leading the funeral procession together with her father, as perhaps befitted a male survivor; Anne and Charlotte walked behind. Keeper joined the Brontë family in its pew while the service was read, then took up his station outside Emily's empty bedroom, and howled. Greyfriars Bobby, a Skye terrier who sat by his master's Edinburgh graveside for fourteen years, was immortalized by a Victorian fountain (and dogs' watering hole). Bobby's statue has become a major tourist attraction, vying for popularity with the local castle. Nor is this popularity simply a by-product of the Victorian fashion in mourning. In the twentieth century, Hachiko, an Akita who belonged to a professor at Tokyo University, became the Greyfriars Bobby of his era. It had been Hachiko's custom to meet his master's subway train every night, and after his master died, in 1925, Hachiko went to the station and waited faithfully each evening until his own death, in 1934. A statue of Hachiko, paid for by his admirers, now stands at the subway exit.

A more recent canine mourner seemed at times the most eloquent and straightforward witness in the O. J. Simpson trial. Nicole Brown Simpson's own Akita became the focus of days of testimony centering on what the witness Pablo Fenjves referred to as the dog's "plaintive wail," which a reporter described as a "truly memorable phrase, one that simultaneously captures the sadness beneath the circus, undergirds the prosecution's case and offers a morsel of poetry amid the cop talk, Californiaspeak and legalese." The lead prosecutor Marcia Clark's "eyes lit up," according to Fenjves, when he first spoke of a "plaintive wail," and prosecutors later insisted that he use those words in his testimony. "That's a very important phrase," Clark's associate Cheri Lewis said. It was as if only the dog could tell the truth, the whole truth, and nothing but the truth.

Of course, the behavior of some of these animals, if it were to be faithfully followed by human beings, would strike us as distinctly odd and perhaps psychologically unsound. It's one thing for Hachiko to meet his master's train for nine years; it's another for a bereaved human being to do so. Get on with your life, we say, and we mean it. But we can demand—and receive—from dogs a highly gratifying devotion that we no longer feel comfortable about demanding from one another. In addition, these icons of absolute fidelity offer us a sense of scale. The dog, by being "superhuman" in realms like constancy and loyalty, gives us permission to temporize, vacillate, and even fail.

It's worth noting that the first "humane society" began, in the eighteenth century, as an organization to benefit people, not animals. The dogs were the guards, not the guarded; the Royal Humane Society was founded in London in

1774 for the rescue of drowning persons. Thus a portrait entitled *A Distinguished Member of the Humane Society*, by the famed dog artist Edwin Landseer, pictures a placid and handsome Newfoundland lying on a pier by the water's edge. (The Newfie, together with the mastiff, was the nineteenth century's hero dog of choice.) Today's humane societies, including some that date back more than a hundred years, are "societies for the prevention of cruelty to animals"; significantly, they were founded in both England and America shortly after the abolition of human slavery and involved many of the same activists.

There is something right about using the word "humane" to describe the impulse to protect animals. The mistreatment of defenseless dogs arouses in us profound emotions of empathy and outrage. All our own fears of betrayal and abandonment leap immediately to mind. Only the other evening, I saw a local news feature about two dogs, nicknamed by their rescuers Mama and Baby, who had been tied to a tree in a densely wooded area and left to die. The reporter herself was in manifest distress, and explained that Baby reminded her of her own beloved dog.

Whether leashed or unleashed in life, the dog roams at large in our cultural imagination. An abandoned dog can break our hearts in ways that human strays all too often no longer do. Yet, at the same time, the dog offers a kind of emotional and practical microclimate in which we can make manageable a host of problems that in other areas of life seem overwhelming or out of control: health insurance, day care, preschool, homelessness, depression, euthanasia. The president of the National Psychological Association for Psychoanalysis has observed ruefully, "How ironic that we seem to care more about the happiness of animals than humans."

But is it ironic? Or is it just another way of locating and pursuing human pleasures—like love—that seem increasingly hard to come by? As the market for pet products and services booms, the notion of spending so much time and money on dogs strikes many people as vain, as another way of "putting on the dog" by competing in ostentatious expense. No doubt the human comedy in the cavalcade of pet paraphernalia has as much to do with excesses of capitalism as with excesses of emotion. Why should it be more peculiar to have seven different kinds of dog leash than seven different kinds of Barbie doll? The fortunes of people and dogs have been linked for centuries, and if our own century has a sometimes risible way of showing as much, that is a sign of the century's folly, not the dog-lover's.

In the end, it is not substitution or anthropomorphism that produces the human love of dogs and the current preoccupation with them in our culture. The pathos of lost, unwanted, abandoned, neglected, or maltreated animals—from Homer's loyal Argus to yesterday's Mama and Baby—speaks, somehow, to the rootlessness and nostalgia inherent in the postmodern condition. Blessedly, dogs are free of irony and are strangers to cynicism (despite the etymology of the word from the Greek *kynikos*, "doglike"). In a relentlessly ironic age, their uncritical demeanor is perhaps just what we need. It is with dogs that, very often, we permit ourselves feelings of the deepest joy and the deepest sorrow. "Dogs are not our whole life," Roger Caras writes in *Dog People*, "but they make our lives whole." In this sense—so one could almost claim—it is the dog that makes us human.

Lassie used to come home every week, often

having rescued Mom or Timmy from some scrape on the way. Now our welcome mats display two-dimensional collies—or Labradors, or Afghans ("available in fifteen breeds")—and working dog owners call home to speak to their pets on the answering machine. Home is where the dog is. If the dog brings back the fifties in a miniaturized form, it's because the dog is what we would like to have been to our parents: totally lovable, totally loved. The puppy represents what the yuppie fantasizes about childhood, what the older person fantasizes about youth, what the city-dweller fantasizes about the country, what the weary workaholic fantasizes about freedom, what the human spouse or partner fantasizes about spontaneity, emotional generosity, and togetherness. In soft-focus television commercials, and at the front door, the dog, leash patiently in mouth, is always waiting for you.

| 1996 |

## WISDOM TINGED WITH JOY

Out of the mouths of city dogs
have come some useful truths.
Barks and whines—noise to some—
are fraught with ancient wisdom.

A dog, to share his basic instinct,
will warn, say, of the landlord
at the door to spoil your day.
"Don't open," he barks. In vain.

When the van is loaded: laptop, mattresses,
    and microwave,
a wise dog rides in stoic silence
to the new (smaller) apartment

where joyously he soon resumes
his job of watching over rooms.

—DOROTHEA TANNING    | 2006 |

"Yes, I'm talking to you. I believe you're
the only Sparky in the house."

# DOG LANGUAGE

IAN FRAZIER

Cycle Dog Food, a product of the Pet Foods Division of the General Foods Corporation, sponsored a K-9 Frisbee Disc Catch and Fetch Contest in the Central Park Sheep Meadow on a recent Saturday:

"You're my sweet dog. You're my sweet dog! Yes, you are. Yes . . . you . . . *are!* You want to wear a nice red bandanna around your neck, like that dog there and that dog there and that dog over there? Do you? You want me to wear a T-shirt with my picture and your picture on it, like that owner over there? Huh? You want your own fan club, like that dog named Morgan? You want your own cheering section, with people who cheer when you run after the Frisbee and who jump in the air when you jump in the air to catch the Frisbee? Maybe if you get to be National Champion Frisbee-Catcher, like that dog Ashley Whippet, you could be a Good-Will Ambassador for Cycle Dog Food, the way he is. Is that what you want? I know what you want. You want a Liv-A-Snap. You feel you're not getting your proper Liv-A-Snappage. Here's a nice Liv-A-Snap. Sit up. Here you—Whoa! Almost took my finger off. You certainly are insistent about getting proper Liv-A-Snappage. You want me to buy you some nice Cycle Dog Food? Now, I can't buy you Cycle 1, because that's 'for a puppy's special growing needs,' and I can't buy you Cycle 3, because that's diet dog food, for overweight dogs, and I can't buy you Cycle 4, because that's for old dogs, so I guess I'd have to buy you Cycle 2—'specially formulated for your dog's active years.' Are you in your active years? I should say so! If I threw you the Frisbee, would you show just how active your active years are? Would you run straight to the concession stand, like that basset hound? Would you knock over the man from Channel 4, like that half collie, half German shepherd? Would you run over and sniff that bush? Would you make me grab you by the tail and wrestle you to the ground before you gave back the Frisbee? Would you bounce in the air like a Super Ball, the way that poodle is doing? Would you stop running if I threw it too far, like that terrier? Would you discuss those pictures of the moons of Jupiter that Voyager 2 sent back? The ones with the erupting volcanoes? Huh? Would you? You are silent, but your eyes speak volumes. You're my sweet dog! Yes, you are!"

| 1979 |

BAD DOGS

# From "THE PET DEPARTMENT"

## JAMES THURBER

*The idea for the department was suggested by the daily pet column in the* New York Evening Post, *and by several others.*

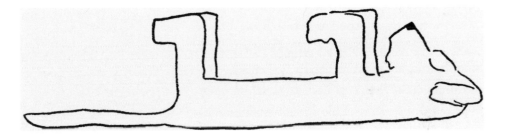

Q. I enclose a sketch of the way my dog, William, has been lying for two days now. I think there must be something wrong with him. Can you tell me how to get him out of this?

Mrs. L. L. G.

A. I should judge from the drawing that William is in a trance. Trance states, however, are rare with dogs. It may just be ecstasy. If at the end of another twenty-four hours he doesn't seem to be getting anywhere, I should give him up. The position of the ears leads me to believe that he may be enjoying himself in a quiet way, but the tail is somewhat alarming.

Q. My husband, who is an amateur hypnotizer, keeps trying to get our bloodhound under his control. I contend that this is not doing the dog any good. So far he has not yielded to my husband's influence, but I am afraid that if he once got under, we couldn't get him out of it.

A. A. T.

A. Dogs are usually left cold by all phases of psychology, mental telepathy, and the like. Attempts to hypnotize this particular breed, however, are likely to be fraught with a definite menace. A bloodhound, if stared at fixedly, is liable to gain the impression that it is under suspicion, being followed, and so on. This upsets bloodhound's life by completely reversing its whole scheme of behavior.

Q. My police dog has taken to acting very strange, on account of my father coming home from work every night for the past two years and saying to

him, "If you're a police dog, where's your badge?," after which he laughs (my father).

Ella R.

A. The constant reiteration of any piece of badinage sometimes has the same effect on present-day neurotic dogs that it has on people. It is dangerous and thoughtless to twit a police dog on his powers, authority, and the like. From the way your dog seems to hide behind tables, large vases, and whatever that thing is that looks like a suitcase, I should imagine that your father has carried this thing far enough—perhaps even too far.

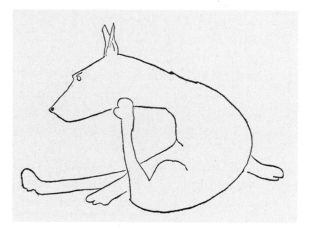

Q. The fact that my dog sits this way so often leads me to believe that something is preying on his mind. He seems always to be studying. Would there be any way of finding out what this is?

Arthur

A. Owing to the artificially complex life led by city dogs of the present day, they tend to lose the simpler systems of intuition which once guided all breeds, and frequently lapse into what comes very close to mental perplexity. I myself have known some very profoundly thoughtful dogs. Usually, however, their problems are not serious and I should judge your dog has merely mislaid something and wonders where he put it.

Q. No one has been able to tell us what kind of dog we have. I am enclosing a sketch of one of his two postures. He only has two. The other one is the same as this except he faces in the opposite direction.

Mrs. Eugenia Black

A. I think that what you have is a cast-iron lawn dog. The expressionless eye and the rigid pose are characteristic of metal lawn animals. And that certainly is a cast-iron ear. You could, however, remove all doubt by means of a simple test with a hammer and a cold chisel, or an acetylene torch. If the animal chips, or melts, my diagnosis is correct.

Q. Mr. Jennings bought this beast when it was a pup in Montreal for a St. Bernard, but I don't think it is. It's grown enormously and is stubborn about letting you have anything, like the bath towel it has its paws on, and the hat, both of which belong to Mr. Jennings. He got it that bowling ball to play with but it doesn't seem to like it. Mr. Jennings is greatly attached to the creature.

Mrs. Fanny Edwards Jennings

A. What you have is a bear. While it isn't my bear, I should recommend that you dispose of it. As these animals grow older they get more and more adamant about letting you have anything until finally there might not be anything in the house you could call your own—except possibly the bowling ball. Zoos use bears. Mr. Jennings could visit it.

Q. Sometimes my dog does not seem to know me. I think he must be crazy. He will draw away, or show his fangs, when I approach him.

H. M. Morgan, Jr.

A. So would I, and I'm not crazy. If you creep up on your dog the way you indicate in the drawing, I can understand his viewpoint. Put your shirt in and straighten up; you look as if you had never seen a dog before, and that is undoubtedly what bothers the animal. These maladjustments can often be worked out by the use of a little common sense.

Q. I have three Scotch terriers which take things out of closets and down from shelves, etc. My veterinarian advised me to gather together all the wreckage, set them down in the midst of it, and say, "Ba-ad Scotties!" This, however, merely seems to give them a kind of pleasure. If I spank one, the other two jump me—playfully, but they jump me.

Mrs. O. S. Proctor

A. To begin with, I question the advisability of having three Scotch terriers. They are bound to get you down. However, it seems to me that you are needlessly complicating your own problem. The Scotties probably think that you are trying to enter into the spirit of their play. Their inability to comprehend what you are trying to get at will in the end make them melancholy, and you and the dogs will begin to drift farther and farther apart. I'd deal with each terrier, and each object, separately, beginning with the telephone, the disconnection of which must inconvenience you sorely.

| 1930 |

*"I'm very sorry, Madam,*
*but the one in the middle is stuffed, poor fellow."*

Feb. 12, 1966

THE NEW YORKER

Price 35 cents

Kovarsky

# DOG TROUBLE

## CATHLEEN SCHINE

Four years ago, I was in a relationship that everyone who cared about me considered abusive. I was covered with bruises and scars. When my older son came home from college, he was greeted with a scene of loud, belligerent menace. My younger son, who still lived with us, tried to reach out, but more often than not his kindness was met by violence. My mother was terrified and refused to set foot in our house. In fact, no one came to visit us anymore. Nor were we welcome at anyone else's house. Even a short walk on the street held the threat of an ugly brawl. At night, I lay in bed, felt the warmth of his body beside me, and tried not to move. I didn't want to set him off. He was volatile, unpredictable. But I felt responsible for him. And, against all odds, I loved him.

He was not my husband, with whom I had just split up. Nor was he my boyfriend. (I had made one of those unforeseen middle-aged discoveries and was living with a woman.) My looming, destructive, desperate, and compelling companion was not even a human being. He was a dog. Or, as my friends and family pointed out, he was "just" a dog.

He appeared to be a lovely little dog, about two and a half years old, when we first saw him. It was a spring day, and he stood at the end of a long line of caged dogs in a Los Angeles pet-supply store, all strays to be adopted, all barking and yapping and hurling themselves against their wire enclosures. But he neither barked nor yapped. He stood politely, his head cocked expectantly. He wagged his tail in vigorous anticipation. When I picked him up, he squirmed with joy and lunged, ecstatic, licking my face, overwhelming me with a wave of urgent, instant love.

"Why do you want a dog?" my mother asked me. "I know why you want a dog. Because your son is going to college." She looked at me pityingly. "When you went to college, I got a geranium."

Buster, which is what we named him, was a seventeen-pound bowlegged mutt with a nondescript coat of short brown hair and a bulldog chest. His tail was far too long for his body, a dachshund's tail. One ear stood up, the other flopped down. His face had the big, worried eyes of a Chihuahua, the anxious furrowed brow of a pug, and the markings of a German shepherd. He yodelled like a beagle and shook his toys with the neck-wrenching vigor of a pit bull terrier. A tough stray missing two toes on his left hind foot, he had been picked up in South L.A. and dumped in the city pound, where, we were told, larger dogs stole his food, until, the day before he was to be euthanized, he was saved by a private rescue group that tried to find a home for him. After we discovered Buster, a representative of the group came to our house to make sure it was safe for the dog. She neglected to tell us that the dog was not safe for us. Perhaps the rescuers were blinded by hope, since we had lifted the dog from his crate and hugged and kissed him with no ill effect. Perhaps they were confused. They had so many dogs to place in homes. Perhaps they were simply desperate.

I grew up reading books about heroic collies. It was from the novels of the popular writer Albert Payson Terhune, treasured by my father before me, that I learned the word "puttee." Terhune would don a pair to walk through the grounds of Sunnybank. I also learned about "carrion," in which his dogs would roll luxuriously, and a "veranda," on which they would sit of an evening, curled contentedly at the feet of their god. Sunnybank was two generations and several classes and ethnic groups away from my world. Terhune, who in the books referred to himself as the Master, raised collies on a sprawling estate in northern New Jersey, which in his novels was called The Place. As impeccably bred as Sunnybank Lad, the Master claimed ancestors who had come to the New World from Holland and England in the seventeenth century. Terhune heatedly defended the rights of dogs and trees, but he was not a man of the people. There is a wonderful story by James Thurber describing the Master's highborn rage ("like summer thunder") when a Mr. Jacob R. Ellis and family, Midwestern tourists come to take a gander at Sunnybank in their Ford sedan, ran over the beloved champion Sunnybank Jean. And the Master's disgust for Negroes and the "rich city dweller of sweatshop origin" was virulent and unashamed. But I noticed none of that as a child, for we had collies, too. Our patient, plodding dogs with their matted ruffs in no way resembled the grand animals of the novels, but they did follow my brother and me protectively around the neighborhood. Would they have leaped at the throat of an attacker, like Buff of "Buff: A Collie" or Lad in "The Juggernaut"? Would they have instinctively guided stolen sheep back into their proper herd? Or wandered for months, living on squirrels, looking for me, their only true Mistress? One of them took long walks every day with an inmate from the sanitarium just down the road. They herded children during recess at an elementary school nearby. They wandered for miles until someone from several towns away would check their tags and call us to come get them, at which point they would greet us with unalloyed, and unsurprised, joy. This was my background with dogs: they were in the background. Or they were in books.

Then one afternoon when I was eight, and unaccountably home alone, sitting in front of the Admiral TV with its big round knobs, watching *The Mickey Mouse Club,* my chin resting on my knees, Laurie, our small mahogany-colored collie, poked her nose in my face. I pushed her away. She whined and whimpered. I ignored her. She pushed my shoulder, hard. She licked my face, pushed again, barked, ran frantically to the door and back, whining, licking, nudging, until I tore myself away from the television and allowed myself to be herded through the kitchen and to the front door, where the dog planted her feet, barking and wagging her tail, until I understood. Smoke and flames were billowing from the bedroom hallway. Our squat little collie had saved my life.

Devotion to a dog like that is not hard for anyone to understand. But how do you explain your devotion to a dog who is not man's best friend? Who is neither noble nor loyal? There is a popular training book called *No Bad Dogs,* but what happens when one is indeed bad and he belongs to you? What happens when bad dogs happen to good, or at least conscientious, people? When an animal defies kindness, defies the culture of therapy, and refuses to be redeemed?

On our very first evening with the little stray, we proudly placed his bowl of food on the kitchen floor. He rushed toward it, poking his muzzle eagerly into the organic human-grade kibble. We watched him, happy that we had rescued him from his hard, hungry life. There is something profoundly satisfying about taking in a creature no one else wants, a delicious flicker of moral superiority, and the surprisingly powerful pleasure of generosity. We watched our dog, a bit smug, perhaps, but, as I look back at the two of us, a new couple opening our lives to a needy dog, I feel only compassion. We had no idea what lay in store. Suddenly, Buster lifted his Chihuahua head. He jerked his pug face back toward his dachshund tail. He bared his pit-bull fangs, and—this all happened in seconds—savagely growling, as if another dog were threatening to move in on his meal, he lunged for his own tail, for his own flank, for his back foot. He whirled, a blur of snarling and slashing. It was a full-blown dogfight, the worst I had ever seen, and he was having it with himself.

That night, Buster jumped up on the bed, crawled under the covers, rested his head on the pillow like a little man, and fell asleep. Around three o'clock, I sat up, terrified. A deep angry roar swept over my face. It was Buster, his eyes rolling, pursuing something that wasn't there. Sleeping with Buster, we soon discovered, was like sleeping with a Vietnam vet who suffers from post-traumatic-stress disorder. Demons haunted Buster's sleep. The first time we left him alone in the house, we returned half an hour later to find him panting, foaming at the mouth, licking his new, self-inflicted wounds on a sofa covered with blood. And so, almost as soon as we got Buster, we began the quest to save him.

Over the next year and a half, we had Buster's

legs and spine and tail X-rayed; we had him tested for every conceivable kind of worm and fed him a hypo-allergenic diet of pure venison and sweet potatoes. We consulted a chiropractor and an acupuncturist. We took him to The Body-Works with Veronica for Alexander technique and Feldenkrais. I searched the Internet for dog behaviorists and tried spray bottles of water and jars of noisy coins, clickers, herbal remedies, even aromatherapy. I typed "self-mutilation + dog" into Google, and articles in veterinary journals about paw licking and scratching came up. If only that were the problem, I thought. I typed in "Obsessive-compulsive disorder + dog" and consulted, by e-mail and phone, vets and animal behaviorists from all over the country. We watched *Emergency Vets* on Animal Planet, hoping we'd see some clue to Buster's problems. We watched *Animal Precinct,* both heartened by and envious of all the bony, beaten, scarred, one-eyed dogs who caressed the hands of strangers and frolicked tenderly with babies when given half a chance. The only thing we didn't try was a pet psychic. But sometimes, late at night, even that seemed plausible.

We couldn't leave Buster at home, but when we took him with us in the car he threw himself against the window in an attempt to attack every bicycle, motorcycle, rollerblade, and shopping cart we passed. If it rained, he tried to subdue the windshield wipers. Parking-garage attendants pulled back when one of us handed them our ticket through the window while the other hung onto the snarling cur. When we fed Buster, we had to stand with a leg on either side, touching his flanks, to reassure him, we hoped, that no one was lurking behind his tail waiting to steal his food. But when, after a while, that, too, failed, and we began feeding Buster one piece of kibble at a time, he bit the hand that fed him. He bit the hand that groomed him. He bit the hand that petted him. After each attack, he would whimper and grovel, licking our faces. If you said, "Kisses" to Buster, he would hurl himself at you to lick your face. When you whistled, he sang along, yodelling comically. He was terrified of men, especially men with hats and, embarrassingly, black men, but he was also afraid of women and children, and he hated other dogs.

Buster slept splayed companionably across your torso if you lay on the couch reading. I thought he was beautiful. He had filled out. His chest was smooth and muscular, his coat shining. When he slept on me like that, momentarily calm, I was momentarily full of hope. One day, the young woman who lived next door reached in the car window to pet him, and he lunged at her, tearing a deep gash in her hand. She was unbelievably understanding, the wound did not require stitches, there was no lawsuit. But we were frantic, and ashamed.

A new vet told us he could tell by the dog's teeth that he had had distemper when he was a puppy. Perhaps this had caused neurological damage. He couldn't be sure. But he was sure about

one thing. "Your dog bites," the vet said. "Dogs that bite almost always continue to bite." Then he said, "If this were my dog, I would put him to sleep."

In the waiting room the day the vet told us to euthanize Buster, I saw an ad for a trainer in a local pet newsletter. Her name was Cinimon and she worked with rescued, hopeless, vicious pit bulls. We called her as soon as we got home.

Cinimon, a tan blonde with a pierced tongue, arrived with short-short cutoff jeans, an exposed midriff, and combat boots. She talked to us for hours, purposely ignoring Buster until he approached her, then handling him with incredible gentleness. She said we had to establish dominance over Buster now that he was in our pack. Her approach was not radical. We should put him in a crate at night and make him earn his treats by doing something, anything, even if it was as simple as sitting when told. Cinimon was full of hope and enthusiasm. I could not help seeing Cinimon, her delicious, oddly spelled name, and her own blooming California good health, as a promise of what Buster could hope for. The vet was probably right, but Buster would be the exception. Cinimon, a Valkyrie from the Valley, a girl with a household full of docile monsters, would make it so. Her training program was a reasonable behavior-modification approach. It made sense. To Cinimon. To us. Just not to Buster.

Buster was becoming a full-time job or, more precisely, a whole life. We went to bed at night worrying about him. Had he got enough exercise? Did exercise tire him out and calm him down, as it was supposed to, or did it hurt his damaged foot and stress his awkward anatomy? Would he sleep through the night, or would he wake and chase his demons and slash my calf in his confused fury? If we put him in his bed on the

## BAWLED OUT

Thomas Wolfe, the novelist, has just taken an apartment at 865 First Avenue, in the rather nice neighborhood near Fiftieth Street. Going down in the elevator the other morning, he was joined by a lady with a big police dog. The dog took an immediate liking to Mr. Wolfe, and began jumping up on him and kissing him. Mr. Wolfe, who is only moderately fond of dogs, pushed this one away, whereat the lady spoke up sharply. "Wolfe!" she said. "You great, obnoxious beast!" Being a gentleman, Mr. Wolfe made no reply, but he was terribly hurt. He spent the rest of the day wandering along the waterfront in the rain, bumping into warehouses and brooding, like a character in one of his own novels. However, the matter was cleared up when he returned home that evening. The elevator man explained that the police dog is named Wolf, which, when you say it fast, sounds pretty much like "Wolfe." The lady, Mrs. Sabine Baring-Gould, was bawling out the dog and not the novelist, whom, as a matter of fact, she rather admires.    | 1937 |

floor, would he fall asleep this time, or would he spin and spin and spin, tearing wildly at himself? We had an obligation to him. We had an obligation to innocent bystanders. Had we pursued every possible road to recovery? Did our umbrella insurance cover liability for dog bites? Should we put him to sleep?

In the morning, he would snuggle up and lay his head across my neck, snoring gently, his breath soft and sweet. He played in the morning, too, chasing toys and shaking them like dying rats. During the day, he snoozed, threw himself angrily against the glass doors to the front garden when the mailman walked by, threw himself angrily at his own back legs, at his long tail, at his deformed foot, at his good feet, at our feet. He sat when we told him to, looking up innocently. He was innocent: that was the most painful part. He was a vicious dog; even we would have to agree. He was destructive and dangerous, and if he had been a larger dog we would have had no choice but to put him down. But he was as innocent as a babe, baffled by his own behavior, terrified of everything that moved. He had been a lost dog. He was still a lost dog.

Then Cinimon suggested Prozac. In the months that followed, we consulted three vets, two psychopharmacologists, and a psychiatrist. We slapped peanut butter around Prozac, Buspar, Elavil, Effexor, Xanax, and Clomicalm, feeding the pills to Buster in a variety of doses and combinations. Even when they seemed to have some positive effect, it would last only a little while. Eventually, the violent behavior would return, worse than ever.

In September, we returned to New York. On the plane, the man in front of me tapped his headphones. Static? Up and down the aisle, people jiggled their headphones, wondering where the strange, ominous rumble came from. It came from under my seat, where a five-hour unilateral dogfight was taking place. At the airport, I put Buster's case on the floor while we waited for the luggage. Someone screamed. I looked back. The case was whirling across the floor, unguided, an eerie missile of snarling desperation.

There are a million or so dogs in New York City. About thirty of them live on our block on the Upper West Side of Manhattan. We have a laundromat, two dry cleaners, two churches, two dentists, a senior center, a Malaysian restaurant, a Korean market, a bakery, and a store that sells cheap leather jackets. A homeless man of regular habits lives in the doorway of the Lutheran church. He does not have a dog. But the gay men who live in the brownstone next door with their five children have two beagles. A woman down the block has a West Highland terrier, a retired champion, whom she took in when the dog's owner, a close friend, died suddenly, though she lives in one room and already had a shepherd mix named Tulip, after the heroine of J. R. Ackerley's obsessively brilliant *My Dog Tulip*. There is an Afghan and an Italian greyhound with legs as spindly as pipe cleaners whose owner rides a bicycle to work. There is a blind miniature schnauzer who wobbles down the sidewalk without leash or supervision until, from a doorway, his owner hollers, "Henry!" and he totters home. There is a man who is in thrall to his young golden retriever; a three-legged yellow lab; two handsome young men with a Brussels griffon puppy; a man who lives with his mother and three tiny scruffy mutts; and a heavily tattooed window-washer with a racing bike whose shepherd mix just died. One woman who leans carefully on a cane and smiles beatifically from beneath pure-white hair gives gentle advice in a soft Irish brogue while Waldo, her Boston terrier, waits patiently, staring with his round bug eyes. And there is a woman with a warm and generous smile and a rich, cultured German accent who walks her aging Pekinese, Lord Byron, four times a day no matter how terrible the weather, a Holocaust survivor whose view of life is so beneficent I sometimes wait outside her building hoping she will materialize and provide wise counsel.

I don't know the names of all our neighbors, but I know the names of their dogs. I do not go out to dinner or to the movies with the neighbors, as I do with my friends. I don't make dates with them. I don't have to. I know I will see one or two or more of them every day. The dogs on the block gambol happily toward a puddle of urine to sniff and amplify, then sniff and be sniffed, twisting

until their leashes are laced like ribbons on a Maypole. Towering above them in choking humidity or cutting wind or hushed snow, the owners say hello, comment on the humidity or the wind or the snow, discuss the latest catastrophe in the city, admire each other's animals, occasionally drop some highly personal remark about physical illness, a child, a parent, a divorce, nod sympathetically, and move on to scrape up a small, neat coil of excrement into an inside-out Fairway bag. New York City, on my block, is as small a town as Andy and Opie's Mayberry. And it was Buster who introduced me to its citizens, lunging at saintly old ladies, storming wheelchairs and strollers, his hair bristling and his teeth bared. Everyone knew him. Everyone had advice. But, mostly, everyone had sympathy. When I saw Waldo or Lord Byron coming down the street, my heart beat faster and I felt tears of gratitude forming, for their owners, women who have seen hardship and evil, would reassure me that there was hope. With patience, they said softly, there was hope.

But Buster was not getting better. We contacted an animal behaviorist recommended to us by the New York Animal Hospital. He arrived with a Snoot Loop, a contraption he was marketing that was very similar to the better known Gentle Leader, a kind of bridle with a strap that tightens around the muzzle of a dog when he pulls. He charged us hundreds of dollars, the Snoot Loop cut into Buster's nose, leaving a bloody welt, and the issue of self-mutilation was not addressed. My girlfriend, Janet, and I, outcasts everywhere but our one little block, began to argue about what to do, how to train Buster, what to feed him, when to feed him. Exhausted,

discouraged, we resorted to the wisdom of our forebears, smacking the dog with a rolled-up newspaper when he attacked himself, or us. It was not effective.

One day, I took Buster to the dog run in Riverside Park near Eighty-second Street. We could let him loose there only when no other dogs were around. On this particular fall day, when the sky was a solemn gray and the leaves were dead on the ground around us, as brown as the dirt, I sat on a bench in the section reserved for small dogs and threw a hard red rubber ball for Buster. We had spent a disastrous Thanksgiving at my aunt's house in Massachusetts. Buster had come with us. Whom could we have left him with? We were assigned a bedroom, and a large sign was taped to our door warning anyone who dared to enter not to let the dog exit. The day we left, we walked out of the room, loaded down with our bags and with Buster on his leash. We had been vigilant and tense for three days and had been rewarded with a Thanksgiving free of bloodshed. There was a great flurry of relieved family hugs and kisses, my two-year-old nephew waddled bumpily toward us, squealing, Buster lunged for him, leaped back with a mouthful of soggy diaper, whimpered while my nephew wailed, and we skulked off in disgrace.

Now I sat on the park bench and watched Buster. My sister-in-law and brother were barely speaking to me. My mother thought I was disturbed. My nephew was terrified of dogs. Janet and I were squabbling. My children were disgusted. Buster chased the ball happily, brought it back, waited until I threw it again, and again, just like a normal healthy dog. With his grinning face, one ear up and one flopped jauntily over his eye, his wriggling body and wagging tail, you would never know. That was one of the problems. People saw him and rushed over, cooing and crowing, hands stretched out to pet the adorable little dog. He would stiffen, growl, bare

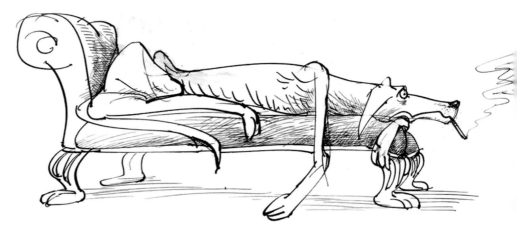

his teeth and lunge, all in a sickening second. When someone came within five feet, I would say something. At first, I struggled with the right wording. "He's unpredictable," I said. Or, "He's afraid of strangers." Sometimes, "He's aggressive." But all of these warnings seemed to leave an opportunity for people to test whether they might be the one special person he was not afraid of or aggressive toward, the unpredicted friend. Finally, I started saying, simply, "He bites."

"He bites," I said when a young woman came into the dog run with a bichon puppy, a cottony ball who bounced around her feet. Then I got up

to leash Buster and take him away. But she put the bichon on her lap and told me not to worry about it. She was benevolent, awash with the joy of a merry new puppy. I thanked her. And then I felt it coming. I tried to stop myself, but I knew I was helpless. And, as I had done so many times before to so many unsuspecting strangers, I began to tell her the tale of Buster. I could hear the high note of panic, the rhythm of hysteria and desperation in my voice. I had heard something like it at playgrounds and bus stops from parents whose children threw sand or tantrums or took drugs or shoplifted or were flunking out of school. But the pitch, the speed of the chatter, the insistence on detail—I recognized that from some-

where else, from strangers approaching me on the street to tell me their life stories: from crazy people. I listened to myself and I heard a crazy woman.

Once again, a vet, this time our New York vet, told us to put the dog to sleep. "Your dog," said Dr. Raclyn, a holistic practitioner who does not give up easily, "is deeply disturbed." One evening when I brought Buster back into the building from his walk, I bumped into one of my neighbors, Virginia Hoffmann, a dog trainer. I blurted out that the dog was miserable, we were miserable, there was no hope. Virginia, who started out as an English teacher, became a trainer after having to deal with her own unhappy puppy. She had become more and more interested, more and more skilled, until one day she quit her day job. Here was someone, I thought, who could understand what we were going through. I asked her if she would help us. I wanted to give it one last try, to spend six months working seriously and consistently with Buster. He would never be sane, I recognized that. But maybe, just maybe, we could reduce the threshold of his suffering to make it bearable for him, and for us. Virginia took pity on us and agreed. She wanted to help us, she said, to help Buster, and she would learn from the experience. But she was very clear about one thing. She offered no guarantees.

"I found a trainer for Buster," I said to my mother.

"Who? Clyde Beatty?"

Trim and neat, straightforward and calm, Virginia had a soothing effect on me. Perhaps she would on Buster, too. I had already considered another dog trainer who lived on the block. He had written several books and had a Catskill-comedian spiel that I found very engaging. His fee was so high that I tried one of his books first and discovered that his system required throwing things at your dog, to which approach Buster responded by attacking the suggested keys or wallet or paperback book that was launched at him, and then cowering in confusion. Another dog trainer I once ran into on the East Side told me she knew just what to do: lift Buster by the back legs and whack him across the jaw hard enough so it rattled. Then she gave me her card and walked on. I gratefully turned to Virginia, with her soft, firm voice and endless sympathy. She came three or four times a week.

Janet was in L.A. a lot then, and my day was centered on the dog. I approached him with a glove attached to a wooden spoon, rewarding him when he didn't bite it. I used toys as a reward instead of food. I let him carry his toys in his mouth when we went outside, on the theory that he would be hard-pressed to bite with his mouth full. He learned the commands "touch" and "leave it." I taught him to go to his bed, to stay, to heel, to jump through a yellow hula hoop. Clyde Beatty, indeed. All of this training had a goal—to give the dog something better to think about than his own fear. To give him confidence. To give him a better sense of his own deformed body. And to give us authority and control. I learned how to break up each task into tiny parts. We tried to get him used to wearing a muzzle, which he hated and would trigger one of his fits, by leaving it on for seconds at a time and rewarding him with a squirt of Cheese Whiz. I wished I had employed Virginia to help in child rearing. For, in addition to training, she taught me not simply to impose or demand but to observe. Virginia suggested that I keep a journal, noting the frequency and intensity of Buster's fits: the details of his misery. Which side of himself did he attack? What might have provoked it? A noise? A touch? A smell? I timed the violent fits. I noted the weather, the time of the day, his position. How long since he'd eaten? Drunk? And then I made him come to me, or stay sitting as I walked away, or jump through a hoop. Buster was a wonderful pupil, smart and willing and obedient. He was an exceptionally well-trained mad dog.

I couldn't wait until Virginia arrived for a lesson. When she walked through the door, my real day began. She brought me articles from veterinary behavioral journals. She relayed relevant anecdotes from friends and colleagues. I loved meeting Buster's big, alert dark eyes and recognizing a quick, happy understanding. Buster bit

Virginia on the first visit. I had my Buster kit of butterfly bandages and Neosporin handy. Though he seemed to sense that here was someone sent to help him, he could never tolerate more than about twenty minutes of work. So the rest of the time we went over the behavior charts like sailors checking the stars.

Janet and I began going out only to places where we could take Buster with us, eating at outdoor cafés in the rain and the bitter wind. But then Buster bit the waiter at Señor Swanky's, and we stopped. We resorted to placing a large plastic collar shaped like an ice-cream cone around his neck when we left him alone. Used by vets to keep dogs from licking their wounds, the plastic cone worked more like blinkers for Buster: he was unable to see, much less bite, his hindquarters. One night, when I had brought Buster to my mother's house in Connecticut (tolerated out of motherly pity and because it was the only way she would get to see me), I put him in his collar and went to visit an old friend. Ten minutes later, my cell phone rang.

"I'm locked in my room with the door closed," my mother said. "Your dog is in the living room having a fit." She sounded terrified.

When I got home, the dog was a blur of foam and fur. I ended up wrapping him in a blanket, the only way I could get near him without being bitten, and holding him on my chest in bed for four hours, trying to soothe him while he panted and trembled. I held him and I cried.

We could no longer leave Buster in his Elizabethan collar. He had another episode that required the blanket wrapped around him, the hours of trembling and rolling eyes. Virginia pointed me to an experiment that had been done with autistic children, in which they were wrapped tightly to help them regain awareness of their own bodies. She found an unlikely product called Anxiety Wrap, a suit for dogs, which worked on the same principle. She said that really the next step would be contacting a research veterinary school and handing Buster over for brain scans and further study. "Would you be doing that for his sake?" she asked. "Or your own? That's always the hard question."

It was a good question. Buster had become an intellectual puzzle, a challenge I could not let go of. He was my companion, certainly. The intensity of his need made the bond between us urgent and powerful. And I felt a responsibility, it was true. You cannot throw away an animal because he is sick. But there was also a little pool of vanity involved, and that insistent, stubborn optimism, a cultural trait, I suppose, that demands constant improvement. I would save this dog because, in a just world, I ought to be able to save him. It was a kind of humanitarian hubris. My dog was miserable. I insisted he get better.

We euthanized Buster eighteen months after we'd got him. We petted him as he stood on the vet's stainless-steel examining table. He wagged his tail and licked our hands. After giving him an IV dose of Valium, Dr. Raclyn added sodium pentobarbitol. Buster turned on him with one last snarl, looked back at us, wagged his tail again, crumpled into our arms, and was gone.

It took six months before we had either the heart or the courage to do it, but we decided to get another dog, a puppy this time. We searched Internet rescue sites and visited the A.S.P.C.A., the city pound, and the North Shore Animal League. There were enormous, sad-eyed shepherd mixes and venerable poodle mixes and hopeful bull-terrier mixes. Lab mixes leaped and whippet mixes shivered. We should have taken them all. We should have taken every puppy, too, although their fat, gigantic paws foretold their gigantic

futures. What we couldn't find was a puppy who would stay small enough for our bicoastal commute. Sometimes we took Virginia with us to guide us, to protect us from falling under the spell of another charismatic but impossible dog. All the best, sweetest dogs we know are rescued dogs; nevertheless—a little guiltily, a little nervously—we drove to Frederick, Maryland, and picked up a tiny ten-week-old Cairn terrier. We named him Hector. A few months later, on the coldest morning of the coldest winter in decades, I took Hector to Central Park. There was smooth, slick snow on the ground. We made our way to Hearnshead Rock, a scenic jog of boulders rolling out into the lake. In spring, deep-yellow irises rise up there. In winter, the cove lets ducks and swans escape the wind. On this dark, achingly cold morning, the lake was almost completely frozen. The silver ice and the silver sky were cut in two by the skyline, and only in the crook of the rocks, where hundreds of ducks swam in circles, had the gray water been prevented from freezing. There were buffleheads and scoters and coots and even a wood duck. There was a great blue heron standing, not a foot from shore, as still as the black trees. The dog and I had been watching this tableau for twenty minutes or so when suddenly the heron shot his head into the shallow water, then snapped his neck back into its looping posture, a large fish dangling

from his beak. He swallowed it. We watched the fish, a protrusion inching slowly down the bird's elegant throat, and then we walked home through silent woods, catching each other's eye now and then, checking in, companionable and intimate, sharing the exhilarating quiet. Hector, trotting beside me in the snow, was, like Buster, just a dog. And if, at that moment, I didn't know exactly how to explain why people want to own dogs, with all the inconvenience and heartache attached, I felt that here, at least, was a clue.

Hector prances along the street Buster skulked, greeting neighbors and strangers and men in hats and toddlers in snowsuits. He loves everyone and everyone loves him. I often think of Buster, and it breaks my heart. People say, "You did everything you could." But did we? What about Phenobarbital, even though every vet recommended against it? What about the autism suit? We should have moved to the country or sent him to the man in San Diego who leads a pack of dogs through the hills. What *about* the pet psychic? Then Hector pounces on an empty forty-ounce Budweiser can, almost as big as he is, and carries it proudly home. He kisses babies like a politician. He comes in peace.

| 2004 |

# PEACOCK

## ALEXANDRA FULLER

In the early nineties, it was possible to walk along the Zambian side of the upper Zambezi River without seeing many people—just a couple of fishermen, children out hunting for rats, or women in search of mopane worms. On the Zimbabwean side, blond savanna reached extravagantly into the distance and elephants often ventured out from the shelter of the bush to drink. Zambia, however, was considerably poorer than Zimbabwe in those days; anything remotely edible on our shore was quickly harvested, and large animals were scarce. Traditionally, ordinary people would not have eaten certain animals—hippos, for example—but a long ache of hunger had eroded the luxury of cultural norms and now nothing was exempt from culinary consideration.

An elderly Belgian aristocrat (unstitched from the wealth of her family by wars and bad luck) owned land here, where the river quickened into rapids as it made its way toward the waterfalls the locals called Mosi-oa-Tunya, "the smoke that thunders." Madame was a refugee of colonialism, remaindered from Zaire, but too possessed by Africa to return to Europe. She lived with several untrustworthy servants and a ragtag menagerie of peacocks, monkeys, dogs, cats, ducks, geese, chickens, and parrots.

My husband, Charlie, and I rented the cottage at the end of Madame's plot. There was only sporadic electricity and no running water—inconveniences that we happily overlooked in our excitement at finding ourselves beyond the reaches of the nearest town. Livingstone, at that time, was a noisy, disgruntled place. A riot had recently broken out in a textile factory and the Indian owners had been badly beaten up. Indians—the only community that seemed to thrive in difficult economic times—were universally mistrusted by their jealous Zambian neighbors.

While Charlie left each morning to run boat trips below Victoria Falls, I stayed in the cottage with our infant daughter and a mixed-breed dog called Liz. Madame quickly established the parameters of her relationship with me—we were to be cordial but formal—visiting each other by written invitation only. Ours was a friendship born of a mutual antipathy for society (we both preferred animals), and we gradually developed a genuine fondness for each other.

Then Liz killed a duck (she was caught in the act by Madame, her mouth lined with bloody feathers). Clough, Madame's gardener, brought over a brusque note on the afternoon of the murder, along with an invoice. Embarrassed, I sent cash and an apology by return post. Liz was confined to the barracks, except at night when she slept with us outside, where we had moved our bed to take advantage of the river breeze.

The following week, Liz allegedly killed a few more ducks and a half-dozen chickens. Madame, faced with such grave losses, came to see me without a letter of warning. The dog had acquired a taste for her livestock, she declared. I was responsible for "damages." Clough wrung his hands, and I knew, without a doubt, who was responsible for the killing spree. But Madame was scrupulously loyal to all her servants. To speak against them, I knew, was to speak against Madame herself! So I paid up with more apologies and a promise to keep Liz with me at all times.

When a peacock was killed several nights later—sent plummeting from its roost in a paperbark tree—I finally summoned up the courage to protest. "But, Madame," I said, "Liz could hardly have climbed all the way up there to kill a peacock."

"Clough found the body," Madame insisted. "He has taken it to be buried."

"Cooked, you mean," I muttered.

"Pardon?"

"Nothing," I said, counting out kwacha notes from my dwindling household budget.

Another peacock and two peahens met their deaths before I confronted Clough: "I know you're eating them."

"No." Clough mustered a look of indignation.

"It wasn't Liz."

"I am not the one. We can't eat peacocks. They are"—he searched for an excuse—"taboo for us."

"How can they be taboo? They aren't even native to this country. They're from India. How can something from India be taboo to you? Taboo means it must be something from your own culture."

Clough's face cleared. "Exactly. In our culture, we Zambians hate Indians. They are even worse than you. We wouldn't eat something of their country."

But the carnage stopped after that and my friendship with Madame survived, although very little else did. Eventually, Liz was killed by baboons, Madame sold the farm as a tourist camp, and we left Zambia for the less colorful comforts of the States.

| 2006 |

# WHAT THE DOG SAW

## MALCOLM GLADWELL

In the case of Sugar v. Forman, Cesar Millan knew none of the facts before arriving at the scene of the crime. That is the way Cesar prefers it. His job was to reconcile Forman with Sugar, and, since Sugar was a good deal less adept in making her case than Forman, whatever he learned beforehand might bias him in favor of the aggrieved party.

The Forman residence was in a trailer park in Mission Hills, just north of Los Angeles. Dark wood panelling, leather couches, deep-pile carpeting. The air-conditioning was on, even though it was one of those ridiculously pristine Southern California days. Lynda Forman was in her sixties, possibly older, a handsome woman with a winning sense of humor. Her husband, Ray, was in a wheelchair, and looked vaguely ex-military. Cesar sat across

from them, in black jeans and a blue shirt, his posture characteristically perfect.

"So how can I help?" he said.

"You can help our monster turn into a sweet, lovable dog," Lynda replied. It was clear that she had been thinking about how to describe Sugar to Cesar for a long time. "She's ninety percent bad, ten percent the love. . . . She sleeps with us at night. She cuddles." Sugar meant a lot to Lynda. "But she grabs anything in sight that she can get, and tries to destroy it. My husband is disabled, and she destroys his room. She tears clothes. She's torn our carpet. She bothers my grandchildren. If I open the door, she will run." Lynda pushed back her sleeves and exposed her forearms. They were covered in so many bites and scratches and scars and scabs that it was as if she had been tortured. "But I love her. What can I say?"

Cesar looked at her arms and blinked: "Wow."

Cesar is not a tall man. He is built like a soccer player. He is in his mid-thirties, and has large, wide eyes, olive skin, and white teeth. He crawled across the border from Mexico fourteen years ago, but his English is exceptional, except when he gets excited and starts dropping his articles—which almost never happens, because he rarely gets excited. He saw the arms and he said, "Wow," but it was a "wow" in the same calm tone of voice as "So how can I help?"

Cesar began to ask questions. Did Sugar urinate in the house? She did. She had a particularly destructive relationship with newspapers, television remotes, and plastic cups. Cesar asked about walks. Did Sugar travel, or did she track—and when he said "track" he did an astonishing impersonation of a dog sniffing. Sugar tracked. What about discipline?

"Sometimes I put her in a crate," Lynda said.

"And it's only for a fifteen-minute period. Then she lays down and she's fine. I don't know how to give discipline. Ask my kids."

"Did your parents discipline you?"

"I didn't need discipline. I was perfect."

"So you had no rules. . . . What about using physical touch with Sugar?"

"I have used it. It bothers me."

"What about the bites?"

"I can see it in the head. She gives me that look."

"She's reminding you who rules the roost."

"Then she will lick me for half an hour where she has bit me."

"She's not apologizing. Dogs lick each other's wounds to heal the pack, you know."

Lynda looked a little lost. "I thought she was saying sorry."

"If she was sorry," Cesar said, softly, "she wouldn't do it in the first place."

It was time for the defendant. Lynda's granddaughter, Carly, came in, holding a beagle as if it were a baby. Sugar was cute, but she had a mean, feral look in her eyes. Carly put Sugar on the carpet, and Sugar swaggered over to Cesar, sniffing his shoes. In front of her, Cesar placed a newspaper, a plastic cup, and a television remote.

Sugar grabbed the newspaper. Cesar snatched it back. Sugar picked up the newspaper again. She jumped on the couch. Cesar took his hand and "bit" Sugar on the shoulder, firmly and calmly. "My hand is the mouth," he explained. "My fingers are the teeth." Sugar jumped down. Cesar stood, and firmly and fluidly held Sugar down for an instant. Sugar struggled, briefly, then relaxed. Cesar backed off Sugar lunged at the remote. Cesar looked at her and said, simply and briefly, "Sh-h-h." Sugar hesitated. She went for the plastic cup. Cesar said, "Sh-h-h." She dropped it. Cesar motioned for Lynda to bring a jar of treats into the room. He placed it in the middle of the floor and hovered over it. Sugar looked at the treats and then at Cesar. She began sniffing, inching closer, but an invisible boundary now stood between her and the prize. She circled and circled but never came closer than three feet. She looked as if she were about to jump on the couch. Cesar shifted his weight, and blocked her. He took a step toward her. She backed up, head lowered, into the furthest corner of the room. She sank down on her haunches, then placed her head flat on the ground. Cesar took the treats, the remote, the plastic cup, and the newspaper and placed them inches from her lowered nose. Sugar, the one-time terror of Mission Hills, closed her eyes in surrender.

"She has no rules in the outside world, no boundaries," Cesar said, finally. "You practice exercise and affection. But you're not practicing exercise, discipline, and affection. When we love someone, we fulfill everything about them. That's loving. And you're not loving your dog." He stood up. He looked around. "Let's go for a walk."

Lynda staggered into the kitchen. In five minutes, her monster had turned into an angel.

"Unbelievable," she said.

Cesar Millan runs the Dog Psychology Center out of a converted auto mechanic's shop in the industrial zone of South-Central Los Angeles. The center is situated at the end of a long narrow alley, off a busy street lined with bleak warehouses and garages. Behind a high green chain-link fence is a large concrete yard, and everywhere around the yard there are dogs. Dogs basking in the sun. Dogs splashing in a pool.

Dogs lying on picnic tables. Cesar takes in people's problem dogs; he keeps them for a minimum of two weeks, integrating them into the pack. He has no formal training. He learned what he knows growing up in Mexico on his grandfather's farm in Sinaloa. As a child, he was called *el Perrero*, "the dog boy," watching and studying until he felt that he could put himself inside the mind of a dog. In the mornings, Cesar takes the pack on a four-hour walk in the Santa Monica mountains: Cesar in front, the dogs behind him; the pit bulls and the Rottweilers and the German shepherds with backpacks, so that when the little dogs get tired Cesar can load them up on the big dogs' backs. Then they come back and eat. Exercise, then food. Work, then reward.

"I have forty-seven dogs right now," Cesar said. He opened the door, and they came running over, a jumble of dogs, big and small. Cesar pointed to a bloodhound. "He was aggressive with humans, really aggressive," he said. In a corner of the compound, a Wheaton terrier had just been given a bath. "She's stayed here six months because she could not trust men," Cesar explained. "She was beat up severely." He idly scratched a big German shepherd. "My girlfriend here, Beauty. If you were to see the relationship between her and her owner." He shook his head. "A very sick relationship. A *Fatal Attraction* kind of thing. Beauty sees her and she starts scratching her and biting her, and the owner is, like, 'I love you, too.' That one killed a dog. That one killed a dog, too. Those two guys came from New Orleans. They attacked humans. That pit bull over there with a tennis ball killed a Labrador in Beverly Hills. And look at this one—one eye. Lost the eye in a dogfight. But look at him now." Now he was nuzzling a French bulldog. He was happy—and so was the Labrador killer from Beverly Hills, who was stretched out in the sun, and so was the aggressive-toward-humans bloodhound, who was lingering by a picnic table with his tongue hanging out. Cesar stood in the midst of all the dogs, his back straight and his shoulders square. It was a prison yard. But it was the most peaceful prison yard in all of California. "The whole point is that everybody has to stay calm, submissive, no matter what," he said. "What you are witnessing right now is a group of dogs who all have the same state of mind."

Cesar Millan is the host of *Dog Whisperer*, on the National Geographic television channel. In every episode, he arrives amid canine chaos and leaves behind peace. He is the teacher we all had in grade school who could walk into a classroom filled with rambunctious kids and get everyone to calm down and *behave*. But what did that teacher have? If you'd asked us back then, we might have said that we behaved for Mr. Exley because Mr. Exley had lots of rules and was really strict. But the truth is that we behaved for Mr. DeBock as well, and he wasn't strict at all. What we really mean is that both of them had that indefinable thing called presence—and if you are going to teach a classroom full of headstrong ten-year-olds, or run a company, or command an army, or walk into a trailer home in Mission Hills where a beagle named Sugar is terrorizing its owners, you have to have presence or you're lost.

Behind the Dog Psychology Center, between the back fence and the walls of the adjoining buildings, Cesar has built a dog run—a stretch of grass and dirt as long as a city block. "This is our Chuck E. Cheese," Cesar said. The dogs saw Cesar approaching the back gate, and they ran, expectantly, toward him, piling through the narrow door in a hodgepodge of whiskers and wagging tails. Cesar had a bag over his shoulder, filled with tennis balls, and a long orange plastic ball scoop in his right hand. He reached into the bag with the scoop, grabbed a tennis ball, and flung it in a smooth practiced motion off the wall of an adjoining warehouse. A dozen dogs set off in ragged pursuit. Cesar wheeled and threw another ball, in the opposite direction, and then a third, and then a fourth, until there were so many balls in the air and on the ground that the pack had turned into a yelping, howling, leaping, charging frenzy. Woof. Woof, woof, woof. *Woof.* "The game should be played five or ten minutes, maybe fifteen minutes," Cesar said. "You begin. You end. And you don't ask, 'Please stop.' You demand that it stop." With that, Cesar gathered himself, stood stock still, and let out a short whistle: not a casual whistle but a whistle of

I'M NOT GIVING YOU THE PAW— I'M FLIPPING YOU THE BIRD.

GREGORY

authority. Suddenly, there was absolute quiet. All forty-seven dogs stopped charging and jumping and stood as still as Cesar, their heads erect, eyes trained on their ringleader. Cesar nodded, almost imperceptibly, toward the enclosure, and all forty-seven dogs turned and filed happily back through the gate.

Last fall, Cesar filmed an episode of *Dog Whisperer* at the Los Angeles home of a couple named Patrice and Scott. They had a Korean jindo named JonBee, a stray that they had found and adopted. Outside, and on walks, JonBee was well behaved and affectionate. Inside the house, he was a terror, turning viciously on Scott whenever he tried to get the dog to submit.

"Help us tame the wild beast," Scott says to Cesar. "We've had two trainers come out, one of whom was doing this domination thing, where he would put JonBee on his back and would hold him until he submits. It went on for a good twenty minutes. This dog never let up. But, as soon as he let go, JonBee bit him four times. . . . The guy was bleeding, both hands and his arms. I had another trainer come out, too, and they said, 'You've got to get rid of this dog.' "

Cesar goes outside to meet JonBee. He walks down a few steps to the back yard. Cesar crouches down next to the dog. "The owner was a little concerned about me coming here by myself," he says. "To tell you the truth, I feel more comfortable with aggressive dogs than insecure dogs, or fearful dogs, or panicky dogs. These are actually the guys who put me on the map." JonBee comes up and sniffs him. Cesar puts a leash on him. JonBee eyes Cesar nervously and starts to poke around.

Cesar then walks JonBee into the living room. Scott puts a muzzle on him. Cesar tries to get the dog to lie on its side—and all hell breaks loose. JonBee turns and snaps and squirms and spins and jumps and lunges and struggles. His muzzle falls off. He bites Cesar. He twists his body up into the air, in a cold, vicious fury. The struggle between the two goes on and on. Patrice covers her face. Cesar asks her to leave the room. He is standing up, leash extended. He looks like a wrangler, taming a particularly ornery rattlesnake. Sweat is streaming down his face. Finally, Cesar gets the dog to sit, then to lie down, and then, somehow, to lie on its side. JonBee slumps, defeated. Cesar massages JonBee's stomach. "That's all we wanted," he says.

What happened between Cesar and JonBee? One explanation is that they had a fight, alpha male versus alpha male. But fights don't come out of nowhere. JonBee was clearly reacting to something in Cesar. Before he fought, he sniffed and explored and watched Cesar—the last of which is most important, because everything we know about dogs suggests that, in a way that is true of almost no other animals, dogs are students of human movement.

The anthropologist Brian Hare has done experiments with dogs, for example, where he puts a piece of food under one of two cups, placed several feet apart. The dog knows that there is food to be had, but has no idea which of the cups holds the prize. Then Hare points at the right cup, taps on it, looks directly at it. What happens? The dog goes to the right cup virtually every time. Yet when Hare did the same experiment with chimpanzees—an animal that shares 98.6 percent of our genes—the chimps couldn't get it right. A dog will look at you for help, and a chimp won't.

"Primates are very good at using the cues of the same species," Hare explained. "So if we were able to do a similar game, and it was a chimp or another primate giving a social cue, they might do better. But they are not good at using human cues when you are trying to cooperate with them. They don't get it: 'Why would you ever tell me where the food is?' The key specialization of dogs, though, is that dogs pay attention to humans, when humans are doing something very human, which is sharing information about something that someone else might actually want." Dogs aren't smarter than chimps; they just have a different attitude toward people. "Dogs

---

## DOG-EARED

An acquaintance of ours who is the director of a small-town library upstate added to his stacks, not long ago, a book called *The Secret of Cooking for Dogs*. The volume had to be retired after its very first loan, he reports, because it had been chewed into unreadability.    | 1965 |

---

are really interested in humans," Hare went on. "Interested to the point of obsession. To a dog, you are a giant walking tennis ball."

A dog cares, deeply, which way your body is leaning. Forward or backward? Forward can be seen as aggressive; backward—even a quarter of an inch—means nonthreatening. It means you've relinquished what ethologists call an "intention movement" to proceed forward. Cock your head, even slightly, to the side, and a dog is disarmed. Look at him straight on and he'll read it like a red flag. Standing straight, with your shoulders squared, rather than slumped, can mean the difference between whether your dog obeys a command or ignores it. Breathing even and deeply—rather than holding your breath—can mean the difference between defusing a tense situation and igniting it. "I think they are looking at our eyes and where our eyes are looking, and what our eyes look like," the ethologist Patricia McConnell, who teaches at the University of

Wisconsin, Madison, says. "A rounded eye with a dilated pupil is a sign of high arousal and aggression in a dog. I believe they pay a tremendous amount of attention to how relaxed our face is and how relaxed our facial muscles are, because that's a big cue for them with each other. Is the jaw relaxed? Is the mouth slightly open? And then the arms. They pay a tremendous amount of attention to where our arms go."

In the book *The Other End of the Leash*, McConnell decodes one of the most common of all human-dog interactions—the meeting between two leashed animals on a walk. To us, it's about one dog sizing up another. To her, it's about two dogs sizing up each other after first sizing up their respective owners. The owners "are often anxious about how well the dogs will get along," she writes, "and if you watch them instead of the dogs, you'll often notice that the humans will hold their breath and round their eyes and mouths in an 'on alert' expression. Since these behaviors are expressions of offensive aggression in canine culture, I suspect that the humans are unwittingly signalling tension. If you exaggerate this by tightening the leash, as many owners do, you can actually cause the dogs to attack each other. Think of it: the dogs are in a tense social encounter, surrounded by support from their own pack, with the humans forming a tense, staring, breathless circle around them. I don't know how many times I've seen dogs shift their eyes toward their owners' frozen faces, and then launch growling at the other dog."

When Cesar walked down the stairs of Patrice and Scott's home then, and crouched down in the back yard, JonBee *looked* at him, intently. And what he saw was someone who moved in a very particular way. Cesar is fluid. "He's beautifully organized intra-physically," Karen Bradley, who heads the graduate dance program at the

University of Maryland, said when she first saw tapes of Cesar in action. "That lower-unit organization—I wonder whether he was a soccer player." Movement experts like Bradley use something called Laban Movement Analysis to make sense of movement, describing, for instance, how people shift their weight, or how fluid and symmetrical they are when they move, or what kind of "effort" it involves. Is it direct or indirect—that is, what kind of attention does the movement convey? Is it quick or slow? Is it strong or light—that is, what is its intention? Is it bound or free—that is, how much precision is involved? If you want to emphasize a point, you might bring your hand down across your body in a single, smooth motion. But how you make that motion greatly affects how your point will be interpreted by your audience. Ideally, your hand would come down in an explosive, bound movement—that is, with accelerating force, ending abruptly and precisely—and your head and shoulders would descend simultaneously, so posture and gesture would be in harmony. Suppose, though, that your head and shoulders moved upward as your hand came down, or your hand came down in a free, implosive manner—that is, with a kind of a vague, decelerating force. Now your movement suggests that you are making a point on which we all agree, which is the opposite of your intention. Combinations of posture and gesture are called phrasing, and the great communicators are those who match their phrasing with their communicative intentions—who understand, for instance, that emphasis requires them to be bound and explosive. To Bradley, Cesar had beautiful phrasing.

There he is talking to Patrice and Scott. He has his hands in front of him, in what Laban analysts call the sagittal plane—that is, the area directly in front of and behind the torso. He then leans forward for emphasis. But as he does he lowers his hands to waist level, and draws them toward his body, to counterbalance the intrusion of his posture. And, when he leans backward again, the hands rise up, to fill the empty space. It's not the kind of thing you'd ever notice. But, when it's pointed out, its emotional meaning is unmistakable. It is respectful and reassuring. It communicates without being intrusive. Bradley was watching Cesar with the sound off, and there was one sequence she returned to again and again, in which Cesar was talking to a family, and his right hand swung down in a graceful arc across his chest. "He's dancing," Bradley said. "Look at that. It's gorgeous. It's such a gorgeous little dance.

"The thing is, his phrases are of mixed length," she went on. "Some of them are long. Some of them are very short. Some of them are explosive phrases, loaded up in the beginning and then trailing off. Some of them are impactive—building up, and then coming to a sense of impact at the end. What they are is appropriate to the task. That's what I mean by 'versatile.'"

Movement analysts tend to like watching, say, Bill Clinton or Ronald Reagan; they had great phrasing. George W. Bush does not. During this year's State of the Union address, Bush spent the entire speech swaying metronomically, straight down through his lower torso, a movement underscored, unfortunately, by the presence of a large vertical banner behind him. "Each shift ended with this focus that channels toward a particular place in the audience," Bradley said. She mimed, perfectly, the Bush gaze—the squinty, fixated look he reserves for moments of great solemnity—and gently swayed back and forth. "It's a little primitive, a little regressed." The combination of the look, the sway, and the gaze was, to her mind, distinctly adolescent. When people say of Bush that he seems eternally boyish, this is in part what they're referring to. He *moves* like a boy, which is fine, except that, unlike such movement masters as Reagan and Clinton, he can't stop moving like a boy when the occasion demands a more grown-up response.

"Mostly what we see in the normal population is undifferentiated phrasing," Bradley said. "And then you have people who are clearly preferential in their phrases, like my husband. He's Mr. Horizontal. When he's talking in a meeting, he's back. He's open. He just goes into this, this same long thing"—she leaned back, and spread her arms out wide and slowed her speech—"and it doesn't change very much. He works with people who understand him, fortunately." She laughed. "When we meet someone like this"—she nodded at Cesar, on the television screen—"what do we do? We give them their own TV series. Seriously. We reward them. We are drawn to them, because we can trust that we can get the message. It's not going to be hidden. It contributes to a feeling of authenticity."

Back to JonBee, from the beginning—only this time with the sound off. Cesar walks down the stairs. It's not the same Cesar who whistled and brought forty-seven dogs to attention. This occasion calls for subtlety. "Did you see the way he walks? He drops his hands. They're close to his side." The analyst this time was Suzi Tortora, the author of *The Dancing Dialogue.* Tortora is a New York dance-movement psychotherapist, a tall, lithe woman with long dark hair and beautiful phrasing. She was in her office on lower Broadway, a large, empty, panelled room. "He's very vertical," Tortora said. "His legs are right under his torso. He's not taking up any space. And he slows down his gait. He's telling the dog, 'I'm here by myself. I'm not going to

rush. I haven't introduced myself yet. Here I am. You can feel me.'" Cesar crouches down next to JonBee. His body is perfectly symmetrical, the center of gravity low. He looks stable, as though you couldn't knock him over, which conveys a sense of calm.

JonBee was investigating Cesar, squirming nervously. When JonBee got too jumpy, Cesar would correct him, with a tug on the leash. Because Cesar was talking and the correction was so subtle, it was easy to miss. Stop. Rewind. Play. "Do you see how rhythmic it is?" Tortora said. "He pulls. He waits. He pulls. He waits. He pulls. He waits. The phrasing is so lovely. It's predictable. To a dog that is all over the place, he's bringing a rhythm. But it isn't a panicked rhythm. It has a moderate tempo to it. There was room to wander. And it's not attack, attack. It wasn't long and sustained. It was quick and light. I would bet that with dogs like this, where people are so afraid of them being aggressive and so defensive around them, that there is a lot of aggressive strength directed at them. There is no aggression here. He's using strength without it being aggressive."

Cesar moves into the living room. The fight begins. "Look how he involves the dog," Tortora said. "He's letting the dog lead. He's giving the dog room." This was not a Secret Service agent wrestling an assailant to the ground. Cesar had his body vertical, and his hand high above JonBee holding the leash, and, as JonBee turned and snapped and squirmed and spun and jumped and lunged and struggled, Cesar seemed to be moving along with him, providing a loose structure for his aggression. It may have looked like a fight, but Cesar wasn't fighting. And what was JonBee doing? Child psychologists talk about the idea of regulation. If you expose healthy babies, repeatedly, to a very loud noise, eventually they will be

able to fall asleep. They'll become habituated to the noise: the first time the noise is disruptive, but, by the second or third time, they've learned to handle the disruption, and block it out. They've regulated themselves. Children throwing tantrums are said to be in a state of dysregulation. They've been knocked off-kilter in some way, and cannot bring themselves back to baseline. JonBee was dysregulated. He wasn't fighting; he was throwing a tantrum. And Cesar was the understanding parent. When JonBee paused, to catch his breath, Cesar paused with him. When JonBee bit Cesar, Cesar brought his finger to his mouth, instinctively, but in a smooth and fluid and calm motion that betrayed no anxiety. "Timing is a big part of Cesar's repertoire," Tortora went on. "His movements right now aren't complex. There aren't a lot of efforts together at one time. His range of movement qualities is limited. Look at how he's narrowing. Now he's enclosing." As JonBee calmed down, Cesar began caressing him. His touch was firm but not aggressive; not

so strong as to be abusive and not so light as to be insubstantial and irritating. Using the language of movement—the plainest and most transparent of all languages—Cesar was telling JonBee that he was safe. Now JonBee was lying on his side, mouth relaxed, tongue out. "Look at that, look at the dog's face," Tortora said. This was not defeat; this was relief.

Later, when Cesar tried to show Scott how to placate JonBee, Scott couldn't do it, and Cesar made him stop. "You're still nervous," Cesar told him. "You are still unsure. That's how you become a target." It isn't as easy as it sounds to calm a dog. "There, there," in a soothing voice, accompanied by a nice belly scratch, wasn't enough for JonBee, because he was reading gesture and posture and symmetry and the precise meaning of touch. He was looking for clarity and consistency. Scott didn't have it. "Look at the tension and aggression in his face," Tortora said, when the camera turned to Scott. It was true. Scott had a long and craggy face, with high, wide cheekbones and

*"They're all sons of bitches."*

pronounced lips, and his movements were taut and twitchy. "There's a bombardment of actions, quickness combined with tension, a quality in how he is using his eyes and focus—a darting," Tortora said. "He gesticulates in a way that is complex. There is a lot going on. So many different qualities of movement happening at the same time. It leads those who watch him to get distracted." Scott is a character actor, with a list of credits going back thirty years. The tension and aggression in his manner made him interesting and complicated—which works for Hollywood but doesn't work for a troubled dog. Scott said he loved JonBee, but the quality of his movement did not match his emotions.

For a number of years, Tortora has worked with Eric (not his real name), an autistic boy with severe language and communication problems.

Tortora video-taped some of their sessions, and in one, four months after they started to work together, Eric is standing in the middle of Tortora's studio in Cold Spring, New York, a beautiful dark-haired three-and-a-half-year-old, wearing only a diaper. His mother is sitting to the side, against the wall. In the background, you can hear the soundtrack to *Riverdance,* which happens to be Eric's favorite album. Eric is having a tantrum.

He gets up and runs toward the stereo. Then he runs back and throws himself down on his stomach, arms and legs flailing. Tortora throws herself down on the ground, just as he did. He sits up. She sits up. He twists. She twists. He squirms. She squirms. "When Eric is running around, I didn't say, 'Let's put on quiet music.' I can't turn him off, because he can't turn off," Tortora said. "He can't go from zero to sixty and then back down to zero. With a typical child, you might say, 'Take a deep breath. Reason with me'—and that might work. But not with children like this. They are in their world by themselves. I have to go in there and meet them and bring them back out."

Tortora sits up on her knees, and faces Eric. His legs are moving in every direction, and she takes his feet into her hands. Slowly, and subtly, she begins to move his legs in time with the music. Eric gets up and runs to the corner of the room and back again. Tortora gets up and mirrors his action, but this time she moves more fluidly and gracefully than he did. She takes his feet again. This time, she moves Eric's entire torso, opening the pelvis in a contra-lateral twist. "I'm standing above him, looking directly at him. I am very symmetrical. So I'm saying to him, I'm stable. I'm here. I'm calm. I'm holding him at the knees and giving him sensory input. It's firm and clear. Touch is an incredible tool. It's another way to speak."

She starts to rock his knees from side to side. Eric begins to calm down. He begins to make slight adjustments to the music. His legs move more freely, more lyrically. His movement is starting to get organized. He goes back into his mother's arms. He's still upset, but his cry has softened. Tortora sits and faces him—stable, symmetrical, direct eye contact.

His mother says, "You need a tissue?"

Eric nods.

Tortora brings him a tissue. Eric's mother says that she needs a tissue. Eric gives his tissue to his mother.

"Can we dance?" Tortora asks him.

"O.K.," he says, in a small voice.

It was impossible to see Tortora with Eric and not think of Cesar with JonBee: here was the same extraordinary energy and intelligence and

personal force marshalled on behalf of the helpless, the same calm in the face of chaos, and, perhaps most surprising, the same gentleness. When we talk about people with presence, we often assume that they have a strong personality—that they sweep us all up in their own personal whirlwind. Our model is the Pied Piper, who played his irresistible tune and every child in Hamelin blindly followed. But Cesar Millan and Suzi Tortora play different tunes, in different situations. And they don't turn their back, and expect others to follow. Cesar let JonBee lead; Tortora's approaches to Eric were dictated by Eric. Presence is not just versatile; it's also reactive. Certain people, we say, "command our attention," but the verb is all wrong. There is no commanding, only soliciting. The dogs in the dog run wanted someone to tell them when to start and stop; they were refugees from anarchy and disorder. Eric wanted to enjoy *Riverdance*. It was his favorite music. Tortora did not say, "Let us dance." She asked, "Can we dance?"

Then Tortora gets a drum, and starts to play. Eric's mother stands up and starts to circle the room, in an Irish step dance. Eric is lying on the ground, and slowly his feet start to tap in time with the music. He gets up. He walks to the corner of the room, disappears behind a partition, and then reenters, triumphant. He begins to dance, playing an imaginary flute as he circles the room.

When Cesar was twenty-one, he travelled from his home town to Tijuana, and a "coyote" took him across the border, for a hundred dollars. They waited in a hole, up to their chests in water, and then ran over the mudflats, through a junk yard, and across a freeway. A taxi took him to San Diego. After a month on the streets, grimy and dirty, he walked into a dog-grooming salon and got a job, working with the difficult cases and sleeping in the offices at night. He moved to Los Angeles, and took a day job detailing limousines while he ran his dog-psychology business out of a white Chevy Astrovan. When he was twenty-three, he fell in love with an American girl named Illusion. She was seventeen, small, dark, and very beautiful. A year later, they got married.

"Cesar was a macho-istic, egocentric person who thought the world revolved around him," Illusion recalled, of their first few years together. "His view was that marriage was where a man tells a woman what to do. Never give affection. Never give compassion or understanding. Marriage is about keeping the man happy, and that's where it ends." Early in their marriage, Illusion got sick, and was in the hospital for three weeks. "Cesar visited once, for less than two hours," she said. "I thought to myself, This relationship is not working out. He just wanted to be with his dogs." They had a new baby, and no money. They separated. Illusion told Cesar that she would divorce him if he didn't get into therapy. He agreed, reluctantly. "The therapist's name was Wilma," Illusion went on. "She was a strong African-American woman. She said, 'You want your wife to take care of you, to clean the house. Well, she wants something, too. She wants your affection and love.'" Illusion remembers Cesar scribbling furiously on a pad. "He wrote that down. He said, 'That's it! It's like the dogs. They need exercise, discipline, *and* affection.'" Illusion laughed. "I looked at him, upset, because why the hell are you talking about your dogs when you should be talking about us?"

"I was fighting it," Cesar said. "Two women against me, blah, blah, blah. I had to get rid of the fight in my mind. That was very difficult. But that's when the light bulb came on. Women have their own psychology."

Cesar could calm a stray off the street, yet, at least in the beginning, he did not grasp the simplest of truths about his own wife. "Cesar related to dogs because he didn't feel connected to people," Illusion said. "His dogs were his way of feeling like he belonged in the world, because he wasn't people friendly. And it was hard for him to get out of that." In Mexico, on his grandfather's farm, dogs were dogs and humans were humans: each knew its place. But in America dogs were treated like children, and owners had shaken up the hierarchy of human and animal. Sugar's problem was Lynda. JonBee's problem was Scott. Cesar calls that epiphany in the therapist's office the most important moment in his life, because it was the moment when he understood that to succeed in the world he could not just be a dog whisperer. He needed to be a people whisperer.

For his show, Cesar once took a case involving a Chihuahua named Bandit. Bandit had a large, rapper-style diamond-encrusted necklace around his neck spelling "Stud." His owner was Lori, a voluptuous woman with an oval face and large, pleading eyes. Bandit was out of control, terrorizing guests and menacing other dogs. Three trainers had failed to get him under control.

Lori was on the couch in her living room as she spoke to Cesar. Bandit was sitting in her lap. Her teen-age son, Tyler, was sitting next to her.

"About two weeks after his first visit with the vet, he started to lose a lot of hair," Lori said. "They said that he had Demodex mange." Bandit had been sold to her as a show-quality dog, she recounted, but she had the bloodline checked, and learned that he had come from a puppy mill. "He didn't have any human contact," she went on. "So for three months he was getting dipped every week to try to get rid of the symptoms." As she spoke, her hands gently encased Bandit. "He would hide inside my shirt and lay his head right by my heart, and stay there." Her eyes were moist. "He was right here on my chest."

"So your husband cooperated?" Cesar asked. He was focussed on Lori, not on Bandit. This is what the new Cesar understood that the old Cesar did not.

"He was our baby. He was in need of being nurtured and helped and he was so scared all the time."

"Do you still feel the need of feeling sorry about him?"

"Yeah. He's so cute."

Cesar seemed puzzled. He didn't know why Lori would still feel sorry for her dog.

Lori tried to explain. "He's so small and he's helpless."

"But do you believe that *he* feels helpless?"

Lori still had her hands over the dog, stroking him. Tyler was looking at Cesar, and then at his mother, and then down at Bandit. Bandit tensed. Tyler reached over to touch the dog, and Bandit leaped out of Lori's arms and attacked him, barking and snapping and growling. Tyler, startled, jumped back. Lori, alarmed, reached out, and—this was the critical thing—put her hands around Bandit in a worried, caressing motion, and lifted him back into her lap. It happened in an instant.

Cesar stood up. "Give me the space," he said, gesturing for Tyler to move aside. "Enough dogs attacking humans, and humans not really blocking him, so he is only becoming more narcissistic. It is all about him. He owns you." Cesar was about as angry as he ever gets. "It seems like you are favoring the dog, and hopefully that is not the truth. . . . If Tyler kicked the dog, you would correct him. The dog is biting your son, and you are not correcting hard enough." Cesar was in em-

phatic mode now, his phrasing sure and unambiguous. "I don't understand why you are not putting two and two together."

Bandit was nervous. He started to back up on the couch. He started to bark. Cesar gave him a look out of the corner of his eye. Bandit shrank. Cesar kept talking. Bandit came at Cesar. Cesar stood up. "I have to touch," he said, and he gave Bandit a sharp nudge with his elbow. Lori looked horrified.

Cesar laughed, incredulously. "You are saying that it is fair for him to touch us but not fair for us to touch him?" he asked.

Lori leaned forward to object.

"You don't like that, do you?" Cesar said, in his frustration speaking to the whole room now. "It's not going to work. This is a case that is not going to work, because the owner doesn't want to allow what you normally do with your kids. . . . The hardest part for me is that the father or mother chooses the dog instead of the son. That's hard for me. I love dogs. I'm the dog whisperer. You follow what I'm saying? But I would never choose a dog over my son."

He stopped. He had had enough of talking. There was too much talking, anyhow. People saying, "I love you," with a touch that didn't mean "I love you." People saying, "There, there," with gestures that did not soothe. People saying, "I'm your mother," while reaching out to a Chihuahua instead of their own flesh and blood. Tyler looked stricken. Lori shifted nervously in her seat. Bandit growled. Cesar turned to the dog and said "Sh-h-h." And everyone was still.

| 2006 |

# BULLDOG

*Fiction*

## ARTHUR MILLER

He saw this tiny ad in the paper: "Black Brindle Bull puppies, $3.00 each." He had something like ten dollars from his housepainting job, which he hadn't deposited yet, but they had never had a dog in the house. His father was taking a long nap when the idea crested in his mind, and his mother, in the middle of a bridge game when he asked her if it would be all right, shrugged absently and threw a card. He walked around the house trying to decide,

and the feeling spread through him that he'd better hurry, before somebody else got the puppy first. In his mind, there was already one particular puppy that belonged to him—it was his puppy and the puppy knew it. He had no idea what a brindle bull looked like, but it sounded tough and wonderful. And he had the three dollars, though it soured him to think of spending it when they had such bad money worries, with his father gone bankrupt again. The tiny ad hadn't mentioned how many puppies there were. Maybe there were only two or three, which might be bought by this time.

The address was on Schermerhorn Street, which he had never heard of. He called, and a woman with a husky voice explained how to get there and on which line. He was coming from the Midwood section, and the elevated Culver line, so he would have to change at Church Avenue. He wrote everything down and read it all back to her. She still had the puppies, thank God. It took more than an hour, but the train was almost empty, this being Sunday, and with a breeze from its open wood-framed windows it was cooler than down in the street. Below in empty lots he could see old Italian women, their heads covered with red bandannas, bent over and loading their aprons with dandelions. His Italian school friends said they were for wine and salads. He remembered trying to eat one once when he was playing left field in the lot near his house, but it was bitter and salty as tears. The old wooden train, practically unloaded, rocked and clattered lightly through the hot afternoon. He passed above a block where men were standing in driveways watering their cars as though they were hot elephants. Dust floated pleasantly through the air.

The Schermerhorn Street neighborhood was a surprise, totally different from his own, in Midwood. The houses here were made of brownstone, and were not at all like the clapboard ones on his block, which had been put up only a few years before or, in the earliest cases, in the twenties. Even the sidewalks looked old, with big squares of stone instead of cement, and bits of grass growing in the cracks between them. He could tell that Jews didn't live here, maybe because it was so quiet and unenergetic and not a soul was sitting outside to enjoy the sun. Lots of windows were wide open, with expressionless people leaning on their elbows and staring out, and cats stretched out on some of the sills, many of the women in their bras and the men in underwear trying to catch a breeze. Trickles of sweat were creeping down his back, not only from the heat but also because he realized now that he was the only one who wanted the dog, since his parents hadn't really had an opinion and his brother, who was older, had said, "What are you, crazy, spending your few dollars on a puppy? Who knows if it will be any good? And what are you going to feed it?" He thought bones, and his brother, who always knew what was right or wrong, yelled, "Bones! They have no teeth yet!" Well, maybe soup, he had mumbled. "Soup! You going to feed a puppy *soup*?" Suddenly he saw that he had arrived at the address. Standing there, he felt the bottom falling out, and he knew it was all a mistake, like one of his dreams or a lie that he had stupidly tried to defend as being real. His heart sped up and he felt he was blushing and walked on for half a block or so. He was the only one out, and people in a few of the windows were watching him on the empty street. But how could he go home after he had come so far? It seemed he'd been travelling for weeks or a year. And now to get back on the subway with nothing? Maybe he ought at least to get a look at the puppy, if the woman would let him. He had looked it up in the Book of Knowledge, where they had two full pages of dog pictures, and there had been a white English bulldog with bent front legs and teeth that stuck out from its lower jaw, and a little black-and-white Boston bull, and a long-nosed pit bull, but they had no picture of a brindle bull. When you came down to it, all he really knew about brindle bulls was that they would cost three dollars. But he had to at least get a look at him, his puppy, so he went back down the block and rang the basement doorbell, as the woman had told him to do. The sound was so loud it startled him, but he felt if he ran away and she came out in time to see him it would be even more embarrassing, so he stood there with sweat running down over his lip.

An inner door under the stoop opened, and a woman came out and looked at him through the dusty iron bars of the gate. She wore some kind of gown, light-pink silk, which she held together with one hand, and she had long black hair down to her shoulders. He didn't dare look directly into her face, so he couldn't tell exactly what she looked like, but he could feel her tension as she stood there behind her closed gate. He felt she could not imagine what he was doing ringing her bell and he quickly asked if she was the one who'd put the ad in. Oh! Her manner changed right away, and she unlatched the gate and pulled it open. She was shorter than he and had a peculiar smell, like a mixture of milk and stale air. He followed her into the apartment, which was so dark he could hardly make out anything, but he could hear the high yapping of puppies. She had to yell to ask him where he lived and how old he was, and when he told her thirteen she clapped a hand over her mouth and said that he was very tall for his age, but he couldn't understand why this seemed to embarrass her, except that she may have thought he was fifteen, which people sometimes did. But even so. He followed her into the kitchen, at the back of the apartment, where finally he could see around him, now that he'd been out of the sun for a few minutes. In a large cardboard box that had been unevenly cut down to make it shallower he saw three puppies and their mother, who sat looking up at him with her tail moving slowly back and forth. He didn't think she looked like a bulldog, but he didn't dare say so. She was just a brown dog with flecks of black and a few stripes here and there, and the puppies were the same. He did like the way their little ears drooped, but he said to the woman that he had wanted to see the puppies but hadn't made up his mind yet. He really didn't know what to do next, so, in order not to seem as though he

didn't appreciate the puppies, he asked if she would mind if he held one. She said that was all right and reached down into the box and lifted out two puppies and set them down on the blue linoleum. They didn't look like any bulldogs he had ever seen, but he was embarrassed to tell her that he didn't really want one. She picked one up and said, "Here," and put it on his lap.

He had never held a dog before and was afraid it would slide off, so he cradled it in his arms. It was hot on his skin and very soft and kind of disgusting in a thrilling way. It had gray eyes like tiny buttons. It troubled him that the Book of Knowledge hadn't had a picture of this kind of dog. A real bulldog was kind of tough and dangerous, but these were just brown dogs. He sat there on the arm of the green upholstered chair with the puppy on his lap, not knowing what to do next. The woman, meanwhile, had put herself next to him, and it felt like she had given his hair a pat, but he wasn't sure because he had very thick hair. The more seconds that ticked away the less sure he was of what to do. Then she asked if he would like some water, and he said he would, and she went to the faucet and ran water, which gave him a chance to stand up and set the puppy back in the box. She came back to him holding the glass and as he took it she let her gown fall open, showing her breasts like half-filled balloons, saying she couldn't believe he was only thirteen. He gulped the water and started to hand her back the glass, and she suddenly drew his head to her and kissed him. In all this time, for some reason, he hadn't been able to look into her face, and when he tried to now he couldn't see anything but a blur and hair. She reached down to him and a shivering started in the backs of his legs. It got sharper, until it was almost like the time he touched the live rim of a light socket while trying to remove a broken bulb. He would never be able to remember getting down on the carpet—he felt like a waterfall was smashing down on top of his head. He remembered getting inside her heat and his head banging and banging against the leg of her couch. He was almost at Church Avenue, where he had to change for the elevated Culver line, before realizing she hadn't taken his three dollars, and he couldn't recall agreeing to it but he had this small cardboard box on his lap with a puppy mewling inside. The scraping of nails on the cardboard sent chills up his back. The woman, as he remembered now, had cut two holes into the top of the box, and the puppy kept sticking his nose through them.

His mother jumped back when he untied the cord and the puppy pushed up and scrambled out, yapping. "What is he doing?" she yelled, with her hands in the air as though she were about to be attacked. By this time, he'd lost his fear of the puppy and held him in his arms and let him lick his face, and seeing this his mother calmed down a bit. "Is he hungry?" she asked, and stood with her mouth slightly open, ready for anything, as he put the puppy on the floor again. He said the puppy might be hungry, but he thought he could eat only soft things, although his little teeth were as sharp as pins. She got out some soft cream cheese and put a little piece of it on the floor, but the puppy only sniffed at it and peed. "My God in Heaven!" she yelled, and quickly got a piece of newspaper to blot it up with. When she bent over that way, he thought of the woman's heat and was ashamed and shook his head. Suddenly her name came to him—Lucille—which she had told him when they were on the floor. Just as he was slipping in, she had opened her

eyes and said, "My name is Lucille." His mother brought out a bowl of last night's noodles and set it on the floor. The puppy raised his little paw and tipped the bowl over, spilling some of the chicken soup at the bottom. This he began to lick hungrily off the linoleum. "He likes chicken soup!" his mother yelled happily, and immediately decided he would most likely enjoy an egg and so put water on to boil. Somehow the puppy knew that she was the one to follow and walked behind her, back and forth, from the stove to the refrigerator. "He follows me!" his mother said, laughing happily.

On his way home from school the next day, he stopped at the hardware store and bought a puppy collar for seventy-five cents, and Mr. Schweckert threw in a piece of clothesline as a leash. Every night as he fell asleep, he brought out Lucille like something from a secret treasure box and wondered if he could dare phone her and maybe be with her again. The puppy, which he had named Rover, seemed to grow noticeably bigger every day, although he still showed no signs of looking like any bulldog. The boy's father thought Rover should live in the cellar, but it was very lonely down there and he would never stop yapping. "He misses his mother," his mother said, so every night the boy started him off on  some rags in an old wash basket down there, and when he'd yapped enough the boy was allowed to bring him up and let him sleep on some rags in the kitchen, and everybody was thankful for the quiet. His mother tried to walk the puppy in the quiet street they lived on, but he kept tangling the rope around her ankles, and because she was afraid to hurt him she exhausted herself following him in all his zigzags. It didn't always happen, but many times when the boy looked at Rover he'd think of Lucille and could almost feel the heat again. He would sit on the porch steps stroking the puppy and think of her, the insides of her thighs. He still couldn't imagine her face, just her long black hair and her strong neck.

One day, his mother baked a chocolate cake and set it to cool on the kitchen table. It was at least eight inches thick, and he knew it would be delicious.  He was drawing a lot in those days, pictures of spoons and forks or cigarette packages or, occasionally, his mother's Chinese vase with the dragon on it, anything that had an interesting shape. So he put the cake on a chair next to the table and drew for a while and then got up and went outside for some reason and got involved with the tulips he had planted the previous fall that were just now showing their tips. Then he decided to go look for a practically new baseball he had mislaid the previous summer and which he was sure, or pretty sure, must be down in the cellar in a cardboard box. He had never really got down to the bottom of that box, because he was always distracted by finding something he'd forgotten he had put in there. He had started down into the cellar from the outside entrance, under the back porch, when he noticed that the pear tree, which he had planted two years before, had what looked like a blossom on one of its slender branches. It amazed him, and he felt proud and successful.

He had paid thirty-five cents for the tree on Court Street and thirty cents for an apple tree, which he planted about seven feet away, so as to be able to hang a hammock between them someday. They were still too thin and young, but maybe next year. He always loved to stare at the two trees, because he had planted them, and he felt they somehow knew he was looking at them, and even that they were looking back at him. The back yard ended at a ten-foot-high wooden fence that surrounded Erasmus field, where the semi-pro and sandlot teams played on weekends, teams like the House of David and the Black Yankees and the one with Satchel Paige, who was famous as one of the country's greatest pitchers except he was a Negro and couldn't play in the big leagues, obviously. The House of Davids all had long beards—he'd never understood why, but maybe they were Orthodox Jews, although they didn't look it. An extremely long foul shot over right field could drop a ball into the yard, and that was the ball it had occurred to him to search for, now that spring had come and the weather was warming up. In the basement, he found the box and was immediately surprised at how sharp his ice skates were, and recalled that he had once had a vise to clamp the skates side by side so that a stone could be rubbed on the blades. He pushed aside a torn fielder's glove, a hockey goalie's glove whose mate he knew had been lost, some pencil stubs and a package of crayons, and a little wooden man whose arms flapped up and down when you pulled a string. Then he heard the puppy yapping over his head, but it was not his usual sound—it was continuous and very sharp and loud. He ran upstairs and saw his mother coming down into the living room from the second floor, her dressing gown flying out behind her, a look of fear on her face. He could hear the scraping of the puppy's nails on the linoleum, and he rushed into the kitchen. The puppy was running around and around in a circle and sort of screaming, and the boy could see at once that his belly was swollen. The cake was on the floor, and most of it was gone. "My cake!" his mother screamed, and picked up the dish with the remains on it and held it up high as though to save it from the puppy, even though practically nothing was left. The boy tried to catch Rover, but he slipped away into the living room. His mother was behind him yelling "The carpet!" Rover kept running, in wider circles now that he had more space, and foam was forming on his muzzle. "Call the police!" his mother yelled. Suddenly, the puppy fell and lay on his side, gasping and making little squeaks with each breath. Since they had never had a dog and knew nothing about veterinarians, he looked in the phone book and found the A.S.P.C.A. number and called them. Now he was afraid to touch Rover, because the puppy snapped at his hand when it got close and he had this foam on his mouth. When the van drew up in front of the house, the boy went outside and saw a young guy removing a little cage from the back. He told him that the dog had eaten practically a whole cake, but the man had no interest and came into the house and stood for a moment looking down at Rover, who was making little yips now but was still down on his side. The man dropped some netting over him and when he slipped him into the cage, the puppy tried to get up and run. "What do you think is the matter with him?" his mother asked, her mouth turned down in revulsion, which the boy now felt in himself. "What's the matter with him is he ate a cake," the man said. Then he carried the cage out and

slid it through the back door into the darkness of the van. "What will you do with him?" the boy asked. "You want him?" the man snapped. His mother was standing on the stoop now and overheard them. "We can't have him here," she called over, with fright and definiteness in her voice, and approached the young man. "We don't know how to keep a dog. Maybe somebody who knows how to keep him would want him." The young man nodded with no interest either way, got behind the wheel, and drove off.

The boy and his mother watched the van until it disappeared around the corner. Inside, the house was dead quiet again. He didn't have to worry anymore about Rover doing something on the carpets or chewing the furniture, or whether he had water or needed to eat. Rover had been the first thing he'd looked for on returning from school every day and on waking in the morning, and he had always worried that the dog might have done something to displease his mother or father. Now all that anxiety was gone and, with it, the pleasure, and it was silent in the house.

He went back to the kitchen table and tried to think of something he could draw. A newspaper lay on one of the chairs, and he opened it and inside saw a Saks stocking ad showing a woman with a gown pulled aside to display her leg. He started copying it and thought of Lucille again. Could he possibly call her, he wondered, and do what they had done again? Except that she would surely ask about Rover, and he couldn't do anything but lie to her. He remembered how she had cuddled Rover in her arms and even kissed his nose. She had really loved that puppy. How could he tell her he was gone? Just sitting and thinking of her he was hardening up like a broom handle and he sud-

## DON'T DO THAT

It was bring-your-own if you wanted anything
hard, so I brought Johnnie Walker Red
along with some resentment I'd held in
for a few weeks, which was not helped
by the sight of little nameless things
pierced with toothpicks on the tables,
or by talk that promised to be nothing
if not small. But I'd consented to come,
and I knew what part of the house
their animals would be sequestered,
whose company I loved. What else can I say,

except that old retainer of slights and wrongs,
that bad boy I hadn't quite outgrown—
I'd brought him along, too. I was out
to cultivate a mood. My hosts greeted me,
but did not ask about my soul, which was when
I was invited by Johnnie Walker Red
to find the right kind of glass, and pour.
I toasted the air. I said hello to the wall,
then walked past a group of women
dressed to be seen, undressing them
one by one, and went up the stairs to where

the Rottweilers were, Rosie and Tom,
and got down with them on all fours.
They licked the face I offered them,
and I proceeded to slick back my hair
with their saliva, and before long
I felt like a wild thing, ready to mess up
the party, scarf the hors d'oeuvres.
But the dogs said, No, don't do that,
calm down, after a while they open the door
and let you out, they pet your head, and
        everything
you might have held against them is gone,
and you're good friends again. Stay, they said.

—Stephen Dunn    | 2009 |

denly thought what if he called her and said his family were thinking of having a second puppy to keep Rover company? But then he would have to pretend he still had Rover, which would mean two lies, and that was a little frightening. Not the lies so much as trying to remember, first, that he still had Rover, second, that he was serious about a second puppy, and, third, the worst thing, that when he got up off Lucille he would have to say that unfortunately he couldn't actually take another puppy because . . . Why? The thought of all that lying exhausted him. Then he visualized being in her heat again and he thought his head would explode, and the idea came that when it was over she might insist on his taking another puppy. Force it on him. After all, she had not accepted his three dollars and Rover had been a sort of gift, he thought. It would be embarrassing to refuse another puppy, especially when he had supposedly come back to her for exactly that reason. He didn't dare go through all that and gave up the whole idea. But then the thought crept back again of her spreading apart on the floor the way she had, and he returned to searching for some reason he could give for not taking another puppy after he had supposedly come all the way across Brooklyn to get one. He could just see the look on her face on his turning down a puppy, the puzzlement or, worse, anger. Yes, she could very possibly get angry and see through him, realizing that all he had come for was to get into her and the rest of it was nonsense, and she might feel insulted. Maybe even slap him. What would he do then? He couldn't fight a grown woman. Then again, it now occurred to him that by this time she might well have sold the other two puppies, which at three dollars were pretty inexpensive. Then what? He began to wonder, suppose he just called her up and said he'd like to come over again and see her, without mentioning any puppies? He would have to tell only one lie, that he still had Rover and that the family all loved him and so on. He could easily remember that much. He went to the piano and played some chords, mostly in the dark bass, to calm himself. He didn't really know how to play, but he loved inventing chords and letting the vibrations shoot up his arms. He played, feeling as though something inside him had sort of shaken loose or collapsed altogether. He was different than he had ever been, not empty and clear anymore but weighted with secrets and his lies, some told and some untold, but all of it disgusting enough to set him slightly outside his family, in a place where he could watch them now, and watch himself with them. He tried to invent a melody with the right hand and find matching chords with the left. By sheer luck, he was hitting some beauties. It was really amazing how his chords were just slightly off, with a discordant edge but still in some way talking to the right-hand melody. His mother came into the room full of surprise and pleasure. "What's happening?" she called out in delight. She could play and sight-read music and had tried and failed to teach him, because, she believed, his ear was too good and he'd rather play what he heard than do the labor of reading notes. She came over to the piano and stood beside him, watching his hands. Amazed, wishing as always that he could be a genius, she laughed. "Are you making this up?" she almost yelled, as though they were side by side on a roller coaster. He could only nod, not daring to speak and maybe lose what he had somehow snatched out of the air, and he laughed with her because he was so completely happy that he had secretly changed, and unsure at the same time that he would ever be able to play like this again.

| 2001 |

CHILDREN OF
CELEBRITY CANINES

BRITTANY:
Daughter of Lassie. Hopes to become an actress/model. Not completely without talent, but close.

LANCE:
Benji's offspring. At the moment, wants to be a rock-and-roll drummer. A borderline sociopathic ne'er-do-well.

ROVER:
Son of Andalusian Dog. Happy and well adjusted. Nothing at all like his dad.

R. Chast

# SCOOPED

LAUREN COLLINS

Michael Brandow, a freelance dog-walker in the Village, hadn't had much luck interesting publishers in a nonfiction manuscript that he'd been working on for the past eight years. In 2006, in the course of his research, he called Alan Beck, a professor of animal ecology at Purdue. Beck happens to edit a line of books about the bond between humans and animals for P.U. Press, and he told Brandow that he'd give the manuscript a look. "I read it and thought, This is a really neat book," Beck said recently. "So I wrote to our publisher and said, 'Over the years, I've given you a lot of shit, but this is a good one.'" The result is a three-hundred-and-thirty-nine-page social history entitled *New York's Poop Scoop Law: Dogs, the Dirt, and Due Process.* Its bibliography cites, among others, Caro; Scorsese; *Dog Run: A Publication of the Washington Square Dog Run Association;* and Glickman, L. T., Shofer, F. S., "Zoonotic Visceral and Ocular Larva Migrans," *Veterinary Clinics of North America: Small Animal Practice,* Vol. 17, No. 1, January, 1987. Brandow has dedicated the book to "My sweet Samantha," his shepherd-chow-beagle bitch.

*Dogs, the Dirt, and Due Process* comes out on August 1st, the thirtieth anniversary (a hundred and thirtieth or so, in dog years) of Section 1310 of the New York State Public Health Law, which formally decrees, "It shall be the duty of each dog owner . . . to remove any feces left by his dog on any sidewalk, gutter, street, or other public area," and which, informally, accounts for the abundance of tightly knotted Gristedes bags in local trash cans. (Pre-1310, the largely ignored "curbing" rule held that animals were supposed to go in the gutter.) Brandow, on the phone the other day from Montreal, where he is spending the summer, admitted that "a lot of people just rolled their eyes" at the mention of his subject, but he sees the law, and the "civil war" that surrounded its adoption, as an urban parable. Notwithstanding a few groaners ("Tension filled the air like the smell of feces that radiated from the pavement,"

"The number one complaint was number two"), the story—which begins in Nutley, New Jersey, in 1971 (some citizens band together against a neighborhood Great Dane), crosses the Hudson (a hundred and twenty-five tons of dog shit *a day* clotting the sidewalks of "Dung City"!), skips to Albany (Koch kicks the issue upstate after the City Council fails to take action), and culminates in New York's becoming the first big city to force owners to clean up after their dogs—makes a fine Empire State procedural.

There was the usual bureaucratic gridlock: Koch inherited the problem from Beame, who inherited it from Lindsay, a waffler on canine concerns, according to Brandow, whose "known pet affiliations were minimal." Tin-eared functionaries, too: "You got *five* cats? And a *dog*?" one city official asked a woman at a hearing. "Christ. What you need is a good man." Then you had your community activists—Max Schnapp, of POPA (Pet Owners Protective Association), a labor organizer and the owner of two Great Danes (Tiger and Sampson), a pet crow (Mitzvah), three rabbits (Pinkie, Dutchie, unnamed), a white mouse (Piggy), a baby squirrel (Elmer Wiggley), a gerbil, and half a dozen alley cats (Mau Mau, Nebisch, Sister, Freddy the Freeloader, Monty Wooley), vs. Fran Lee, the founder of Children Before Dogs—grinding out their small-bore issues on the grand stage. "It was an amazing time," Beck, who was the director of the Bureau of Animal Affairs for the city from 1975 to 1980, recalled. "I was actually caught in the crossfire when dog feces were being thrown back and forth." (Gross but true: Lee, at a public debate, got smacked in the head by a loaded baggie.)

For the book, Beck was happy to share his collection of memorabilia, including various cleanup devices, some of which, Brandow writes, were modelled on fruit pickers. "The drawings, they're like looking at eighteenth-century flying contraptions or something," he said. "There was one that supposedly had some sort of mechanical jaws and a flashlight attachment for evening scooping."

Amid Doggy Tongs, Pooch Scoops, and Scoop de Doos, there is an original pooper scooper: U.S. Patent #3,685,088, formal title "Means for Collecting a Dog's Excrement by the Dog's Owner or Walker." A cardboard shovel strapped to the hand by rubber bands, it was invented by Henry Doherty, an unemployed office manager from Wayne, New Jersey, and, while the Lindsay administration endorsed the contrivance, it is not Brandow's preferred method. "I think it's a waste of money," Brandow said. "I steal as many bags as I can from the Korean grocer when I go there to buy vegetables."

| 2008 |

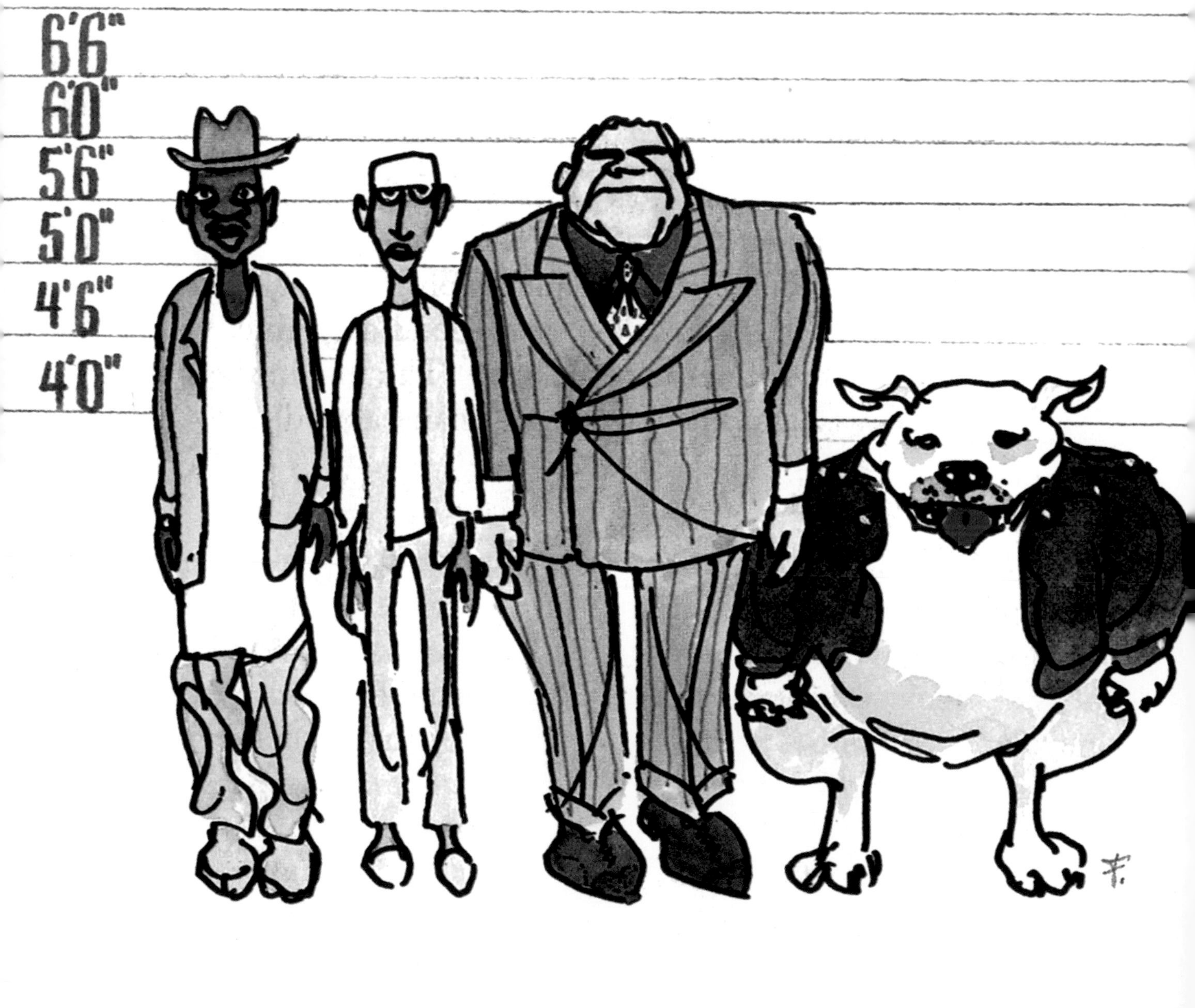
6'6"
6'0"
5'6"
5'0"
4'6"
4'0"

# TROUBLEMAKERS

## MALCOLM GLADWELL

One afternoon last February, Guy Clairoux picked up his two-and-a-half-year-old son, Jayden, from day care and walked him back to their house in the west end of Ottawa, Ontario. They were almost home. Jayden was straggling behind, and, as his father's back was turned, a pit bull jumped over a back-yard fence and lunged at Jayden. "The dog had his head in its mouth and started to do this shake," Clairoux's wife, JoAnn Hartley, said later. As she watched in horror, two more pit bulls jumped over the fence, joining in the assault. She and Clairoux came running, and he punched the first of the dogs in the head, until it dropped Jayden, and then he threw the boy toward his mother. Hartley fell on her son, protecting him with her body. "JoAnn!" Clairoux cried out, as all three dogs descended on his wife. "Cover your neck, cover your neck." A neighbor, sitting by her window, screamed for help. Her partner and a friend, Mario Gauthier, ran outside. A neighborhood boy grabbed his hockey stick and threw it to Gauthier. He began hitting one of the dogs over the head, until the stick broke. "They wouldn't stop," Gauthier said. "As soon as you'd stop, they'd attack again. I've never seen a dog go so crazy. They were like Tasmanian devils." The police came. The dogs were pulled away, and the Clairouxes and one of the rescuers were taken to the hospital. Five days later, the Ontario legislature banned the ownership of pit bulls. "Just as we wouldn't let a great white shark in a swimming pool," the province's attorney general, Michael Bryant, had said, "maybe we shouldn't have these animals on the civilized streets."

Pit bulls, descendants of the bulldogs used in the nineteenth century for bull baiting and dogfighting, have been bred for "gameness," and thus a lowered inhibition to aggression. Most dogs fight as a last resort, when staring and growling fail. A pit bull is willing to fight with little or no provocation. Pit bulls seem to have a high tolerance for pain, making it possible for them to fight to the point of exhaustion. Whereas guard dogs like German shepherds usually attempt to restrain those they perceive to be threats by biting and holding, pit bulls try to inflict the maximum amount of damage on an opponent. They bite, hold, shake, and tear. They don't growl or assume an aggressive facial expression as warning. They just attack. "They are often insensitive to behaviors that usually stop aggression," one scientific review of the breed states. "For example, dogs not bred for fighting usually display defeat in combat by rolling over and exposing a light underside. On several occasions, pit bulls have been reported to disembowel dogs offering this signal of submission." In epidemiological studies of dog bites, the pit bull is overrepresented among dogs known to have seriously injured or killed human beings, and, as a result, pit bulls have been banned or restricted in several Western European countries, China, and numerous cities and municipalities across North America. Pit bulls are dangerous.

Of course, not all pit bulls are dangerous. Most don't bite anyone. Meanwhile, Dobermans and Great Danes and German shepherds and Rottweilers are frequent biters as well, and the dog that recently mauled a Frenchwoman so badly that she was given the world's first face transplant was, of all things, a Labrador retriever. When we say that pit bulls are danger-ous, we are making a generalization, just as insurance companies use generalizations when they charge young men more for car insurance than the rest of us (even though many young men are perfectly good drivers), and doctors use generalizations when they tell overweight middle-aged men to get their cholesterol checked (even though many overweight middle-aged men won't experience heart trouble). Because we don't know which dog will bite someone or who will have a heart attack or which drivers will get in an accident, we can make predictions only by generalizing. As the legal scholar Frederick Schauer has observed, "painting with a broad brush" is "an often inevitable and frequently desirable dimension of our decision-making lives."

Another word for generalization, though, is "stereotype," and stereotypes are usually not considered desirable dimensions of our decision-making lives. The process of moving from the specific to the general is both necessary and perilous. A doctor could, with some statistical support, generalize about men of a certain age and weight. But what if generalizing from other traits—such as high blood pressure, family history, and smoking—saved more lives? Behind each generalization is a choice of what factors to leave in and what factors to leave out, and those choices can prove surprisingly complicated. After the attack on Jayden Clairoux, the Ontario government chose to make a generalization about pit bulls. But it could also have chosen to generalize about powerful dogs, or about the kinds of people who own powerful dogs, or about small children, or about back-yard fences—or, indeed, about any number of other things to do with dogs and people and places. How do we know when we've made the right generalization?

In July of last year, following the transit bombings in London, the New York City Police Department announced that it would send officers into the subways to conduct random searches of passengers' bags. On the face of it, doing random searches in the hunt for terrorists—as opposed to being guided by generalizations—seems like a silly idea. As a columnist in *New York* wrote at the time, "Not just 'most' but nearly every jihadi who has attacked a Western European or American target is a young Arab or Pakistani man. In other words, you can predict with a fair degree of certainty what an Al Qaeda terrorist looks like. Just as we have always known what Mafiosi look like—even as we understand that only an infinitesimal fraction of Italian-Americans are members of the mob."

But wait: do we really know what mafiosi look like? In *The Godfather*, where most of us get our knowledge of the Mafia, the male members of the Corleone family were played by Marlon Brando, who was of Irish and French ancestry, James Caan, who is Jewish, and two Italian-Americans, Al Pacino and John Cazale. To go by *The Godfather*, mafiosi look like white men of European descent, which, as generalizations go, isn't terribly helpful. Figuring out what an Islamic terrorist looks like isn't any easier. Muslims are not like the Amish: they don't come dressed in identifiable costumes. And they don't look like basketball players; they don't come in predictable shapes and sizes. Islam is a religion that spans the globe.

"We have a policy against racial profiling," Raymond Kelly, New York City's police commissioner, told me. "I put it in here in March of the first year I was here. It's the wrong thing to do, and it's also ineffective. If you look at the London bombings, you have three British citizens of Pakistani descent. You have Germaine Lindsay, who is Jamaican. You have the next crew, on July 21st, who are East African. You have a Chechen woman in Moscow in early 2004 who blows herself up in the subway station. So whom do you profile? Look at New York City. Forty percent of New Yorkers are born outside the country. Look at the diversity here. Who am I supposed to profile?"

Kelly was pointing out what might be called profiling's "category problem." Generalizations involve matching a category of people to a behavior or trait—overweight middle-aged men to heart-attack risk, young men to bad driving. But, for that process to work, you have to be able both to define and to identify the category you are generalizing about. "You think that terrorists aren't aware of how easy it is to be characterized by ethnicity?" Kelly

*"Artie, they took my bowl."*

*"Yes, you're my best friend, and no, I'm not lending you forty thousand dollars."*

went on. "Look at the 9/11 hijackers. They came here. They shaved. They went to topless bars. They wanted to blend in. They wanted to look like they were part of the American dream. These are not dumb people. Could a terrorist dress up as a Hasidic Jew and walk into the subway, and not be profiled? Yes. I think profiling is just nuts."

Pit-bull bans involve a category problem, too, because pit bulls, as it happens, aren't a single breed. The name refers to dogs belonging to a number of related breeds, such as the American Staffordshire terrier, the Staffordshire bull terrier, and the American pit bull terrier—all of which share a square and muscular body, a short snout, and a sleek, short-haired coat. Thus the Ontario ban prohibits not only these three breeds but any "dog that has an appearance and physical characteristics that are substantially similar" to theirs; the term of art is "pit bull–type" dogs. But what does that mean? Is a cross between an American pit bull terrier and a golden retriever a pit bull–

type dog or a golden retriever–type dog? If thinking about muscular terriers as pit bulls is a generalization, then thinking about dangerous dogs as anything substantially similar to a pit bull is a generalization about a generalization. "The way a lot of these laws are written, pit bulls are whatever they say they are," Lora Brashears, a kennel manager in Pennsylvania, says. "And for most people it just means big, nasty, scary dog that bites."

The goal of pit-bull bans, obviously, isn't to prohibit dogs that look like pit bulls. The pit-bull appearance is a proxy for the pit-bull temperament—for some trait that these dogs share. But "pit bullness" turns out to be elusive as well. The supposedly troublesome characteristics of the pit-bull type—its gameness, its determination, its insensitivity to pain—are chiefly directed toward other dogs. Pit bulls were not bred to fight humans. On the contrary: a dog that went after spectators, or its handler, or the trainer, or any of the other people involved in making a dogfighting dog a good dogfighter was usually put down. (The rule in the pit-bull world was "Man-eaters die.")

A Georgia-based group called the American Temperament Test Society has put twenty-five thousand dogs through a ten-part standardized drill designed to assess a dog's stability, shyness, aggressiveness, and friendliness in the company of people. A handler takes a dog on a six-foot lead and judges its reaction to stimuli such as gunshots, an umbrella opening, and a weirdly dressed stranger approaching in a threatening way.

Eighty-four percent of the pit bulls that have been given the test have passed, which ranks pit bulls ahead of beagles, Airedales, bearded collies, and all but one variety of dachshund. "We have tested somewhere around a thousand pit bull–type dogs," Carl Herkstroeter, the president of the A.T.T.S., says. "I've tested half of them. And of the number I've tested I have disqualified one pit bull because of aggressive tendencies. They have done extremely well. They have a good temperament. They are very good with children." It can even be argued that the same traits that make the pit bull so aggressive toward other dogs are what make it so nice to humans. "There are a lot of pit bulls these days who are licensed therapy dogs," the writer Vicki Hearne points out. "Their stability and resoluteness make them excellent for work with people who might not like a more bouncy, flibbertigibbet sort of dog. When pit bulls set out to provide comfort, they are as resolute as they are when they fight, but what they are resolute about is being gentle. And, because they are fearless, they can be gentle with anybody."

Then which are the pit bulls that get into trouble? "The ones that the legislation is geared toward have aggressive tendencies that are either bred in by the breeder, trained in by the trainer, or reinforced in by the owner," Herkstroeter says. A mean pit bull is a dog that has been turned mean, by selective breeding, by being cross-bred with a bigger, human-aggressive breed like German shepherds or Rottweilers, or by being conditioned in such a way that it begins to express hostility to human beings. A pit bull is dangerous to people, then, not to the extent that it expresses its essential pit bullness but to the extent that it deviates from it. A pit-bull ban is a generalization about a generalization about a trait that is not, in fact, general. That's a category problem.

One of the puzzling things about New York City is that, after the enormous and well-publicized reductions in crime in the mid-1990s, the crime rate has continued to fall. In the past two years, for instance, murder in New York has declined by almost 10 percent, rape by 12 percent, and burglary by more than 18 percent. Just in the last year, auto theft went down 11.8 percent. On a list of two hundred and forty cities in the United States with a population of a hundred thousand or more, New York City now ranks two hundred-and-twenty-second in crime, down near the bottom with Fontana, California, and Port St. Lucie, Florida. In the 1990s, the crime decrease was attributed to big obvious changes in city life and government—the decline of the drug trade, the gentrification of Brooklyn, the successful implementation of "broken windows" policing. But all those big changes happened a decade ago. Why is crime *still* falling?

The explanation may have to do with a shift in police tactics. The N.Y.P.D. has a computerized map showing, in real time, precisely where serious crimes are being reported, and at any moment the map typically shows a few dozen constantly shifting high-crime hot spots, some as small as two or three blocks square. What the N.Y.P.D. has done, under Commissioner Kelly, is to use the map to establish "impact zones," and to direct newly graduated officers—who used to be distributed proportionally to precincts across the city—to these zones, in some cases doubling the number of officers in the immediate neighborhood. "We took two-thirds of our graduating class and linked them with experienced officers, and focussed on those areas," Kelly said. "Well, what has happened is that over time we have averaged about a thirty-five percent crime reduction in impact zones."

For years, experts have maintained that the

incidence of violent crime is "inelastic" relative to police presence—that people commit serious crimes because of poverty and psychopathology and cultural dysfunction, along with spontaneous motives and opportunities. The presence of a few extra officers down the block, it was thought, wouldn't make much difference. But the N.Y.P.D. experience suggests otherwise. More police means that some crimes are prevented, others are more easily solved, and still others are displaced—pushed out of the troubled neighborhood—which Kelly says is a good thing, because it disrupts the patterns and practices and social networks that serve as the basis for law-breaking. In other words, the relation between New York City (a category) and criminality (a trait) is unstable, and this kind of instability is another way in which our generalizations can be derailed.

Why, for instance, is it a useful rule of thumb that Kenyans are good distance runners? It's not just that it's statistically supportable today. It's that it has been true for almost half a century, and that in Kenya the tradition of distance running is sufficiently rooted that something cataclysmic would have to happen to dislodge it. By contrast, the generalization that New York City is a crime-ridden place was once true and now, manifestly, isn't. People who moved to sunny retirement communities like Port St. Lucie because they thought they were much safer than New York are suddenly in the position of having made the wrong bet.

The instability issue is a problem for profiling in law enforcement as well. The law professor David Cole once tallied up some of the traits that Drug Enforcement Administration agents have used over the years in making generalizations about suspected smugglers. Here is a sample:

Arrived late at night; arrived early in the morning; arrived in afternoon; one of the first to deplane; one of the last to deplane; deplaned in the middle; purchased ticket at the airport; made reservation on short notice; bought coach ticket; bought first-class ticket; used one-way ticket; used round-trip ticket; paid for ticket with cash; paid for ticket with small denomination currency; paid for ticket with large denomination currency; made local telephone calls after deplaning; made long distance telephone call after deplaning; pretended to make telephone call; traveled from New York to Los Angeles; traveled to Houston; carried no luggage; carried brand-new luggage; carried a small bag; carried a medium-sized bag; carried two bulky garment bags; carried two heavy suitcases; carried four pieces of luggage; overly protective of luggage; disassociated self from luggage; traveled alone; traveled with a companion; acted too nervous; acted too calm; made eye contact with officer; avoided making eye contact with officer; wore expensive clothing and jewelry; dressed casually; went to restroom after deplaning; walked rapidly through airport; walked slowly through airport; walked aimlessly through airport; left airport by taxi; left airport by limousine; left airport by private car; left airport by hotel courtesy van.

Some of these reasons for suspicion are plainly absurd, suggesting that there's no particular rationale to the generalizations used by D.E.A. agents in stopping suspected drug smugglers. A way of making sense of the list, though, is to think of it as a catalogue of unstable traits. Smugglers may once have tended to buy one-way tick-

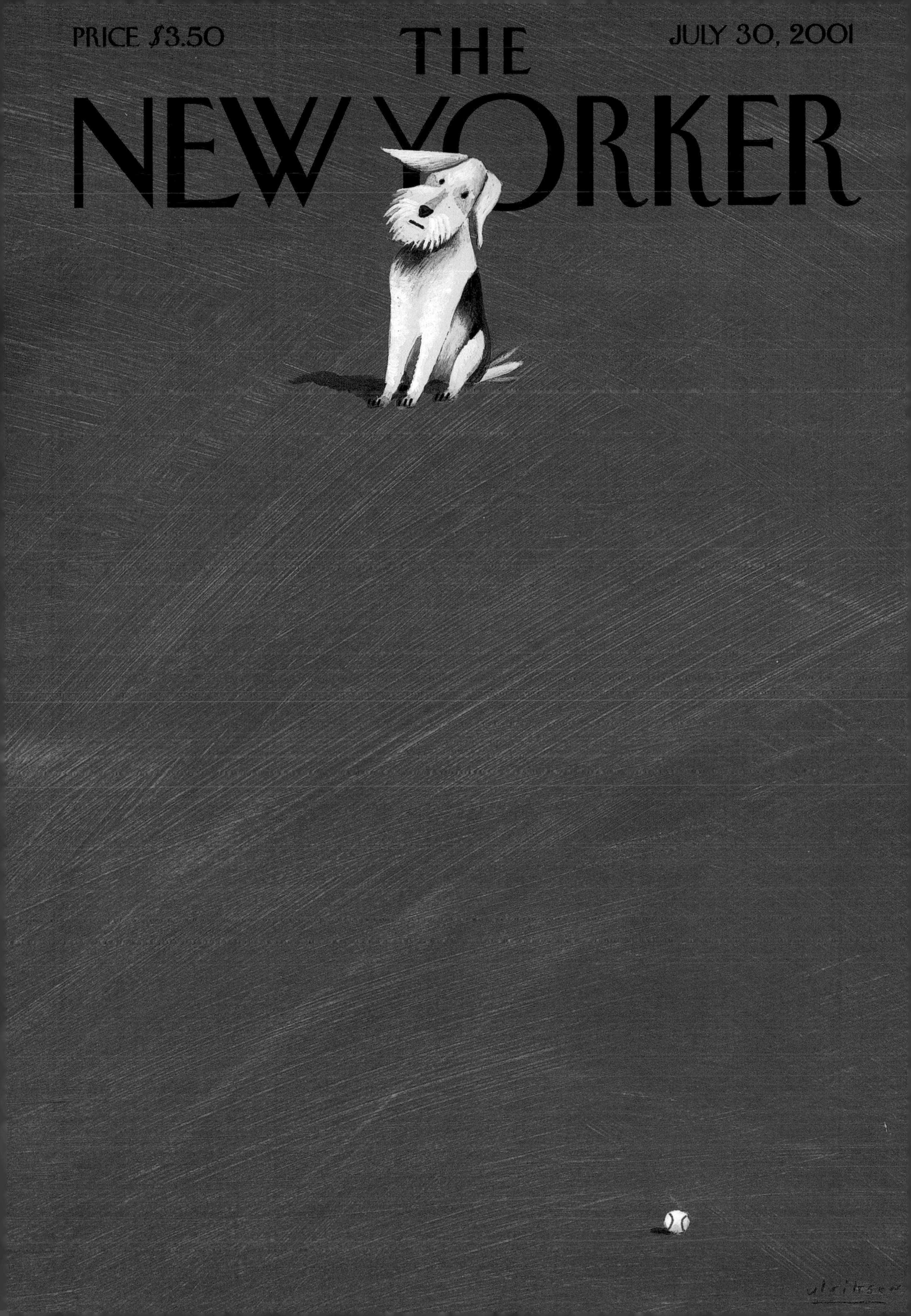
PRICE $3.50
THE
NEW YORKER
JULY 30, 2001

ets in cash and carry two bulky suitcases. But they don't have to. They can easily switch to round-trip tickets bought with a credit card, or a single carry-on bag, without losing their capacity to smuggle. There's a second kind of instability here as well. Maybe the reason some of them switched from one-way tickets and two bulky suitcases was that law enforcement got wise to those habits, so the smugglers did the equivalent of what the jihadis seemed to have done in London, when they switched to East Africans because the scrutiny of young Arab and Pakistani men grew too intense. It doesn't work to generalize about a relationship between a category and a trait when that relationship isn't stable—or when the act of generalizing may itself change the basis of the generalization.

Before Kelly became the New York police commissioner, he served as the head of the U.S. Customs Service, and while he was there he overhauled the criteria that border-control officers use to identify and search suspected smugglers. There had been a list of forty-three suspicious traits. He replaced it with a list of six broad criteria. Is there something suspicious about their physical appearance? Are they nervous? Is there specific intelligence targeting this person? Does the drug-sniffing dog raise an alarm? Is there something amiss in their paperwork or explanations? Has contraband been found that implicates this person?

You'll find nothing here about race or gender or ethnicity, and nothing here about expensive jewelry or deplaning at the middle or the end, or

*"The dog ate my magnetic insoles."*

walking briskly or walking aimlessly. Kelly removed all the unstable generalizations, forcing customs officers to make generalizations about things that don't change from one day or one month to the next. Some percentage of smugglers will *always* be nervous, will *always* get their story wrong, and will *always* be caught by the dogs. That's why those kinds of inferences are more reliable than the ones based on whether smugglers are white or black, or carry one bag or two. After Kelly's reforms, the number of searches conducted by the Customs Service dropped by about 75 percent, but the number of successful seizures improved by 25 percent. The officers went from making fairly lousy decisions about smugglers to making pretty good ones. "We made them more efficient and more effective at what they were doing," Kelly said.

Does the notion of a pit-bull menace rest on a stable or an unstable generalization? The best data we have on breed dangerousness are fatal dog bites, which serve as a useful indicator of just how much havoc certain kinds of dogs are causing. Between the late 1970s and the late 1990s, more than twenty-five breeds were involved in fatal attacks in the United States. Pit-bull breeds led the pack, but the variability from year to year is considerable. For instance, in the period from 1981 to 1982 fatalities were caused by five pit bulls, three mixed breeds, two St. Bernards, two German-shepherd mixes, a pure-bred German shepherd, a husky type, a Doberman, a Chow Chow, a Great Dane, a wolf-dog hybrid, a husky mix, and a pit-bull mix—but no Rottweilers. In 1995 and 1996, the list included ten Rottweilers, four pit bulls, two German shepherds, two huskies, two Chow Chows, two wolf-dog hybrids, two shepherd mixes, a Rottweiler mix, a mixed breed, a Chow Chow

mix, and a Great Dane. The kinds of dogs that kill people change over time, because the popularity of certain breeds changes over time. The one thing that doesn't change is the total number of the people killed by dogs. When we have more problems with pit bulls, it's not necessarily a sign that pit bulls are more dangerous than other dogs. It could just be a sign that pit bulls have become more numerous.

"I've seen virtually every breed involved in fatalities, including Pomeranians and everything else, except a beagle or a basset hound," Randall Lockwood, a senior vice-president of the A.S.P.C.A. and one of the country's leading dog-bite experts, told me. "And there's always one or two deaths attributable to malamutes or huskies, although you never hear people clamoring for a ban on those breeds. When I first started looking at fatal dog attacks, they largely involved dogs like German shepherds and shepherd mixes and St. Bernards—which is probably why Stephen King chose to make Cujo a St. Bernard, not a pit bull. I haven't seen a fatality involving a Doberman for decades, whereas in the 1970s they were quite common. If you wanted a mean dog, back then, you got a Doberman. I don't think I even saw my first pit-bull case until the middle to late 1980s, and I didn't start seeing Rottweilers until I'd already looked at a few hundred fatal dog attacks. Now those dogs make up the preponderance of fatalities. The point is that it changes over time. It's a reflection of what the dog of choice is among people who want to own an aggressive dog."

There is no shortage of more stable generalizations about dangerous dogs, though. A 1991 study in Denver, for example, compared a hundred and seventy-eight dogs with a history of biting people with a random sample of a hundred and seventy-eight dogs with no history of biting.

## WALKING THE DOG: A DIATRIBE

I have never seen a cicada, but nothing so pollutes
the night with noise as those self-absorbed, ear-baiting singers,
even in the night of a big wind, not the blurbs
of trees, shaking and shouting their leaves at each other,
not the girlish swish of tires on a street distorted to highway,
nor, in gusts, all the clattery trash set out at curbs,
There is nothing so loud, not the *Boo! Wawboooo!* of a coonhound,
whose throat, shaped for sounding the hunt through miles of thicket,
is leashed to the suburbs.

They are being natural, the cicadas. Need more be said?
And the eye that must take its delight, what weather then is this
for its succoring stroll? Hound and I walk in a gross
distortion of shapes and shadows, which lunge in the light-and-black
of night and storm and one street lamp. Too close to the sidewalk,
plantings of pyracantha spread an emboss,
over their mean thorns, of elaborate foliage and berries.
What do they know of what is insufferable
in their ignorant gloss?

Yet they lash as we linger to take in the violent evening.
Back home, my skin crawls with the sense that I've been through something.
Woven between hedges and tree rows there are, even in windstorms,
strings of light tension I broke, and I brush at the invisible
felt facts of my journey, I feel for the invisible makers,
hoping to finger webs, threads, spiders, worms.
How do I know what I've done, how does anyone know
what breakthrough or heartbreak has been accomplished in a dark
where there are no forms?

—MONA VAN DUYN    | 1972 |

The breeds were scattered: German shepherds, Akitas, and Chow Chows were among those most heavily represented. (There were no pit bulls among the biting dogs in the study, because Denver banned pit bulls in 1989.) But a number of other, more stable factors stand out. The biters were 6.2 times as likely to be male than female, and 2.6 times as likely to be intact than neutered.

The Denver study also found that biters were 2.8 times as likely to be chained as unchained. "About twenty percent of the dogs involved in fatalities were chained at the time, and had a history of long-term chaining," Lockwood said. "Now, are they chained because they are aggressive or aggressive because they are chained? It's a bit of both. These are animals that have not had an opportunity to become socialized to people. They don't necessarily even know that children are small human beings. They tend to see them as prey."

In many cases, vicious dogs are hungry or in need of medical attention. Often, the dogs had a history of aggressive incidents, and, overwhelmingly, dog-bite victims were children (particularly small boys) who were physically vulnerable to attack and may also have unwittingly done things to provoke the dog, like teasing it, or bothering it while it was eating. The strongest connection of all, though, is between the trait of dog viciousness and certain kinds of dog owners. In about a quarter of fatal dog-bite cases, the dog owners were previously involved in illegal fighting. The dogs that bite people are, in many cases, socially isolated because their owners are socially isolated, and they are vicious because they have owners who want a vicious dog. The junk-yard German shepherd—which looks as if it would rip your throat out—and the German-shepherd guide dog are the same breed. But they are not the same dog, because they have owners with different intentions.

"A fatal dog attack is not just a dog bite by a big or aggressive dog," Lockwood went on. "It is usually a perfect storm of bad human-canine interactions—the wrong dog, the wrong background, the wrong history in the hands of the wrong person in the wrong environmental situation. I've been involved in many legal cases involving fatal dog attacks, and, certainly, it's my impression that these are generally cases where everyone is to blame. You've got the unsupervised three-year-old child wandering in the neighborhood killed by a starved, abused dog owned by the dogfighting boyfriend of some woman who doesn't know where her child is. It's not old Shep

sleeping by the fire who suddenly goes bonkers. Usually there are all kinds of other warning signs."

Jayden Clairoux was attacked by Jada, a pit-bull terrier, and her two pit-bull–bullmastiff puppies, Agua and Akasha. The dogs were owned by a twenty-one-year-old man named Shridev Café, who worked in construction and did odd jobs. Five weeks before the Clairoux attack, Café's three dogs got loose and attacked a sixteen-year-old boy and his four-year-old half brother while they were ice skating. The boys beat back the animals with a snow shovel and escaped into a neighbor's house. Café was fined, and he moved the dogs to his seventeen-year-old girlfriend's house. This was not the first time that he ran into trouble last year; a few months later, he was charged with domestic assault, and, in another incident, involving a street brawl, with aggravated assault. "Shridev has personal issues," Cheryl Smith, a canine-behavior specialist who consulted on the case, says. "He's certainly not a very mature person." Agua and Akasha were now about seven months old. The court order in the wake of the first attack required that they be muzzled when they were outside the home and kept in an enclosed yard. But Café did not muzzle them, because, he said later, he couldn't afford muzzles, and apparently no one from the city ever came by to force him to comply. A few times, he talked about taking his dogs to obedience classes, but never did. The subject of neutering them also came up—particularly Agua, the male—but neutering cost a hundred dollars, which he evidently thought was too much money, and when the city temporarily confiscated his animals after the first attack it did not neuter them, either, because Ottawa does not have a policy of preemptively neutering dogs that bite people.

On the day of the second attack, according to some accounts, a visitor came by the house of Café's girlfriend, and the dogs got wound up. They were put outside, where the snowbanks were high enough so that the back-yard fence could be readily jumped. Jayden Clairoux stopped and stared at the dogs, saying, "Puppies, puppies." His mother called out to his father. His father came running, which is the kind of thing that will rile up an aggressive dog. The dogs jumped the fence, and Agua took Jayden's head in his mouth and started to shake. It was a textbook dog-biting case: un-neutered, ill-trained, charged-up dogs, with a history of aggression and an irresponsible owner, somehow get loose, and set upon a small child. The dogs had already passed through the animal bureaucracy of Ottawa, and the city could easily have prevented the second attack with the right kind of generalization—a generalization based not on breed but on the known and meaningful connection between dangerous dogs and negligent owners. But that would have required someone to track down Shridev Café, and check to see whether he had bought muzzles, and someone to send the dogs to be neutered after the first attack, and an animal-control law that insured that those whose dogs attack small children forfeit their right to have a dog. It would have required, that is, a more exacting set of generalizations to be more exactingly applied. It's always easier just to ban the breed.

| 2006 |

*"This isn't tap water, is it?"*

# From METAMORPHOSES

*Fiction*

## JOHN CHEEVER

Larry Actaeon was built along classical lines: curly hair, a triangulated nose, and a large and supple body, and he had what might be described as a Periclean interest in innovation. He designed his own sailboat (it had a list to port), ran for mayor (he was defeated), bred a Finnish wolf bitch to a German shepherd dog (the American Kennel Club refused to list the breed), and organized a drag hunt in Bullet Park, where he lived with his charming wife and three children. He was a partner in the investment-banking firm of Lothard and Williams, where he was esteemed for his shrewd and boisterous disposition.

Lothard and Williams was a highly conservative shop with an unmatched reputation for probity, but it was unconventional in one respect. One of the partners was a woman. This was a widow named Mrs. Vuiton. Her husband had been a senior partner, and when he died she had asked to be taken into the firm. In her favor were her intelligence, her beauty, and the fact that had she withdrawn her husband's interest from the partnership, it would have been missed. Lothard, the most conservative of them all, supported her candidacy, and she was taken in. Her intellect was formidable, and was fortified by her formidable and immaculate beauty. She was a stunning woman, in her middle thirties, and brought more than her share of business to the firm. Larry didn't dislike her—he didn't quite dare to—but that her good looks and her musical voice were more effective in banking than his own shrewd and boisterous manner made him at least uneasy.

The partners in Lothard and Williams—they were seven—had their private offices arranged around the central offices of Mr. Lothard. They had the visual old-fashioned appurtenances—walnut desks, portraits of dead partners, dark walls and carpets. The six male partners all wore watch chains, stickpins, and high-crowned hats. Larry sat one afternoon in this atmosphere of calculated gloom, weighing the problems of a long-term bond issue that was in the house and having a slow sale, and suddenly it crossed his mind that they might unload the entire issue on a pension-fund customer. Moved by his enthusiasm, his boisterousness, he strode through Mr. Lothard's outer office and impetuously opened the inner door. There was Mrs. Vuiton, wearing nothing but a string of beads. Mr. Lothard was at her side, wearing a wristwatch. "Oh, I'm terribly sorry!" Larry said, and he closed the door and returned to his own desk.

The image of Mrs. Vuiton seemed incised in his memory, burnt there. He had seen a thousand naked women, but he had never seen one so stunning. Her skin had a luminous and pearly whiteness that he could not forget. The pathos and beauty of the naked woman established itself in his memory like a strain of music. He had beheld something that he should not have seen, and Mrs. Vuiton had glared at him with a look that was wicked and unholy. He could not shake or rationalize away the feeling that his blunder was disastrous; that he had in some way stumbled into a transgression that would demand compensation and revenge. Pure enthusiasm had moved him to open the door without knocking; pure enthusiasm, by his lights, was a blameless impulse. Why should he feel himself surrounded by trouble, misfortune, and disaster? The nature of man was concupiscent; the same thing might be going on in a thousand offices. What he had seen was commonplace, he told himself. But there had been nothing commonplace about the whiteness of her skin or her powerful and collected stare. He repeated to himself that he had done nothing wrong, but underlying all his fancies of good and evil, merits and rewards, was the stubborn and painful nature of things, and he knew that he had seen something that it was not his destiny to see.

He dictated some letters and answered the telephone when it rang, but he did nothing worthwhile for the rest of that afternoon. He spent some time trying to get rid of the litter that his Finnish wolf bitch had whelped. The Bronx Zoo was not interested. The American Kennel Club said that he had not introduced a breed, he had produced a monstrosity. Someone had informed him that jewellers, department stores, and museums were policed by savage dogs, and he telephoned the security departments of Macy's, Cartier's, and the Museum of Modern Art, but they all had dogs. He spent the last of the afternoon at his window, joining that vast population of the blunderers, the bored—the empty-handed barber, the clerk in the antique store nobody ever comes into, the idle insurance salesman, the failing haberdasher—all of those

thousands who stand at the windows of the city and watch the afternoon go down. Some nameless doom seemed to threaten his welfare, and he was unable to refresh his boisterousness, his common sense.

He had a directors' dinner meeting on the East Side at seven. He had brought his evening clothes to town in a suit box, and had been invited to bathe and change at his host's. He left his office at five and, to kill time and if possible cheer himself, walked the two or three miles to Fifty-seventh Street. Even so, he was early, and he stopped in a bar for a drink. It was one of those places where the single women of the neighborhood congregate and are made welcome; where, having tippled sherry for most of the day, they gather to observe the cocktail hour. One of the women had a dog. As soon as Larry entered the place, the dog, a dachshund, sprang at him. The leash was attached to a table leg, and he struck at Larry so vigorously that he dragged the table a foot or two and upset a couple of drinks. He missed Larry, but there was a great deal of confusion, and Larry went to the end of the bar farthest from the ladies. The dog was excited, and his harsh, sharp barking filled the place. "What are you thinking of, Smoky?" his mistress asked. "What in the world are you thinking of? What's become of my little doggy? This can't be my little Smoky. This must be another doggy. . . ." The dog went on barking at Larry.

"Dogs don't like you?" the bartender asked.

"I breed dogs," Larry said. "I get along very well with dogs."

"It's a funny thing," the bartender said, "but I never heard that dog bark before. She's in here every afternoon, seven days a week, and that dog's always with her, but this is the first time there's ever been a peep out of him. Maybe if you took your drink into the dining room."

"You mean I'm disturbing Smoky?"

"Well, she's a regular customer. I never saw you before."

"All right," Larry said, putting as much feeling as he could into his consent. He carried his drink through a doorway into the empty dining room and sat at a table. The dog stopped barking as soon as he was gone. He finished his drink and looked around for another way to leave the place, but there was none. Smoky sprang at him again when he went out through the bar, and everyone was glad to see such a troublemaker go.

The apartment house where he was expected was one he had been in many times, but he had forgotten the address. He had counted on recognizing the doorway and the lobby, but when he stepped into the lobby he was faced with the sameness of those places. There was a black-and-white floor, a false fireplace, two English chairs, and a framed landscape. It was all familiar, but he realized that it could have been one of a dozen lobbies, and he asked the elevator man if this was the Fullmers' house. The man said "Yes," and Larry stepped into the car. Then, instead of ascending to the tenth floor where the Fullmers lived, the car went down. The first idea that crossed Larry's mind was that the Fullmers

might be having their vestibule painted and that, for this or for some other inconvenience or change, he would be expected to use the back elevator. The man slid the door open onto a kind of infernal region, crowded with heaped ashcans, broken perambulators, and steampipes covered with ruptured asbestos sleeving. "Go through the door there and get the other elevator," the man said.

"But why do I have to take the back elevator?" Larry asked.

"It's a rule," the man said.

"I don't understand," Larry said.

"Listen," the man said. "Don't argue with me. Just take the back elevator. All you deliverymen always want to go in the front door like you owned the place. Well, this is one building where you can't. The management says all deliveries at the back door, and the management is boss."

"I'm not a deliveryman," Larry said. "I'm a guest."

"What's the box?"

"The box," Larry said, "contains my evening clothes. Now take me up to the tenth floor where the Fullmers live."

"I'm sorry, Mister, but you *look* like a deliveryman."

"I am an investment banker," Larry said, "and I am on my way to a directors' meeting, where we are going to discuss the underwriting of a forty-four-million-dollar bond issue. I am worth nine hundred thousand dollars. I have a twenty-two-room house in Bullet Park, a kennel of dogs, two riding horses, three children in college, a twenty-two-foot sailboat, and five automobiles."

"Jesus," the man said.

After Larry had bathed, he looked at himself in the mirror to see if he could detect any change in his appearance, but the face in the glass was too familiar; he had shaved and washed it too many times for it to reveal any secrets. He got through dinner and the meeting, and afterward had a whiskey with the other directors. He was still, in a way that he could not have defined, troubled at having been mistaken for a deliveryman, and hoping to shift his unease a little he said to the man beside him, "You know, when I was coming up in the elevator tonight I was mistaken for a deliveryman." His confidant either didn't hear, didn't comprehend, or didn't care. He laughed loudly at something that was being said across the room, and Larry, who was used to commanding attention, felt that he had suffered another loss.

He took a taxi to Grand Central and went home on one of those locals that seem like a roundup of the spiritually wayward, the drunken, and the lost. The conductor was a corpulent man with a pink face and a fresh rose in his buttonhole. He had a few words to say to most of the travellers.

"You working the same place?" he asked Larry.

"Yes."

"You rush beer up in Yorktown, isn't that it?"

"No," Larry said, and he touched his face with his hands to see if he could feel there the welts, lines, and other changes that must have been worked in the last few hours.

"You work in a restaurant, don't you?" the conductor asked.

"No," Larry said quietly.

"That's funny," the conductor said. "When I saw the soup-and-fish I thought you was a waiter."

It was after one o'clock when he got off the train. The station and the cab-stand were shut, and only a few cars were left in the parking lot. When he switched on the lights of the small European car he used for the station, he saw that they burned faintly, and as soon as he pressed the starter they faded to nothing with each revolution of the motor. In the space of a few minutes, the battery gave up the ghost. It was only a little less than a mile to his house, and he really didn't mind the walk. He strode briskly along the empty streets and unfastened the gates to his driveway. He was fastening them when he heard the noise of running and panting and saw that the dogs were out.

The noise woke his wife, who, thinking that he had already come home, called to him for help. "Larry! Larry, the dogs are out! The dogs are out! Larry, please come quickly, the dogs are out and I think they're after someone!" He heard her calling him as he fell, and saw the yellow lights go on in the windows, but that was the last he saw.

| 1963 |

*"On the Internet, nobody knows you're a dog."*

# WORSE THAN HIS BITE

ERIC KONIGSBERG

Good schools, abundant day-care options, probably more discarded chicken bones per block than you'll find in any other town: the relative lack of green space notwithstanding, it was possible, until recently, to consider New York City an excellent place for dogs. That may soon change, however, now that Mayor Bloomberg has proposed a series of new noise-control amendments. Along with curtailing the excesses of ice-cream-truck drivers and dub-reggae enthusiasts, his plan calls for an enforced limit of ten minutes—five minutes at night—when it comes to barking dogs. After that, a dog's owner may be deemed in violation of the law and issued a ticket or a fine.

"There have typically been a lot of dog complaints to the 311 line," Jordan Barowitz, the Mayor's spokesman, explained the other day. "Last month, for instance, there were eleven hundred and forty-nine calls under the category 'animal noise.' And then, let's see here, 'animal noise, chronic': four hundred and fourteen. That month was a bit heavier than April. September, October, it's very high. It drops in November, but it bounces back up in December. Maybe they get excited about the holidays."

Currently, the city's noise code reads, "No person shall permit an animal, including a bird, under his or her control to cause unnecessary noise." This, needless to say, is a little vague. "It produces problems from an enforcement standpoint," Barowitz said. The city's Department of Environmental Protection, which drafted the proposed legislation, examined the laws in several other cities before deciding on the ten-minute rule. Charles Sturcken, the D.E.P.'s public-affairs director, said, "Seattle has some of the more advanced measures in the country. Hawaii apparently has very quiet noise codes. Atlanta has a ten-minute-duration law anytime for barking, or up to half an hour for intermittent barking. Palo Alto, it's also ten minutes. We thought that was reasonable."

Reasonable for people, maybe. To a dog, the ten- and five-minute limits might seem arbitrary, and a little harsh: even in dog years, five minutes of barking is thirty-five minutes, which falls just short of the standard therapeutic hour. What's more, the Mayor's proposal ignores the archetype of the barking dog as hero ("Lassie, Dad's hurt! Get help!"), and the fact that raising a ruckus is what a lot of dogs have been bred to do.

Some breeds are more vocal than others. According to a study published in 1965 by the animal behaviorists John Paul Scott and John L. Fuller, the lowest "threshold of stimulation" belongs to the cocker spaniel. A cocker spaniel puppy fighting with a litter mate over a bone barked nine hundred and seven times in ten minutes. The quietest dog in the study was the African basenji, which almost never barks (the most vocal basenji racked up twenty low-pitched "woof"s in the bone-fight test), a trait the animal is believed to have developed over many generations of hiding from leopards. Jean Martin, a basenji breeder in Tully, New York, says that she gets a lot of calls from New Yorkers shopping for a bark-less dog. "Basenjis don't bark, but they can scream. They can howl. And they can yodel."

It is not easy to stop a dog from barking. Though a recent study published in *Science* indicated that dogs may understand human language, in one case comprehending more than two hundred words, anecdotal evidence suggests that the phrases "Shut up,"

"Knock it off," and "Put a sock in it" are not among them. For that reason, counter-barking can be big business. Andrea Arden, a trainer, says, "I get probably two or three calls a day from people with a barking problem. They say, 'You need to get back to me immediately. I only get one more warning, and then I'm out of my building.'" The most popular quick fix is a special collar that emits a spray of citronella oil whenever its wearer barks (it is activated by sound vibrations). "Those are fine," Arden says. "But I'm worried people will resort to desperate measures—shock collars, tranquillizers, wiring the dog's mouth shut. The absolute cruellest thing you can do is debarking—that's when the vocal cords are cut. You hear about that a lot with beagles. I personally don't know any vets in town who do that, but it happens. And I have no doubt that the noise restrictions will mean people start giving their dogs up to shelters."

"I'm sure I'll be getting the calls," said Darryl Vernon, a lawyer in midtown, who for twenty years has represented dog owners in all kinds of legal actions. "The landlords will say, 'This is governmental ratification, and I'm going to use it to sue and evict dog owners and raise the rent.' Until now, I've never had a client get a violation from the city for barking. It's mainly for odors."

| 2004 |

## TENNIS BALL

IN THE GRAVEYARD /26

*/ said hello again,*

I parked by Jane's grave in June, under oaks and birches,
and ~~told her I loved her,~~ and went walking with Gussie
past stones and flowers and the grave with the plastic
chickens. (Somebody ~~loved~~ somebody who loved chickens.)
Gus stopped and stared: A woman's long bare legs
stretched up at the edge of the graveyard, a man's body
heaving between them.       Gus considered an inspection,
so I clicked my fingers, as softly as I could, to distract him,
and became the embarrassed cause of *coitus interruptus.*
Walking to the car, I peeked. She was restarting him, her
head moving up and down. It was a June day, leaves full,
Gus healthy and gay, chasing a tennis ball, my wife dead.

I parked by the grave in September, under oaks and birches,
and said hello again, and went walking with Gussie

past markers, roses, and the grave with plastic chickens.
(Somebody loved somebody who loved chickens.)

Gus stopped and stared: a woman's long bare legs
stretched up at the edge of the graveyard, a man's body

heaving between them. Gus considered checking them out,
so I clicked my fingers, softly as I could, to distract him,

and became the unintending source of coitus interruptus.
Walking to the car, I peeked. She was re-starting him, her

head riding up and down. It was a fine day, leaves red,
Gus healthy and gay, refusing to give up his tennis ball.

—DONALD HALL   | 2005 |

IN THE GRAVEYARD /32

I parked by the grave in June, under oaks and birches,
and said hello again, and went walking with Gussie
past stones and flowers and the grave with the plastic
chickens. (Somebody loved somebody who loved chickens.)
Gus stopped and stared: A woman's long bare legs
stretched up at the edge of the graveyard, a man's body
heaving between them.       Gus considered an inspection,
so I clicked my fingers, as softly as I could, to distract him,
and became the unintending cause of *coitus interruptus.*
Walking to the car, I peeked. She was restarting him, her
head moving up and down. It was a June day, leaves full,
Gus healthy and gay, chasing a ~~tennis ball, while the motor~~
~~still runs, keeping the car cool by the headstone.~~

*teasing me*
*with it.*

*/ keeping it, ~~from me~~ — teasing*

IN THE GRAVEYARD /33

I parked by the grave in June, under oaks and birches,
and said hello again, and went walking with Gussie
past stones and flowers and the grave with the plastic
chickens. (Somebody loved somebody who loved chickens.)
Gus stopped and stared: A woman's long bare legs
stretched up at the edge of the graveyard, a man's body
heaving between them.       Gus considered an inspection,
so I clicked my fingers, as softly as I could, to distract him,
and became the unintending cause of *coitus interruptus.*
Walking to the car, I peeked. It was a June day, leaves full,
head moving up and down. It was a June day, leaves full,
Gus healthy and gay, ~~chasing a ball, keeping it, teasing~~

*playing keepaway with his tennis ball.*
*a*

IN THE GRAVEYARD /39

*/ me*

I parked by ~~the~~ grave in June, under oaks and birches,
and said hello again, and went walking with Gussie
past stones and flowers and the grave with the plastic
chickens. (Somebody loved somebody who loved chickens.)
Gus stopped and stared: A woman's long bare legs
stretched up at the edge of the graveyard, a man's body
heaving between them.       Gus considered checking them out,
so I clicked my fingers, as softly as I could, to distract him,
and became the unintending cause of *coitus interruptus.*
Walking to the car, I peeked. She was restarting him, her
head ~~moving~~ up and down. It was a June day, leaves full,
Gus healthy and gay, running to ~~catch~~ his tennis ball.

*fetch me*

# MAN BLAMES DOG

## BEN McGRATH

Pity the poor dog. In this time of heightened fear—of drugs, of bombs, of the things we humans might do to one another—man increasingly asks so much of him. Last week, dog crews patrolled New York's subway tunnels, while along our borders new graduates of the Canine Enforcement Training Center—Belgian Malinois, German shepherds, Labrador retrievers—were out sniffing, in numbers and locations not to be disclosed, for chemical weapons. In return, man has had little to offer but gratitude. And these days even the gratitude seems to be in short supply. Last Monday's news of a Hell's Kitchen night-club drug sting was noteworthy, not least because of the revelation that the offending club, Sound Factory, had been busted before, and had been allowed to remain open on the condition that, among other things, it employ a dog to do what its human owners, out of common business sense, wouldn't do: turn away 70 percent of their potential customers—the portion of club-goers, on an average night, who are drug users, according to police estimates.

In a triumphant press conference, Police Commissioner Ray Kelly announced that at the time of this most recent raid Sound Factory's supposed detector dog had been found to be "asleep on the job, as usual," while transactions for Ecstasy, cocaine, and other narcotics were conducted inside.

"The dog hasn't been arrested," Kenneth Aronson, Sound Factory's attorney, was quick to point out. (The club owner and two associates have been.) But in the court of public opinion the pooch was as good as guilty, its reputation in the scent-detection community shot.

"I was very upset about that," Stephanie Kramer, the culprit's personal handler, said late last week. "I e-mailed the Commissioner about what he said. That was an unfair statement." Kramer is a franchisee of Interquest Detection Canines, "the nation's oldest and largest canine detection and drug dog firm." She said the dog's name is Fanta. Fanta is a she, a seven-year-old black Labrador of Eastern European descent. She has been "doing drugs" for a year and a half, ever since she completed her training, in Texas. She lives with Kramer in eastern Pennsylvania, about an hour and a half's drive from Sound Factory. She does most of her scent work at schools and offices.

"You have to understand, the club was so slow that night," Kramer explained. "There was something going on—a big party in Miami, I think—so there were maybe two hundred people inside." (Keep in mind that Sound Factory has four floors and thirty thousand square feet.) "They started the raid at about six in the morning," Kramer continued. By then, Fanta had already been on the job for five hours, on top of the long commute. "So, yeah, she was sleeping. There's nothing for her to do. Am I supposed to tell her to stand at attention? I can't explain to her that she must stay awake for no reason."

And, anyway, "an adult dog sleeps seventy percent of the time," Kenneth Aronson, the attorney, said.

Fanta's job, it turns out, was not to sniff people (that was up to the bouncers) but to sniff their bags. "We had a couple alerts that turned out to be residual odors," Kramer said, reflecting on Fanta's year of service with the club. (Kramer has not been paid for the night of the sting, and wants her seven hundred and fifty dollars.) But Fanta, for whatever reason, never found any drugs while stationed at this alleged "stash house." Which does raise questions about her efficacy.

Kramer reports that, the same week Fanta got caught snoozing, she found six hundred dollars' worth of marijuana in the parking lot of a high school in Pennsylvania. But Fanta is unable to recognize the scents of GHB (the so-called date-rape drug) or ketamine (Special K), and when it comes to Ecstasy "there has to be quite a lot of it, because she only smells the methamphetamine traces." ("You and I go into someone's home and they're preparing beef stew—we smell beef stew," Steve Browand, a drug-dog expert with the New York Security Service Group, explained. "The dog goes in, he recognizes the beef, he recognizes the carrots, he recognizes the peas, he recognizes the potatoes. He separates the ingredients.") Pot is not exactly the chief concern of the nightlife police.

"An important function of the dog is as more of a deterrent," Aronson said. "If people see a drug-smelling dog, they turn around and they get rid of what they have. They put it back in their car, or they throw it down the sewer. Or maybe they take it." And then, sufficiently giddy, perhaps they return to the line and greet the dog with affection.

"Most people wanted to pet her," Kramer said. "She rolls right over on her back and you could rub her belly."

In the end, Fanta was probably not the right gal for the job, but "to me, she's a good dog," Kramer said.

| 2004 |

# CHABLIS

*Fiction*

## DONALD BARTHELME

My wife wants a dog. She already has a baby. The baby's almost two. My wife says that the baby wants the dog.

My wife has been wanting a dog for a long time. I have had to be the one to tell her that she couldn't have it. But now the baby wants a dog, my wife says. This may be true. The baby is very close to my wife. They go around together all the time, clutching each other tightly. I ask the baby, who is a girl, "Whose girl are you? Are you Daddy's girl?" The baby says, "Momma," and she doesn't just say it once, she says it repeatedly, "Momma Momma Momma." I don't see why I should buy a hundred-dollar dog for that damn baby.

The kind of dog the baby wants, my wife says, is a cairn terrier. This kind of dog, my wife says, is a Presbyterian like herself and the baby. Last year the baby was a Baptist—that is, she went to the Mother's Day Out program at the First Baptist twice a week. This year she is a Presbyterian because the Presbyterians have more swings and slides and things. I think that's pretty shameless and I have said so. My wife is a legitimate lifelong Presbyterian and says that makes it O.K.: way back when she was a child she used to go to the First Presbyterian in Evansville, Illinois. I didn't go to church, because I was a black sheep. There were five children in my family and the males rotated the position of black sheep among us, the oldest one being the black sheep for a while while he was in his D.W.I. period or whatever and then getting grayer as he maybe got a job or was in the service and

141

then finally becoming a white sheep when he got married and had a grandchild. My sister was never a black sheep, because she was a girl.

Our baby is a pretty fine baby. I told my wife for many years that she couldn't have a baby because it was too expensive. But they wear you down. They are just wonderful at wearing you down, even if it takes years, as it did in this case. Now I hang around the baby and hug her every chance I get. Her name is Joanna. She wears Oshkosh overalls and says "no," "bottle," "out," and "Momma." She looks most lovable when she's wet, when she's just had a bath and her blond hair is all wet and she's wrapped in a beige towel. Sometimes when she's watching television she forgets that you're there. You can just look at her. When she's watching television, she looks dumb. I like her better when she's wet.

This dog thing is getting to be a big issue. I said to my wife, "Well you've got the baby. Do we have to have the damn dog too?" The dog will probably bite somebody, or get lost. I can see myself walking all over our subdivision asking people, "Have you seen this brown dog?" "What's its name?" they'll say to me, and I'll stare at them coldly and say, "Michael." That's what she wants to call it, Michael. That's a silly name for a dog and I'll have to go looking for this possibly rabid animal and say to people, "Have you seen this brown dog? Michael?" It's enough to make you think about divorce.

What's that baby going to do with that dog that it can't do with me? Romp? I can romp. I took her to the playground at the school. It was Sunday and there was nobody there, and we romped. I ran, and she tottered after me at a good pace. I held her as she slid down the slide. She groped her way through a length of big pipe they have there set in concrete. She picked up a feather and looked at it for a long time. I was worried

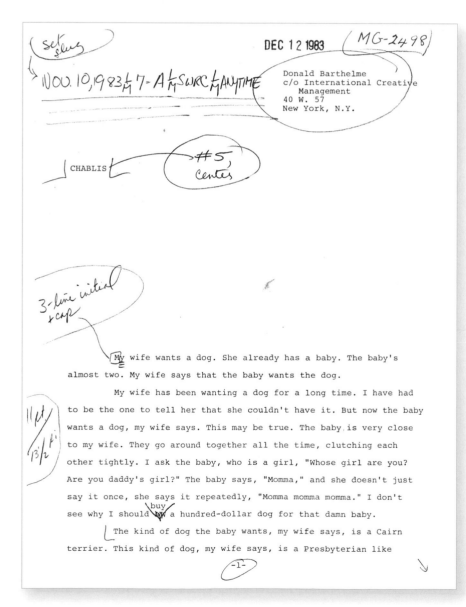

that it might be a diseased feather but she didn't put it in her mouth. Then we ran some more over the patched bare softball field and through the arcade that connects the temporary wooden classrooms, which are losing their yellow paint, to the main building. Joanna will go to this school someday, if I stay in the same job.

I looked at some dogs at Pets-A-Plenty, which has birds, rodents, reptiles, and dogs, all in top condition. They showed me the cairn terriers. "Do they have their prayer books?" I asked. This woman clerk didn't know what I was talking about. The cairn terriers ran about two ninety-five per, with their papers. I started to ask if they had any illegitimate children at lower prices, but I could see that it would be useless and the woman already didn't like me, I could tell.

What is wrong with me? Why am I not a more natural person, like my wife wants me to be? I sit up, in the early morning, at my desk on the second floor of our house. The desk faces the street. At five-thirty in the morning, the runners are already out, individually or in pairs, running toward rude red health. I'm sipping a glass of Gallo Chablis with an ice cube in it, smoking, worrying. I worry that the baby may jam a kitchen knife into an electrical outlet while she's wet. I've put those little plastic plugs into all the electrical outlets, but she's learned how to pop them out.

I've checked the Crayolas. They've made the Crayolas safe to eat—I called the head office in Pennsylvania. She can eat a whole box of Crayolas and nothing much will happen to her. If I don't get the new tires for the car, I can buy the dog.

I remember the time, thirty years ago, when I put Herman's mother's Buick into a cornfield, on the Beaumont highway. There was a car coming at me in my lane, and I didn't hit it, and it didn't hit me. I remember veering to the right and down into the ditch and up through the fence and coming to rest in the cornfield and then getting out to wake Herman and the two of us going to see what the happy drunks in the other car had come to, in the ditch on the other side of the road. That was when I was a black sheep, years and years ago. That was skillfully done, I think. I get up, congratulate myself in memory, and go in to look at the baby.

| 1983 |

## DOG

They say, my dog, your love is pure,
And like my taxes will endure,

That when your eyes with ardor burn,
It is not food for which they yearn

But only recognition, which
Is breath of life to dog or bitch.

Yet am I still uneasy, since
I see a likeness there—and wince.

—Virginia Woods Bellamy   | 1937 |

# DOWN THE LEASH

## ANGELICA GIBBS

Blanche Saunders, a dark-haired, wiry, youthful-looking woman of forty-five with a pronounced affinity for black standard poodles, is this country's best-known practitioner of Obedience Training, an up-and-coming branch of pedagogy that she has been instrumental in popularizing in America during the past fifteen years. Among Miss Saunders' professional acquaintances—dog fanciers whose affinities range all the way from Afghan hounds to Yorkshire terriers—the word "obedience" has but one meaning. It denotes the social polish that a qualified trainer can impart to a dog through the medium of his owner, or at least to any dog able and willing to react cooperatively to such exclamations as "Hup!" (or "Hop!"), "Pfui!" (or "Phooey!"), and "Heel!," to sit or lie motionless for prolonged periods while interlopers do their best to distract him, to bound over a series of hurdles with a dumbbell gripped between his teeth, and otherwise either to control himself or channel his energies along more or less useful lines in everyday life. Since, unlike more traditional systems of education, Obedience Training involves a chain of command, rather than direct communication between teacher and pupil, Miss Saunders can't exactly be classified as a dog trainer. Instead, she thinks of herself as a trainer of dog owners, those ineffectual bipeds whose only reason for existence is to act as intermediaries between her and their dogs. Some dog owners who have undergone the rigors of Obedience Training have been inclined to view the program as discriminatory, for the certificates and degrees Miss Saunders doles out upon the completion of her courses are awarded not to the owners but to their pets. Most owners, however, accept their anomalous status with good grace and when their dogs are guilty of a fault, or in extreme cases a flunk-out, sportingly insist that they and not their pets are to blame.

All this is as it should be, in the opinion of Obedience Training experts, but they often wish that dog owners, in their day-to-day dealings with their pets, would take a firmer stand. The Obedience Training people point out that dogs, as opposed to cats, are fundamentally amenable to being bossed around and that it is therefore not becoming for dog owners to take a subservient attitude toward the whims of their animals. According to this view, the dog owners of America, by allowing their dogs to precede them through doorways, to monopolize and muddy their furniture, to take sips from their cocktails or tidbits from their tables, and to intimidate, or even bite, their guests, not only have managed to lose the respect of their maladjusted animals but have become one of the major educational challenges of our day. There can be no denying that Miss Saunders has met this challenge with praiseworthy vigor, and from every conceivable angle. She has put in her most direct pedagogical licks in New York, where since 1944 she has been conducting Obedience Training courses, each consisting of nine lessons, in various armories and gymnasiums, mostly under the sponsorship of the A.S.P.C.A. The tuition for a course, for which Miss Saunders receives a fee of anywhere up to five hundred dollars, depending on the size of the class, is nine dollars. To date, about twenty-two hundred men,

women, and adolescents have turned up for these courses, snaked along by their dogs and clinging to the wrong, or hind, end of the leash. "By the time they've finished the nine lessons," an A.S.P.C.A. official said proudly the other day, "the relative positions on the leashes have been reversed in at least two-thirds of the cases."

A considerably larger group of dog owners has had its eyes opened to the merits of Obedience work through a manual Miss Saunders has written, called *Training You to Train Your Dog*, published by Doubleday in 1946 and listed by the *Times* last December as a "hidden best seller," meaning that it belongs, along with dictionaries and cookbooks, in that enviable category of books that, though they never reach the best-seller lists, continue to be bought in respectable quantities over a long period of time. So far, forty thousand copies of Miss Saunders' book have been sold. In addition to fulfilling the obligation implicit in its title, this volume has an unexpected appeal for its purchasers, many of whom ordinarily have little time for reading anything farther afield than the *American Kennel Gazette* and *Leash and Collar*, in that it gives them a nodding acquaintance with the prose style of Walter Lippmann. Mr. Lippmann dashed off a preface for it not long after Miss Saunders made a trip to Washington to induce the Lippmanns' black standard poodle, Brioche, to stop biting the columnist's secretaries. "To [those] who cannot or will not train their own dogs, [this] book ought to carry conviction that for dogs, as well as for others, education and discipline are not accompaniments of tyranny but are necessary to the pursuit of happiness," Lippmann wrote resoundingly.

Along with other wide-awake modern educators, Miss Saunders has recently begun employing audio-visual aids in her teaching. Her most successful effort in this branch of instruction has been a series of three 16-mm. films produced, in both black-and-white and color, by United Specialists, Inc., a firm in which she is associated with Louise Branch, who owns it and who, happily, is not only a fellow poodle fancier but a photographer. The three films, collectively also called "Training You to Train Your Dog" and billed by the producers as a "five-bark picture, a real bow-wow!," are designed to drive home the points made by Miss Saunders' manual, and they are available separately or in complete sets, the cost in the latter case being two hundred and ten dollars for a black-and-white version or five hundred and seventy dollars in color. *Puppy Trouble*, the first of the series, covers, as set forth in its subtitle, the "Kindergarten and Grade School Training Stage" of a dog, and the voice of Helen Hayes, a poodle owner herself, has been dubbed in, expressing the presumed thoughts of the starring puppy, who, it was found, could not be relied upon to respond vocally at the proper moments and was not quite as comprehensible even when he did. "Some very cute little touches," as Miss Saunders described them over the radio not long ago, resulted from this collaboration. "In one scene, where the puppy was getting his first bath," Miss Saunders went on, "Miss Hayes made her voice shiver so realistically you could almost hear the little fellow tremble." The second

---

Overheard in Central Park, stout dowager to drooping toy poodle: "I told you not to talk to strangers!"

| 1963 |

---

United Specialists film, called *Basic Obedience Instruction* and subtitled "High School and Prep School Training Stage," and the third, called *Advanced Obedience Instruction* and subtitled "College and University Training Stage," have Lowell Thomas on their sound tracks, explaining the steps by which Obedience Training may lead to the granting of degrees represented by initials, analogous to B.A., M.A., and Ph.D., affixed to a dog's name. *Basic Obedience Instruction* depicts Miss Saunders and one of her favorite poodles demonstrating to a number of more or less intelligent-looking dogs and their owners the requirements for the degree of C.D., or Companion Dog—the lowest rung on the academic ladder. These include the heel on leash, the heel free, the recall, the long (one-minute) sit, and the long (three-minute) down. As might be expected, the third film, leading through the halls of higher learning, covers far more esoteric accomplishments, such as the retrieve on flat, the retrieve over obstacle, the speak on command, and the seek-back for lost article, by which the pupil progresses up the ladder to the degree of C.D.X. (Companion Dog, Excellent), then to U.D. (Utility Dog), and finally to U.D.T. (Utility Dog Tracker).

The "Training You to Train Your Dog" films are distributed to the public, usually at a nominal charge, by a number of rather disparate organizations, including the American Meat Institute and the American Museum of Natural History, which buy the reels from United Specialists. One of the distributors, the Gaines Dog Research Center, maintained by the makers of Gaines dog foods, estimates that through its facilities alone at least five hundred thousand people in this country are privileged each year to hear Miss Hayes whimpering in her imaginary tub and to watch one of Miss Saunders' talented poodles discriminating, at the command of his mistress, between a scented and an unscented gardening glove. These performances have undoubtedly proved instructive to a further, unestimated number of people in Norway, Sweden, Denmark, Belgium, Switzerland, Holland, Cuba, Mexico, Brazil, and Venezuela, where the movies have also been distributed. The most recent request for them from abroad came in to United Specialists, to the gratification and mystification of everyone there, from the Rajkumar Preatum Sherjung, of Bijnor, United Provinces, India, who demanded the whole works, *Puppy Trouble* and all.

Obedience Training is of Teutonic origin, and because it involves not only a good deal of canine regimentation but downright physical coercion on the part of the handler, who uses a choke collar to induce a dog to fall in with his wishes, its opponents frequently claim that its ranks consist of what they describe as Prussian types, or people desirous chiefly of imposing their wills forcibly on others. Obedience trainers, these detractors say, are imbued with top-sergeant, or bulldog, tendencies, to a man, or woman. But though Miss Saunders is considered in dog-fancying circles to be the embodiment of what is reverently termed "trainer personality," there is little in her manner to suggest the top sergeant and there is absolutely nothing of the bulldog about her. A dog-show official who is at his most articulate within his own very special frame of reference once said of Miss Saunders that she combines all the commendable qualities, both physical and temperamental, that are customarily associated with the terrier group—the slimness and stamina of the wirehair, the pleasing facial contours and limpid eyes of the cairn, the activity and gameness of the Border, and the amiability of the Dandie Dinmont—an opinion concurred in

by the majority of her admirers but highly disconcerting to a minority who hold that Miss Saunders, since she is a confirmed poodle fancier, should bear a resemblance to her favorite, rather than to an alien, type of dog.

One attribute that Miss Saunders shares with no breed of terrier is her voice, which is low and husky. It is seldom raised in anger, but there is a perceptible undercurrent of annoyance in it when she's dealing with dog owners en masse. This is especially noticeable when she is confronted, in one of the various armories and gymnasiums in which she works, by a bunch of would-be trainers who, to judge, by their actions, couldn't impose their collective wills on a tame mouse. At the start of such a class, Miss Saunders usually manages to employ the most moderate of the three tones of voice she advocates for Obedience Training; namely, the coaxing. "Let's try to improve just a *little* on our sit-stay this week," she'll say into a portable microphone she uses, addressing the thirty-odd dog owners lined up in front of her with their pets (ranging in size from Great Danes to Chihuahuas), each of which is stationed, in conformance with Obedience protocol, beside his owner's left knee. As the owners timidly beseech their charges to plunk themselves down on their haunches by way of participating in the sit-stay, Miss Saunders emits a gusty sigh, well amplified by the microphone, and resorts to the second, or demanding, tone of voice.
"Come on, see to it your dogs sit!" she says firmly. "String them down on that leash. Who's supposed to be training who around here,
anyway?" When, in consequence of resisting a good deal of tugging on choke collars, most of the dogs have decided that it's in their best interests to sit down, the owners drop their leashes

and back gingerly away to a distance of fifteen or twenty feet, uttering what they fondly believe to be forceful requests to the dogs to stay put. At this point, two or three representatives of the more flighty breeds are likely to begin frolicking about the arena, and Miss Saunders is obliged to fall back on the third, or commanding, tone. "Bring your dogs back! *Make* them sit! *Snap* them down! See that they stay!" she shouts lustily into the microphone. "Put a little conviction in your voice for a change! No diplomas for *you* if you can't learn a simple exercise like this!"

Although this threat obtains results in most cases, each class is very apt to include at least one overwrought lady dog owner who not only is unable to make any impression whatever on her charge but may even burst into tears as she pursues him around the floor. When this occurs, Miss Saunders sets her microphone down with a crash, mutters "My goodness *sakes*!"—her strongest exclamation—and strides forward to take over the delinquent dog. Seizing his leash, she gives it a brisk tug, remarks matter-of-factly that the dog isn't boss around the place, as he seems to think, and repeats the sit-stay command. Sometimes a brief clash of wills ensues. More often, the dog gives Miss Saunders a speculative look and quietly falls in with her wishes, leaving his owner with the suspicion that something occult has taken place in her presence.

The effectiveness of Miss Saunders' trainer personality, as manifested in her direct dealings with dogs, is difficult even for experts to explain, but it is generally conceded that she is the fortunate possessor of what those in the know refer to as "dog hands." This attribute, they say, is a matter of rapport, of which, as the late Josef Weber, of Princeton, New Jersey, one of the most noted of all German-born trainers in this country, said in a still widely quoted apothegm, "It yoost goes

down the leash." In addition to being endowed with dog hands, or leash rapport, Miss Saunders is said to be able to anticipate to an uncanny degree the way a dog will act in almost any set of circumstances. In this way she averts many of the crises—dogfights, for example—that often harass less intuitive trainers. Despite her talent for keeping intellectually one jump ahead of a dog, however, she hasn't been able to wholly avoid one perennial training hazard—plain dogbite. At one time or another, representatives of practically every recognized breed, and quite a few mutts, too, have sunk their fangs into various portions of Miss Saunders, mistaking her, possibly, for an owner devoid of trainer personality. From a canine point of view, the results of these onslaughts have been unrewarding. "A dogbite to Blanche is as a mosquito bite to you or me," a man from the A.S.P.C.A. told a dog owner who was taking a breather during a training session one evening not long ago. By way of example, he cited an occasion on which Miss Saunders was driving him and a dog of hers home after a class. As she stopped for a traffic light, she complained mildly of a disagreeable tickling sensation in one foot. When they reached his home, she got out and examined her foot under a street light. She discovered that the toe of one of her substantial leather brogues had been gnawed open and a wound inflicted that would have disabled the average person for a week. Miss Saunders' only reaction was a relatively casual "My goodness *sakes*!" Then she bade the A.S.P.C.A. man a polite good night and leaped back into her car.

As Miss Saunders frequently points out in her training manual, the element of surprise is an all-important one in the master-dog relationship. It is also one of which she has always taken fullest advantage. In this field, as a trainer, she presupposes a good deal of ingenuity, alertness, and

agility on the owner's part. If a dog is too vocal, for instance, and sets up a clamor the minute the owner leaves the house, Miss Saunders advises the owner to put on his hat and coat, shut the dog in the living room, stride to the outside door, slam it, and then sneak back noiselessly to the living-room door. "At the first sound [the dog] makes, call out, 'Stop that!'" she counsels. "This may come as such a surprise that he will probably be quiet the rest of the day, trying to figure out how you got back into the house without his knowing it." Miss Saunders also recommends some rather unusual items of equipment for startling dogs out of their shortcomings and making them ponder the singular requests of mankind. Among these are mousetraps (to be placed on sacrosanct chairs or couches), short lengths of chain (to be tossed at a dog's hindquarters if he barks when the doorbell or telephone rings), carriage whips (to be used in breaking dogs of chasing automobiles), and BB guns (to be aimed, it should be noted at once, not at but away from an erring pet). Illustrating the use of a BB gun, Miss Saunders tells in her manual of a distressingly loud-mouthed poodle who was an inmate of a kennel she once ran. "I crept inside the kennel with a BB gun," she recalls. "For fully twenty minutes I stood in total blackness with the BB gun pointed toward the wooden door of the pen. . . . Then when [the dog] decided it was time to begin [barking] again I pulled the trigger. In the dead of night the little pellet sounded like an exploding firecracker when it hit the door. From then on there was perfect silence."

In the hands of an impetuous or highly nervous dog owner, a BB gun might well turn out to be a dangerous, or even lethal, weapon. In Miss Saunders' hands, never. She has been distinguished for both her marksmanship and her aplomb with firearms ever since the memorable day when, at the age of fifteen, she first hefted a rifle. As she recalls the incident, she was summoned out of a high-school history class and asked to pinch-shoot for a friend in a rifle match. After taking only two practice shots, both of them bull's-eyes, she entered the match, and wound up with two firsts—high score for girls and high score for boys and girls. To Miss Saunders' classmates, this was not a violently surprising accomplishment, for she had already established herself as proficient in sports, having earned a position on five of the school's six championship athletic teams for girls. It is Miss Saunders' suspicion that her athletic aptitude was a result of trying to hold her own in a household in which the

"What other tricks does he need?"

Shanahan

other offspring consisted of seven older brothers and one older sister. She became a member of this top-heavy brood on September 12, 1906, in the town of Easton, Maine, where her father, the Reverend Abram Saunders, was the Baptist minister. After his death, in 1916, the family moved to Detroit, where she attended high school, ending up with excellent marks as well as a shelfful of trophies. Upon graduating, in 1924, she got a summer job on a small farm near Brewster, in Putnam County, New York, owned by Ethel Perrin, a family friend and the founder of the department of physical education in the Detroit public-school system. Tending Miss Perrin's livestock proved so congenial to Miss Saunders that she decided to learn more about the subject and, accordingly, enrolled that autumn in Massachusetts Agricultural College, which is now a part of the University of Massachusetts. There she majored in animal husbandry and poultry raising, and took side courses in engineering, carpentry, and automobile repairing. As part of its curriculum, the college insisted that its students take jobs on farms for at least six months of each year. Such was the local reputation Miss Saunders had achieved while working on the Perrin place that she had little difficulty finding a berth for herself as first in command of a fifty-acre farm in the vicinity of Brewster.

During the next ten years, while still an undergraduate and afterward, Miss Saunders worked on farms in and near Putnam County. This period of her life is recorded in considerable detail in several plump photograph albums that she treasures. A few of the snapshots in them show Miss Saunders—wearing overalls and looking handsome, healthy, and supremely contented— perched atop this or that item of farm machinery. Most of the pictures, however, are of animals, including calves named Precious, Marjorie, Sylvia,

and Edna; Jerushe, a very photogenic shoat; Muffit, a stolid work horse; and innumerable anonymous milch cows—all of which, she feels, were in some measure responsible, by giving her a working knowledge of animal psychology, for her present skill in handling dogs. She believes, for example, that a flock of White Leghorns, shown in the albums in their various stages of development, laid the foundation for her ability to move casually and almost soundlessly among high-strung dogs. Most often, when looking through the albums, Miss Saunders turns to the photographs of some Boston terriers she encountered during her farm training, to whom she taught such tricks as begging, jumping over sticks, and balancing tennis balls on their noses. She frequently says that although she'd never heard of Obedience work at the time, these terriers—notably one named Tagalong, a performer of the highest calibre—provided her with the equivalent of a kindergarten, or even a grade-school, course in the subject.

Regrettably, there's no photograph to record the afternoon, in the autumn of 1934, when Miss Saunders unknowingly took the plunge into what was to be her lifework, and experienced in the process the first faint intimations of her affinity for poodles. "I was working up in a haymow on a farm near Brewster that afternoon when a car with a rather large, intelligent-looking dog and a woman in it pulled into the barnyard," she has since recalled. "I came running down, and the dog was introduced to me as Tango of Piperscroft, an apricot standard poodle. I said, 'You mean *that's* a poodle? I thought they were horrid little white things with runny eyes.' " When the matter of Tango had been settled, Miss Saunders learned that her bipedal caller was Mrs. White-house Walker, of Bedford Hills, who owned the poodle and was, indeed, the leading exponent of standard poodles in this country. Now she was pioneering in Obedience work with Tango and the other poodles she had in her poodle kennel, the Carillon, at Bedford Hills. Her visit to the Brewster barnyard was prompted by the fact that she had advertised in the *Rural New-Yorker* for a kennel maid at twenty dollars a month, and Miss Saunders had answered the ad. "I must have been getting a little bored with heavy animals, I guess," Miss Saunders says. "Anyway, until I saw that ad, I'd never thought of working with dogs. If anyone had suggested it, I'd have said, 'My goodness *sakes*, not *me!*' Of course, I didn't know it then, but Tango was a very important dog—the granddaddy of Obedience in America."

The granddaddy of Obedience in America, important though he was, wasn't a perfect physical specimen, being a shade too wide in the rear, but he was presentable enough to overcome Miss Saunders' anti-poodle bias. The week after Tango and Mrs. Walker called on her, she went to help out around the Carillon, and within a month she had been elevated to the role of kennel manager. During that period, her personality underwent the sort of metamorphosis that Obedience people consider one of the most valuable by-products of their specialty. Commenting admiringly on this, Mrs. Walker said the other day, "When Blanche first came to the Carillon, she was a shy, demure little thing, without much self-confidence. But as soon as she'd worked a couple of weeks with Carillon Epreuve—Glee, for short, and the most nervous and timid of all our bitches—she simply blossomed out. That's the beauty of Obedience. It gives one poise. Takes one out of oneself. Glee

was completely transformed, too. She ended up as the first dog in the United States, of any breed, to get her C.D., her C.D.X., and her U.D."

Having Miss Saunders to run her kennel for her left Mrs. Walker free to devote her full energies to alerting the dog fanciers of America to the merits of Obedience—a task of some magnitude, for at that time most people on this side of the Atlantic were under the impression that the only reasonable goals of formal dog training were police work, sheepherding, hunting, and retrieving. Only a few months before the arrival of Miss Saunders at the Carillon, Mrs. Walker had taken her first step toward advancing her theory that a dog should be well behaved as well as utilitarian by giving an informal demonstration of Obedience on the lawn of her father's estate, in Mount Kisco. Not long after that, she had succeeded in talking the officials of the North Westchester Kennel Club into letting her put on a similar affair as a part of their annual all-breed show. The small group of dogs and owners starring in this exhibition were rather uncertain about what they were up to, for their training was based solely on Mrs. Walker's hazy recollection of some Obedience tests she had once watched in England, but even so they walked away with the show. "The spectator appeal was so fantastic that nobody paid any attention to the judging of the breeds," Mrs. Walker afterward reported triumphantly to a friend.

Inspired by this coup, Mrs. Walker left Miss Saunders in charge of the kennel and hopped the next boat for England, where she headed straight for Tango's birthplace, the Piperscroft Kennels, near Horsham. Here Mrs. Grace E. L. Boyd, the owner of the kennels, put her star Obedience dog, King Leo of Piperscroft, through his paces for Mrs. Walker's edification. Next, Mrs. Boyd took her guest to meet a neighbor, a Captain Radcliffe, who had been influential in introducing Obedience Training tests into England from Germany. Under the Captain's guidance, Mrs. Walker mastered the subject, from hup to pfui, in about three weeks. Then she hopped a boat home. During the crossing, she stayed in her berth, outlining in her mind the first set of American Obedience rules. These were modifications of the English rules, which, numbering among their requirements such feats as scaling walls, retrieving objects over six-foot hurdles, and refusing food from strangers, Mrs. Walker considered too exacting. When she got home, she set about with renewed vigor serving as an evangel of Obedience and soon succeeded in stirring up so much interest among dog fanciers in this country that she was unable to deal singlehanded with the requests for information that inundated Bedford Hills. She was relieved to find that Miss Saunders had become infected by her enthusiasm and was able to take over all the correspondence while Mrs. Walker was in the field plugging her hobby.

In 1936, Mrs. Walker gathered a number of small East Coast Obedience groups she had helped organize into the Obedience Test Club, with headquarters at Bedford Hills, and introduced its members to the intricacies of a scoring system she had worked out for Obedience trials—the exhibitions, most often held in connection with bench shows, that determine the eligibility of the competing dogs for degrees. That same year, the officials of the American Kennel Club, who had been viewing this newfangled aspect of the dog business with skeptical aloofness, apparently came to the conclusion that their organization was better equipped than was the relatively insignificant Obedience Test Club

to handle all the red tape connected with Obedience records and scoring systems and with the dispensing of degrees. They therefore announced that the A.K.C., whose official sanction carried almost overpowering weight among dog fanciers, would recognize Obedience Training, but only if it was given by clubs that paid the organization a fee of two hundred and fifty dollars. To the chagrin of those who had got in on the ground floor of Obedience, the A.K.C. declined to recognize the accomplishments of dogs who had already forged ahead in Obedience Test Club classes, which made it necessary for those luckless animals to re-enroll as novices and compete all over again, under a slightly different scoring system. The A.K.C.'s appearance on the scene also had the effect of automatically disqualifying any dog with a bar sinister in its background from earning recognized degrees, no matter how talented it might be. The unfortunate owners of dogs in this category nonetheless managed to keep their chins up, and continued to form Obedience clubs—unsponsored ones, which awarded a tactfully worded certificate rather than a degree. A few years later, their morale was raised considerably when a woolly-coated little dog named Squeaky, a stray adopted by Dr. Mary Julian White, then of New York and now a psychiatrist practicing in Washington, was shown on the cover of the *American Kennel Gazette*, along with two dogs of unquestionable ancestry, in a photograph taken during an intermission in an Obedience demonstration put on by Miss Saunders in Rockefeller Plaza. Since Squeaky was, and still is, the only mutt ever to be thus honored by the magazine, the photograph caused a furore which hasn't yet died down completely. Nowadays, the staff of the *Gazette* is noncommittal when questioned about *l'affaire* Squeaky, but some defenders of the publication's editorial integrity claim that Squeaky is, to the expert eye, no mutt at all but a representative of a rare Tibetan breed, the Lhasa Apso. (Squeaky's owner, too, likes to think of him as a Lhasa, but, as a psychiatrist, feels obliged to admit that her thinking may be wishful.) Miss Saunders, however, who originally trained him, is an outright dissenter. "Now, look, that dog's no more Lhasa than I am," she said the other day. "Last month, in Canada, I met up with a *real* Lhasa, and he didn't look a bit like Squeaky. When he lived in New York, Squeaky used to be clipped to look sort of like a schnauzer, but he isn't that, either. He's just a terribly talented mutt, and that's how he got into my Rockefeller Plaza demonstration, and met up with that photographer."

Dazed but not done in at having their Obedience baby taken out of their hands by the A.K.C., Mrs. Walker and Miss Saunders, a resilient pair, swiftly began adjusting themselves to the new order of things. One of the marked advantages of being nestled under the maternalistic wing of the A.K.C., they realized, was the circumstance that from that time on Obedience trials could be held without any quibble at all in conjunction with A.K.C.-sponsored bench shows, the most fertile possible spots for long-range Obedience proselytization. In the matter of purebreds versus crossbreeds, both women were, and are, leniently disposed toward mutts; Miss Saunders, in fact, in later years, after her prestige as an Obedience trainer was such that she could get along without the cachet of A.K.C. backing, pretty much threw in her lot with the A.S.P.C.A., which makes no distinction between purebred and mongrel and can therefore award only certificates, and the majority of the classes she conducts today are held under its auspices. At the time, however, as thoroughbred-poodle fanciers and breeders, both she and Mrs. Walker had to

admit that the A.K.C.'s discriminatory stand had its points, and before long the Obedience Test Club's literature was proclaiming that its ultimate aim was "to demonstrate the usefulness of the purebred dog as the companion and guardian of man and not the ability of the dog to acquire facility in the performance of mere tricks." In order to further this aim, Mrs. Walker and Miss Saunders embarked, in the fall of 1937, on a trek that has become legendary in the dog world. Rigging up a twenty-one-foot trailer with all the installations of a well-run dog-diet kitchen, they hitched it to Mrs. Walker's car and set out in the company of Glee and two other blue-ribbon poodles—Ch. Carillon Joyeux and Ch. Carillon Boncœur—to give their demonstrations in communities where, as Miss Saunders puts it, "the word 'obedience' had never been heard before." These included most of the focal spots on the Southwestern dog-show circuit—Wichita Falls, Dallas, San Antonio, Houston, Galveston, Fort Worth, and Los Angeles. It was a lighthearted trip, as well as a successful one from a missionary point of view. "In that part of the country, dog people are rather like circus people," Miss Saunders later told some friends. "Just a big, happy family. On their way to shows, and going home, they shouted to each other from car to car, and often pulled up by the side of the road to compare notes on their dogs."

Ten weeks and some ten thousand miles later, the peripatetic kennel, its personnel intact, returned to Bedford Hills, greatly to the relief of several of the community's human inhabitants, who had considered the venture a perilous one and who now gathered about to shudder delightedly over the two women's accounts of its hazards, such as a Texas sandstorm that clogged all the drains in the trailer, and encounters, in several remote spots, with hoboes who, peering in the trailer's windows, reeled back when con-

*"May I keep my collar on?"*

fronted by the merry faces of Boncœur, Glee, and Joyeux. As a more or less direct outcome of the trip, the number of Obedience trials held in conjunction with dog shows doubled within the next few months. The long-range results of the two travellers' efforts were recently pointed up in some figures released by the A.K.C., showing that since 1936 it has awarded to representatives of a hundred and eight of the hundred and eleven officially recognized breeds 6,550 C.D.s, 1,680 C.D.X.s, 460 U.D.s, and 296 O.D.T.s, and that in all, during that time, well over fifty thousand purebred dogs have competed in Obedience trials. While Obedience people regard these statistics as impressive, they also see in them a challenge to intensify their campaigning, especially when they reflect upon the fact that the total number of dogs in the United States is somewhere around twenty-two million, about five million of them purebreds and the rest kitchen cousins, or mutts.

Not long ago, the editor of *Dog World*—"If It's about Dogs, Write to *Dog World*"—explained to a reader, who had taken him at his word, that Obedience trials in this country have proved to be "a vitamin for the dog-breeding and showing field." He might well have added that Miss Saunders' achievements both in Obedience work and in poodle breeding are an almost perfect case in point. At the time Miss Saunders took over as manager of the Carillon, poodles were comparatively rare in America; only a hundred and thirty-four of them—possibly a third of the country's total—were registered in the A.K.C.'s studbook. As a pupil, and then as an instructor, in Mrs. Walker's Bedford Hills Obedience Training classes, and later as a judge at Obedience trials, Miss Saunders became convinced that poodles constitute an eminently satisfactory breed for Obedience work, owing to two pronounced traits—their anxiety to please their masters and their intelligence, a term rather loosely applied by breeders to dogs who take readily to training and are able to retain what they have learned. Although it is impossible to put a finger on all the factors that determine the popularity of a given breed of dog, it is at present generally agreed that the increasingly frequent and successful appearances of poodles in Obedience trials in this country have had a decidedly tonic effect on their sale. By 1944, the number of poodle registrations had risen to 465, and by 1946 to 1,186; last year, the total was 3,195. A while ago, in reply to a letter inquiring about the total number of poodles now owned in this country, and, more specifically, in New York City, Arthur Frederick Jones, editor of the *American Kennel Gazette*, wrote, "I would estimate that now living in the United States there are about 14,000 Poodles of all sizes. This is estimated on the registrations over the last ten years, Poodles not usually dying too young. It would be practically impossible to estimate the number in New York City, other than to say that, aside from Southern California, and a few in the

Middle West, the metropolitan area contains the bulk of America's Poodle population."

In 1943, Miss Saunders felt that the time had come to strike out on her own. By then, it was obvious that a local, and possibly a national, poodle vogue was in the making. At the instigation of Mrs. Walker, who had decided to close the Carillon, because of the difficulties of keeping it going in wartime, Miss Saunders came to New York and rented a house in the East Fifties, where she opened an establishment for the care and training of poodles. The shingle she hung out bore the Carillon name, bequeathed her by her former employer. She also brought with her, as an additional gift from Mrs. Walker, a poodle bitch named Ch. Carillon Colline—better known as just Colline—who was to be entrusted with the task of perpetuating the Carillon strain. Within a short time, the new Carillon, where Miss Saunders clipped, shampooed, manicured, boarded, and trained poodles (along with an occasional maverick from some alien breed), became immensely successful; its clientele included the pets not only of some of the most prosperous people in the city but of several well-known out-of-towners, among them some Wilmington du Ponts, who flew a number of poodles here regularly by private plane for their Carillon appointments. From the point of view of Colline, however, an urban base of operations offered serious disadvantages when offspring began to arrive, just as it has to many another young matron. This situation was remedied in 1946, when Miss Saunders and her photographer friend and business associate, Miss

Branch, while in the throes of planning the first of their Obedience pictures, hit upon the idea of setting up yet another Carillon kennel, on an estate Miss Branch shares with other

## THE VISITOR

Young couple in Cambridge who have been collecting modern black-and-white prints for several years arranged this summer, after a good deal of trouble, to have John McAndrew, director of the Wellesley College Art Museum, drive over and evaluate them. There was a heavy rainstorm on the appointed evening and they were afraid he wouldn't come, but he did, and when they opened the door, he was standing there dripping, and so was a shaggy, standard-size black poodle. The hostess let them both in, and the director introduced himself, whereas the poodle just shook himself, showering three rare British prints and two Swedish ones. In the living room, Mr. McAndrew had a highball, and the poodle sat beside him, eying him affectionately and making a wet smudge first on the carpet and then on the cream-colored sofa, when he leaned against that. They went upstairs to view the rest of the collection, and the poodle came along, stopping in the bathroom for a drink of water. "Shouldn't I get him a pan or something from the kitchen?" asked the hostess uncertainly. "Oh, he seems to be able to take care of himself," said the museum man, chuckling. "I suppose that's one of the advantages of being a big dog."

The poodle then wandered into the nursery and rubbed his head against a sleeping baby. The hostess gave her husband a this-has-gone-far-enough look, but the husband gave her a he-seems-to-like-the-collection look, so she merely guided the poodle out of the nursery and shut the door. Downstairs, Mr. McAndrew praised the collection warmly, asked permission to exhibit it this fall, and made arrangements for his new friends to visit him later on that week. It had stopped raining, and the husband walked him to his car, while the wife went to the kitchen to get some damp cloths. She found the poodle there, accepting tidbits from the cook. Just as Mr. McAndrew was about to drive off, she rushed out of the house, holding the poodle by the collar and screaming, "He's forgotten his dog!" The director looked at the young couple in a dazed way. "My dog?" he said mildly. "He was standing on your doorstep when I came up. I detest dogs." The poodle, while this was going on, nodded pleasantly to all three people and trotted on his way.    | 1952 |

members of her family, in Pawling. By this time, Miss Saunders was working ten hours a day in her Manhattan establishment, in addition to running training classes for the A.S.P.C.A. once a week and judging Obedience trials on the side, and was therefore able to devote only weekends to the development of the Pawling project. Even so, she contrived to find time to draw up the architectural plans for the kennel, which started on a small scale but has been expanded over the years to accommodate sixty poodles, and which features such amenities of canine living as an electric dishwasher in its kitchen and ultraviolet lights over its whelping pens. A month or so ago, she expanded this operation by buying a ten-acre place near Bedford, which she is also calling the Carillon and where she plans to keep the kennel's puppies. The show stock will remain in Pawling.

Colline, now an extraordinarily agile matriarch of fourteen, no longer has any active duties around the Carillon, but she roams the premises with an air of marked, and justifiable, smugness. Occasionally, she is accompanied on her rambles by the most illustrious of all her offspring, Ch. Carillon Jester (C.D., C.D.X., U.D.T.), a handsome black standard poodle whose entire life has been consecrated to the cause of Obedience. Ever since he first posed, in his late puppyhood, for the illustrations for Miss Saunders' training manual, Jester has been in the public eye almost without surcease, performing in Obedience movies, barking fetchingly at Miss Saunders' request on radio programs, heisting dumbbells on Faye Emerson's television show, and tracking down gardening gloves, handkerchiefs, and other items of Obedience paraphernalia at large-scale Obedience exhibitions in such places as Madison Square Garden and Yankee Stadium. In the opinion of Obedience people, gatherings for the observance of National Dog Week and Be Kind to Animals Week would be hollow occasions indeed were it not for the presence of Jester, who inevitably has his audience in his pocket.

The advanced state of development to which Obedience Training has succeeded in bringing Jester's talents is readily explained in the light of the evolution of his breed. Over the centuries, poodles have been distinguishing themselves for their savoir-faire in the hunting field, in circuses, on the stage, and in the laps of royalty. Poodles were once primarily used as retrievers of waterfowl, as Miss Saunders is about to point out in what she describes as "an unusually straight-from-the-shoulder dog book," on which she is collaborating with Mrs. John Cross, Jr., the dachshund-fancying wife of the bench-show chairman of the Westminster Kennel Club. The book will also scotch the widely held notion that poodles originated in France. Actually, they originated in Germany; their name is derived either from the German *Pudel*, meaning puddle, or from *puddeln*, to splash in water. The poodle's elaborate clip, which has been the target of much facetious comment from the uninitiated, dates back to its retrieving days, when it was adopted as a practical measure, to keep the animals from sinking under the weight of their coats as they dived into rivers or lakes to retrieve birds. Shortly before the French Revolution, poodles were taken up wholeheartedly by the ladies of the court at Versailles. As a result, the breed attained an aura of preciousness that still clings to it, obscuring what Miss Saunders feels is its true utilitarian worth. She regards it as lamentable that a lot of latter-day poodle owners have persisted in taking a frivolous attitude toward their pets, especially in the matter of discipline. "Of course [my Miss Matilda] is spoiled," Mrs. James Lowell Oakes, Jr., blithely admits in *The Book of the Poodle*, one of

*"I can't explain it. I see that guy coming up the walkway and I go postal."*

the many recently published volumes devoted to rhapsodic appraisals of the breed. "She is going to school and learning Obedience Training . . . but I do not want her ever to lose her love of people. I do not want her to stop jumping up on the back of our love seat or barking at our car."

Whimsical and overindulgent dog owners, although a notably free-spending group when it comes to providing comfort for their pets, nevertheless cause Miss Saunders a good deal of anguish. She suffers greatly in this respect at nearly all the Obedience Training classes she conducts, and perhaps most of all on those nights when she presides over a series of classes open only to poodles, sponsored by the Poodle Obedience Training Club of Greater New York, an organization of some seventy-five poodle fanciers, each of whom is convinced that his dog is superior on every count to all other poodles. As Jester's owner, Miss Saunders is able to ignore and even to smile at this communal fantasy, but she has found it extremely difficult to overlook some other, far more serious misapprehensions that members of the group cling to. On one recent all-poodle evening, for example, when the class convened in the gymnasium of the Washington Irving High School, on Irving Place, it became apparent as the novice division paraded before her, with only three more sessions to go before graduation, that the owners had been cherishing the illusion that their dogs were far too smart to need to bother their heads about the homework assigned them. "My goodness *sakes*!" Miss Saunders said rather early in the evening. "Where's this class been for the last four weeks? My all-breed class last night had only had a couple of lessons and *their* dogs heeled perfectly, on and off leash. Don't any of you ever work your dogs at home?"

"It's been raining a lot," explained the owner of a gray miniature with a red ribbon on its top-knot.

"So what?" Miss Saunders said. "Your poodle can heel in the living room, can't he?"

Meanwhile, at the far end of the gymnasium, where a number of folding chairs had been set out, the members of the advanced, or utility, division were assembling. As Miss Saunders continued with the novice lesson ("Turn! Turn! Snap! Praise! *Command* when you start! Get those leads slack!"), one of the most enthusiastic of the local poodle fanciers, Count Alexis Pulaski, made an impressive entrance. In his retinue were Ch. Pulaski's Masterpiece (U.D.), Deauville Coquette, and Pulaski  Master's Pinocchio, three of his finest gray miniatures; their handler, Miss Lucy Copestake; and Miss Dorothy Dorn, head of the dog department at Hammacher Schlemmer, who was staggering under the weight of several large suit boxes, which turned out to contain various articles of canine apparel. As the newcomers seated themselves, Ch. Carillon Jester, tethered nearby, set up a prolonged howl.

"What goes on over there?" Miss Saunders inquired irritably from her end of the gymnasium.

"Jester's teaching my Cocoa bad tricks," complained the young and pretty owner of a brown standard two seats away from the Count.

"Well, I can't believe my ears," Miss Saunders said. "Jester never howls unless he's interested in being a daddy. Slap his nose, somebody. Now, class, make your corrections again, and make them *severe!*"

The novice trainers obediently shouted "Heel!" at their dogs, with various degrees of conviction, and on the sidelines Miss Dorn opened the largest of the suit boxes and lifted out some poodle-size navy-blue serge sailor collars, ornamented with white rick-rack braid and red stars.

"Adorable!" cried Cocoa's owner.

"My dogs are going to wear these collars at next week's cocktail party at the Coq Rouge," the Count explained to her. "Masterpiece is to be guest of honor. Did you know he makes about ten thousand a year in stud fees?"

"No! Really?" exclaimed the young woman.

"Less noise over there!" Miss Saunders called bitterly into her microphone. "This isn't a tea party, it's a class,"

"We'll try on Co-quette's costume first," said Miss Dorn in a stage whisper, and proceeded to squeeze that sleepy and reluctant animal into a black velvet jacket, ornamented with ermine tails. "She's gained a good deal of weight," she added doubtfully.

"Try to make her walk," said the Count. "I want to see the effect."

"If the buttons are moved over, she can get away with it," Miss Dorn assured him.

"We'll diet her," the Count said.

"If there isn't less noise over there, somebody's going to have to leave," Miss Saunders said balefully as Jester commenced howling again.

"I don't think you'd better work Masterpiece tonight," the Count said to Miss Copestake as the novice division began to straggle off the floor. "He got a little overexcited at the photographer's today."

"O.K.," Miss Copestake replied.

"If things go like this next week, we won't have any graduation, I warn you!" Miss Saunders shouted after her retreating novices. "Now I'd like the advanced class out here, if I can manage to have a little peace and quiet." Then, slamming down her microphone on a table in front of her and lighting a cigarette, she remarked sotto-voce to a friend standing nearby, "Well, *poodles* are intelligent, anyway. I often like to remind myself of that."

| *1951* |

STEINBERG

# TOP DOGS

# A PREFACE TO DOGS

## JAMES THURBER

As soon as a wife presents her husband with a child, her capacity for worry becomes acuter: she hears more burglars, she smells more things burning, she begins to wonder, at the theatre or the dance, whether her husband left his service revolver in the nursery. This goes on for years and years. As the child grows older, the mother's original major fear—that the child was exchanged for some other infant at the hospital—gives way to even more magnificent doubts and suspicions: she suspects that the child is not bright, she doubts that it will be happy, she is sure that it will become mixed up with the wrong sort of people.

This insistence of parents on dedicating their lives to their children is carried on year after year in the face of all that dogs have done, and are doing, to prove how much happier the parent-child relationship can become, if managed without sentiment, worry, or dedication. Of course, the theory that dogs have a saner family life than humans is an old one, and it was in order to ascertain whether the notion is pure legend or whether it is based on observable fact that I have for four years made a careful study of the family life of dogs. My conclusions entirely support the theory that dogs have a saner family life than people.

In the first place, the husband leaves on a woodchuck-hunting expedition just as soon as he can, which is very soon, and never comes back. He doesn't write, makes no provision for the care or maintenance of his family, and is not liable to prosecution because he doesn't. The wife doesn't care where he is, never wonders if he is thinking about her, and although she may start at the slightest footstep, doesn't do so because she is hoping against hope that it is he. No lady dog has ever been known to set her friends against her husband, or put detectives on his trail.

This same lack of sentimentality is carried out in the mother dog's relationship to her young. For six weeks—but only six weeks—she looks after them religiously, feeds them (they came clothed), washes their ears, fights off cats, old women, and wasps that come nosing around, makes the bed, and rescues the puppies when they crawl under the floor boards of the barn or get lost in an old boot. She does all these things, however, without 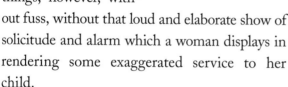 out fuss, without that loud and elaborate show of solicitude and alarm which a woman displays in rendering some exaggerated service to her child.

At the end of six weeks, the mother dog ceases to lie awake at night harking for ominous sounds; the next morning she snarls at the puppies after breakfast, and routs them all out of the house. "This is forever," she informs them, succinctly. "I have my own life to live, automobiles to chase, grocery boys' shoes to snap at, rabbits to pursue. I can't be washing and feeding a lot of big six-weeks-old dogs any longer. That phase is definitely over." The family life is thus terminated, and the mother dismisses the children from her mind—frequently as many as eleven at one time—as easily as she did her husband. She is now free to devote herself to her career and to the novel and astonishing things of life.

In the case of one family of dogs that I observed, the mother, a large black dog with long ears and a keen zest for living, tempered only by an immoderate fear of toads and turtles, kicked ten puppies out of the house at the end of six weeks to the day—it was a Monday. Fortunately for my observations, the puppies had no place to go, since they hadn't made any plans, and so they just hung around the barn, now and again trying to patch things up with their mother. She refused, however, to entertain any proposition leading to a resumption of home life, pointing out firmly that she was, by inclination, a chaser of bicycles and a hearth-fire watcher,  both of which activities would be insupportably cluttered up by the presence of ten helpers. The bicycle-chasing field was overcrowded, anyway, she explained, and the hearth-fire-watching field even more so. "We could chase parades together," suggested one of the dogs, but she refused to be touched, snarled, and drove him off.

It is only for a few weeks that the cast-off puppies make overtures to their mother in regard to the reestablishment of a home. At the end of that time, by some natural miracle that I am unable clearly to understand, the puppies suddenly one day don't recognize their mother any more, and she doesn't recognize them. It is as if they had never met, and is a fine idea, giving both parties a clean break and a chance for a fresh start. Once, some months after this particular family had broken up and the pups had been sold, one of them, named Liza, was brought back to "the old nest" for a visit. The mother dog of course didn't recognize the puppy and promptly bit her in the hip.

They had to be separated, each grumbling something about you never know what kind of dogs you're going to meet. Here was no silly, affecting reunion, no sentimental tears, no bitter intimations of neglect, or forgetfulness, or desertion.

If a pup is not sold or given away, but is brought up in the same household with its mother, the two will fight bitterly, sometimes twenty or thirty times a day, for maybe a month. This is very trying to whoever owns the dogs, particularly if they are sentimentalists who grieve because mother and child don't know each other. The condition finally clears up: the two dogs grow to tolerate each other and, beyond growling a little under their breath about how it takes all kinds of dogs to make up a world, get along fairly well together when their paths cross. I know of one mother dog and her half-grown daughter who sometimes spend the whole day together hunting woodchucks, although they don't speak. Their association is not sentimental, but practical, and is based on the fact that it is safer to hunt woodchucks in pairs than alone. These two dogs start out together in the morning, without a word, and come back together in the evening, when they part, without saying good night, whether they have had any luck or not. Avoidance of farewells, which are always stuffy and sometimes painful, is another thing in which it seems to me dogs have better sense than people.

Well, one day the daughter, a dog about ten months old, seemed, by some prank of nature which again I am unable clearly to understand, for a moment or two, to recognize her mother, after all those months of oblivion. The two had just started out after a fat woodchuck who lives in the orchard. Something got wrong with the daughter's ear—a long, floppy ear. "Mother," she said, "I wish you'd look at my ear." Instantly the other dog bristled and growled. "I'm not your mother," she said, "I'm a woodchuck-hunter." The daughter grinned. "Well," she said, just to show that there were no hard feelings, "that's not my ear, it's a motorman's glove."

| 1932 |

*"For Heaven's sake, why
don't you go outdoors
and trace something?"*

# THE DOG STAR

## SUSAN ORLEAN

R in Tin Tin was born on a battlefield in the Meuse Valley, in
eastern France, in September, 1918. The exact date isn't certain,
but when Leland Duncan found the puppy, on September 15th,
he was still blind and nursing, and was nearly bald. The Meuse Valley
was a terrible place to be born that year. In most other circumstances,
the valley—plush and undulating, checkered with dairy farms—would
have been inviting, but it rolls to the German border, and in 1918 it
was at the center of the First World War.

Lee Duncan was a country boy, a third-generation Californian.
One of his grandmothers was a Cherokee, and one grandfather had
come west with Brigham Young. The family ranched, farmed,
scratched out some kind of living. Lee's mother, Elizabeth, had married his father, Grant Duncan, when she was eighteen, in 1891. Lee
was born in 1893, followed, three years later, by his sister, Marjorie.
The next year, Grant took off and was never heard from again. Lee
was a great keeper of notes and letters and memos and documents. In
thousands of pages, which include a detailed memoir—a rough draft
for the autobiography he planned to write and the movie he hoped
would be made about his life—there is only one reference to his father,
and even that is almost an aside.

After Grant abandoned Elizabeth, she was unable to care for her
children. She left them in an orphanage in Oakland. Neither she nor
the children knew if they would ever be reunited. It wasn't until three
years later that she would reclaim them.

In 1917, Duncan joined the Army. He was assigned to the 135th Aero Squadron, as a gunnery corporal, and was sent to the French front. His account of this time is soldierly and understated, but he vividly recalled the morning of September 15, 1918, when he was sent to inspect the ruins of a German encampment. "I came upon what might have been headquarters for some working dogs," he wrote. As he strolled around, he saw a hellish image of slaughter: about a dozen dogs, killed by artillery shells. But hiding nearby was a starving, frantic German shepherd female and a litter of five puppies.

From the moment he found the dogs, Duncan considered himself a lucky man. He marvelled at the story, turning it over like a shiny stone, watching it catch the light. He thought about that luck when it came to naming the two puppies he eventually kept for himself—the prettiest ones, a male and a female. He called them Rin Tin Tin and Nanette, after the good-luck charms that were popular with soldiers in France—a pair of dolls, made of yarn or silk, named in honor of two young lovers who, it was said, had survived a bombing in a Paris railway station at the start of the war.

In May, 1919, after the Armistice, Duncan returned to the United States. It would have been easier to leave the "war orphans" behind, but, he later wrote, "I felt there was something about their lives that reminded me of my own life. They had crept right into a lonesome place in my life and had become a part of me." Before they reached California, however, Nanette developed pneumonia and died, and Duncan got another German shepherd puppy, named Nanette II, to keep Rin Tin Tin company. After Duncan had been back home for a while in Los Angeles, where Elizabeth was then living, he began to feel restless and anxious. He experienced spasms, probably as a result of his war service, and he found it difficult to work. His one pleasure was to train Rinty, as he called him, to do tricks.

By then, Rinty, a rambunctious, bossy dog, was nearly full-grown. He had lost his puppy fluffiness; his coat was lustrous and dark, nearly black, with gold marbling on the legs and chin and chest. His tail was as bushy as a squirrel's. He wasn't overly tall or broad, his legs weren't particularly muscular or long, but he was powerful and nimble, as light on his feet as a mountain goat. His ears were comically large, tulip-shaped, and set far apart on a wide skull. His face was more arresting than beautiful, his expression pitying and generous and a little sorrowful, as if he were viewing with charity and resignation the whole enterprise of living.

German shepherds were a relatively new breed, and very new in this country, but their popularity was growing quickly. Duncan got to know other shepherd fanciers, and helped found the Shepherd Dog Club of California. He decided to enter Rinty in a show at the Ambassador Hotel, in Los Angeles. An acquaintance named Charley Jones asked if he could come along. He had just developed a type of slow-motion camera, and he wanted to try it out by filming Rinty.

Rin Tin Tin and a female shepherd named Marie were competing in a jump-off for first place in the "working dog" part of the show. The bar was set at eleven and a half feet. The judge and show officials gathered beside it for a close look. Marie took her turn, and flew up and over. Rin Tin Tin then squared off for his leap. "Charley Jones had his camera on Rinty as he made his jump and as he came down on the other side," Duncan wrote. The dog had cleared the bar at almost twelve feet, sailing over the head of the judge and several others, and winning the competition.

Something about watching Rin Tin Tin being filmed stuck with Duncan. In the weeks that followed, he was seized by a desire to get the dog to Hollywood. "I was so excited over the motion picture idea that I found myself thinking of it night and day," he wrote.

In 1922, Duncan married a wealthy socialite named Charlotte Anderson, who owned a stable and a champion horse called Nobleman. The couple had probably met at a dog or a horse show. Still, the marriage was curious. Duncan was good-looking and was always described as a likable man, but he spent all of his time with his dog. It's hard to imagine him presenting an alluring package to a woman like Anderson, who was sophisticated, older than Duncan—he was twenty-eight, she was in her mid-thirties—and had been married before. It's even harder to picture Duncan having a romantic life; he made no mention of it, or of Anderson, in his memoir.

Duncan's devotion was to his dog. When he wasn't training Rinty to follow direction—which he did for hours every day—he took him to Poverty Row, in Hollywood, where the less established studios were. The two of them walked up and down the street, knocking on doors, trying to interest someone in using Rinty in a film. This wasn't as implausible as it might sound: in those years, bit players were often plucked from the crowds that gathered at the studio gates. Moreover, in 1921, a German shepherd named Strongheart had made a spectacular and profitable appearance in *The Silent Call*. Strongheart was the first German shepherd to star in a Hollywood film, and his grave, gallant manner and the still-novel look of German shepherds caused a sensation. The dogs were now as sought after in Hollywood as blond starlets. Duncan probably brushed past other young men with their own trained German shepherds, all inspired by Strongheart, as he went from door to door.

Then Duncan got a break: he secured a small part for Rinty in a melodrama called *The Man from Hell's River*. Rinty—who is not in the cast list but is mentioned in the *Variety* review as "Rin Tan"—plays a sled-dog team leader belonging to Pierre, a Canadian Mountie.

In time, Rin Tin Tin made twenty-three silent films. Copies of only six of those films are known to exist today. *The Man from Hell's River* is not among them. All we have is the movie's "shot list," which was a guide for the film editor. Parts of it read like a sort of silent-film found poetry:

Long shot dog on tree stump
Long shot wolf
Long shot prairie
Long shot dog runs and exits
Long shot deer
Long shot dog
Medium shot girl
Close-up shot little monkey.

And, at the end:

Med shot dog and puppies
Med close-up more puppies
Med shot people and dogs.

Rinty was soon cast in another film, *My Dad*, a run-of-the-mill "snow," which is what silents set in wintry locations were called. It, too, was a small part, but, for the first time, he was given a film credit. In the cast list, he appeared thus:

Rin-Tin-Tin. . . . . . . . . . . . . By Himself.

Finally, Duncan got through the door at Warner Bros. One of the smallest studios, Warner Bros. had been founded in 1918 by four brothers from Youngstown, Ohio, who set up shop in a drafty barn on Sunset Boulevard. That day, Harry Warner was directing a scene that included a wolf. The animal had been borrowed from the zoo and was not performing well. According to James English's 1949 book, *The Rin Tin Tin Story*, Duncan rubbed dirt into Rinty's fur to make him look like a wolf, and persuaded Warner to give Rinty a chance to try the scene. Rinty performed brilliantly, and Warner liked what he saw. He agreed to look at a script that Duncan had been working on for Rinty, entitled "Where the North Begins." While writing it, Duncan had studied the dog's facial expressions. He was convinced that Rinty could be taught to act a part—not just to carry a story through action but "to register emotions and portray a real character with its individual loves, loyalties, and hates." A few weeks later, Duncan got a letter from the studio: Warner wanted to produce his screenplay and cast Rin Tin Tin in the lead.

Production began almost immediately, with Chester Franklin, an accomplished director, in charge. Claire Adams, Walter McGrail, and Pat Hartigan—silent-film stalwarts—were cast opposite Rinty. The film was shot mostly in the High Sierras. "It didn't seem like work," Duncan wrote. "Even Rinty was bubbling over with happiness out here in the woods and snow." Rinty sometimes bubbled too much, chasing foxes into snowdrifts, and, once, attacking a porcupine, which filled his face with quills. Otherwise, Duncan was proud of the dog's performance, which included a twelve-foot jump—higher than the one at the Ambassador Hotel.

To advertise the film, Warner Bros. distributed promotional material to theatre owners which included ads, guidelines for publicity stunts, and feature stories for local newspapers. The features were meant to make the filming of the movie seem almost as dramatic as the movie:

HUNGRY WOLVES SURROUND CAMP
*Movie Actors in Panic When Pack Bays at Them*

GREAT RISK OF LIFE IN FILMING PICTURE

THE MOVIES NO BED OF ROSES
*Chester Franklin, Director, Tells Hard-Luck Story of Blizzard.*

The publicity stunts, which studio marketing people referred to as "exploitation," included suggestions that theatre owners "get a crate and inside it put a puppy or a litter of them" for the lobby ("You will be sure to get a crowd"); partner with a Marine recruiter and place signs outside the recruiting office saying "WHERE THE NORTH BEGINS AT THE [BLANK] THEATRE *is a thrilling picture of red-blooded* ADVENTURE. *Your adventure will begin when you join the marines and see the world*"; or, as one, titled "HOLDING UP PEDESTRIANS," proposed, "Get a man to walk along the principal streets of the city stopping pedestrians and asking them the question, 'Where Does the North Begin?' and upon their answering (or even not answering) he can . . . tell them it begins at your playhouse."

When *Where the North Begins* was released nationwide, *Variety* declared, "Here is a cracking good film for almost any audience. . . . It has the conventional hero and the conventional heroine, but Rin-Tin-Tin is the show. . . . A good many close-ups are given the dog and in all of them he holds the attention of the audience closely." Another review praised Rinty's eyes, saying that they conveyed something "tragic, fierce, sad and . . . a nobility and degree of loyalty not credible in a person."

The *Times* was more ambivalent, and made the first comparison between Rin Tin Tin and Strongheart: "This dog engages in a pantomimic

struggle that is not always impressive, at least not nearly as realistic as the work of Strongheart," but adding that Rin Tin Tin "is a remarkable animal, with splendid eyes and ears, and he seems to be wondering what all this acting is about." *Motion Picture Magazine*'s story "The Rival of Strongheart" went further, noting that Rin Tin Tin "is now competing with Strongheart for the canine celluloid honors."

The film was a hit, earning more than four hundred thousand dollars. Strongheart had set the pace, but Rin Tin Tin had become a star. Thousands of fan letters were arriving at Warner Bros. each week. *Where the North Begins* was playing all over the country, and, as was typical with popular films, most theatres extended its run as long as people kept showing up; movies were

such a new form of entertainment that a hit film was a spectacle, a national event that everyone wanted to view. Still, the movie wasn't at the level of Strongheart's *The Silent Call*, which had broken attendance records in Los Angeles, where it was shown eight times a day for thirteen weeks.

Most of the German shepherds who followed Strongheart and Rin Tin Tin in Hollywood had just a burst of fame and then were forgotten. Among the many dozens were Wolfheart and Braveheart, Wolfang and Duke; Fang, Fangs, Flash, and Flame; Thunder, Lightning, Lightnin', and Lightnin' Girl; Ace the Wonder Dog, Captain the King of Dogs, and Kazan the Dog Marvel. They played serious, heroic figures in films that, like them, are now mostly forgotten: *Aflame in the Sky, Courage of the North, The Silent Code, Avenging Fangs, Fangs of Destiny, Wild Justice.*

In real life, too, the dog hero was having its day. In 1923, Bobbie the Oregon Wonder Dog walked alone for six months from Indiana to Oregon, to find his owners; in 1925, a sled dog named Balto led a team carrying diphtheria antitoxin to Nome, Alaska, saving the town from an epidemic; in 1928, Buddy, the nation's first Seeing Eye dog, began guiding a young blind man named Morris Frank.

Even so, Rin Tin Tin was singled out. He was praised by everyone from the director Sergei Eisenstein, who posed for a photograph with him, to the poet Carl Sandburg, who was working as a film critic for the Chicago *Daily News.* "A beautiful animal, he has a power of expression in his every movement that makes him one of the leading pantomimists of the screen," Sandburg wrote, adding that Rinty was "phenomenal" and "thrillingly intelligent." Warner Bros. got thousands of requests for pictures of Rinty, which were signed with a paw print and a line written in Duncan's spidery hand: "Most faithfully, Rin Tin Tin."

From the start, Rin Tin Tin was admired as an actor but was also seen as a real dog, a genetic model; everyone, it seemed, wanted a piece of him. He and Nanette, who often appeared on-screen as his "wife," mated, and Duncan distributed the puppies among some of Rin Tin Tin's most celebrated fans. Greta Garbo and Jean Harlow each owned a Rin Tin Tin descendant, as did W. K. Kellogg, the cereal magnate.

To promote *Where the North Begins* and subsequent movies, the studio sent Duncan and the dog on promotional tours around the country. They appeared at hospitals and orphanages, gave interviews, and visited animal shelters and schools. When describing a visit to one shelter, Duncan sounded as if he were telling the story of his own childhood through Rin Tin Tin. "Perhaps if I could have understood, I might have heard Rinty telling these other less fortunate dogs of how his mother failed in her terrific struggle to keep her little family together. Or

*"Don't you get it? It was never about the stick—I sent you there to find yourself."*

how he, as a little war orphan, had found a kin-
dred spirit in his master and friend, also a half-
orphan." Of course, Rin Tin Tin's mother had
actually succeeded in keeping her family together
in the bombed-out kennel. It was Duncan's
mother who, for a time, had failed in her struggle.

In the evening, Duncan and Rinty would go
to a theatre where a Rin Tin Tin movie was playing, and afterward come onstage. Duncan usually began by explaining how he had trained the
dog: "There are persons who have said I must
have been very cruel to Rinty in order to get him
to act in the pictures," especially in the scenes
where the dog is shown "groveling in the dust,
shrinking away, his tail between his legs," which
Rinty did in *Where the North Begins* and in many
films that followed. Duncan would then demonstrate how he worked with the dog, saying that it
was best to use a low voice with "a tone of mild
entreaty." He didn't believe in bribing Rin Tin
Tin with food or excessive praise: he rewarded
him by letting him play with a squeaky rubber
doll he had first given to Rinty when he was a
puppy. At this point in the show, Duncan would
run Rinty through some of his tricks—his
belly-crawling, his ability to stand stock-still for
minutes on end, his range of expressions from
anger to delight to dread.

One such night, according to a writer named
Francis Rule, Duncan began by calling Rinty,
and then, for laughs, scolded him after he strolled
lazily onstage, stretched, and yawned. "There
then followed one of the most interesting exhibitions I have ever witnessed," Rule wrote, in
*Picture-Play Magazine*. As Duncan led Rinty
through a series of acting exercises, "there was
between that dog and his master as perfect an
understanding as could possibly exist between
two living beings." Duncan "scarcely touched
him during the entire proceedings—he stood

about eight feet away and simply gave directions.
And it fairly took your breath away to watch that
dog respond, his ears up unless told to put them
down and his eyes intently glued on his master.
There was something almost uncanny about it."

Everywhere Duncan and Rinty appeared,
the dog was treated like a dignitary. In New York,
Mayor Jimmy Walker gave him a key to the city.
In Portland, Oregon, he was welcomed as "a distinguished canine visitor," and was met at the
train station by the city's school superintendent,
the chief of police, and the head of the local Humane Society. Then Rinty made a statesmanlike
pilgrimage to the grave of Bobbie the Oregon
Wonder Dog. During the ceremony, according to
one report, "Rin Tin Tin with his own teeth
placed the flowers on Bobbie's grave and then in
a moment's silence laid his head on the cross
marking the resting place of the dog." The next
day, at Portland's Music Box Theatre, Rinty was
presented with the Abraham Lincoln humanitarian award and medal for distinguished service.

In 1924, the studio began work on *Find Your Man*.
The director was Mal St. Clair, and the writer
was, in the words of Jack Warner, a "downy-
cheeked youngster who looked as though he had
just had the bands removed from his teeth so he
could go to the high school prom." The youngster
was Darryl Zanuck, the son of a professional
gambler; Zanuck had come to Hollywood from
Nebraska, when he was seventeen. One of his first
jobs was writing ads for Yuccatone Hair Restorer.
His slogan, "You've Never Seen a Bald-Headed
Indian," helped make Yuccatone a success, until
bottles of the hair tonic fermented and exploded
in twenty-five drugstores, and the company was
driven out of business. Zanuck left advertising to
work for the director Mack Sennett and, later, for
Charlie Chaplin. Mal St. Clair had also worked

with Sennett, and several of his films had included dogs.

The movie that Zanuck had in mind was set in a remote timber camp. He and St. Clair acted it out for Harry Warner, with Zanuck playing the part of the dog. With Warner's approval, production started almost immediately. Billed as "Wholesome Melodrama At Its Very Best" that starred "Rin Tin Tin the Wonder Dog," the movie was a "box office rocket," in Jack Warner's words.

The next Rin Tin Tin movie, *Lighthouse by the Sea*, was also written by Zanuck and released in 1924. It concerned a pretty girl and her father, a lighthouse keeper who is going blind. Warner Bros. even held screenings for the blind. There was a narrator onstage who described the action and read the intertitle cards, which included "He's so tough I have to feed him manhole covers for biscuits!," "This pup can whip his weight in alligators—believe me!," and "I thought you said that flea incubator could fight!"

Zanuck always acknowledged that Rin Tin Tin had given him his entree into Warner Bros., but he later told interviewers that he disliked the dog and hated writing for him. Even so, he wrote at least ten more scripts for Rinty, all of them great successes. By the time he was twenty-five, Zanuck was running the studio.

Rinty's films were so profitable that Warner Bros. paid him two thousand dollars a week; even at that, Rin Tin Tin was a bargain. Around the Warner Bros. lot, he was called "the mortgage lifter," because every time the studio was in financial straits it released a Rin Tin Tin movie and the income from it set things right again. Duncan was given every privilege: he was driven to the set each day, and he had an office on the Warner Bros. lot, where he sifted through the fan mail and the little mementos that arrived for Rin Tin Tin.

Duncan had never imagined this part of the equation. He started buying snappy clothes and cars. He bought land in Beverly Hills and built a house for himself and his mother. The house is now gone, and it's hard to know much about it; in his memoir, Duncan talked mostly about the kennel he built for the dogs. Then he bought a house in North Hollywood for his sister, Marjorie. His biggest splurge was on a beach house in a gated section of Malibu, where his neighbors were Hollywood stars.

On top of the movie income, Rinty was signed to endorsement deals. An executive from Chappel Brothers, which had recently introduced Ken-L Ration, the first commercial canned dog food, was so eager to have Rin Tin Tin as a spokesperson that, in a meeting with Duncan, he ate a can of it to demonstrate its tastiness. Duncan was convinced. Rinty was featured in ads for Ken-L Ration, Ken-L-Biskit, and Pup-E-Crumbles brands, with the slogan "My Favorite Food! Most Faithfully, Rin Tin Tin."

Of the six Rin Tin Tin silent films still available, the most memorable is *Clash of the Wolves* (1925). Rinty plays a half-dog, half-wolf named Lobo, who is living in the wild as the leader of a wolf pack. The film begins with a vivid and disturbing scene of a forest fire, which drives Lobo and his pack, including Nanette and their pups, from their forest home to the desert ranchlands, where they prey on cattle to survive. The ranchers hate the wolves, especially Lobo; a bounty of a hundred dollars is offered as a reward for his hide. In the meantime, a young mineral prospector named Dave arrives in town. A claim jumper who lusts after Dave's mineral discovery (and Dave's girlfriend, Mae) soon schemes against him. Mae happens to be the daughter of the rancher who is most determined to kill Lobo and who also doesn't like Dave.

The wolves, led by Lobo, attack a steer, and the ranchers set out after them. The chase is fast and frightening, and when Rin Tin Tin weaves through the horses' churning legs it looks as if he were about to be trampled. He outruns the horses, his body flattened and stretched as he bullets along the desert floor, and, if you didn't see the little puffs of dust when his paws touch the ground, you'd swear he was floating. He scrambles up a tree—a stunt so startling that it has to be replayed a few times to believe it. Can dogs climb trees? Evidently. At least, certain dogs can. And they can climb down, too, and then tear along a rock ridge, and then come

*"He was abandoned in the D.C. area as a puppy and raised by a pack of senators."*

to a halt at the narrow crest of the ridge. The other side of the gorge looks miles away. Rin Tin Tin stops, pivots; you feel him calculating his options; then he crouches and leaps, and the half-second before he lands safely feels long and fraught. His feet touch ground and he scrambles on, but moments later he plummets off the edge of another cliff, slamming through the branches of a cactus, collapsing in a heap, with a cactus needle skewered through the pad of his foot.

The action is thrilling, but the best part of the movie is the quieter section, after Rin Tin Tin falls. He limps home, stopping every few steps to lick his injured paw; his bearing is so abject that it is easy to understand why Duncan felt the need to explain that it was just acting. Rin Tin Tin hobbles into his den and collapses next to Nanette, in terrible pain.

In an earlier scene in the movie, one of the wolves is injured and the pack musters around

him. At first, it looks as if they were coming to his aid, but, suddenly, their actions seem more agitated than soothing, and just then an intertitle card flashes up, saying simply, "The Law of the Pack. Death to the wounded wolf." So we know that the other wolves will kill Lobo if they realize that he's injured. Rinty and Nanette try to work on the cactus needle in his paw surreptitiously. But the pack senses that something is wrong. Finally, one of them approaches, a black look on his face, ready to attack. Rinty draws himself up and snarls. The two animals freeze, and then Rinty snarls again, almost sotto voce, as if he were saying, "I don't care what you think you know about my condition. I am still the leader here." The murderous wolf backs off.

The rest of the plot is a crosshatch of misperception and treachery. Rinty, fearing that he will still be killed by his pack and attract harm to Nanette and their pups, leaves, so that he might die alone, and his wobbling, wincing departure is masterly acting. Dave comes upon Rinty as he is on his death walk. Knowing there is a bounty for the dog, he pulls out his gun, but then gives in to his sympathy for the suffering animal and removes the cactus thorn. (Charles Farrell, who played Dave, must have been a brave man; Rinty was required to snap and snarl at him in that scene, and there are a few snaps when Rinty looks like he's not kidding.) Dave's decision to save Lobo is of great consequence, because, of course, Lobo ends up saving Dave's life. Lobo chooses to be a dog—a guardian—and protect Dave, rather than give in to his wolf impulse to be a killer.

The film has its share of silliness—a scene in which Rinty wears a beard as a disguise to avoid being identified as Lobo, for example—and, to the modern eye, the human acting is stilted. But *Clash of the Wolves* shows why so many millions of people fell in love with Rin Tin Tin.

By the middle of the twenties, the movie business had grown into one of the ten biggest industries in the United States. According to the historian Ann Elwood, almost a hundred million movie tickets were sold each week, to a population of a hundred and fifteen million. In 1928, Warner Bros. was worth sixteen million dollars; two years later, it was worth two hundred million. It still had the reputation of being second-rate, compared with Paramount or M-G-M, but it was expanding and innovating. It had launched a chain of movie palaces, with orchestras and elaborate, thematic décor—Arabian nights in one theatre, Egyptian days or Beaux Arts Paris in another—and, best of all, air-conditioning,

which was rare in public buildings, and even rarer in private homes.

In 1927, four Rin Tin Tin films were released, and during breaks in the production schedule Duncan and Rinty were on the road doing stage appearances. Duncan hardly had a life at home. Charlotte Anderson had filed for divorce. She said she didn't like Rinty, and didn't like competing with him. In the proceedings, she charged that Duncan didn't love her or her horses: "All he cared for was Rin Tin Tin," she testified. An article in the Los Angeles *Times* noted, "Evidently, Rin Tin Tin's company was so much pleasure to Duncan that he considered Mrs. Duncan's presence rather secondary."

Otherwise, the year was a high point for Duncan. The four films—*A Dog of the Regiment, Jaws of Steel, Tracked by the Police,* and *Hills of Kentucky*—were box-office hits as well as critical successes. The Academy Awards were presented for the first time two years later, and, according to Hollywood legend, Rinty received the most votes for best actor. But members of the Academy, anxious to establish that the awards were serious and important, decided that giving an Oscar to a dog did not serve that end. (The award went to Emil Jannings.)

Even without the Oscar, Rinty was in the news all the time. He was frequently given an honorific: the King of Pets; the Famous Police Dog of the Movies; the Dog Wonder; the Wonder Dog of the Stage and Screen; the Wonder Dog of All Creation; the Mastermind Dog; the Marvelous Dog of the Movies; and America's Greatest Movie Dog. In 1928, a review of Rin Tin Tin's film *A Race for Life* began with the question "Strongheart who?"

| 2011 |

# THE OWNER OF BEN FINNEY

## ALEXANDER WOOLLCOTT

Those of you who go to Antibes this summer will find that once slumbrous cape aswarm with the conspicuous. Thanks to the ever reliable herd instinct of the human species, the manager of the Hotel du Cap needs only smile and rub his hands at this curious veering of the summer tourists to his once deserted corner of the Riviera.

You will see Lloyd Osbourne, indistinguishable from a lizard on the sunbaked rocks in front of his terra-cotta home. You will see Mary Garden or Lily Langtry, perhaps, running over from Monte Carlo to a dinner party at the Cap. You will see the Dwight Deere Wimans (late of Moline, Ill.) and the Archibald MacLeishes taking up an unconscionable part of the *plage* with their respective young. You will see Mrs. James Hazen Hyde, bearing up with remarkable fortitude under the continual annoyance of being mistaken for Marie Tempest. And you will even see Marie Tempest herself. You will see Elsie de Wolfe (Lady Mendl, to you) throning away in La Garoupe, the largest villa at the Cap. Oh these, and Montemezzi, perhaps, and Moronzoni, and Walter Ellis of New Orleans, and Benjamin Strong of the Federal Reserve Bank, and (so as to have a little of everything) Dudley Field Malone.

But it is none of these you will remember longest. The unforgettable habitué of Antibes is Egon. He has been wintering and springing in New York, and you could see him almost any day if you dropped in at the White Horse Tavern in West Forty-fifth Street, where he rather made a point of keeping an eye on the coatroom, being, I think, the only coatroom attendant in town who could dispose of a troublesome customer, or merely knock off for the day, by a neat standing broad jump over the counter. But, with the coming of spring to West Forty-fifth Street, Egon began to betray a nostalgia for Antibes and made it clear enough that he had to meet a friend over there. Victorio, the coatroom boy at the Algonquin, was to have departed in April for six months of painting in Paris. I shouldn't be at all surprised if Egon got the idea from him.

Egon is seven years old. He is one of the largest and most powerful German police dogs ever bred in the kennels of Berlin. Even when he was very young, he cost as much as a high-powered automobile. He has been owned since he was a yearling by Benjamin Ficklin Finney, Jr., sometime student in residence at the University of Virginia and, later, a captain in the United States Marines in France where, I need hardly add, he was popularly known as Finney la Guerre.

Benjamin Ficklin Finney, Sr., stays the year round in Sewanee, Tenn., where he is the Regent of the University of the South. Benjamin Ficklin Finney, Jr., having inherited (from his mother) the famous Penelo Plantation at Tarboro, N.C., stays nowhere at all very long and, to put it in a nutshell, does nothing at all.

When last heard from, Massa Ben, as the old planter is sometimes called, was on his way into the depths of Indo-China, with a rifle over his shoulder and a commission from the Chicago Field Museum to come out with the pelt of some animal that most stay-at-homes would think of as not really being worth all that trouble.

You may possibly have read of Massa Ben in the tabloids, for he has been variously reported, at one time or another, as engaged to Betty Compson, Marilyn Miller, Ruth Goldbeck, Constance Talmadge and, in fact, practically everyone, with the possible exception of Mrs. Leslie Carter. But, for the most part, Finney is as inconspicuous as the husband of some famous star. He is known all over the world just as that nice-looking young man who owns Egon. Egon, in turn, has an excessively high opinion of the value of his master to society, tempered, to be sure, by his occasional suspicion that Massa Ben is not quite bright and will probably get drowned in the Mediterranean if Egon is not there to keep an eye on him.

Indeed, Egon's single social gaucherie derives from his arrant assumption that he is the only good swimmer in the world. This made him more than a little trying when I first met him in Antibes. That was before the days of the congestion caused by the comparatively recent notion that all the best people naturally spend the summer in that still somewhat surprised portion of the Riviera. In those days, the silence of the Antibes nights was broken only by the sweet music of the nightingales and the cries of the wounded borne faintly on the wind from the Casino at Juan les Pins; the silence of the mornings only by the sound of Tennessee's own Grace Moore firmly practicing the scales in her pink villa at the Cap.

The Honorable Montague Norman, Governor of the Bank of England, would gather his peignoir about him, proceed majestically down the leafy footway from the hotel, pause on the rocks for a bit of sun and then cleave the turquoise depths with his venerable person. He might get out quite a distance when Egon would hurry forward, wearing his Drat-the-man-he's-in-again expression. Failing utterly to conceal his deep enjoyment of this further load of responsibility thrown upon him by the incompetence of the human race, he would run out on the spring-

board, throw up his head in a clamor of scolding and then leap into the sea, heading like a destroyer toward the unsuspecting financier. A little later, a coastful of lazy human molluscs would chuckle at the spectacle of the Honorable Montague Norman being helplessly delivered on shore.

I have heard people, with dry bathing-suits, loudly wonder why swimmers thus lent themselves to Egon's palpable exhibitionism. They were foolish, it seems, to let themselves be rescued. I myself used to say that, until the day came when I had grown so dear to him that he just could not bear the thought of my drowning out there in the Mediterranean. It is quite useless to resist. You know the trick the life guards are taught when they must deal with the witless and hampering struggles of a drowning person. The life guard must haul back with his free hand, sock the little struggler on the jaw and then, undis-turbed, tow his unconscious form to shore. It is an old trick along the beaches of the world, and Egon learned it early. Of course he does not knock you unconscious. He merely strokes your bare skin with his paws until you shriek with agony, and, in crises, he bites you. You yourself would soon abandon the notion of resistance if you could see this fiend in canine form, only slightly smaller than Man o' War, bearing down on you with the resolution of the Twentieth Century Limited and wearing, when you try playfully to evade him, an expression of wordless rage that fairly chills the blood. "Oh, well," you say, "if that's the way you feel about it," and you put a consenting hand on his still angry hackles. At that gesture of surrender, he circles like a wherry and heads for shore, the very throb of his engine suggesting that he could take on a few dozen more if need be.

Of course, he himself is no mean swimmer. When urged, he makes a pretty forty-foot dive from the high rocks, first devoting some time to a preliminary barking, which is part genuine misgivings, part excitement and part sheer showmanship, because it would be so foolish to dive until enough people were looking that way. But in the end he does dive, clean and straight and proud as Lucifer.

And he rides a surf board. He cannot mount one unaided, but I have seen Scott Fitzgerald help his floundering efforts to get on. Then Fitzgerald would slip off into the water and Egon would ride alone, balancing expertly and terribly pleased with himself. Indeed, he can thus circle the bay indefinitely, provided only that Ben Finney is in the motor boat in plain sight. Otherwise, after a minute, you can fairly see Egon's eyes cloud with a worry as to where that fool Finney of his is. Fallen into the water, perhaps, and probably going down for the last time. It is too much. Egon will turn around, scan the sea, lose his balance in consequence and pitch crestfallen and furious into the water. By the time he comes up for air, the motor boat is half way to Cannes.

There was a time when serious thought was given to the notion of starring Egon in the movies, in order that, in the course of time, he might succeed the ageing Rin Tin Tin as John Barrymore succeeded Forbes-Robertson. Indeed, once when he was spending the winter in Florida a few years ago, he wandered impromptu into a picture that the late Barbara La Marr was making there and came close to running away with her triumph. It was quite evident that (in the pattern of the favorite Hollywood bedtime story) he could easily step from movie extra to star overnight. If nothing came of this project, I suspect it was because the roving Finney would not stay in one country long enough to let Egon have a career.

Probably it is just as well, for Hollywood compels its dog stars to perform only the most routine heroics, and a really interesting scenario—something that Egon could have got his teeth into, as I believe the actors phrase it—would never have been suffered to reach the production stage.

Finney will probably come out of Indo-China and head straight for Antibes before the summer is half gone. It is planned that Egon should meet him there. It was first suggested that I act as escort on his return to the Riviera, but I declined, though not for fear of his getting lost while in my charge. You do not even have to tether Egon, for, if only you will give him his leash to take charge of, he regards it as a point of honor to pretend he is tied up. It is, however, comparatively easy to steal him if you happen to know his one weakness. He will get into any automobile.

But once that has been accomplished, the thief's troubles are only beginning. For it just is not possible to own Egon inconspicuously. More than once a taxi driver in discharging a fare has noticed with surprise and pleasure that a large and obviously valuable police dog has stepped quietly in through the still open door and settled himself on the seat as though affably waiting to be driven somewhere. You can easily imagine the sequence of thoughts which then visits that driver. Probably his first impulse is to turn down his flag and ask what address. His second, perhaps, is to howl with fear. His third is to drive quietly home and present the creature to his wife and kiddies. It is then that misgivings come, for you cannot take Egon even as far as the nearest lamp post without drawing a crowd. And when, as has happened several times, his mysterious disappearance is broadcast over the radio, he is instantly and even thankfully returned, with some implausible story about having been found astroll in Long Island City.

Nor, if I declined him as a traveling companion for this summer, was it because he is any nuisance to have around. Indeed, he can be a positive convenience. For instance, you could meet anyone you wish to on the boat by taking Egon for one turn around the promenade deck. He has been Massa Ben's entire social credentials for some years past and he has done even more for him than that. Once when Finney lost his passport and had to get across three pesky little frontiers without one, he and Egon would merely descend from the train on the wrong side while the other passengers were docilely filing through the inspection line. Each time when sundry officials noticed this evasion and bustled importantly forward to investigate it, Finney would just whisper some magical word in Egon's ear and Egon would leap murderously forward, in the manner and with the general effect of the Hound of the Baskervilles. Each time the officials seemingly thought it best to drop the whole matter.

It was, therefore, no fear of his being a nuisance that bade me forswear the considerable pleasure and social importance to be derived from crossing the Atlantic with Egon. I merely wished to avoid the personal grief which, sooner or later, is the inevitable portion of his every interim boss. When he is in New York, for instance, he hangs around with William Zelcer, who owns the White Horse Tavern. They are great friends, and every morning Zelcer goes to the trouble of driving the full circuit of Central Park so that, by loping behind, Egon can get his exercise. Then Egon returns the compliment by waiting gloomily in the carriage-starter's shack outside the New York Athletic Club while Zelcer is inside getting

*his* exercise. He sleeps on the floor at the foot of Zelcer's bed at the Hotel Hawthorne and sometimes, when he is very crafty, on the bed itself, although it is no easy task for him to hoist his vast and guilty bulk onto the counterpane without being noticed. He keeps trying, however, and, as I have said, he is good enough to look after things in the coat-room at the Tavern.

But if Finney should walk in from Indo-China tomorrow, Egon would not only cut Zelcer dead on the street, but if there were the *contretemps* of a meeting at some party, he would growl ominously and show his fangs in order to make it a matter of record (to Zelcer, to Finney and to whomever it might concern) just where his affections are centred, for better for worse, for richer for poorer, in sickness and in health—world without end.

| *1928* |

# HIS LIFE AS A DOG

REBECCA MEAD

To look at Spencer Beglarian, an actor who lives in Los Angeles, you would not guess that he has been typecast as a dog. Beglarian isn't especially canine in appearance—he is slight and neat, with dark hair and gray eyes, and does not bound or slobber as a matter of course. Beglarian, though, is on his way to being the acting world's go-to "dog" guy, in the same way that, say, Jack Black is Hollywood's go-to smart-and-funny fat guy. He has appeared as a dog three times recently: first in a Los Angeles production of *Stray Dog Story,* a play by Robert Chesley, in which he had the part of Buddy, a dog who has been turned into a gay man but retains a canine heart and mind; as Sparky the Dog-Man, in an episode of *Sabrina, the Teenage Witch;* and now, in his most substantial dog role so far, in *Dog Days,* a short film that will be screened in New York next week, as part of the Independent Feature Project's Buzz Cuts series. The film, directed by Ellie Lee, and based on a short story by Judy Budnitz, is an unsettling family drama set in a grim, post-nuclear American town, and Beglarian plays a man who has taken on the persona of a stray dog named Prince. He hangs around outside a family's home on his hands and knees, wearing a dog suit, hoping for scraps of food and affection. In the process, he serves as a mirror of the family members' humanity or inhumanity. The role is a demanding one: like a real dog, Beglarian has to communicate without speaking, although, unlike a real dog, he doesn't have a tail to wag.

When he is asked how he goes about inhabiting the character of a dog, Beglarian's nose starts to twitch. "I don't think I have become more doglike physically after playing these roles," he said recently, sitting poolside at a Los Angeles hotel—the kind of place where dogs are not allowed. "But philosophically I have. I look at every dog now, and I connect with dogs as I never did before." Although he has become known as someone who gives good dog, Beglarian says that he has never played the same dog twice. He hasn't even played the same breed twice. "In *Stray Dog,* I imagined I was a Jack Russell terrier—very high-energy," he said. (In the play, he goes to a gay-pride march and starts howling with joy.) "Whereas *Dog Days* was more like a Labrador—older, slower, but just as constant and in-tense in his affec-tion. Then Sparky was one of those Australian sheep-dogs."

Beglarian does not own a dog, so in order to prepare for his roles he does field work. To get ready to play Buddy, he did some sur-veillance at a local Starbucks that is pop-ular with dog walkers. "You really can communicate with dogs if you take time to focus and look in their eyes," he said. For *Dog Days,* his acting coach was a dog that belonged to one of the film's finan-cial backers. "That dog was rather old, but quite loving," he said. During film-ing, Beglarian intentionally ate less, so as to be more convincing as a starving dog-man. And he drew upon the dis-comfort he felt while wearing a furry dog suit in hot weather to convey the misery of being a post-apocalyptic stray.

Beglarian, who is forty, and who teaches and writes in addition to acting, has come away from his dog studies with more than a killer whimper and a con-vincing way of cocking his head. There are, he says, life lessons to be learned from the canine world. "I think you can learn patience from dogs," he said. "How to stay with something with persistence, but not in a ferocious, manic way."

In exploring canine nature, he drew upon an early formative experience. "While I was at Yale drama school, I was very depressed for a time," he ex-plained. "One day, I was in New York, in this really small, split-level apartment that belonged to a friend who was try-ing to make it as an actress. She had a black Lab, and the Lab had a toy. I remember throwing this toy down the stairs. I kept throwing it and throwing it, and there was as much joy on the part of the dog the last time he returned it as there had been the first time. There would have been more joy eternally. It struck me that there's some-thing Zen about that—doing something that might seem menial, but if you have joy in it you are happy. This is a kind of wisdom that dogs have."

| 2001 |

## YOUR FACE ON THE DOG'S NECK

It is early afternoon.
You sit on the grass
with your rough face on the dog's neck.
Right now
you are both as still as a snapshot.
That infectious dog ought to let a fly bother her,
ought to run out in an immense field,
chasing rabbits and skunks,
mauling the cats, licking insects off her rump,
and stop using you up.
My darling, why do you lean on her so?
I would touch you—
that pulse brooding under your madras shirt,
each shoulder the most well-built house,
the arms, thin birches that do not escape the breeze,
the white teeth that have known me,
that wait at the bottom of the brook,
and the tongue, my little fish! . . .
But you are stopped in time.

So I will speak of your eyes,
although they are closed.
Tell me, where is each stubborn-colored iris?
Where are the quick pupils that make
the floor tilt under me?
I see only the lids, as tough as riding boots.
Why have your eyes gone into their own room?
*Good night* they are saying
from their little leathery doors.
Or shall I sing of eyes
that have been ruined with mercy and lust,
and once with your own death,
when you lay bubbling like a caught fish,
sucking on the manufactured oxygen?
Or shall I sing of eyes
that are resting so near the hair
of that hateful animal?
Love twists me, a Spanish flute plays in my blood,
and yet I can see only
your little sleep, an empty place.

But when your eyes open
against the wool stink of her thick hair,
against the faint sickening neck of that dog,
whom I envy like a thief,
what will I ask?
Will I speak up, saying
there is a hurried song, a certain seizure
from which I gasp?
Or will your eyes lie in wait,
little field mice nestling on their paws?
Perhaps they will say nothing,
perhaps they will be dark and leaden,
having played their own game
somewhere else,
somewhere far off.

Oh, I have learned them, and know that
when they open and glance at me
I will turn like a little dancer,
and then, quite simply,
and all by myself,
I will fall,
bound to some mother/father,
bound to your sight,
bound for nowhere
and everywhere.
Or perhaps, my darling,
because it is early afternoon,
I will forget that my voice is full of good people,
forget how my legs could sprawl on the terrace,
forget all that the birds might witness—
the torn dress, the shoes lost in the arbor—
while the neighbor's lawnmower bites and spits out
some new little rows of innocent grass.
Certainly,
I need not speak of it at all.
I will crouch down
and put my cheek near you,
accepting this spayed and flatulent bitch you hold,
letting my face rest in an assembled tenderness
on the old dog's neck.

—ANNE SEXTON    | 1966 |

July 22, 1967

Price 35 cents

THE
NEW YORKER

# RICH BITCH

## JEFFREY TOOBIN

The life of Leona Helmsley presents an object lesson in the truism that money does not buy happiness. Born in 1920, she overcame a hardscrabble youth in Brooklyn to become a successful condominium broker in Manhattan, eventually alighting, in the 1960s, at a firm owned by Harry B. Helmsley, one of the city's biggest real-estate developers. The two married in 1972, and Leona became the public face of their empire, the self-styled "queen" of the Helmsley chain of hotels. In a series of ads that ran in the *Times Magazine* and elsewhere, Helmsley's visage became a symbol of the celebration of wealth in the 1980s. She wouldn't settle for skimpy towels, the ads proclaimed—"Why should you?"

In private, as it turned out, the grinning monarch wasn't just demanding but despotic. Throughout her life, Leona left a trail of ruin—embittered relatives, fired employees, and, fatefully, unpaid taxes. Knowing that the Helmsleys had used company funds to renovate their sprawling mansion, Dunnellen Hall, in Greenwich, Connecticut, disgruntled associates leaked the records to the *Post*. Among the charges billed to the company were a million-dollar dance floor installed above a swimming pool; a forty-five-thousand-dollar silver clock; and a two-hundred-and-ten-thousand-dollar mahogany card table. In 1988, the U.S. Attorney's office charged the couple with income-tax evasion, among other crimes. (Harry Helmsley avoided trial

because of ill health; he died in 1997, at the age of eighty-seven.) At the trial, a housekeeper famously testified that Leona had told her, "We don't pay taxes. Only the little people pay taxes," and the public warmed itself on a tabloid bonfire built under the Queen of Mean. Leona was convicted of multiple counts and served eighteen months in federal prison. In time, following her release, she became largely a recluse, and she died at Dunnellen Hall on August 20, 2007.

After her husband died, Leona Helmsley got a dog named Trouble, a Maltese bitch. In her will, which she signed two years before her death, Helmsley put aside twelve million dollars in a trust to care for Trouble. Further, she directed that, when Trouble died, the dog was to be "buried next to my remains in the Helmsley Mausoleum," at Sleepy Hollow Cemetery, in Westchester County. Helmsley made only a handful of relatively small individual bequests in the will, and left the bulk of her remaining estate to the Leona M. and Harry B. Helmsley Charitable Trust. Based on the figures in court files, that trust may turn out to be worth nearly eight billion dollars, which would make it one of the top ten or so foundations in the United States. (Leona's estate was so large because Harry left his fortune to her.) According to a "mission statement," which Helmsley signed on March 1, 2004, the trust was to make expenditures for "purposes related to the provision of care for dogs." The size of the bequests, to Trouble and to dogs generally, has generated widespread astonishment.

In fact, the clear motivation underlying Leona Helmsley's will—her desire to pass her wealth on to dogs—is more common than might be expected. Pet-lovers (many of whom now prefer the term "animal companion") have engineered a quiet revolution in the law to allow, in effect, non-humans to inherit and spend money. It is becoming routine for dogs to receive cash and real estate in the form of trusts, and there is already at least one major foundation devoted to helping dogs. A network of lawyers and animal activists has orchestrated these changes, largely without opposition, in order to whittle down the legal distinctions between human beings and animals. They are already making plans for the Helmsleys' billions.

For a couple that became emblematic of late-twentieth-century New York, Harry and Leona Helmsley were an unlikely pair. Harry, born in 1909 and raised in the Bronx, was sixteen when he joined a small Manhattan real-estate firm as an office boy for twelve dollars a week, and soon worked his way into a partnership. In 1938, he married the former Eve Green, a widow. Tall, stooped, a workaholic before the term was invented, Helmsley started buying buildings that were, in a way, a reflection of himself—drab but profitable. Often collaborating with a rotating group of partners on different projects, he moved on to a few more glamorous acquisitions, like the Empire State Building, in 1961, but he seemed to go out of his way to avoid calling attention to himself. He and Eve had no children. "My properties are my children," he would say.

Lena Rosenthal, in contrast, was a raucous, disputatious presence seemingly from birth. (She later changed her name to Leona Roberts.) Nearly every aspect of her biography has been challenged, particularly if she was the source for it. She claimed to have worked as a model for Chesterfield cigarettes in her early years, but evidence for that assertion is elusive. She was married three times, but generally acknowledged having had only two husbands. She married Leo Panzirer in 1940, and they divorced twelve years later. Then she married and divorced Joseph Lubin (she usually neglected to mention him at all in later years), before her marriage to Harry Helmsley, who had left his wife of thirty-three years shortly after Leona's arrival at his firm. Leona had one child, Jay Panzirer, who died, of a heart ailment, in 1982, at the age of forty. Jay Panzirer had four children, and these grandchildren survived Leona. The will hints at the tense relationship between her and her only descendants.

Leona had contentious relationships with almost everybody (except Harry). In particular, she came to despise Jay's widow, Mimi, his third wife, for reasons that Mimi later said she never understood. Following Jay's death, the Helmsleys moved immediately to evict Mimi and their eldest grandchild, Craig, from their home in Florida, which was owned by a Helmsley subsidiary. During the next several years, the Helmsleys filed no fewer than six lawsuits against Mimi, asserting that they were entitled to the money in Jay's estate, a distinctly modest sum compared with their own fortune. After five years of rancorous litigation, Leona won about two-thirds of the two hundred and thirty-one thousand dollars at issue. As a result of Leona's legal triumph, each of her grandchildren was left with an inheritance from their father of a little more than four hundred dollars.

In her will, Leona Helmsley was more generous to two of her grandchildren, David

and Walter Panzirer, who were left trusts and bequests worth ten million dollars, on the condition that they visit their father's grave at least once a year. (Jay was buried in the family mausoleum, alongside Harry and Leona.) To make sure that they did, the will stipulated that the trustees "shall have placed in the Helmsley Mausoleum a register to be signed by each visitor." Leona's other two grandchildren, Craig Panzirer and Meegan Panzirer Wesolko, were excluded from any inheritance, "for reasons which are known to them." (The reasons were not disclosed.) That omission led to the first legal skirmish regarding the Helmsley estate. Lawyers for the two disinherited grandchildren filed a notice in Manhattan Surrogate's Court announcing that they planned to challenge the will on the ground that Leona "was not of sound mind or memory and did not have the mental capacity to make a Will" in 2005.

Leona's executors—her surviving brother, Alvin Rosenthal; her grandsons David and Walter Panzirer; her lawyer Sandor Frankel; and John Codey, a family friend—decided to settle

*"You haven't a clue what I'm talking about, do you?"*

the dispute quickly. They agreed to amend the will so that Craig and Meegan also received bequests: four million dollars for Craig, and two million for Meegan. In return, Craig and Meegan agreed to an elaborate confidentiality provision, promising not to "directly or indirectly publish or cause to be published any diary, memoir, letter, story, photograph, interview, article, essay, account or depiction of any kind" concerning the dispute over the will. Likewise, they agreed that all of their "personal correspondence . . . records, tapes, papers and financial information of or relating to" Leona must be given to the estate's lawyers. (Consequently, neither Craig nor Meegan, nor their attorneys, would comment on the dispute.) Still, the conflict among the human beneficiaries of the will was easy to resolve compared with the legal matters relating to dogs.

The modern history of legal rights for animals begins with a chimpanzee named Washoe. "He was the first 'signing chimp,' the first chimpanzee who learned sign language to communicate with people," Victoria Bjorklund, the head of the exempt-organizations practice at the New York law firm of Simpson Thacher & Bartlett, said. "There came a time when he was going to be sent off to be used in medical testing, and there was a lot of distress about that possibility." So Bjorklund and others set up a trust (funded with

*"It's not enough that we succeed. Cats must also fail."*

the proceeds of a book about Washoe), and appointed a guardian to protect him and several other chimps like him. The problem was that New York law said that a guardian could be appointed for a "person with a disability." Was Washoe a "person" under New York law?

The lawyers at Simpson Thacher argued that "the mental, emotional, sociological, and biological characteristics" of Washoe and the other chimps "warrant their treatment as persons" entitled to representation. The lawyers submitted affidavits from such animal experts as Jane Goodall, who said that "chimpanzees are biochemically closer to humans than they are to any other of the great apes." According to the brief in the case, the chimps "are capable of rational thought, communication, and other higher cognitive functions," justifying their treatment as the legal equivalent of minors or disabled humans. In a 1997 decision, the surrogate of Nassau County agreed and appointed a guardian to administer the trust for the benefit of the chimps. "That trust was then respected by the State of Washington, where Washoe lived," Bjorklund said. "We think it was the first trust ever established for the benefit of specific nonhuman primates."

Jane Hoffman, a former associate at Simpson Thacher, had brought the Washoe case to the firm. "The idea was to create a right for a nonhuman animal to receive money—to push the envelope on the law, which at that point had only allowed trusts for the benefit of children or disabled adults," she said. In 1990, Hoffman and a group of other lawyers founded a new committee at the Association of the Bar of the City of New York, on "Legal Issues Pertaining to Animals." One of the first subjects that the committee's members took up was the issue of inheritance. In 1996, they helped change the law to make it easier for any animal—especially a pet—to become

the beneficiary of a trust. Many people wanted to make provisions for the care of their pets in their wills, but the law allowed no simple mechanism to do so. Frances Carlisle, a New York trusts-and-estates lawyer and a member of the committee, pushed the New York State Legislature to allow the creation of "pet trusts," which permit individuals to put aside money and instructions for their pets. New York approved the changes, and now thirty-eight states allow for the creation of such trusts. "We decided we didn't want people to have to leave the disposition of their pets to chance, or a sudden decision, after they died," Carlisle told me. "We want to give people peace of mind about their animals."

The legal movement, which largely focussed on pets, was, of course, symbiotically aligned with the broader animal-rights movement, which also grew in the 1990s. But the theme remained the same—to extend the rights of humans to animals. In a country where most people eat meat, many hunt, and most others give little thought to the legal rights of their pets, the complexities of such a change are considerable. Even pro-animal-rights scholars, like Peter Singer, a professor at Princeton, recognize the difficulties. As Singer said at a recent conference in New York City, "We're talking about beings as different as chimpanzees, pigs, chickens, fish, oysters, and others, and you must recognize those differences." For the moment, the goals of the movement are modest, and largely limited to domestic animals.

"What the law is doing is catching up with the idea that people don't consider their pets property, in the way a car or a chair is," Hoffman told me. "I am not pumping for my cats to be able to vote for McCain or Obama. I'm not saying they could visit me at the hospital, though that's probably a pretty good idea. The right category for pets is closer to children, who can't vote, and can't own property, but you can't inflict pain on them, either. The law is catching up with societal beliefs."

"Leona had never had a dog before she got Trouble," Elaine Silverstein, a co-founder of the Miami agency that created the "queen" advertisements for the Helmsley hotels, told me. "She treated her like a person, and took her everywhere. She would take that dog to bed with her every night." After Helmsley's release from prison, she returned for a time to her hotels' ads, but for one campaign she insisted that Silverstein feature Trouble instead. The ad showed the tiny white dog perched on a red velvet chair, and text that said, " 'Trouble,' the Helmsley's favorite four-legged guest," recommends that you call for reservations. "It didn't make much sense for a dog to endorse a hotel, but that's what Leona wanted," Silverstein said.

Still, Helmsley's relationship with dogs reflected some of the distemper of her dealings with humans. According to Silverstein, one of Helmsley's friends, seeing how much she loved Trouble, gave her another Maltese, who was named Double Trouble. "But Leona never liked that dog, so she got rid of it," Silverstein said. "That was usually Leona's solution. It was what she did with people."

For all Helmsley's love of Trouble, her will certainly made life complicated for the dog. She stipulated that Trouble, when her time came, join Leona, Harry, and Jay in the family mausoleum. (Leona also established a three-million-dollar trust for the "perpetual care and maintenance" of the mausoleum, directing that it be "acid washed or steam cleaned at least once a year.") According to Carlisle, however, a joint human-canine burial is not possible at Sleepy Hollow. "Under New York law, animals can't be buried in human cemeteries," she said. "Leona could possibly be buried in a pet cemetery with Trouble, but not the other way around. That was an error in the drafting of the will." (Trouble is still alive, so it's not clear where she will be buried.)

The twelve-million-dollar trust for Trouble also created problems. The will stated that custody of Trouble should go to Rosenthal, Leona's brother, or to her grandson David, and the trust agreement directed them to "provide for the care, welfare and comfort of Trouble at the highest standard." But neither man wanted the dog. After the will was made public, Trouble received death threats, which may have had something to do with their refusal. (Both men declined to comment.) So the trustees had to find the dog a home. Moreover, the bequest to Trouble was so self-evidently excessive for a single, aging dog that the trustees decided to take steps to reduce it.

As a guardian for Trouble, the trustees settled on Carl Lekic, who is the general manager of the Helmsley Sandcastle Hotel, in Sarasota, Florida. According to his affidavit in the case, Lekic had known Trouble since she was born, because Leona spent several months a year, late in life, at the hotel. "When I visited New York on business while Mrs. Helmsley was alive, I would also see Trouble and would pay attention to and play with her," Lekic said. The trustees agreed to pay him five thousand dollars a month to take care of Trouble. Lekic estimated annual security costs for the dog of a hundred thousand dollars, grooming costs of eight thousand dollars, food costs of twelve hundred dollars, and veterinary care of up to eighteen thousand dollars.

But how many years would Trouble likely live? To answer this question, the trustees sought an affidavit from Dr. E. F. Thomas, Jr., Trouble's veterinarian. Trouble was nine years old in early 2008 and had, according to Thomas, "several on-going medical problems," including hypothyroidism and compromised kidney function. In the light of her medical issues, and the patterns of Maltese generally, Thomas estimated that Trouble was likely to live only three to five more years. In all, then, Lekic and the trustees concluded, only two million dollars of the trust's principal would suffice to cover all of Trouble's needs. On April 30, 2008, Judge Renee Roth, the New York surrogate who is supervising the Helmsley will, approved the reduction of ten million dollars in the trust. (If there is any leftover money in Trouble's trust following her demise, it goes to the Helmsley charitable trust.)

The local tabloids responded to Roth's ruling with feigned sympathy for Trouble's loss of ten million dollars. But some in the legal world of pet trusts saw the surrogate's decision as a substantial victory for their cause "One of the greatest moments in my life was when the judge awarded two million in the Helmsley case," said Rachel Hirschfeld, a New York trusts-and-

estates lawyer and the operator of petriarch.com, a Web site for pet owners. "It's not the reduction that's important; it's that the judge said two million was appropriate. It's a landmark case, for a judge to be able to say that we have a case for that amount of money."

The amount of money for Trouble, while substantial, pales compared with the sums at issue in the Leona M. and Harry B. Helmsley Charitable Trust. According to the estimate submitted in court by the trustees, the proceeds are between three and eight billion dollars. In the final years of her life, Leona appears to have given considerable thought to the trust, and to have reordered her priorities in a dog-focussed way.

To make her intentions clear for the trust, she signed two mission statements, which have not previously been made public. On September 16, 2003, Leona signed a document that listed three goals for the planned expenditures. The money was to go first "to the provision of care for dogs." The second was more conventional: "the provision of medical and health care services for indi-

*"Westminster's over, Shep—it's all about possums now."*

gent people, with emphasis on providing care to children." A third category covered "such other charitable activities as the Trustee shall determine." About six months later, however, Helmsley changed her mind. On March 1, 2004, she signed a new mission statement that revoked the previous one, and made one significant change. She now omitted the second purpose—medical care for the indigent, especially children—and left only the purpose of caring for dogs and the catch-all third category.

What this means for how the trust will operate is far from clear. "A mission statement is really just guidance to the trustees," Victoria Bjorklund, of Simpson Thacher, said. "It's not binding on them. It would only be binding if it was in the will itself." Still, the mission statement should have an influence on how the trustees allocate the funds. "The fact that she took out the care of children means to me that she probably experienced a change in her priorities that she expressed that way," Bjorklund went on. "And there is a general-purposes clause that says the trustees can use the funds for anything that would be charitable. So they don't have to use the money only for the care of dogs, but she is certainly indicating that it's a priority." The trust is not yet operating or making grants, and people familiar with the work of the trustees say that they are still trying to figure out what to do.

The animal-rights movement in New York is, however, already gathering proposals for how to use the money. The most detailed ideas so far come from Jane Hoffman. In 2002, the former corporate lawyer founded the group now known as the Mayor's Alliance for NYC's Animals, a not-for-profit organization that works as a public-private partnership with more than a hundred and forty animal-rescue groups and shelters around the city. "We are committed to making New York 'no-kill,' one community at a time," she told me, using the movement's term for eliminating euthanasia as a means of population control for any kind of animal.

To run the operations of the alliance, Hoffman secured a $25.4-million grant over seven years from Maddie's Fund, the largest-endowed dog-and-cat-centered foundation in America, which was created in 1999 by the founder of PeopleSoft software, Dave Duffield, and his wife, Cheryl. The Duffields have endowed the foundation with more than three hundred million dollars and made grants of more than seventy-one million dollars. According to the fund's Web site, "The Foundation makes good on a promise the Duffields made to their beloved Miniature Schnauzer, Maddie, to give back to her kind in dollars that which Maddie gave to them in companionship and love."

Hoffman and other animal-rights supporters have been nursing a grudge for years against the Doris Duke Charitable Foundation. Duke, the tobacco heiress, died in 1993 and left much of her wealth to a foundation that now has assets of about two billion dollars. In her will, Duke spoke of her interest in the "prevention of cruelty to children or to animals" and in "promoting anti-vivisectionism." (Duke's pets included two camels and a leopard, as well as several dogs.) The Duke foundation has a program to combat child abuse, but it has never invested in an animal-welfare program. Claire Baralt, a communications officer for the foundation, points out that the will says that support of animal rights was optional, not mandatory. According to Hoffman, however, "Doris Duke is a good example of how a testator's intent has been thwarted. You know that person was extremely attached to her animals, but, at the end of the day, the trustees have made sure that very little has gone from that

PRICE $3.95

THE

NEW YORKER

MAR. 10, 2003

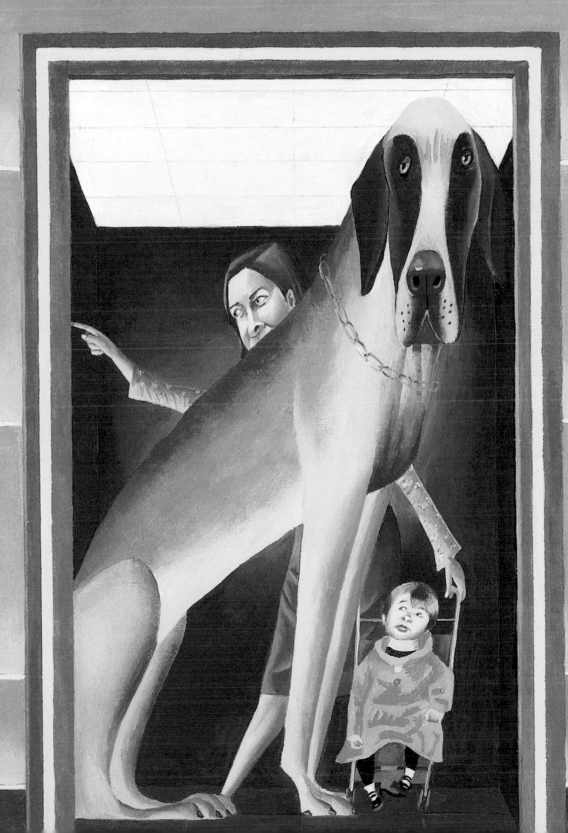

estate to animals. If you judge animal need against human need, human need is going to win most of the time, because we are human. We want to make sure the same mistakes are not made with Helmsley.

"The thing that I'm trying to get people to realize is this is not bling for dogs," Hoffman went on. "When you think about it, five to eight billion dollars isn't that much. Foundations are required to give out at least five percent of their assets every year, so we're talking about two hundred and fifty million to four hundred million dollars." This vast sum, which would dwarf the proceeds of Maddie's Fund, could finance a great deal of medical research on or about dogs, but most of the ideas so far involve establishing no-kill policies for strays. Thanks in part to the efforts of the members of Hoffman's alliance to foster adoptions and spaying and neutering, the percentage of animals killed in New York City shelters has dropped from 74 percent, in 2002, to 43 percent, in 2007. Hoffman would like to use the Helmsley money to buy more spay-neuter vans, at two hundred thousand dollars each, and windowed vans for adoption events, at a hundred and seventy thousand dollars apiece; and to establish a "special Leona Helmsley Memorial Veterinary Hospital for needy pets," at twenty million dollars a year, "providing medical treatment, inoculations, and training to help low-income families care for their dogs and create safer and more humane communities." Hoffman wants to take these ideas nationwide. "A Leona Helmsley Trust dedicated to helping make the U.S. 'no kill' could actually achieve its goal in a remarkably short amount of time," she said.

Hoffman's enthusiasm obscures the fundamental moral question about how Helmsley hoped to dispose of her fortune. The way Leona

altered her mission statement places the issue in especially stark terms. Version one proposed helping dogs and ailing poor children; version two—the final version—cut out the children and gave everything to the dogs. Is there any justification for such a calculation? Or does Helmsley's change, along with the broader vogue for pet bequests, reflect a decadent moment in our history?

"In the nineteenth century, when the robber barons started modern American philanthropy, there were no tax deductions, no incentives from the government to give, just the growing idea that with wealth comes social and moral obligation," Vartan Gregorian, the president of the Carnegie Corporation and a veteran of the New York philanthropic scene, said. "They could spend their money any way they wanted, but, once we started giving tax deductions, which amounted to a publicly approved subsidy, you had to prove that the money was going for a philanthropic purpose, but that is so broad that you can give to almost anything.

"When you see a gift like Leona's, it's individualism carried to iconography," Gregorian went on. "The whole idea that individuals can do whatever they want is part of the American psyche. It's left to individual decision-making. That you can give to this sector of society, which is animals, as opposed to the other sector, which is human beings, tells you something about her and about the times in which we live."

The specific nature of Leona's gift appears consistent with the pervasive misanthropy of her life and her will. This was a woman, after all, who at her trial was quoted as saying about a contractor who was owed thirteen thousand dollars for installing a custom-made barbecue pit at the Helmsley estate and wanted to be paid because he had six children, "Why doesn't he keep his pants on? He wouldn't have so many problems." (In his opening statement at the trial, her defense attorney said, "I don't believe Mrs. Helmsley is charged in the indictment with being a tough bitch.") In the light of her vast wealth, the bequests to her relatives were grudging, small, and controlling, particularly the insistence that two of Jay Panzirer's children visit his grave each year. As in life, Leona's disdain for others contrasted with her nearly fetishistic obsession with her husband. (While Harry was alive, she held an annual ball to celebrate his birthday, known as the "I'm Just Wild About Harry" party.) The transfer of this kind of obsessive affection from Harry to Trouble seems apparent. The twelve-million-dollar trust for the dog is bigger than any other single bequest in the will. On the whole, the will reflects contempt for humanity as much as love of dogs.

Under the law, certainly, it was Helmsley's right to divvy up her money any way she wanted. And she is not the first wealthy person to use a will to show a preference for dogs over humans. Rumors abound about major bequests to pets, although facts are difficult to pin down. Natalie Schafer, the actress who played Lovey, the millionaire's wife, on *Gilligan's Island,* is said to have left her estate for the care of her dog. ("It is still getting residuals," Rachel Hirschfeld said.) Toby Rimes, a New York dog, is said to have inherited about eighty million dollars, and Kalu, a pet chimpanzee in Australia, may have received a bequest of a hundred and nine million dollars. (A widely reported story that a German dog named Gunther IV inherited more than a hundred million dollars appears to be a hoax.)

Is it right to give so much money to a dog—or to dogs generally? And what is the limit of such dispensations to pets? Will there come a time when dogs can sue for a new guardian—or to avoid being put to sleep? One philosopher draws a distinction between the needs of Trouble and those of dogs as a whole. Helmsley "did a disservice to the people in the dog world and to dogs generally by leaving such an enormous amount of money for her own dog," Jeff McMahan, who teaches philosophy at Rutgers University, said. "To give even two million dollars to a single little dog is like setting the money on fire in front of a group of poor people. To bestow that amount of money is contemptuous of the poor, and that may be one reason she did it.

"But to give such a large sum of money to dogs generally is not frivolous," McMahan went on. "I think it shows some misplaced priorities, but many bequests do. In a world where there is starvation and poverty, you can say that it's wrong to give money to universities, or museums, or, worst of all, to divide it up for your children and heirs who are already rich. Welfare for dogs is better than more pampering of the rich. It may indicate misplaced moral priorities, but it's not frivolous or silly. It's disgraced by the context, but the two bequests should be separately evaluated."

Throughout her life, Leona Helmsley demonstrated not just a lack of affection for her fellow-humans but an absence of understanding as well. The irony is that, for all that her will purports to show her love for Trouble, Leona didn't seem to understand dogs very well, either. "What is funny about giving all this money to one dog is that it doesn't deal with the fact that the dog is going to be sad that Leona died," Elizabeth Harman, who teaches philosophy at Princeton, said. "What would make this dog happy is for a loving family to take it in. The dog doesn't want the money. The money will just make everyone who deals with the dog strange."

| 2008 |

# SMALL-TOWN LIFE

### GEORGE W. S. TROW

There has been a dog emporium, named Canine Styles, on the west side of Lexington Avenue between Sixty-third Street and Sixty-fourth Street since 1959. We know this for a fact. Some people used to call it Ursula's, but now everyone calls it Canine Styles. A dog emporium is not a pet shop. You don't buy *dogs* at Canine Styles—you buy *things* for dogs. And a few things for cats. And you pay a fairly high price to have your dog groomed and his hair cut there. Continuities and threads of tradition exist at Canine Styles. The cutting of your dog's hair, for instance, will be undertaken by the head dog groomer, Edith Hoeltz, who has been at it on this block, at this exact spot on Lexington, for thirty years. Mrs. Hoeltz is tallish and has a strong German accent. She has short blond hair and bangs. We saw her the other day in a social atmosphere, dogless, chatting with people, acting like a friendly person. Whenever we'd seen her before, she had been in her professional posture: with scissors, grooming a dog. When Mrs. Hoeltz grooms a dog, she leans over it, and her expression is serious, devoted, and *eternal*. Socially, standing upright and chatting, Mrs. Hoeltz has the attractive in-transit look that human beings have at social gatherings where they feel at home. When Mrs. Hoeltz is grooming a dog, she seems to be saying to herself "Is now and ever shall be." Something like that.

Lexington Avenue looks a little eternal here, a little like a Christmas treat. Around Canine Styles on the west side of Lexington are Albert & Sons Prime Meats & Poultry, Eastside Shoe Service, Plaza Watch & Jewelry, DiPierre Corsetry, and Phone Boutique. There are homeless people on the street, and, of course, Phone Boutique, but there's not much we can't deal with. Of all ideas, New York as small town is the strangest, perhaps, but it is a sustainable one right here on Lexington.

The other day, we were walking on Lexington and we ran into Mark Drendel, who is the proprietor of Canine Styles. Mr. Drendel was walking determinedly. Mr.

Drendel parts his hair in the middle. He was wearing a brown plaid sports jacket. He was born in 1959, the year Ursula opened her shop.

"Who was Ursula?" we asked.

"Ursula Lehnhardt."

"When did you buy Canine Styles?"

"I bought it eighteen months ago."

"How did you get the idea of buying a dog store?"

"I passed somebody, this guy, on Columbus, walking a dog, and I asked where the dog was groomed, and he said Ursula's.

"You go from nothing to running the place?"

"That's right."

To create a sense of the small town in New York, we thought, takes this kind of will to power.

Mr. Drendel looked up at the sky and said, "There's no greater feeling in the whole world than to be dressed in a full set of tails and have a lady on your arm and you are leading her onto the dance floor," he said. "She is dressed in the most beautiful gown, completely jewelled. You take her out on the

So I took my dog there, and it turned out to be a major career change for me. I knew I wanted to do something dog-related. They needed sales help in the front of the store, and I got the job. In two, three weeks, I knew I wanted to own the store. I knew it would be a great place and I could change my life there. That was the beginning of March. On June 27th, I closed the deal—signed the papers and bought the store. One minute, I was new sales help, and the next minute I owned the store."

We learned that Mr. Drendel grew up in Memphis. In 1976, he began to take classes at the Ambassador Dance School in Memphis. He became obsessed with ballroom dancing and ballroom-dancing competitions. He ended up as the dance director of the school. "That's what I tend to do everywhere," he said.

floor and spin her and watch her twirl around, curtsy to the audience, and you take her into dance position and begin to do the most beautiful foxtrot or waltz. It's two or three minutes of the most incredible moments of your life. It's my first love, although I don't do it anymore."

"When did you first visit New York?"

"When I was eighteen."

"What did you do after ballroom dancing?"

"I owned a place called the Car Salon, in Austin, Texas. People came to get their cars washed, and I gave them complimentary cocktails. Then the bottom fell out of the economy in Texas, so I came to New York."

As we left Mr. Drendel, we were thinking, Well, a part of the bottom may have fallen out of the economy in New York, too.

But we passed by Canine Styles later in the day and we saw a party—a Christmas party. It was all a matter of women and their dogs. We saw papillons, English bulldogs, Shih Tzus, bichons frises, Yorkshire terriers, Maltese (eleven of them), French poodles, a Jack Russell terrier, a Gordon setter (the largest dog at the party), a wire-haired fox terrier, a schnauzer, a Norwich terrier, a West Highland white terrier, a cocker spaniel. People were dressed up. It looked as if the shop had been dressed up. Someone was taking *pictures*. Flashbulbs went off. We moved closer. Flashbulbs were going off in what is normally the grooming area. "Alice. Look, Alice. Smile. Good girl, Alice," a woman was saying. We saw Edith Hoeltz smiling and talking. We continued our walk down Lexington Avenue. Plaza Watch & Jewelry. Phone Boutique. Di-Pierre Corsetry. The image of the flashbulbs going off in the grooming area of Canine Styles stayed with us. And the idea of Mrs. Hoeltz grooming dogs on that spot for thirty years straight stayed with us, and Mr. Drendel coming into her life and her coming into his. We thought that if New York is to work as a community it will take all that—flashbulbs, a party, Mrs. Hoeltz's dedication, and Mr. Drendel's magical ability to walk right in and take over. Then we thought about Mr. Drendel and his various careers, and realized that what we were seeing on Lexington Avenue was the spirit of competitive ballroom dancing.

| 1991 |

# TALLYHO!

## E. J. KAHN, JR.

Among the things I do not ordinarily do on wintry Sunday afternoons is to take long walks. The other weekend I broke this tradition rather violently by taking a walk fourteen miles long with a group of Long Islanders who spend their Sunday afternoons following an over-conscientious pack of beagles. We covered this distance, a little more than half the length of a marathon race, over an area replete with obstacles, and for several days afterward I had difficulty walking at all, even on a Persian rug.

I was introduced to beagling by an agile friend of mine who is known in beagling circles as Brownie. She is a member of the Buckram Beagles, an organization which has kennels at Brookville, Long Island, containing thirty hunting beagles and, at the moment, eighteen puppies, who are being trained to devote most of the rest of their lives to the demolition of jack rabbits. There are twenty-six packs of beagles in this country, and four of them, including the Buckram Beagles, are run on a joint-ownership basis. It costs about $4,500 a year to maintain the Buckram pack, and the organization's forty members, most of whom are Long Islanders, pay annual dues of $50 each. Additional income is provided by eighty-five "subscribing" members, who are not permitted to vote at meetings but, for $15 apiece or $30 a family, are entitled to run their legs off every Wednesday and Sunday afternoon from October 1st to April 1st. Beagling is too strenuous a sport to be carried on under a hot summer sun, and even on cool August and September days it might inflict serious damage on crops growing in fields that happen to lie in its path. On Wednesdays, only a handful of women, children, and gentlemen of leisure go beagling; on Sundays, there is usually a group of from fifty to a hundred, ranging in age from children of eleven to venerable sportsmen and women whose stamina is equal to that of any rabbit. The Buckram group have been doing this sort of thing since 1934 and never miss a Sunday, being as determined to fulfill their schedules as a college football team. To avoid monotony, these beaglers change their hunting grounds almost every Sunday. In seven years they have run over most of the big Long Island estates, some of them belonging to members and some to friends. Once, last winter, desiring a change, they persuaded T.W.A. to lend them a couple of large air-

## ROUNDABOUT

Eight-year-old girl was showing some of her school artwork to a family friend, who complimented her on her excellent rendition of a dog. "I really can't draw a dog," she said, "so when I have to have a dog, I just draw a horse, and it always looks like a dog."

| 1952 |

planes and flew from LaGuardia Field to Camden, New Jersey, for an afternoon's outing, ferrying the beagles in a forward compartment. The trip over was rough and many of the members, on alighting, were green; the hounds appeared to enjoy the excursion and frisked around the New Jersey countryside just as if it had been Old Westbury.

Brownie began some time back to urge me to go beagling with her, pointing out that there is really nothing like fresh air. She is as avid a beagler as you could ask for; last winter, while recovering from a broken foot, she hobbled out every Sunday and managed somehow to participate in the chase. She is not bothered by the sight of a lot of dogs killing a rabbit, and once told me cheer-

fully that after the beagles have eaten their prey, which they do with gusto, they look "like the grooms in *Macbeth*." Brownie is a literary girl and, when not beagling, writes books for children in which there are quite a few sentimental references to rabbits, which she is apt to describe as "soft, cuddly bunnies." On her desk she keeps a pad, or hind foot, of a jack rabbit; the foot has been mounted by a taxidermist on a small wooden plaque. The beagles of which she is part owner have eaten rabbits in rose gardens, hothouses, swimming pools, and tennis courts, and they eat so thoroughly that pads, or masks (heads), can be salvaged only if one of the leaders of the hunt grabs the rabbit away from the hounds. Beaglers are as fond of masks and pads as other hunters are of moose heads. One member of the Buckram group, an acquisitive girl who went to England two years ago to romp with various beagle packs, returned with a dozen masks, which she has scattered around her house like ashtrays.

Before going beagling, I decided to acquaint myself slightly with some of the terms of the sport and borrowed a book from Brownie entitled *The Art of Beagling*, by J. Otho Paget, an Englishman. I found out, first of all, that it is improper to refer to a beagle in action as a dog; whatever the sex, a beagle is a hound. To confuse things further, all jack rabbits—synonymous with hares—are known as "she." The followers of the hounds are called the field. The men who control the hunt are the Master, the whips, and the huntsman. The Buckram Beagles have two Masters, who have dictatorial authority over both hounds and field. The whips keep the pack from wandering off irrelevantly during hunts and keep the field from getting too close to the hounds. When the field is ordered to halt during a run, the pause is known as a check. The huntsman, customarily a professional, is on more intimate terms with the pack than anyone else; he feeds them, grooms them, nurses them, and can recognize them all. According to Paget, the choice of a competent huntsman is as difficult to make as the choice of a competent wife; according to one member of the Buckram Beagles I queried on this subject, Paget is guilty of understatement. "Huntsmen are created by

*"I find that incessant barking eases the pain."*

God," he said. When a beagle uses his vocal chords, I learned from the book, he does not bark; he gives tongue, or he opens. A statement like "Chieftain didn't hark to Destiny when he opened" makes perfect sense to an experienced beagler; it means simply that a hound named Destiny cried out upon scenting a rabbit, and that another hound named Chieftain neglected to help Destiny track down the prey. A beagle, also, never wags his tail; he feathers his stern.

On a recent Sunday, I met Brownie around noon and we had a hunt breakfast at Schrafft's. I brought along another friend of Brownie's named Woodward—who had never beagled before, either—on the theory that if I dropped far behind the field, he would probably be there to keep me company. It was a cold, cloudy day, and although it looked as if the weather might improve, I remembered a warning I had read in Paget's book: "Never mind how fine the morning, always be prepared for the worst." Woodward and I were both prepared; we each had two sweaters on and two pairs of the heaviest woollen socks we

could find. Brownie was wearing a baggy corduroy outfit and knee-high gaiters, which, she explained to us, were useful when you encountered thorns or brambles. After breakfast we drove out to Brookville, where the field had been instructed to assemble at the gate of an estate belonging to Guy Cary, a Long Island sportsman but a non-beagler. It took us an hour to get there and by the time we arrived most of the field had gathered. There were around seventy-five beaglers, dressed in old, functional clothes: tweedy trousers and skirts, knickerbockers, sweaters and leather jackets, heavy stockings, riding breeches, and the like. A few of the older people carried canes. Most of the crowd were the kind you see at horse shows. Brownie introduced Woodward and me to the Co-Masters of the hunt, Morgan Wing, Jr., a young banker, and John C. Baker, Jr., a young insurance adjuster. Both of them were wearing dark-green hunting coats, stocks, white corduroy trousers, and black sneakers. Wing had on a black velvet cap with a ribbon at its back tied in a bowknot; Baker had on an ordinary checked cap. There were five other men in similar livery who, Brownie told me, were

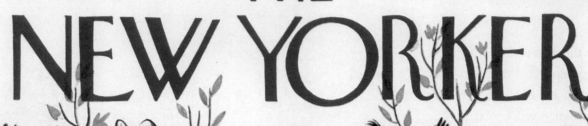

the huntsman and the whips. All five carried whips, and the huntsman, the only professional among them, also carried a small-size hunting horn.

A couple of minutes after we got to the gate, a station wagon with a screened rear compartment and with "Buckram Beagles" neatly lettered on one door drew up. When its back was opened twenty-odd dogs spilled out and scrambled about excitedly. They had floppy ears and their color was a mixture of black, brown, and white. Brownie told me they were fourteen-and-a-quarter-inch beagles. The height of a beagle is the distance from his shoulder to the ground, and fourteen and a quarter inches is considered desirable because taller hounds with longer legs might run too fast for the average field. While we were discussing the relative speeds of hounds and men (hounds are faster), the huntsman blew a sharp note on his horn and, with the hounds clustered at his heels, started to walk rapidly down a lane leading out of Mr. Cary's estate. The pack went ahead across a highway, through somebody's back yard, and, sniffing industriously, out onto a large, rolling meadow which had a number of jumping fences on it. A girl named Dot, to whom we had been introduced at the gate, told me that the meadow and the jumps belonged to Ambrose Clark and that the Meadow Brook Cup Race was held there every year. Dot, a bare-kneed outdoors girl, said, while we ambled along, that she knew more about fox-hunting than beagling. Horses are her favorite animals, and she said that over the weekend she had already shod a couple of them. "What else did you do?" asked Brownie. "Well, I mended a few wagons," said Dot. We walked on down a hill and, at the foot of it, ran up against a clump of barberry bushes. Some of the field detoured around them, but Brownie, Dot, Woodward, and I pushed through, all of us emerging

unscathed except Dot, who came out with both knees scratched and bloody. She seemed totally unconcerned about this and refused to accept Woodward's offer of a handkerchief as a bandage. "It's just a healthy glow," she said. After going up a hill, we started across some ploughed land that was muddy and slippery. Mr. Baker asked us to spread out over it. "A hare was seen here yesterday!" he shouted. While spreading, I chatted briefly with William Rochester, one of the whips, who was trying to compute the day's attendance for the group's records and kept looking back to see if anyone had been permanently caught in the barberry bushes. When I left him a moment later, Brownie whispered to me in awed tones, "He is the only man who can crack a whip while he's running."

We went along for an hour, walking, jogging, and climbing over or through fences, while the hounds moped around several yards ahead of us without getting on the trail of a hare or anything else. Brownie told me that this was unusual. On most days the hounds manage fairly quickly to pick up the scent of at least a cottontail, which beaglers regard as unworthy of their attention, except on Wednesdays. There are too few hares on Long Island to satisfy the Buckram Beagles; there are so few, in fact, that the field thinks it can recognize a couple it has chased and failed to catch. A couple of months ago the pack caught up with one that its followers had named Flora, after pursuing her for many cold afternoons. The beaglers had grown fond of her and used to cry "Go it, Flora!" in the heat of a chase. They were all sorry to see Flora killed. "Morgan Wing just cried," Brownie told me.

After covering the first four or five miles, the field was pretty well distributed over the countryside, with five or six hundred yards separating the hounds from the last stragglers. Most of the beaglers travelled in small groups and there were quite a few striding along all by themselves. Brownie explained that one of the advantages of the sport is that if you are in a mood for solitude and don't want to talk to anybody, you don't have to. The majority of beaglers are not that unsocial; they talk to each other like anyone else. There was an extreme instance of sociability not long ago when a male whip and a lady whip, after admiring each other's green coats for several Sundays, got married. The conversations I overheard as we walked along were unromantic. They concerned horses, regiments, gardens, Long Island social activities, drinking, and the war. Two girls who had evidently been down South were chatting about beagling. "I had a *marvellous* time in Virginia," said one. "I hunted with a different pack every day." "It was simply *divine* in Maryland," said the other. "We started to hunt at nine and didn't finish till four in the afternoon."

Brownie told me that the weather was satisfactory for hunting, although our lack of success up to that point didn't indicate it. The ground was damp and the air was cold, a combination that would have produced a rich, clinging scent had there been any hares around. Beagles are supposed to hunt only with their noses; it is regarded as poor form for them to lift their heads at all, and they have been known to lose track of a rabbit when it was in plain sight of the whole field. I was beginning to think we would never meet up with a rabbit when the hounds suddenly gave tongue and lit out for a patch of woods, with the huntsman, the Masters, the whips, and the field scrambling after them. We stopped talking and ran. Somebody gasped out, without changing his stride, that a jack had been viewed on a knoll. We plunged into the woods, where the huntsman was yelling to a hound who had strayed from the pack on some investigation of his own, "Come on, come, come away, come, brave boy!" As we rushed down a path, stumbling over roots of trees, we passed a horseman, who seemed startled and embarrassed by the unexpected traffic. As soon as the hounds had crossed his trail, they began to dash around in aimless circles and Mr. Wing ordered us to check. He said that the horse's scent had undoubtedly crossed the jack's. Mr. Baker went on a short distance by himself, bending over and sniffing intently at the ground, like a beagle. A small boy grabbed a lady by the hand and asked, "Mother, have we lost the bait?" His mother looked pained.

After scouting around for a while, the Masters concluded that they *had* lost the bait and prepared gloomily to call it an uneventful day. It was after five and the sky was beginning to darken. We turned back dejectedly and were recrossing Ambrose Clark's meadow when a large rabbit which had been squatting there leaped up and raced down a slope. Half a dozen people screamed "Tallyho!"—which was precisely the word to scream—and stood at attention, with their arms, in proper beagling fashion, stiffly outstretched toward the spot where the jack had first been seen. Woodward, who wanted to be helpful but didn't know the correct manner of expression, shouted, "There goes a rabbit!," and a few people glared at him.

The huntsman blew hard into his horn and the hounds milled around him, feathering their sterns. It took them a few moments to pick up the scent, and then they opened loudly and rushed off in the direction the rabbit had taken. When they got to the bottom of the slope, they scurried, to our amazement, into another patch of woods. We had clearly seen the rabbit head in exactly the opposite direction. The whips, who were as surprised as anyone else, summoned the hounds

from the woods by whipping at their heels and calling their names and practically pushed them back on the rabbit's course. "This is more like steering a pack of dogs after a rabbit than being led by the dogs," said Woodward.

The hounds, having retrieved the scent, dashed up a hill and into still another wood. We went right in after them, with a couple of the green-coated men shouting "Hoo!" and "Hoy!" and "Cooee!" and others cautioning us not to get too close. Rabbits frequently run in circles and if the field gets too close are apt to turn and run right through somebody's legs, the whole pack hurtling along behind. I knew from Paget's book that human scent is strong enough to obscure rabbit scent, and I had been told by Brownie that any humans who inadvertently got into the middle of the chase were supposed to stand absolutely still, or, in beagle parlance, to freeze, since scent increases with motion. We froze two or three times in the woods while we watched the rabbit swerve back and forth through the trees, with the hounds sometimes only ten or fifteen feet behind her. When the rabbit resumed running in a fairly straight line, we resumed running too. Now and then the rabbit would obligingly go along a narrow path through the brush, which made it easier for us, but some of the beaglers, who felt that single-file progress was too slow, made their own paths, pushing along through the underbrush with one arm held protectingly in front of their faces. (Dot, the girl with the scratched knees, had a solution of her own for making rapid trips through narrow channels. Whenever she thought she was being held up unduly by the people in front of her, she would shout commandingly, "Hold hard! 'Ware hounds!" At that everybody else would freeze and she would blithely slip past, as if she had official business up ahead.) It seemed unlikely that the rabbit would escape, since there were no disturbing horse scents around, but she was saved by a cottontail who crossed her scent and momentarily confused the hounds, most of whom started off after the cottontail. The huntsman blew his horn desperately. "Hold till the hounds get on again!" a whip shouted, and we froze.

At six-thirty, when the hounds were still trying to get back on, the whips and Masters conferred and decided it was time to quit, although Mr. Baker said hopefully, "If we wait half an hour, we'll have a moon." It was completely dark then, and there was no trace of a moon. Mr. Wing finally announced formally that we would call it a day. "It's getting late and we have a long way to go," he said. "How long?" somebody asked. "Three miles," said Mr. Wing. We left the whips, who were calling the hounds together, and with Mr. Wing leading the way we started to walk back to our cars. Brownie, who was examining a two-inch gash on one knee, said that we had already covered eleven miles and asked me how my legs felt. They felt like lead. Our progress was slow and silent, except when one girl got stuck to a thorny bush and said stoically to her escort, "Yank me loose. Just yank." He pulled; she came loose, rubbed her leg, and limped on. A quarter of a mile from our starting point, a car with a tattered Willkie sticker on its rear window drove up a back road out of the darkness and offered us a lift. Ten of us got in and on it. "I never saw you look better," said Brownie to Woodward as she collapsed on the rear seat. "I never felt worse," said Woodward. I said nothing.

| 1941 |

# SHOW DOG

## SUSAN ORLEAN

f I were a bitch, I'd be in love with Biff Truesdale. Biff is perfect. He's friendly, good-looking, rich, famous, and in excellent physical condition. He almost never drools. He's not afraid of commitment. He wants children—actually, he already has children and wants a lot more. He works hard and is a consummate professional, but he also knows how to have fun.

What Biff likes most is food and sex. This makes him sound boorish, which he is not—he's just elemental. Food he likes even better than sex. His favorite things to eat are cookies, mints, and hotel soap, but he will eat just about anything. Richard Krieger, a friend of Biff's who occasionally drives him to appointments, said not long ago, "When we're driving on I-95, we'll usually pull over at McDonald's. Even if Biff is napping, he always wakes up when we're getting close. I get him a few plain hamburgers with buns—no ketchup, no mustard, and no pickles. He loves hamburgers. I don't get him his own French fries, but if I get myself fries I always flip a few for him into the back."

If you're ever around Biff while you're eating something he wants to taste—cold roast beef, a Wheatables cracker, chocolate, pasta, aspirin, whatever—he will stare at you across the pleated bridge of his nose and let his eyes sag and his lips tremble and allow a little bead of drool to percolate at the edge of his mouth until you feel so crummy that you give him some. This routine puts the people who know him in a quandary, because Biff has to watch his weight. Usually, he is as skinny as

Kate Moss, but he can put on three pounds in an instant. The holidays can be tough. He takes time off at Christmas and spends it at home, in Attleboro, Massachusetts, where there's a lot of food around and no pressure and no schedule and it's easy to eat all day. The extra weight goes to his neck. Luckily, Biff likes working out. He runs for fifteen or twenty minutes twice a day, either outside or on his Jog-Master. When he's feeling heavy, he runs longer, and skips snacks, until he's back down to his ideal weight of seventy-five pounds.

Biff is a boxer. He is a show dog—he performs under the name Champion Hi-Tech's Arbitrage—and so looking good is not mere vanity; it's business. A show dog's career is short, and judges are unforgiving. Each breed is judged by an explicit standard for appearance and temperament, and then there's the incalculable element of charisma in the ring. When a show dog is fat or lazy or sullen, he doesn't win; when he doesn't win, he doesn't enjoy the ancillary benefits of being a winner, like appearing as the celebrity spokesmodel on packages of Pedigree Mealtime with Lamb and Rice, which Biff will be doing soon, or picking the best-looking bitches and charging them six hundred dollars or so for his sexual favors, which Biff does three or four times a month. Another ancillary benefit of being a winner is that almost every single weekend of the year, as he travels to shows around the country, he gets to hear people applaud for him and yell his name and tell him what a good boy he is, which is something he seems to enjoy at least as much as eating a bar of soap.

Pretty soon, Biff won't have to be so vigilant about his diet. After he appears at the Westminster Kennel Club's show, this week, he will retire from active show life and work full time as a stud. It's a good moment for him to retire. Last year, he won more shows than any other boxer, and also more than any other dog in the purebred category known as Working Dogs, which also includes Akitas, Alaskan malamutes, Bernese mountain dogs, bullmastiffs, Doberman pinschers, giant schnauzers, Great Danes, Great Pyrenees, komondors, kuvaszok, mastiffs, Newfoundlands, Portuguese water dogs, Rottweilers, St. Bernards, Samoyeds, Siberian huskies, and standard schnauzers. Boxers were named for their habit of standing on their hind legs and punching with their front paws when they fight. They were originally bred to be chaperons—to look forbidding while being pleasant to spend time with. Except for show dogs like Biff, most boxers lead a life of relative leisure. Last year at Westminster, Biff was named Best Boxer and Best Working Dog, and he was a serious contender for Best in Show, the highest honor any show dog can hope for. He is a contender to win his breed and group again this year, and is a serious contender once again for Best in Show, although the odds are against him, because this year's judge is known as a poodle person.

Biff is four years old. He's in his prime. He could stay on the circuit for a few more years, but by stepping aside now he is making room for his sons Trent and Rex, who are just getting into the business, and he's leaving while he's still on top. He'll also spend less time in airplanes, which is the one part of show life he doesn't like, and more time with his owners, William and Tina Truesdale, who might be persuaded to waive his snacking rules.

Biff has a short, tight coat of fox-colored fur, white feet and ankles, and a patch of white on his chest roughly the shape of Maine. His muscles are plainly sketched under his skin, but he isn't bulgy. His face is turned up and pushed in, and has a

*"I can't sleep."*

dark mask, spongy lips, a wishbone-shaped white blaze, and the earnest and slightly careworn expression of a small-town mayor. Someone once told me that he thought Biff looked a little bit like President Clinton. Biff's face is his fortune. There are plenty of people who like boxers with bigger bones and a stockier body and taller shoulders —boxers who look less like marathon runners and more like weight-lifters—but almost everyone agrees that Biff has a nearly perfect head.

"Biff's head is his father's," William Truesdale, a veterinarian, explained to me one day. We were in the Truesdales' living room in Attleboro, which overlooks acres of hilly fenced-in fields. Their house is a big, sunny ranch with a stylish pastel kitchen and boxerabilia on every wall. The Truesdales don't have children, but at any given moment they share their quarters with at least a half-dozen dogs. If you watch a lot of dog-food commercials, you may have seen William—he's the young, handsome, dark-haired veterinarian declaring his enthusiasm for Pedigree Mealtime while his boxers gallop around.

"Biff has a masculine but elegant head," Wil-

liam went on. "It's not too wet around the muzzle. It's just about ideal. Of course, his forte is right here." He pointed to Biff's withers, and explained that Biff's shoulder-humerus articulation was optimally angled, and bracketed his superb brisket and forelegs, or something like that. While William was talking, Biff climbed onto the couch and sat on top of Brian, his companion, who was hiding under a pillow. Brian is an English toy Prince Charles spaniel who is about the size of a teakettle and has the composure of a hummingbird. As a young competitor, he once bit a judge—a mistake Tina Truesdale says he made because at the time he had been going through a little mind problem about being touched. Brian, whose show name is Champion Cragmor's Hi-Tech Man, will soon go back on the circuit, but now he mostly serves as Biff's regular escort. When Biff sat on him, he started to quiver. Biff batted at him with his front leg. Brian gave him an adoring look.

"Biff's body is from his mother," Tina was saying. "She had a lot of substance."

"She was even a little extreme for a bitch," William said. "She was rather buxom. I would call her zaftig."

"Biff's father needed that, though," Tina said. "His name was Tailo, and he was fabulous. Tailo had a very beautiful head, but he was a bit fine, I think. A bit slender."

"Even a little feminine," William said, with feeling. "Actually, he would have been a really awesome bitch."

The first time I met Biff, he sniffed my pants, stood up on his hind legs and stared into my face, and then trotted off to the kitchen, where someone was cooking macaroni. We were in Westbury, Long Island, where Biff lives with Kimberly Pastella, a twenty-nine-year-old professional handler, when he's working. Last year, Kim and Biff went to at least one show every weekend. If they drove, they took Kim's van. If they flew, she went coach and he went cargo. They always shared a hotel room.

While Kim was telling me all this, I could hear Biff rummaging around in the kitchen. "Biffers!" Kim called out. Biff jogged back into the room with a phony look of surprise on his face. His tail was ticking back and forth. It is cropped so that it is about the size and shape of a half-smoked stogie. Kim said that there was a bitch downstairs who had been sent from Pennsylvania to be bred to one of Kim's other clients, and that Biff could smell her and was a little out of sorts. "Let's go," she said to him. "Biff, let's go jog." We went into the garage, where a treadmill was set up with Biff's collar suspended from a metal arm. Biff hopped on and held his head out so that Kim could buckle his collar. As soon as she leaned toward the power switch, he started to jog. His nails clicked a light tattoo on the rubber belt.

Except for a son of his named Biffle, Biff gets along with everybody. Matt Stander, one of the founders of *Dog News,* said recently, "Biff is just

*"First, they do an on-line search."*

very, very personable. He has a je ne sais quoi that's really special. He gives of himself all the time." One afternoon, the Truesdales were telling me about the psychology that went into making Biff who he is. "Boxers are real communicators," William was saying. "We had to really take that into consideration in his upbringing. He seems tough, but there's a fragile ego inside there. The profound reaction and hurt when you would raise your voice at him was really something."

"I *made* him," Tina said. "I made Biff who he is. He had an overbearing personality when he was small, but I consider that a prerequisite for a great performer. He had such an *attitude!* He was like this miniature *man!*" She shimmied her shoulders back and forth and thrust out her chin. She is a dainty, chic woman with wide-set eyes and the neck of a ballerina. She grew up on a farm in Costa Rica, where dogs were considered just another form of livestock. In 1987, William got her a Rottweiler for a watchdog, and a boxer, because he had always loved boxers, and Tina decided to dabble with them in shows. Now she makes a monogrammed Christmas stocking for each animal in their house, and she watches the tape of Biff winning at Westminster approximately once a week. "Right from the beginning, I made Biff think he was the most fabulous dog in the world," Tina said.

"He doesn't take after me very much," William said. "I'm more of a golden retriever."

"Oh, he has my nature," Tina said. "I'm very strong-willed. I'm brassy. And Biff is an egotistical, self-centered, selfish person. He thinks he's very important and special, and he doesn't like to share."

Biff is priceless. If you beg the Truesdales to name a figure, they might say that Biff is worth around a hundred thousand dollars, but they will also point out that a Japanese dog fancier recently handed Tina a blank check for Biff. (She immediately threw it away.) That check notwithstanding, campaigning a show dog is a money-losing proposition for the owner. A good handler gets three or four hundred dollars a day, plus travel expenses, to show a dog, and any dog aiming for the top will have to be on the road at least a hundred days a year. A dog photographer charges hundreds of dollars for a portrait, and a portrait is something that every serious owner commissions, and then runs as a full-page ad in several dog-show magazines. Advertising a show dog is standard procedure if you want your dog or your presence on the show circuit to get well known. There are also such ongoing show-dog expenses as entry fees, hair-care products, food, health care, and toys. Biff's stud fee is six hundred dollars. Now that he will not be at shows, he can be bred several times a month. Breeding him would have been a good way for him to make money in the past, except that whenever the Truesdales were enthusiastic about a mating they bartered Biff's service for the pick of the litter. As a result, they now have more Biff puppies than Biff earnings. "We're doing this for posterity," Tina says. "We're doing it for the good of all boxers. You simply can't think about the cost."

On a recent Sunday, I went to watch Biff work at one of the last shows he would attend before his retirement. The show was sponsored by the Lehigh Valley Kennel Club and was held in a big, windy field house on the campus of Lehigh University, in Bethlehem, Pennsylvania. The parking lot was filled with motor homes pasted with life-size decals of dogs. On my way to the field house, I passed someone walking an Afghan hound wearing a snood, and someone else wiping down a Saluki with a Flintstones beach towel. Biff was napping in his crate—

a fancy-looking brass box with bright silver hardware and with luggage tags from Delta, USAir, and Continental hanging on the door. Dogs in crates can look woeful, but Biff actually likes spending time in his. When he was growing up, the Truesdales decided they would never reprimand him, because of his delicate ego. Whenever he got rambunctious, Tina wouldn't scold him—she would just invite him to sit in his crate and have a time-out.

On this particular day, Biff was in the crate with a bowl of water and a gourmet Oinkeroll. The boxer judging was already over. There had been thirty-three in competition, and Biff had won Best in Breed. Now he had to wait for several hours while the rest of the working breeds had their competitions. Later, the breed winners would square off for Best in Working Group. Then, around dinnertime, the winner of the Working Group and the winners of the other groups—sporting dogs, hounds, terriers, toys, non-sporting dogs, and herding dogs—would compete for Best in Show. Biff was stretched out in the crate with his head resting on his forelegs, so that his lips draped over his ankle like a café curtain. He looked bored. Next to his crate, several wire-haired fox terriers were standing on tables getting their faces shampooed, and beyond them a Chihuahua in a pink crate was gnawing on its door latch. Two men in white shirts and dark pants walked by eating hot dogs. One of them was gesturing and exclaiming, "I thought I had good dachshunds! I thought I had *great* dachshunds!"

Biff sighed and closed his eyes.

While he was napping, I pawed through his suitcase. In it was some dog food; towels; an electric nail grinder; a whisker trimmer; a wool jacket in a lively pattern that looked sort of Southwestern; an apron; some antibiotics; baby oil; coconut-oil coat polish; boxer chalk powder; a copy of *Dog News;* an issue of *ShowSight* magazine, featuring an article subtitled "Frozen Semen—Boon or Bane?" and a two-page ad for Biff, with a full-page, full-color photograph of him and Kim posed in front of a human-size toy soldier; a spray bottle of fur cleanser; another Oinkeroll; a rope ball; and something called a Booda Bone. The apron was for Kim. The baby oil was to make Biff's nose and feet glossy when he went into the ring. Boxer chalk powder—as distinct from, say, West Highland–white-terrier chalk powder—is formulated to cling to short, sleek boxer hair and whiten boxers' white markings. Unlike some of the other dogs, Biff did not need to travel with a blow dryer, curlers, nail polish, or detangling combs, but, unlike some less sought-after dogs, he did need a schedule. He was registered for a show in Chicago the next day, and had an appointment at a clinic in Connecticut the next week to make a semen deposit, which had been ordered by a breeder in Australia. Also, he had a date that same week with a bitch named Diana who was about to go into heat. Biff has to book his stud work after shows, so that it doesn't interfere with his performance. Tina Truesdale told me that this was typical of all athletes, but everyone who knows Biff is quick to comment on how professional he is as a stud. Richard Krieger, who was going to be driving Biff to his appointment at the clinic in Connecticut, once told me that some studs want to goof around and take forever but Biff is very businesslike. "Bing, bang, boom," Krieger said. "He's in, he's out."

"No wasting of time," said Nancy Krieger, Richard's wife. "Bing, bang, boom. He gets the job done."

After a while, Kim showed up and asked Biff if he needed to go outside. Then a handler who is a friend of Kim's came by. He was wearing a

black-and-white houndstooth suit and was bran-
dishing a comb and a can of hair spray. While
they were talking, I leafed through the show catalogue and read some of the dogs' names to Biff,
just for fun—names like Aleph Godol's Umbra
Von Carousel and Champion Spanktown Little
Lu Lu and Ranchlake's Energizer O'Motown
and Champion Beaverbrook Buster V Broad-
head. Biff decided that he did want to go out, so
Kim opened the crate. He stepped out and
stretched and yawned like a cat, and then he suddenly stood up and punched me in the chest. An
announcement calling for all toys to report to
their ring came over the loudspeaker. Kim's friend
waved the can of hair spray in the direction of a
little white poodle shivering on a table a few yards
away and exclaimed, "Oh, no! I lost track of time!
I have to go! I have to spray up my miniature!"

Typically, dog contestants first circle the ring
together; then each contestant poses individually for the judge, trying to look perfect as the
judge lifts its lips for a dental exam, rocks its
hindquarters, and strokes its back and thighs.
The judge at Lehigh was a chesty, mustached
man with watery eyes and a grave expression. He
directed the group with hand signals that made
him appear to be roping cattle. The Rottweiler
looked good, and so did the giant schnauzer. I
started to worry. Biff had a distracted look on his
face, as if he'd forgotten something back at the
house. Finally, it was his turn. He pranced to the
center of the ring. The judge stroked him and
then waved his hand in a circle and stepped out of
the way. Several people near me began clapping.
A flashbulb flared. Biff held his position for a
moment, and then he and Kim bounded across
the ring, his feet moving so fast that they blurred
into an oily sparkle, even though he really didn't
have very far to go. He got a cookie when he fin-

ished the performance, and another a few minutes later, when the judge wagged his finger at
him, indicating that Biff had won again.

You can't help wondering whether Biff will
experience the depressing letdown that retired
competitors face. At least, he has a lot of stud
work to look forward to, although William
Truesdale complained to me once that the Truesdales' standards for a mate are so high—they require a clean bill of health and a substantial
pedigree—that "there just aren't that many right
bitches out there." Nonetheless, he and Tina are
optimistic that Biff will find enough suitable
mates to become one of the most influential boxer
sires of all time. "We'd like to be remembered as
the boxer people of the nineties," Tina said.
"Anyway, we can't wait to have him home."

"We're starting to campaign Biff's son Rex,"
William said. "He's been living in Mexico, and
he's a Mexican champion, and now he's ready to
take on the American shows. He's very promising. He has a fabulous rear."

Just then, Biff, who had been on the couch,
jumped down and began pacing. "Going somewhere, honey?" Tina asked.

He wanted to go out, so Tina opened the
back door, and Biff ran into the back yard. After
a few minutes, he noticed a ball on the lawn. The
ball was slippery and a little too big to fit in his
mouth, but he kept scrambling and trying to grab
it. In the meantime, the Truesdales and I sat,
stayed for a moment, fetched ourselves turkey
sandwiches, and then curled up on the couch.
Half an hour passed, and Biff was still happily
pursuing the ball. He probably has a very short
memory, but he acted as if it were the most fun
he'd ever had.

| 1995 |

## THE UNRULY THOUGHTS OF THE DOG TRAINER'S LOVER

Into the wheat-thrown fields we lead
the leashed dogs, the well-trained hounds;
they leap to mind through the weedy
Queen Anne's lace. He orders them, "Circle round,
round." I'm a willing believer.

They run together—gray water, tail to mouth—
in wheeling stories. Their frilled jaws
can hold eggs, live rabbits, our wrists. At his brief sign
they make no sound. I am properly awed.
Their paws wear great rings of grass brown.

He wields the commands "Sit," "Stay"
like a stick and a thorn. He can say "Fetch" or "Leave":
they scatter in ashen explosions. Waving
devoted tails like prayer flags, they look for reprieve to me.
I shrug. He gestures "Heel." They come through meticulous paces.

I'm here to reward us all when we lie down,
to roll over into the pasture hay, to carry a sack
of marrow bones tight in my loose
hand. I wear his clothes like khaki
fatigues in the afternoon. He stands his ground.

I hear mongrel packs have taken the roads upstate,
attacking deer at will. But we will go to the kennel show
for blue snapping ribbons. The fairgrounds will shake
under the truck. He'll call the dogs: "Go slowly, hounds.
I said go slow." We all may have made a grave mistake.

—ELIZABETH MACKLIN    | 1980 |

THE UNRULY THOUGHTS OF THE DOG TRAINER'S LOVER
Macklin

Into the wheat thrown fields we lead
the leashed dogs, the well-trained hounds.
They leap to mind through the weedy
Queen Anne's lace. He orders them, Circle round,
round. I'm a willing believer.
They run together--gray water, tail to mouth--
in wheeling stories. Their frilled jaws
can hold eggs, live rabbits, our wrists. At his brief sign
they make no sound. I am properly awed.
Their paws wear great rings of grass brown.

He wields the commands Sit, Stay. He can say Fetch or Leave:
like a stick and a thorn, they look for reprieve to me.
they scatter in ashen explosions, they come through meticulous paces.
devoted tails like prayer flags. Waving
I shrug. He gestures Heel; they come through meticulous paces.

I'm here to reward us all when we lie down,
to roll over into the pasture hay, to carry a sack
of marrow bones tight in my loose
hand. I wear his clothes like khaki fatigues
in the afternoon. He stands his ground.

I hear mongrel packs have taken the roads upstate,
attacking deer at will. But we will go to the kennel show
for blue snapping ribbons. The fairgrounds will shake
under the truck. He'll call the dogs: Go slowly, hounds.
I said go slow. We all may have made a grave mistake.

---

He holds the command to sit, stay, fetch or
like a stick and a thorn; he can say leave:
and they scatter in ashen explosions. Waving
devotions like prayer flags, they look reprieve
at me. He gestures Heel; they go through careful paces.
come through meticulous

---

A long way from the muddy kennel runs,
away from warm straw, but circumscribed.

The Dog Trainer's Lover

Into the wheat-thrown fields we lead
the leashed dogs, the hounds:    (well-trained
they leap to mind through the weedy
queen anne's lace. He orders them, Circle round,
round. willing believers
Pivot like maple seeds

They run together, gray water, tail to mouth,
in wheeling stories. Their frilled jaws can
hold eggs, live rabbits, our wrists. They make no sound
dust laid panting. but good laws
and they wear great brown rings of grass.
devotion
free rein

I'm here to reward us all when we lie down,
to roll over the pasture hay, carry a sack
of marrow bones, tight in my own
loose hand. A long way from the muddy track (much
kennel runs, away from warm straw, we are at home. far

I've heard mongrel packs have taken the roads upstate,
attacking deer at will. So we'll go to the kennel show
for blue, snapping ribbons, and the dogs
sleek, chained wind me down slowly.
Gather the hounds - state,
in control. We may have made a grave mistake.

# REAL DOGS

RICHARD COHEN

In the past, the only recourse for a dog who craved fame was Hollywood. A dog was either a movie dog or a house pet, end of discussion. While a few dogs became celebrities, the vast majority passed through life unknown, leaving behind no more than a handful of memories scattered like bones across back yards and living rooms. Then, in 1990, Chuck Svoboda and Frank Simon, two men working the Southwest border for the United States Customs Service, decided that something had to be done to get some less flashy dogs a little more attention. They discussed the problem with their immediate supervisor, and, as a result, the United States Customs Service issued nine baseball-style trading cards, each picturing a drug-detecting dog and listing the dog's age, breed, seizure record, and most notable achievement. The cards, which are distributed to schoolchildren, show canine agents sniffing tires, standing in pickups, and straining in the glare of the midday Texas sun. Real dogs solving real problems.

We learned all this from Morris Berkowitz, who is a canine-program manager with the Customs Service and is determined to improve the image of the working dog. "These dogs may not play ball," he likes to say, "but they can do a little trick called 'stop crime.'"

Last April, Milk-Bone Dog Biscuits, part of a division of Nabisco Foods, took the dog-card concept a step further: it named two dozen canine agents to an honorary All-Star team, issued a second set of cards, celebrating these dogs, and began putting them inside boxes of Milk-Bones. A dog handler named August King, who is partnered with a sixty-pound yellow Labrador retriever, claims that the cards could actually work as deterrents to drug trafficking. "When dealers get a look at the dogs stacked against them, they just might change their plans," he told us. Nabisco executives speak in more general terms. "The cards put us on the side of the good dog and good dogs everywhere," a company spokesman said.

All told, three hundred and forty-seven dogs are employed by the Customs Service, and police America's airports, seaports, and border checkpoints. It was twenty-four of those dogs that were chosen as All-Stars. Two New York dogs made the squad. "Rufus and Jack—both are legends, but Rufus is an animal I truly respect," Mr. Berkowitz said. Last year, while searching a cargo truck, Rufus, a sad-eyed springer spaniel, uncovered nine hundred pounds of cocaine, and in the course of his career he has found over eighty million dollars' worth of narcotics. "To understand how remarkable that stat is, you should know that Rufus is at least thirteen years old and that most dogs retire at around nine," Mr. Berkowitz explained. "It's not that they lose their desire; their bodies just won't do what they once did. The retired dogs spend their days like civilian dogs—lying in front of a TV or running around some yard. But Rufus is unstoppable. He's like Nolan Ryan."

In their pictures, the dogs look stern and businesslike—all but Corky. Corky, a member of the All-Stars, is a beige cocker spaniel with floppy ears and thick fur, who looks more like a lapdog than like a customs agent. We asked Mr. Berkowitz why a non-active agent (Corky's card reads "Retired") was named to the All-Star team—wasn't that sort of like sending Bill Bradley to the Olympics? "Corky is not an average agent," Mr. Berkowitz replied. "Corky broke a line many people thought unbreakable. He was the first cute dog to work in Customs. Before Corky, all drug-detection canines were big breeds. Labs or shepherds. But some travellers get spooked by big dogs, so we brought Corky on to sniff. He's passive. If he picks up a scent, he doesn't scratch or claw, he simply sits at the suspect's feet.

Before Corky, our people thought drug dogs had to look a certain way. Big and tough. We don't think that anymore."

In the light of Corky's historical role, many drug-dog fans consider his card the set's most valuable. "All the cards are going to be worth something," Ann Smith, a public-relations manager for Nabisco, told us. "But if you're going to hang on to just one, hang on to Corky." She added that Corky has appeared on the TV show *Top Cops,* reenacting some of his most dramatic cases, among them the discovery of 56.4 pounds of cocaine in an overnight-courier bag at Miami International Airport. "When I was a kid, I collected baseball cards," she said. "My favorite card was Johnny Bench crouched behind home plate. If you want to get my Corky, in addition to Bench you have to give me a Ted Williams and a Babe Ruth."

| 1992 |

# LA FORZA DEL ALPO

### ROGER ANGELL

*(An opera in four acts, conceived prior to successive evenings at the Westminster Kennel Club Show and the Metropolitan Opera)*

CAST

GUGLIELMO—A dashing fox terrier (*tenor*)

MIMI (Ch. Anthracite Sweet-Stuff of Armonk)—A poodle (*soprano*)

DON CANINO (her father)—Another poodle (*baritone*)

BRUTTO—Companion poodle to Don Canino and suitor for the hand of Mimi (*basso*)

FIDOLETTA—A Lhasa Apso. Nurse to Mimi but secretly enamored of Guglielmo. A real bitch (*mezzo*)

SPIQUE—A comical bulldog (*basso bundo*)

DR. FAUSTUS—A veterinary (*tenor*)

CHORUS: Non-sporting, herding, and terrier contestants; judges, handlers, reporters

*(There will be three walks around the block)*

After the disastrous failure of his misbegotten early *Arfeo* at La Scala in the winter of 1843, few expected that Verdi would soon return to the themes of canine anti-clericalism and the proliferation of Labradors (*labbrazazione*), but his discovery of the traditional Sicilian grooming cavatina—as recapitulated in the touching barkarole "Dov'é il mio guinzaglio?" ("I have lost my leash") that closes Act III—appears to have sent him back to work. Verdi's implacable opposition to the Venetian muzzling ordinance of 1850 is to be heard in the rousing

"Again a full moon" chorus that resonates so insistently during Brutto's musings before and after the cabaletta:

*fff*    *Bhou-wou-wou-wou*

At the opening curtain, Guglielmo and Mimi, in adjoining benching stalls, plan their elopement despite the opposition of Don Canino, who has arranged her forthcoming marriage to Brutto despite rumors about the larger male's parentage. After the lovers' tender duet "A cuccia, a cuccia, amore mio" ("Sit! Sit, my love!"), recalling their first meeting at an obedience class, they part reluctantly, with Guglielmo distressed at her anxiety over the nuptials: "Che gelida manina" ("Your icy paw"). Don Canino, enlisting the support of the perfidious Fidoletta, plots to dispatch Guglielmo into the K-9 Corps, and, joined by Brutto, the trio, in "Sotto il nostro albero" ("Under the family tree"), jovially celebrates the value of pedigree.

As the judging begins, Guglielmo, alerted to Don Canino's plot by the faithful Spique, disguises himself as a miniature apricot poodle, but the lovers fail to detect the lurking presence of Don Canino, who has hidden himself among a large entry of Rottweilers in Ring 6. A pitched battle between hostile bands of Lakeland and Bedlington terriers requires the attention of Spique, and in his absence Fidoletta entraps the innocent Guglielmo, who discloses his identity to her. She breaks off their amusing impromptu duet "Non so chi sei" ("I don't know who you are, but I sure like your gait") to fetch the police, but Guglielmo makes good his escape through the loges during

the taping of a Kal Kan commercial—an octet severely criticized in its day, but to which Mascagni makes clear obeisance in his later sestina, "Mangia, Pucci."

Guglielmo, not realizing in the darkness that he has found his way back to his natal kennel in Chappaqua, delivers the dirgelike "Osso Bucco" while digging in the yard, but is elated by news from Spique that he has uncovered certain documents in the back-door garbage compactor. Fidoletta, puzzled, trails the valiant pair as they hasten back to the Garden.

In our turbulent final act, the wedding of Mimi and Brutto is interrupted by the arrival of Dr. Faustus, bearing the purloined A.K.C. documents unearthed by Spique. The good vet declares that the nuptials must halt, because Brutto is in fact not only Mimi's father but (through a separate whelping) her uncle as well. Don Canino, horrified at his own depravity, vows to enter holy orders, and, in a confession, reveals that Brutto is no purebred—"Mira l'occhio azzurro" ("Ol' Blue Eyes")—thanks to a Pomeranian on his dam's side. Dr. Faustus removes Brutto to his laboratory for neutering. Guglielmo, still in disguise, unexpectedly wins a Best of Opposite Sex award in his breed as the lovers are at last united. Guglielmo serenades his Mimi with the "Sono maschio" ("I am a young intact male") as the happy couple, renouncing show biz, envision their future as a breeding pair with a cut-rate puppy mill in the Garden State Mall. Spique, exhausted by so much unlikelihood, falls asleep on the emptied stage, where his sonorous snores ("*Zzzzz*") are joined by those of the audience.

| 1994 |

# MONOLOG PSA ZAPLĄTANEGO W DZIEJE

Są psy i psy. Ja byłem psem wybranym.
Miałem dobre papiery i w żyłach krew wilcza
Mieszkałem na wyżynie wdychając wonie wi
na łąki w słońcu, na świerki po deszczu
i grudy ziemi spod śniegu.

Miałem porządny dom i ludzi na usługi.
Byłem żywiony, myty, szczotkowany,
wyprowadzany na piękne spacery.
Jednak z szacunkiem, bez poufałości.
Każdy dobrze pamiętał, czyim jestem psem.

Byle parszywy kundel potrafi mieć p
Ale uwaga - wara od porównań.
Mój pan był panem jedynym w swoim
Miał okazałe stado chodzące za nir
i zapatrzone w niego z lękliwym p

Dla mnie były uśmieszki ~~a kiepsk~~
z kiepsko skrywaną zazdrością.
Bo tylko ja miałem prawo
witać go w lotnych podskokach
Tylko ja - ~~a~~ żeganać ciągnące zębami na s
Tylko mnie wolno było
z głową na jego kolanach
dostępować głaskania i tarmo
Tylko ja mogłem przy nim sobie udawać
a wtedy on się schylał i sz

Na innych gniewał się częs
Warczał na nich, ujadał, l
biegał od ściany do ścian
Myślę, że lubił tylko mn
i więcej nigdy, nikogo.

Miałem też obowiązki:
Bo zjawiał się na krót
Co go zatrzymywało tam, w dolinach,
odgadywałem
~~Coś~~ mi jednak ~~mówiło~~, że to pilne sprawy,
conajmniej takie pilne ja~~k dla mnie walka~~

Jak dla mnie walka
i wszystkim, co si

Jest los i los. Mój
Nastała ~~wiosna~~ wojna, a ~~po~~
Rozpętała się w domu
Skrzynie, walizki, k
Koła z piskie zjeżdża
Umilkły za zakrętem

Na tarasie płonęły jak
żółte bluzy, opaski z o
i dużo, bardzo dużo prz
z których powypadały ~~sli~~ cho

Snułem się w tym zamęcie
bardziej zdumiony niż zły
Czułem na sierści ~~szybkie~~
Jakbym był psem bezpańsk
natrętnym przybłędą,
którego już od schodów przy

Ktoś zerwał mi obrożę nabija
Ktoś kopnął moją miskę od ki
A potem ktoś ostatni, zanim k
wychylił się z szoferki
i strzelił do mnie dwa razy.

Nawet nie umiał trafić, gdzie
bo umierałam jeszcze długo i bo
w brzęku rozzuchwalonych much.
Ja, pies mojego pana.

# MONOLOGUE OF A DOG ENSNARED IN HISTORY

There are dogs and dogs. I was among the chosen.
I had good papers and wolf's blood in my veins.
I lived upon the heights inhaling the odors of views:
meadows in sunlight, spruces after rain,
and clumps of earth beneath the snow.

I had a decent home and people on call
I was fed, washed, groomed,
and taken for lovely strolls.
Respectfully, though, and *comme il faut.*
They all knew full well whose dog I was.

Any lousy mutt can have a master.
Take care, though—beware comparisons.
My master was a breed apart.
He had a splendid herd that trailed his every step
and fixed their eyes on him in fearful awe.

For me they always had smiles,
with envy poorly hidden.
Since only I had the right to greet him with nimble
    leaps,
only I could say goodbye by worrying his trousers
    with my teeth.
Only I was permitted
to receive scratching and stroking
with my head laid in his lap.
Only I could feign sleep
while he bent over me to whisper something.

He raged at others often, loudly.
He snarled, barked,
raced from wall to wall.
I suspect he liked only me
and nobody else, ever.

I also had responsibilities: waiting, trusting.
Since he would turn up briefly and then vanish.

What kept him down there in the lowlands, I don't
    know.

I guessed, though, it must be pressing business,
at least as pressing
as my battle with the cats
and everything that moves for no good reason.

There's fate and fate. Mine changed abruptly:
One spring came
and he wasn't there.
All hell broke loose at home.
Suitcases, chests, trunks crammed into cars.
The wheels squealed tearing downhill
and fell silent round the bend.

On the terrace scraps and tatters flamed,
yellow shirts, armbands with black emblems,
and lots and lots of battered cartons
with banners tumbling out.

I was adrift in this whirlwind,
more amazed than peeved.
I felt unfriendly glances on my fur.
As if I were a dog without a master,
some pushy stray
chased downstairs with a broom.

Someone tore my silver-trimmed collar off,
someone kicked my bowl, empty for days.
Then someone else, driving away,
leaned out from the car
and shot me twice.

He couldn't even shoot straight,
since I died for a long time, in pain,
to the buzz of impertinent flies.
I, the dog of my master.

—WISLAWA SZYMBORSKA    | 2004 |
(*Translated, from the Polish, by Stanislaw Baranczak
and Clare Cavanagh.*)

# SCRATCH AND SNIFF

IAN FRAZIER

Cell phones smell. You wouldn't think so, but they do. The K-9 Unit of the New Jersey Department of Corrections, while training seven recently acquired cell-phone-sniffing dogs, first put a whole bunch of cell-phone parts in a plastic box to create a kind of sachet of cell-phone scent for use in imprinting. The basic, pervasive cell-phone smell that built up in the closed box was powerful—a sweetish, metallic, ozoney, weird robotic reek. People would never carry such a rank object as a cell phone in their pockets if their noses were as good as a dog's.

To Troy, Ernie, Chance, and the other muscular, well-fed, and extremely enthusiastic dogs who search for illegal cell phones inside New Jersey's thirteen state prisons, the smell of a cell phone is bliss. They love to follow it, love finding its source even more. While held in restraint, just before the search, they emit low, well-disciplined whines of almost unbearable expectation. And when they do find the cell phone—or the cell-phone charger, the earpiece, the battery, or any other related object that somehow picked up cell-phone scent (recently a cell-phone-sniffing dog, though not trained to search for narcotics, found some narcotics that had evidently been stored next to a cell phone)—the dogs react with a panting, whining, scratching happiness greater than any human happiness by a factor similar to that by which a dog's sense of smell is said to be better than ours.

Inside a prison, cell phones defeat some of the purpose of incarceration. They're among the biggest problems prison officials face. Criminals with cell phones continue to run their gangs even while locked up. How do they get the phones? "Oh, gee—all kinds of ways," Thomas Moran, the New Jersey D.O.C. chief of staff, said the other day. "Their friends shoot 'em over the fence with potato guns, fly 'em in on model airplanes, arrows . . . Body cavities, of course, when a girlfriend visits. Packages. Food deliveries. F.C.C. regulations say we can't interfere with cell-phone transmissions by jamming. Going after the illegal phones with dogs is by far the most efficient means."

Recently, the officers of the K-9 Unit held a demonstration with their cell-phone dogs on the grounds of the Albert C. Wagner Youth Correctional Facility, in central Jersey farm country. The officers are so proud of their dogs they beam. As the dogs found cell phones hidden in lockers and near bunks in an un-used dorm building, and sniffed out a dog-tooth-marked cell phone in the weeds of a field, the officers explained the pro-gram.

Captain Matthew Kyle: "We don't want to publicate what the cell-phone smell is exactly. It's an organic substance that's in all cell phones—leave it at that. The dogs can smell it even when it's masked. They can find it if the cell phone's in water, oil, peanut butter—anywhere."

Sergeant William Crampton: "Only time we ever had a dog indicate inaccu-rately was on a diabetic test kit one indi-vidual had."

Officer Donald Mitchell: "We worked with thirteen dogs to get the seven we have now. Some dogs we had to fail out for environmental reasons. The dog can't work in the prison environment. Maybe a dog don't like the slippery floors in the cellblock, or the noise, or the food odors. Some dogs don't like heights. On the top tier of cells you're looking down through a floor grating four or five stories. There's dogs won't walk on that. Or they don't like the heat up there in the sum-mer."

Officer Joseph Nicholas: "All our dogs right now are German shepherds or Labs. We did try one golden retriever, but we had to fail him out. That dog was too easy-going. He'd come in a room on a search and just lay down. We sent him back to the Seeing Eye dog center in Mor-ristown, where all our cell-phone dogs came from. That golden was a lover, not a fighter."

Captain Kyle: "Very few other states have cell-phone-dog programs like ours—Maryland and Virginia are two of them. There's a private contractor in California that trains dogs for cell-phone work, but they charge twenty-one thousand dollars for three dogs. We trained all our dogs our-selves, saving the taxpayers money. Since we started with our first three dogs, in Oc-tober of 2008, we've found a hundred and thirty-three cell phones, a hundred and twenty-eight chargers, and I am not sure how many earpieces, batteries, and other items. We believe that eventually every prison system in the country will be using cell-phone dogs."

| 2009 |

# DOGOLOGY

*Fiction*

## T. CORAGHESSAN BOYLE

### RUMORS

It was the season of mud, drainpipes drooling, the gutters clogged with debris, a battered and penitential robin fixed like a statue on every lawn. Julian was up early, a Saturday morning, beating eggs with a whisk and gazing idly out the kitchen window and into the colorless hide of the day, expecting nothing, when all at once the scrim of rain parted to reveal a dark, crouching presence in the far corner of the yard. At first glance, he took it to be a dog—a town ordinance that he particularly detested disallowed fences higher than three feet, and so the contiguous lawns and flower beds of the neighborhood had become a sort of open savanna for roaming packs of dogs—but before the wind shifted and the needling rain closed in again he saw that he was wrong. This figure, partially obscured by the resurgent forsythia bush, seemed out of proportion, all limbs, as if a dog had been mated with a monkey. What was it, then? Raccoons had been at the trash lately, and he'd seen an opossum wavering down the street like a pale ghost one night after a dreary, overwrought movie Cara had insisted upon, but this was no opossum. Or raccoon, either. It was dark in color, whatever it was—a bear, maybe, a yearling strayed down from the high ridges along the river, and hadn't Ben Ober told him somebody on F Street had found a bear in their swimming pool? He put down the whisk and went to fetch his glasses.

228

A sudden eruption of thunder set the dishes rattling on the drainboard, followed by an uncertain flicker of light that illuminated the dark room as if the bulb in the overhead fixture had gone loose in the socket. He wondered how Cara could sleep through all this, but the wonder was short-lived, because he really didn't give a damn one way or the other if she slept all day, all night, all week. Better she should sleep and give him some peace. He was in the living room now, the gloom ladled over everything, shadows leeching into black holes behind the leather couch and matching armchairs, and the rubber plant a dark ladder in the corner. The thunder rolled again, the lightning flashed. His glasses were atop the TV, where he'd left them the night before while watching a sorry documentary about the children purportedly raised by wolves in India back in the 1920s, two stringy girls in sepia photographs that revealed little and could have been faked, in any case. He put his glasses on and padded back into the kitchen in his stocking feet, already having forgotten why he'd gone to get the glasses in the first place. Then he saw the whisk in a puddle of beaten egg on the counter, remembered, and peered out the window again.

The sight of the three dogs there—a pair of clownish chows and what looked to be a shepherd mix—did nothing but irritate him. He recognized this trio; they were the advance guard of the army of dogs that dropped their excrement all over the lawn, dug up his flower beds, and, when he tried to shoo them, looked right through him as if he didn't exist. It wasn't that he had anything against dogs, per se—it was their destructiveness he objected to, their arrogance, as if they owned the whole world and it was their privilege to do as they liked with it. He was about to step to the back door and chase them off, when the figure he'd first seen—the shadow beneath the forsythia

bush—emerged. It was no animal, he realized with a shock, but a woman, a young woman dressed all in black, with her black hair hanging wet in her face and the clothes stuck to her like a second skin, down on all fours like a dog herself, sniffing. He was dumbfounded. As stunned and amazed as if someone had just stepped into the kitchen and slapped him till his head rolled back on his shoulders.

He'd been aware of the rumors—there was a new couple in the neighborhood, over on F Street, and the woman was a little strange, dashing through people's yards at any hour of the day or night, baying at the moon, and showing her teeth to anyone who got in her way—but he'd dismissed them as some sort of suburban legend. Now here she was, in his yard, violating his privacy, in the company of a pack of dogs he'd like to see shot—and their owners, too. He didn't know what to do. He was frozen in his own kitchen, the omelette pan sending up a metallic stink of incineration. And then the three dogs lifted their heads as if they'd heard something in the distance, the thunder boomed overhead, and suddenly they leaped the fence in tandem and were gone. The woman rose up out of the mud at this point—she was wearing a sodden turtleneck, jeans, a watch cap—locked eyes with him across the expanse of the rain-screened yard for just an instant, or maybe he was imagining this part of it, and then she turned and took the fence in a single bound, vanishing into the rain.

## CYNOMORPH

Whatever it was they'd heard, it wasn't available to her, though she'd been trying to train her hearing away from the ceaseless clatter of the mechanical and tune it to the finer things, the wind stirring in the grass, the alarm call of a fallen nestling, the faintest sliver of a whimper from the dog three houses over, begging to be let out. And her nose. She'd made a point of sticking it in anything the dogs did, breathing deeply, rebooting the olfactory receptors of a brain that had been deadened by perfume and underarm deodorant and all the other stifling odors of civilization. Every smell was a discovery, and every dog discovered more of the world in ten minutes running loose than a human being would discover in ten years of sitting behind the wheel of a car or standing at the lunch counter in a deli or even hiking the Alps. What she was doing, or attempting to do, was nothing short of reordering her senses so that she could think like a dog and interpret the whole world—not just the human world—as dogs did.

Why? Because no one had ever done it before. Whole hordes wanted to be primatologists or climb into speedboats and study whales and dolphins or cruise the veldt in a Land Rover to watch the lions suckle their young beneath the baobabs, but none of them gave a second thought to dogs. Dogs were beneath them. Dogs were common, pedestrian, no more exotic than the housefly or the Norway rat. Well, she was going to change all that. Or at least that was what she'd told herself after the graduate committee rejected her thesis, but that was a long time ago now, two years and more—and the door was rapidly closing.

But here she was, moving again, and movement was good, it was her essence: up over the fence and into the next yard, dodging a clothesline, a cooking grill, a plastic rake, a sandbox, reminding herself always to keep her head down and go quadrupedal whenever possible, because how else was she going to hear, smell, and see as the dogs did? Another fence, and there, at the far end of the yard, a shed, and the dense rust-colored tails of the chows wagging. The rain spat in her face, relentless. It had been coming down steadily most of the night, and now it seemed even heavier, as if it meant to drive her back indoors where she belonged. She was shivering—had been shivering for the past hour, shivering so hard she thought her teeth were coming loose—and as she ran, doubled over in a crouch, she pumped her knees and flapped her arms in an attempt to generate some heat.

What were the dogs onto now? She saw the one she called Barely disappear behind the shed and snake back out again, her tail rigid, sniffing now, barking, and suddenly they were all barking—the two chows and the semi-shepherd she'd named Factitious because he was such a sham, pretending he was a rover when he never strayed more than five blocks from his house, on E Street. There was a smell of freshly turned earth, of compost and wood ash, of the half-drowned worms that Snout the Afghan loved to gobble up off the pavement. She glanced toward the locked gray vault of the house, concerned that the noise would alert whoever lived there, but it was early yet, no lights on, no sign of activity. The dogs' bodies moiled. The barking went up a notch. She ran, hunched at the waist, hurrying.

And then, out of the corner of her eye, she caught a glimpse of A1, the big-shouldered husky who'd earned his name by consuming half a bottle of steak sauce beside an overturned trash can one bright January morning. He was running—but where had he come from? She hadn't seen him all night and assumed he'd been wandering out at the limits of his range, over in Bethel or Georgetown. She watched him streak across the yard, ears pinned back, head low, his path converging with hers until he disappeared behind the shed. Angling round the back of the thing—it was aluminum, one of those prefab articles they sell in the big warehouse stores—she found the compost pile her nose had alerted her to (good, good: she was improving) and a tower of old wicker chairs stacked up six feet high. A1 never hesitated. He surged in at the base of the tower, his jaws snapping, and the second chow, the one she called Decidedly, was right behind him—and then she saw: there was something there, a face with incendiary eyes, and it was growling for its life in a thin continuous whine that might have been the drone of a model airplane buzzing overhead.

What was it? She crouched low, came in close. A straggler appeared suddenly, a fluid sifting from the blind side of the back fence to the yard—it was Snout, gangly, goofy, the fastest dog in the neighborhood and the widest ranger, A1's wife and the mother of his dispersed pups. And then all five dogs went in for the kill.

The thunder rolled again, concentrating the moment, and she got her first clear look: cream-colored fur, naked pink toes, a flash of teeth and burdened gums. It was an opossum, unlucky, doomed, caught out while creeping back to its nest on soft marsupial feet after a night of foraging among the trash cans. There was a roil of dogs, no barking now, just the persistent unravelling growls that were like curses, and the first splintering crunch of bone. The tower of wicker came down with a clatter, chairs upended and scattered, and the dogs hardly noticed. She glanced around her in alarm, but there was nobody to be seen, nothing moving but the million silver drill bits of the rain boring into the ground. Just as the next flash of lightning lit the sky, A1 backed out from under the rumble of chairs with the carcass clenched in his jaws, furiously shaking it to snap a neck that was already two or three times broken, and she was startled to see how big the thing was—twenty pounds of meat, gristle,

bone, and hair, twenty pounds at least. He shook it again, then dropped it at his wife's feet as an offering. It lay still, the other dogs extending their snouts to sniff at it dispassionately, scientists themselves, studying and measuring, remembering. And, when the hairless pink young emerged from the pouch, she tried not to feel anything as the dogs snapped them up one by one.

## CARA

"You mean you didn't confront her?" Cara was in her royal-purple robe—her "wrapper," as she insisted on calling it, as if they were at a country manor in the Cotswolds entertaining Lord and Lady Muckbright instead of in a tract house in suburban Connecticut—and she'd paused with a forkful of mushroom omelette halfway to her mouth. She was on her third cup of coffee and wearing her combative look.

"Confront her? I barely had time to recognize she was human." He was at the sink, scrubbing the omelette pan, and he paused to look bitterly out into the gray vacancy of the yard. "What did you expect me to do, chase her down? Make a citizen's arrest? What?"

The sound of Cara buttering her toast—she might have been flaying the flesh from a bone—set his teeth on edge. "I don't know," she said, "but we can't just have strangers lurking around anytime they feel like it, can we? I mean, there are *laws*—"

"The way you talk you'd think I invited her. You think I like mental cases peeping in the window so I can't even have a moment's peace in my own house?"

"So do something."

"What? You tell me."

"Call the police, why don't you? That should be obvious, shouldn't it? And that's another thing—"

dogs' bodies moiled. The barking went up a notch. She ran, hunched at the waist, hurrying.

And then, out of the corner of her eye, she caught a glimpse of A-1, the big-shouldered husky who'd earned his name by consuming half a bottle of steak sauce beside an overturned trash can one bright ~~cold~~ morning in January, while [January] she looked on in a daze, her fingers numbed, her cheekbones frozen inside the ski mask, A-1 running ~~and where~~ but had he come from? She hadn't seen him He was OK all night and assumed he'd been wandering out at the limits of his range, over in Bethel or Germantown. She watched him ~~come~~ streaking across the yard, ears pinned back, head low, his path converging on hers until he disappeared behind the shed. Angling round the back of the thing—it was aluminum, one of those prefab articles they sell in the big warehouse stores—she found the compost pile her nose had alerted her to (good, good: she was improving) and a tower of old wicker chairs stacked up six feet high.

A-1 ~~never~~ hesitated. He surged in at the stet base of the tower, his jaws snapping, and Decidedly, was right behind him—and the second chow, the one she called incendiary OK then she saw: there was something there, again? a growl isn't really a face with ~~burning~~ eyes, and it was a whine? stet growling for its life in a thin continuous whine that might have been the drone of a model airplane buzzing overhead.

note 3 reps of burning eyes – p.7, p.13

What was it? She crouched low, came in close. A straggler appeared suddenly, a [stet] fluid sifting from the blind side of the back fence to the yard—it was Snout, gangly, goofy, the fastest dog in the neighborhood and the widest ranger, A-1's wife and the mother of his dispersed pups—and all five of the dogs ⊙ And then OK went in for the kill. or lightning? more likely to stet

The thunder rolled again, concentrating the moment, and ~~then~~ she got her first clear look: cream-colored fur, naked pink toes, a flash of teeth and burdened gums. It was an opossum, unlucky, ~~doomed,~~ caught out while creeping back to its nest on soft marsupial feet after a night of foraging among the trash cans. There was a roil of dogs, no barking now, just the persistent unravelling growls that were like curses, and the first splintering crunch of bone. The tower of wicker came down with a clatter, chairs upended and scattered, and the dogs hardly noticed. She glanced around her in alarm, stet but there was nobody to be seen, nothing

That was when the telephone rang. It was Ben Ober, his voice scraping through the wires like a set of hard chitinous claws scrabbling against the side of the house. "Julian?" he shouted. "Julian?"

Julian reassured him. "Yeah," he said, "it's me. I'm here."

"Can you hear me?"

"I can hear you."

"Listen, she's out in my yard right now, out behind the shed with a, I don't know, some kind of wolf, it looks like, and that Afghan nobody seems to know who's the owner of—"

"Who?" he said, but even as he said it he knew. "Who're you talking about?"

"The dog woman." There was a pause, and Julian could hear him breathing into the mouthpiece as if he were deep underwater. "She seems to be—I think she's killing something out there."

## THE WOLF CHILDREN OF MAYURBHANJ

It was high summer, just before the rains set in, and the bush had shrivelled back under the sun till you could see up the skirts of the sal trees, and all that had been hidden was revealed. People began to talk of a disturbing presence in the jungle outside the tiny village of Godamuri in Mayurbhanj district, of a *bhut,* or spirit, sent to punish them for their refusal to honor the authority of the maharaja. This thing had twice been seen in the company of a wolf, a vague pale slash of movement in the incrassating twilight, but it was no wolf itself, of that that eyewitnesses were certain. Then came the rumor that there were two of them, quick, nasty, bloodless things of the night, and that their eyes flamed with an infernal heat that incinerated anyone who looked into them, and panic gripped the countryside. Mothers kept their children close, fires burned in the night. Then, finally, came the news that these

things were concrete and actual and no mere figments of the imagination: their den had been found in an abandoned termitarium in the dense jungle seven miles southeast of the village.

The rumors reached the Reverend J. A. L. Singh, of the Anglican mission and orphanage at Midnapore, and in September, after the monsoon clouds had peeled back from the skies and the rivers had receded, he made the long journey to Godamuri by bullock cart. One of his converts, a Kora tribesman by the name of Chunarem, who was prominent in the area, led him to the site. There, the Reverend, an astute and observant man and an amateur hunter acquainted with the habits of beasts, saw evidence of canine occupation of the termite mound—droppings, bones, tunnels of ingress and egress—and instructed that a machan be built in an overspreading tree. Armed with his dependable 20-bore Westley Richards rifle, the Reverend sat breathlessly in the machan and concentrated his field glasses on the main entrance to the den. The Reverend Singh was not one to believe in ghosts, other than the Holy Spirit, perhaps, and he expected nothing more remarkable than an albino wolf or perhaps a sloth bear gone white with age or dietary deficiency.

Dusk filtered up from the forest floor. Shadows pooled in the undergrowth, and then an early moon rose up pregnant from the horizon to soften them. Langurs whooped in the near distance, cicadas buzzed, a hundred species of beetles, moths, and biting insects flapped round the Reverend's ears, but he held rigid and silent, his binoculars fixed on the entrance to the mound. And then suddenly a shape emerged, the triangular head of a wolf, then a smaller canine head, and then something else altogether, with a neatly rounded cranium and foreshortened face. The wolf—the dam—stretched herself and slunk off into the undergrowth, followed by a pair of wolf cubs and two other creatures, which were too long-legged and rangy to be canids; that was clear at a glance. Monkeys, the Reverend thought at first, or apes of some sort. But then, even though they were moving swiftly on all fours, the Reverend could see, to his amazement, that these weren't monkeys at all, or wolves or ghosts, either.

## DENNING

She no longer bothered with a notepad or the pocket tape recorder she'd once used to document the telling yip or strident howl. These were the accoutrements of civilization, and civilization got in the way of the kind of freedom she required if she was ever going to break loose of the constraints that had shackled field biologists from the beginning. Even her clothes seemed to get in the way, but she was sensible enough of the laws of the community to understand that they were necessary, at least for now. Still, she made a point of wearing the same things continuously for weeks on end—sans underwear or socks—in the expectation that her scent would invest them, and the scent of the pack, too. How could she hope to gain their confidence if she smelled like the prize inside a box of detergent?

One afternoon toward the end of March, as she lay stretched out beneath a weak pale disk of a sun, trying to ignore the cold breeze and concentrate on the doings of the pack—they were excavating a den in the vacant quadrangle of former dairy pasture that was soon to become the J and K blocks of the ever-expanding developments—she heard a car slow on the street a hundred yards distant and lifted her head lazily, as the dogs did, to investigate. It had been a quiet morning and a quieter afternoon, with Al and Snout, as the alpha couple, looking on placidly as Decidedly, Barely, and Factitious alternated the

digging and a bulldog from B Street she hadn't yet named lay drooling in the dark wet earth that flew from the lip of the burrow. Snout had been chasing cars off and on all morning—to the dogs, automobiles were animate and ungovernable, big unruly ungulates that needed to be curtailed—and she guessed that the fortyish man climbing out of the sedan and working his tentative way across the lot had come to complain, because that was all her neighbors ever did: complain.

And that was a shame. She really didn't feel like getting into all that right now—explaining herself, defending the dogs, justifying, forever justifying—because for once she'd got into the rhythm of dogdom, found her way to that sacred place where to lie flat in the sun and breathe in the scents of fresh earth, dung, sprouting grass was enough of an accomplishment for a day. Children were in school, adults at work. Peace reigned over the neighborhood. For the dogs—and for her, too—this was bliss. Hominids had to keep busy, make a buck, put two sticks together, order and structure and *complain,* but canids could know contentment, and so could she, if she could only penetrate deep enough.

Two shoes had arrived now. Loafers, buffed to brilliance and decorated with matching tassels of stripped hide. They'd come to rest on a trampled mound of fresh earth no more than twenty-four inches from her nose. She tried to ignore them, but there was a bright smear of mud or excrement gleaming on the toe of the left one; it *was* excrement, dog—the merest sniff told her that, and she was intrigued despite herself, though she refused to lift her eyes. And then a man's voice was speaking from somewhere high above the shoes, so high up and resonant with authority it might have been the voice of the alpha dog of all alpha dogs—God himself.

The tone of the voice, but not the sense of it,

PRICE $3.95

JUNE 27, 2005

# THE
# NEW YORKER

appealed to the dogs, and the bulldog, who was present and accounted for because Snout was in heat, hence the den, ambled over to gaze up at the trousered legs in lovesick awe. "You know," the voice was saying, "you've really got the neighborhood in an uproar, and I'm sure you have your reasons, and I know these dogs aren't yours—" The voice faltered. "But Ben Ober—you know Ben Ober? Over on C Street? Well, he's claiming you're killing rabbits or something. Or you were. Last Saturday. Out on his lawn?" Another pause. "Remember, it was raining?"

A month back, two weeks ago, even, she would have felt obliged to explain herself, would have soothed and mollified and dredged up a battery of behavioral terms— proximate causation, copulation solicitation, naturalistic fallacy—to cow him, but today, under the pale sun, in the company of the pack, she just couldn't seem to muster the energy. She might have grunted—or maybe that was only the sound of her stomach rumbling. She couldn't remember when she'd eaten last.

The cuffs of the man's trousers were stiffly pressed into jutting cotton prows, perfectly aligned. The bulldog began to lick at first one, then the other. There was the faintest creak of tendon and patella, and two knees presented themselves, and then a fist, pressed to the earth for balance. She saw a crisp white strip of shirt cuff, the gold flash of watch and wedding band.

"Listen," he said, "I don't mean to stick my nose in where it's not wanted, and I'm sure you have your reasons for, for"—the knuckles retrenched to balance the movement of his upper body, a swing of the arm, perhaps, or a jerk of the head—"all this. I'd just say live and let live, but I can't. And you know why not?"

She didn't answer, though she was on the verge—there was something about his voice that was magnetic, as if it could adhere to her and pull her to her feet again—but the bulldog distracted her. He'd gone up on his hind legs with a look of unfocussed joy and begun humping the man's leg, and her flash of epiphany deafened her to what he was saying. The bulldog had revealed his name to her: from now on she would know him as Humper.

"Because you upset my wife. You were out in our yard and I, she— Oh, Christ," he said, "I'm going about this all wrong. Look, let me introduce myself—I'm Julian Fox. We live on B Street, 2236? We never got to meet your husband and you when you moved in. I mean, the developments got so big—and impersonal, I guess—we never had the chance. But if you ever want to stop by, maybe for tea, a drink—the two of you, I mean—that would be, well, that would be great."

## A DRINK ON B STREET

She was upright and smiling, though her posture was terrible and she carried her own smell with her into the sterile sanctum of the house. He caught it immediately, unmistakably, and so did Cara, judging from the look on her face as she took the girl's hand. It was as if a breeze had wafted up from the bog they were draining over on G Street to make way for the tennis courts; the door stood open, and here was a raw infusion of the wild. Or the kennel. That was Cara's take on it, delivered in a stage whisper on the far side of the swinging doors to the kitchen as she fussed with the hors d'oeuvres and he poured vodka for the husband and tap water for the girl: *She smells like she's been sleeping in a kennel.* When he handed her the glass, he saw that there was dirt under her nails. Her hair shone with grease and there were bits of fluff or lint or something flecking the coils of it where it lay massed on her shoulders. Cara tried to draw her into small talk, but she wouldn't draw—she just kept nodding and smiling till the smile had nothing of greeting or joy left in it.

Cara had got their number from Bea Chiavone, who knew more about the business of her neighbors than a confessor, and one night last week she'd got through to the husband, who said his wife was out—which came as no surprise—but Cara had kept him on the line for a good ten minutes, digging for all she was worth, until he finally accepted the invitation to their "little cocktail party." Julian was doubtful, but before he'd had a chance to comb his hair or get his jacket on, the bell was ringing and there they were, the two of them, arm in arm on the doormat, half an hour early.

The husband, Don, was acceptable enough. Early thirties, bit of a paunch, his hair gone in a tonsure. He was a computer engineer. Worked for I.B.M. "Really?" Julian said. "Well, you must know Charlie Hsiu, then—he's at the Yorktown office?"

Don gave him a blank look.

"He lives just up the street. I mean, I could give him a call, if, if—" He never finished the thought. Cara had gone to the door to greet Ben and Julie Ober, and the girl, left alone, had migrated to the corner by the rubber plant, where she seemed to be bent over now, sniffing at the potting soil. He tried not to stare—tried to hold the husband's eye and absorb what he was saying about interoffice politics and his own role on the research end of things ("I guess I'm what you'd call the ultimate computer geek, never really get away from the monitor long enough to put a name to a face")—but he couldn't help stealing a glance under cover of the Obers' entrance. Ben was glad-handing, his voice booming, Cara was cooing something to Julie, and the girl (the husband had introduced her as Cynthia, but she'd murmured, "Call me C.f., capital 'C,' lowercase

'f' ") had gone down on her knees beside the plant. He saw her wet a finger, dip it into the soil, and bring it to her mouth.

While the La Portes—Cara's friends, dull as woodchips—came smirking through the door, expecting a freak show, Julian tipped back his glass and crossed the room to the girl. She was intent on the plant, rotating the terra-cotta pot to examine the saucer beneath it, on all fours now, her face close to the carpet. He cleared his throat, but she didn't respond. He watched the back of her head a moment, struck by the way her hair curtained her face and spilled down the rigid struts of her arms. She was dressed all in black, in a ribbed turtleneck, grass-stained jeans, and a pair of canvas sneakers that were worn through at the heels. She wasn't wearing socks, or, as far as he could see, a brassiere, either. But she'd clean up nicely, that was what he was thinking—she had a shape to her, anybody could see that, and eyes that could burn holes right through you. "So," he heard himself say, even as Ben's voice rose to a crescendo at the other end of the room, "you, uh, like houseplants?"

She made no effort to hide what she was doing, whatever it may have been—studying the weave of the carpet, looking at the alignment of the baseboard, inspecting for termites, who could say?—but instead turned to gaze up at him for the first time. "I hope you don't mind my asking," she said in her hush of a voice, "but did you ever have a dog here?"

He stood looking down at her, gripping his drink, feeling awkward and foolish in his own house. He was thinking of Seymour (or "See More," because as a pup he was always running off after things in the distance), picturing him now for the first time in how many years? Something passed through him then, a pang of regret carried in his blood, in his neurons: Seymour.

He'd almost succeeded in forgetting him. "Yes," he said. "How did you know?"

She smiled. She was leaning back against the wall now, cradling her knees in the net of her interwoven fingers. "I've been training myself. My senses, I mean." She paused, still smiling up at him. "Did you know that when the Ninemile wolves came down into Montana from Alberta they were following scent trails laid down years before? Think about it. All that weather, the seasons, trees falling and decaying. Can you imagine that?"

"Cara's allergic," he said. "I mean, that's why we had to get rid of him. Seymour. His name was Seymour."

There was a long braying burst of laughter from Ben Ober, who had an arm round Don's shoulder and was painting something in the air with a stiffened forefinger. Cara stood just beyond him, with the La Portes, her face glowing as if it had been basted. Celia La Porte looked from him to the girl and back again, then arched her eyebrows wittily and raised her long-stemmed glass of Viognier, as if toasting him. All three of them burst into laughter. Julian turned his back.

"You didn't take him to the pound—did you?" The girl's eyes went flat. "Because that's a death sentence, I hope you realize that."

"Cara found a home for him."

They both looked to Cara then, her shining face, her anchorwoman's hair. "I'm sure," the girl said.

"No, really. She did."

The girl shrugged, looked away from him. "It doesn't matter," she said with a flare of anger. "Dogs are just slaves, anyway."

## KAMALA AND AMALA

The Reverend Singh had wanted to return to the site the following afternoon and excavate the den,

convinced that these furtive night creatures were in fact human children, children abducted from their cradles and living under the dominion of beasts—unbaptized and unsaved, their eternal souls at risk—but urgent business called him away to the south. When he returned, late in the evening, ten days later, he sat over a dinner of cooked vegetables, rice, and dal, and listened as Chunaram told him of the wolf bitch that had haunted the village two years back, after her pups had been removed from a den in the forest and sold for a few annas apiece at the Khuar market. She could be seen as dusk fell, her dugs swollen and glistening with extruded milk, her eyes shining with an unearthly blue light against the backdrop of the forest. People threw stones, but she never flinched. And she howled all night from the fringes of the village, howled so that it seemed she was inside the walls of every hut simultaneously, crooning her sorrow into the ears of each sleeping villager. The village dogs kept hard by, and those that didn't were found in the morning, their throats torn out. "It was she," the Reverend exclaimed, setting down his plate as the candles guttered and moths beat at the netting. "She was the abductress—it's as plain as morning."

A few days later, he got up a party that included several railway men and returned to the termite mound, bent on rescue. In place of the rifle, he carried a stout cudgel cut from a mahua branch. He brought along a weighted net as well. The sun hung overhead. All was still. And then the hired beaters started in, the noise of them racketing through the trees, coming closer and closer until they converged on the site, driving hares and bandicoot rats and the occasional gaur before them. The railway men tensed in the machan, their rifles trained on the entrance to the burrow, while Reverend Singh stood by with a party of diggers to effect the rescue when the time came. It was unlikely that the wolves would have been abroad in daylight, and so it was no surprise to the Reverend that no large animal was seen to run before the beaters and seek the shelter of the den. "Very well," he said, giving the signal, "I am satisfied. Commence the digging."

As soon as the blades of the first shovels struck the mound, a protracted snarling could be heard emanating from the depths of the burrow. After a few minutes of the tribesmen's digging, the she-wolf sprang out at them, ears flattened to her head, teeth flashing. One of the diggers went for her with his spear just as the railway men opened fire from the machan and turned her, snapping, on her own wounds; a moment later, she lay stretched out dead in the dust of the laterite clay. In a trice the burrow was uncovered, and there they were, the spirits made flesh, huddled in a defensive posture with the two wolf cubs, snarling and panicked, scrabbling at the clay with their broken nails to dig themselves deeper. The tribesmen dropped their shovels and ran, panicked themselves, even as the Reverend Singh eased himself down into the hole and tried to separate child from wolf.

The larger of the children, her hair a feral cap that masked her features, came at him biting and scratching, and finally he had no recourse but to throw his net over the pullulating bodies and restrain each of the creatures separately in one of the long, winding *gelaps* the local tribesmen use for winter wear. On inspection, it was determined that the children were females, aged approximately three and six, of native stock, and apparently, judging from the dissimilarity of their features, unrelated. The she-wolf, it seemed, had abducted the children on separate occasions, perhaps even from separate locales, and over the course of some time. Was this the bereaved bitch that Chunarem had reported? the Reverend wondered. Was she acting out of a desire for revenge? Or merely trying, in her own unknowable way, to replace what had been taken from her and ease the burden of her heart?

In any case, he had the children confined to a pen so that he could observe them, before caging them in the back of the bullock cart for the trip to Midnapore and the orphanage, where he planned to baptize and civilize them. He spent three full days studying them and taking notes. He saw that they persisted in going on all fours, as if they didn't know any other way, and that they fled from sunlight as if it were an instrument of torture. They thrust forward to lap water like the beasts of the forest and took nothing in their mouths but bits of twig and stone. At night they came to life and stalked the enclosure with shining eyes like the *bhuts* that half the villagers still believed them to be. They did not know any of the languages of the human species, but communicated with each other—and with their sibling wolves—in a series of grunts, snarls, and whimpers. When the moon rose, they sat on their haunches and howled.

It was Mrs. Singh who named them, some weeks later. They were pitiful, filthy, soiled with their own urine and excrement, undernourished, and undersized. They had to be caged to keep them from harming the other children, and Mrs. Singh, though it broke her heart to do it, ordered them put in restraints, so that the filth and the animal smell could be washed from them, even as their heads were shaved to defeat the ticks and fleas they'd inherited from the only mother they'd ever known. "They need delicate names," Mrs. Singh told her husband, "names to reflect the beauty and propriety they will grow into." She named the younger sister Amala, after a bright-yellow flower native to

Bengal, and the elder Kamala, after the lotus that blossoms deep in the jungle pools.

## RUNNING WITH THE PACK

The sun stroked her like a hand, penetrated and massaged the dark yellowing contusion that had sprouted on the left side of her rib cage. Her bones felt as if they were about to crack open and deliver their marrow and her heart was still pounding, but at least she was here, among the dogs, at rest. It was June, the season of pollen, the air supercharged with the scents of flowering, seeding, fruiting, and there were rabbits and squirrels everywhere. She lay prone at the lip of the den and watched the pups—long-muzzled like their mother and brindled Afghan peach and husky silver—as they worried a flap of skin and fur that

Snout had peeled off the hot black glistening surface of the road and dropped at their feet. She was trying to focus on the dogs—on A1, curled up nose to tail in the trampled weed after regurgitating a mash of kibble for the pups, on Decidedly, his eyes half closed as currents of air brought him messages from afar, on Humper and Factitious—but she couldn't let go of the pain in her ribs and what that pain foreshadowed from the human side of things.

Don had kicked her. Don had climbed out of the car, crossed the field, and stood over her in his suede computer-engineer's ankle boots with the waffle bottoms and reinforced toes and lectured her while the dogs slunk low and rumbled deep in their throats. And, as his voice had grown louder, so, too, had the dogs' voices, until they were a

*"Oh, God! Here comes little Miss Perky."*

chorus commenting on the ebb and flow of the action. When was she going to get her ass up out of the dirt and act like a normal human being? That was what he wanted to know. When was she going to cook a meal, run the vacuum, do the wash—his underwear, for Christ's sake? He was wearing dirty underwear, did she know that?

She had been lying stretched out flat on the mound, just as she was now. She glanced up at him as the dogs did, taking in a piece of him at a time, no direct stares, no challenges. "All I want," she said, over the chorus of growls and low, warning barks, "is to be left alone."

"Left alone?" His voice tightened in a little yelp. "Left alone? You need help, that's what you need. You need a shrink, you know that?"

She didn't reply. She let the pack speak for her. The rumble of their response, the flattened ears and stiffened tails, the sharp, savage gleam of their eyes should have been enough, but Don wasn't attuned. The sun seeped into her. A grasshopper she'd been idly watching as it bent a dandelion under its weight suddenly took flight, right past her face, and it seemed the most natural thing in the world to snap at it and break it between her teeth.

Don let out some sort of exclamation—"My God, what are you doing? Get up out of that, get up out of that now!"—and it didn't help matters. The dogs closed in. They were fierce now, barking in savage recusancy, their emotions twisted in a single cord. But this was Don, she kept telling herself, Don from grad school, bright and buoyant Don, her mate, her husband, and what harm was there in that? He wanted her back home, back in the den, and that was his right. The only thing was, she wasn't going.

"This isn't research. This is bullshit. Look at you!"

"No," she said, giving him a lazy, sidelong look, though her heart was racing, "it's dog shit. It's on your shoes, Don. It's in your face. In your precious computer—"

That was when he'd kicked her. Twice, three times, maybe. Kicked her in the ribs as if he were driving a ball over an imaginary set of uprights in the distance, kicked and kicked again—before the dogs went for him. A1 came in first, tearing at a spot just above his right knee, and then Humper, the bulldog who, she now knew, belonged to the feathery old lady up the block, got hold of his pant leg while Barely went for the crotch. Don screamed and thrashed, all right—he was a big animal, two hundred and ten pounds, heavier by far than any of the dogs—and he threatened in his big animal voice and fought back with all the violence of his big animal limbs, but he backed off quickly enough, threatening still, as he made his way across the field and into the car. She heard the door slam, heard the motor scream, and then there was the last thing she heard: Snout barking at the wheels as they revolved and took Don down the street and out of her life.

## SURVIVAL OF THE FITTEST

"You know he's locked her out, don't you?"

"Who?" Though he knew perfectly well.

"Don. I'm talking about Don and the dog lady?"

There was the table, made of walnut varnished a century before, the crystal vase full of flowers, the speckless china, the meat, the vegetables, the pasta. Softly, so softly he could barely hear it, there was Bach, too, piano pieces—partitas—and the smell of the fresh-cut flowers.

"Nobody knows where she's staying, unless it's out in the trash or the weeds or wherever. She's like a bag lady or something. Bea said Jerrilyn Hunter said she saw her going through the trash one morning. Do you hear me? Are you even listening?"

"I don't know. Yeah. Yeah, I am." He'd been reading lately. About dogs. Half a shelf of books from the library in their plastic covers—behavior, breeds, courting, mating, whelping. He excised a piece of steak and lifted it to his lips. "Did you hear the Leibowitzes' Afghan had puppies?"

"*Puppies?* What in God's name are you talking about?" Her face was like a burr under the waistband, an irritant, something that needed to be removed and crushed.

"Only the alpha couple gets to breed. You know that, right? And so that would be the husky and the Leibowitzes' Afghan, and I don't know who the husky belongs to—but they're cute, real cute."

"You haven't been—? Don't tell me. Julian, use your sense: she's out of her mind. You want to know what else Bea said?"

"The alpha bitch," he said, and he didn't know why he was telling her this, "she'll actually hunt down and kill the pups of any other female in the pack who might have got pregnant, a survival-of-the-fittest kind of thing—"

"She's crazy, bonkers, out of her *fucking* mind, Julian. They're going to have her committed, you know that? If this keeps up. And it will keep up, won't it, Julian? Won't it?"

## THE COMMON ROOM AT MIDNAPORE

At first they would take nothing but raw milk. The wolf pups, from which they'd been separated for reasons both of sanitation and acculturation, eagerly fed on milk-and-rice pap in their kennel in one of the outbuildings, but neither of the girls would touch the pan-warmed milk or rice or the stewed vegetables that Mrs. Singh provided, even at night, when they were most active and their eyes spoke a language of desire all their own.

Each morning and each evening before retiring, she would place a bowl on the floor in front of them, trying to tempt them with biscuits, confections, even a bit of boiled meat, though the Singhs were vegetarians themselves and repudiated the slaughter of animals for any purpose. The girls drew back into the recesses of the pen the Reverend had constructed in the orphanage's common room, showing their teeth. Days passed. They grew weaker. He tried to force-feed them balls of rice, but they scratched and tore at him with their nails and their teeth, setting up such a furious caterwauling of hisses, barks, and snarls as to give rise to rumors among the servants that he was torturing them. Finally, in resignation, and though it was a risk to the security of the entire orphanage, he left the door to the pen open in the hope that the girls, on seeing the other small children at play and at dinner, would soften.

In the meantime, though the girls grew increasingly lethargic—or perhaps because of this—the Reverend was able to make a close and telling examination of their physiology and habits. Their means of locomotion had transformed their bodies in a peculiar way. For one thing, they had developed thick pads of callus at their elbows and knees, and toes of abnormal strength and inflexibility—indeed, when their feet were placed flat on the ground, all five toes stood up at a sharp angle. Their waists were narrow and extraordinarily supple, like a dog's, and their necks dense with the muscle that had accrued there as a result of leading with their heads. And they were fast, preternaturally fast, and stronger by far than any other children of their respective ages that the Reverend and his wife had ever seen. In his diary, for the sake of posterity, the Reverend noted it all down.

Still, all the notes in the world wouldn't matter a whit if the wolf children didn't end their hunger strike, if that was what this was, and the Reverend and his wife had begun to lose hope for them, when the larger one—the one who would become known as Kamala—finally asserted herself. It was early in the evening, the day after the Reverend had ordered the door to the pen left open, and the children were eating their evening meal while Mrs. Singh and one of the servants looked on and the Reverend settled in with his pipe on the veranda. The weather was typical for Bengal in that season, the evening heavy and close, every living thing locked in the grip of the heat, and all the mission's doors and windows standing open to receive even the faintest breath of a breeze. Suddenly, without warning, Kamala bolted out of the pen, through the door, and across the courtyard to where the orphanage dogs were being fed scraps of uncooked meat, gristle, and bone left over from the preparation of the servants' meal, and before anyone could stop her she was down among them, slashing with her teeth, fighting off even the biggest and most aggressive of them until she'd bolted the red meat and carried off the long, hoofed shin-bone of a gaur to gnaw in the farthest corner of her pen.

And so the Singhs, though it revolted them,

*"I really appreciate this . . ."*

fed the girls on raw meat until the crisis had passed, and then they gave them broth, which the girls lapped from their bowls, and finally meat that had been at least partially cooked. As for clothing—clothing for decency's sake—the girls rejected it as unnatural and confining, tearing any garment from their backs and limbs with their teeth, until Mrs. Singh hit on the idea of fashioning each of them a single tight-fitting strip of cloth they wore knotted round the waist and drawn up over their privates, a kind of diaper or loincloth they were forever soiling with their waste. It wasn't an ideal solution, but the Singhs were patient—the girls had suffered a kind of deprivation no other humans had ever suffered—and they understood that the ascent to civilization and light would be steep and long.

When Amala died, shortly after the wolf pups had succumbed to what the Reverend presumed was distemper communicated through the orphanage dogs, her sister wouldn't let anyone approach the body. Looking back on it, the Reverend would see this as Kamala's most human moment—she was grieving, grieving because she had a soul, because she'd been baptized before the Lord and was no wolfling or jungle *bhut* but a human child after all, and here was the proof of it. But poor Amala. Her, they hadn't been able to save. Both girls had been dosed with sulfur powder, which caused them to expel a knot of roundworms up to six inches in length and as thick as the Reverend's little finger, but the treatment was perhaps too harsh for the three-year-old, who was suffering from fever and dysentery at the same time. She'd seemed all right, feverish but calm, and Mrs. Singh had tended her through the afternoon and evening. But when the Reverend's wife came into the pen in the morning Kamala flew at her, raking her arms and legs and driving her back from the straw in which her sis-

ter's cold body lay stretched out like a figure carved of wood. They restrained the girl and removed the corpse. Then Mrs. Singh retired to bandage her wounds and the Reverend locked the door of the pen to prevent any further violence. All that day, Kamala lay immobile in the shadows at the back of the pen, wrapped in her own limbs. When night fell, she sat back on her haunches behind the rigid geometry of the bars and began to howl, softly at first, and then with increasing force and plangency until it was the very sound of desolation itself, rising up out of the compound to chase through the streets of the village and into the jungle beyond.

## GOING TO THE DOGS

The sky was clear all the way to the top of everything, the sun so thick in the trees that he thought it would catch there and congeal among the motionless leaves. He didn't know what prompted him to do it, exactly, but as he came across the field he balanced first on one leg and then the other, to remove his shoes and socks. The grass—the weeds, wildflowers, puffs of mushroom, clover, swaths of moss—felt clean and cool against the lazy progress of his bare feet. Things rose up to greet him, things and smells he'd forgotten all about, and he took his time among them, moving forward only to be distracted again and again. He found her, finally, in the tall nodding weeds that concealed the entrance of the den, playing with the puppies. He didn't say hello, didn't say anything—just settled in on the mound beside her and let the pups surge into his arms. The pack barely raised its collective head.

Her eyes came to him and went away again. She was smiling, a loose, private smile that curled the corners of her mouth and lifted up into the smooth soft terrain of the silken skin under her eyes. Her clothes barely covered her anymore, the turtleneck torn at the throat and sagging across one clavicle, the black jeans hacked off crudely—or maybe chewed off—at the peaks of her thighs. The sneakers were gone altogether, and he saw that the pale-yellow soles of her feet were hard with callus, and her hair—her hair was struck with sun and shining with the natural oil of her scalp.

He'd come with the vague idea—or, no, the very specific idea—of asking her for one of the pups, but now he didn't know if that would do, exactly. She would tell him that the pups weren't hers to give, that they belonged to the pack, and though each of the pack's members had a bed and a bowl of kibble awaiting it in one of the equitable houses of the alphabetical grid of the development springing up around them, they were free here, and the pups, at least, were slaves to no one. He felt the thrusting wet snouts of the creatures in his lap, the surge of their animacy, the softness of the stroked ears, and the prick of the milk teeth, and he smelled them, too, an authentic smell compounded of dirt, urine, saliva, and something else also: the unalloyed sweetness of life. After a while, he removed his shirt, and so what if the pups carried it off like a prize? The sun blessed him. He loosened his belt, gave himself some breathing room. He looked at her, stretched out beside him, at the lean, tanned, running length of her, and he heard himself say, finally, "Nice day, isn't it?"

"Don't talk," she said. "You'll spoil it."

"Right," he said. "Right. You're right."

And then she rolled over, bare flesh from the worried waistband of her cutoffs to the dimple of her breastbone and her breasts caught somewhere in between, under the yielding fabric. She was warm, warm as a fresh-drawn bath, the touch of her communicating everything to him, and the smell of her, too—he let his hand go up under the flap of material and roam over her breasts, and then he bent closer, sniffing.

Her eyes were fixed on his. She didn't say anything, but a low throaty rumble escaped her throat.

## WAITING FOR THE RAINS

The Reverend Singh sat there on the veranda, waiting for the rains. He'd set his notebook aside, and now he leaned back in the wicker chair and pulled meditatively at his pipe. The children were at play in the courtyard, an array of flashing limbs and animated faces, attended by their high, bright catcalls and shouts. The heat had loosened its grip ever so perceptibly, and they were, all of them, better for it. Except Kamala. She was indifferent. The chill of winter, the damp of the rains, the full merciless sway of the sun—it was all the same to her. His eyes came to rest on her where she lay across the courtyard in a stripe of sunlight, curled in the dirt with her knees drawn up beneath her and her chin resting atop the cradle of her crossed wrists. He watched her for a long while as she lay motionless there, no more aware of what she was than a dog or an ass, and he felt defeated, defeated and depressed. But then one of the children called out in a voice fluid with joy, a moment of triumph in a game among them, and the Reverend couldn't help but shift his eyes and look.

(*Some details here are from Charles MacLean's* The Wolf Children: Fact or Fantasy? *and* Wolf-Children and Feral Man, *by the Reverend J. A. L. Singh and Robert M. Zingg.*)

| 2002 |

*"Now play dead."*

PRICE $3.50

# THE NEW YORKER

ulriksen

# DOGTOWN

BEN McGRATH

If you find yourself on the service road of the Major Deegan, in the shadow of the Cross Bronx Expressway, between the train tracks and the Harlem River, and you hear loud barking interspersed with the crowing of roosters, do not be alarmed. Follow your ears (and the flies) to the chain-link fence, and, while noting the "No Trespassing" and "Beware of Dog" signs, introduce yourself politely to whoever might be sitting nearby, at the entrance of what appears to be a canine shantytown—plywood huts, wire cages, tarps, and assorted vehicles packed into half an acre near the base of High Bridge.

The land belongs to the New Tabernacle Baptist Church, which for the past eleven years has run a kind of nonprofit kennel club for urban hunting dogs, carrying on a local, word-of-mouth tradition that dates to around the Second World War. A New Tabernacle volunteer named Lewis Jones (everyone calls him Lou) serves as the chief groundskeeper, tending to, among other things, a charred mound of beer cans that passes for a waste-disposal system. Fifteen dog shanties house about fifty beagles, coon hounds, and Italian mastiffs. At one point, the kennel had an official name—the Highbridge Hunting Club—but its charter has lapsed. The dogs' owners do not pay rent, although donations to the church are encouraged.

One afternoon last week, a man named Peppy (Lou calls him Lucky) was sitting on a rusty bench while facing a pen full of mastiffs that were pawing aggressively at the gate. "These are guard dogs," he said. "The rest are bird dogs, rabbit dogs." (Lou says that the mastiffs are for "hunting the big game, like lions and tigers.") A few roosters wandered around freely, speaking their minds. Peppy had on a green T-shirt with a picture of a snarling dog and the words "Remington Steel: We breed with overseas methods." He said that he'd been raising dogs in the Bronx for almost two years—an arriviste. "There's not too many places in the city you can keep dogs," Peppy said. "If you're into hunting, you heard of this place."

Soon, Peppy's business partner, Ross, arrived, carrying a couple of boxes of syringes, for applying tick and flea repellent. The two men opened the nearest padlock and began attending to their pooches, the most stubborn of whom was named Isabella. A couple of albino cats prowled the perimeter. The roosters kept crowing. "Cats came, I guess, because of the rats," Ross said. "See, the rats will come to try to eat the dog food."

"Got rats down here about the size of an arm," Peppy said. "Cats eat the rats."

"I guess it's just a nature thing," Ross said.

And the roosters? "That's old hunting tradition," Peppy said. "It's a Southern thing."

Guests are not common, and the conversation proceeds at a languid pace. "The A.S.P.C.A. comes down sometimes," Peppy said. "Sanitation comes by to see that it don't smell." Occasionally, someone from a rowing club upriver will wander by, having beached at a wet-weather discharge station near the Metro-North rail yards.

"One guy approached us—he wanted to bring some pits," Ross said, referring to pit bulls. "We try to steer clear of that."

"He might be Michael Vick-in' it," Peppy said, referring to the Atlanta Falcons quarterback, who has been indicted on charges of helping to run a dogfighting ring. (Last week, Vick pleaded not guilty.) Peppy and Ross's dogs don't fight, they said, but they do compete. Ross used to breed "Rotts"—Rottweilers. Now he prefers Cane Corsos, a variety of Italian mastiff. "They're the No. 1 guard dog in the world," he said. He also enters them in events organized by the Protection Sports Association. "You got 'weight pull,' 'hard catch,' " he said. Then he described an event in which a man hides behind a tepee and, on command, a dog charges and lunges for the man's arm. Isabella paced and drooled.

A recent visitor, still bewildered upon leaving such a place (the nearest subway stop is twenty-five minutes away on foot, across multiple highways), tried recounting his experience—the hounds, the roosters, the cats, the tepee—to Joseph Pentangelo, a local A.S.P.C.A. official. "You sound like you went to Oz," he said, and added, "You're not allowed to own roosters in New York City." He wasn't aware of the New Tabernacle kennel, but he mentioned that the week before he'd been called to retrieve a horse that had got loose on Pelham Parkway. "This guy appeared to be squatting, keeping it as a pet," Pentangelo said. "He'd made this stable using the box from a delivery truck, and then he fashioned a corral out of wire and police barricade and pickle barrels."

| 2007 |

# FANCIERS

## GEORGE W. S. TROW

Right this minute (if you will join us in the historical present), we are in the Eugenia Room of Sardi's. What a treat. Not many actors physically in sight, although plenty of ghosts. Instead, we see dozens of dog fanciers (members of the Dog Fanciers Club), wonderful and exciting pictorial representations of dogs displayed on stands, a few pieces of dog sculpture standing on their own, and, above all these (like classical busts in a Grinling Gibbons room), pictures from what we have come to think of as Sardi's Permanent Collection—i.e., the real stuff. We start with one of Michael Redgrave, by Don Bevan. "Dear Sardi's, I am happy to be here among my friends" is the inscription.

The dog fanciers also seem to be happy to be with one another. Their club has been in existence for about thirty years. It used to meet at various restaurants, even at the old Statler, but for the last fifteen years it has met exclusively at Sardi's. For a time, the dog fanciers just talked about dogs—American Kennel Club rules and things like that—but three years ago Howard Atlee, the club president, decided that their meetings needed what he calls "event identity," and so now they have an annual show of dog art, and judge the art, and the winning artists receive five hundred dollars and are invited to donate their objects to the Dog Museum, in St. Louis. In order that this story won't be threaded through with unnecessary suspense, we can say that the winners this year are *Stumped*, by Harry C. Weber, which is a bronze sculpture of two Jack Russells writhing around in the wilderness; *Champion American Bull Terrier*, by Babette Joan Kiesel, which is a straightforward portrait; *The Party*, by Jodi Hudspeth, which is a bronze sculpture of three Yorkshire terriers having a kind of birthday party, with a gift box and dog bones and a ball and another small thing, maybe a book, in the foreground; and *Autumn Beauty*, by Stephen J. Hubbell, which is an oil on canvas of a debonair English setter.

O.K. Now we're back in the Eugenia Room. After looking up at Michael Redgrave, we walked cautiously around. We admired a piece of sculpture called *Sighthound,* by Kathleen O'Bryan Hedges, from Great Falls, Virginia. *Sighthound* was very thin and silvery. Then we heard another piece being described as "Matissey" and "Cézanney," and we kept right on going. We talked to Mr. Atlee. "Most people have a picture of a dog, even if they don't have a dog," he said. We have no idea if this is true. Mr. Atlee looked just like Gregory Peck in *To Kill a Mockingbird* as he said it. We were told that Ellen Fisch, who lives in Hewlett, Long Island, and has painted a portrait of Ranger, the Queen Mother's Welsh corgi, and presented it at Clarence House, was there. But we didn't meet her. We did meet Mrs. Edward L. Stone, a distinguished-looking woman, who was one of the judges.

Then we met a real dog fancier, a woman with long dark hair. "Are you fond of dogs?" we asked, because we noticed that she was staring intently at *Sighthound.*

"I live for my dog," she said simply.

"What sort of dog do you have?" we asked.

"A Maltese," she said, and then she tried to clarify for us her relationship to the dog world. "There are things I don't do," she said. "I don't travel to Far Hills in the driving rain so that my dog can compete with other dogs. On the other hand, I do do a lot of what you might call *doting.* I pay a lot of attention to how my dog's hair is washed and cut. On the other hand, I don't act as a chaperon for my dog."

We asked her what she meant by "chaperon."

"Well," she said, "it's like children's social life, where your parents pay for you to go, and you have to go and say hello to the ones brought by other parents."

We said that she seemed to be talking from the dog's point of view.

"Yes, that's what I do do," the woman said.

Then we looked at a painting of a huge white dog walking in a vast area of pale-green-and-amber grass. The artist was Patrick McManus, and quite soon we found ourself talking to him.

"What sort of dog is it?" we asked.

"It's a whippet. It needs to be hung in a room bigger than this one."

"What other kinds of work do you do?"

"I do this. I live hand to mouth. I was a construction worker at one time. I'm a recluse. I don't come out too often." He introduced us to his girlfriend, Baby. "I also write songs and write for a dog magazine," he said.

Lunch was served. There were eleven

tables of dog fanciers. There were party favors on the tables donated by J-B Wholesale Pet Supplies, Inc. One of them was a yellow rubber lion. "A pet would be afraid of it," someone said. We looked over at the head table. There were Mr. Atlee and Mrs. Stone and also Captain Arthur J. Haggerty, who is a famous dog trainer and is famous in another way, too—for looking like Mr. Clean, the cleanser man. He has a big, very bald head.

"I've just been to the Dog Museum, in St. Louis," the woman sitting next to us said. "They just built a new wing. I saw forty years of Snoopy. *Snoopy*, I thought. Anyway, it's a fine museum."

Two of the judges made speeches. Howard Atlee was at the microphone a lot as he introduced people. He announced the winners. We had a chance to have another talk with the serious dog fancier who thinks from the dog's point of view. We asked her what she most liked about the Dog Fanciers Club.

"Well, my favorite book is dedicated to one of the founders of the club," she said. "I can tell you are going to ask what my favorite book is. It's *The Complete Maltese,* by Nicholas Cutillo. It's not an old book, but it deals with antiquity. The Maltese is a very old breed."

"Antiquity?" we asked.

"Antiquity. Mr. Cutillo quotes the Roman poet Martial, who wrote about a Maltese who belonged to a Roman governor of Malta. The Maltese was named Issa. I happen to be able to quote you part of what Martial wrote. He said, 'Issa is

more frolicsome than Catullus' sparrow. Issa is purer than a dove's kiss. Issa is gentler than a maiden, Issa is more precious than Indian gems.' I find that to be very moving. *My* Maltese is more frolicsome than a sparrow, as a matter of fact. I love the name Issa. If I had read this epigram before I named my Maltese, I might have named her Issa. By the way, the epigram ends 'Lest the last days that she sees the light should snatch her from him forever, Publius had her picture painted.' So that justifies the idea of painting a dog's picture."

We were going to ask this serious dog fancier what name she did give her Maltese, but before we could she turned around and disappeared from the Eugenia Room.

We asked Patrick McManus if he ever painted anything other than dogs.

"I did a whole series of construction workers when I was a construction worker," he said.

| 1990 |

# DOG RACE.

... we were both up early when
the big day came. I wandered into the kitchen for a
share but Claud got dressed right away and
went outside to arrange about the straw. The
kitchen was a front room and through the
window I could see the sun just coming
up behind the line of trees on top of the
ridge the other side of the valley. //

~~the moment as it rose behind the trees and
shone through them, just one moment when
they ... the whole crest of the hill seemed
to be on fire.~~ // Each time Claud came past
the window with an armload of straw I
noticed over the rim of the mirror the intent
breathless expression on his face, the great round brown
head thrusting forward at the forehead wrinkled into deep
corrugations right up to the hairline. I'd
seen this look on him once before at
was the evening he's asked Clarice to marry
him. Today he was so excited he even
walked funny, treading softly as though the
around the filling-station were a shade too hot for the
of his feet; as he kept packing more
the back of the van to

# DOG RACE

*Fiction*

## ROALD DAHL

We were both up early when the big day came. I wandered into the kitchen for a shave, but Claud got dressed right away and went outside to arrange about the straw. Through the kitchen window, I could see the sun just coming up behind the line of trees on top of the ridge the other side of the valley.

Each time Claud came past the window with an armload of straw, I noticed over the rim of the mirror the intent, breathless expression on his face, the great round bullethead thrusting forward and the forehead wrinkled into deep corrugations right up to the hairline. I'd only seen this look on him once before and that was the evening he'd asked Clarice to marry him. Today he was so excited he even walked funny, treading softly as though the concrete around the filling station were a shade too hot for the soles of his feet; and he kept packing more and more straw into the back of the van to make it comfortable for Jackie.

Then he came into the kitchen to fix breakfast, and I watched him put the pot of soup on the stove and begin stirring it. He had a long metal spoon and he kept on stirring and stirring, and about every half minute he leaned forward and stuck his nose into that sickly-sweet steam of cooking horseflesh. Then he started putting extras into it—three peeled onions, a few young carrots, a cupful of stinging-nettle tops, a teaspoon of Valentine's Meat Extract, twelve drops of cod-liver oil—and everything he touched was handled very gently with the ends of his big fat fingers as though it might have been a little fragment of Venetian glass. He took some minced horse meat from the icebox, measured one handful into Jackie's bowl, three into the other, and when the soup was ready he shared it out between the two, pouring it over the meat.

It was the same ceremony I'd seen performed each morning for the past five months, but never with such breathless concentration as this. There was no talk, not even a glance my way, and when he turned and went out again to fetch the dogs, even the back of his neck and his shoulders seemed to be whispering, "Oh, Jesus, don't let anything go wrong, and especially don't let me do anything wrong today."

I heard him talking softly to the dogs in the pen as he put the leashes on them, and when he brought them around into the kitchen, they came in prancing and pulling to get at the breakfast, treading up and down with their front feet and waving their enormous tails from side to side like whips.

"All right," Claud said, speaking at last. "Which is it?"

Most mornings he'd offer to bet me a pack of cigarettes, but there were bigger things at stake today, and I knew all he wanted for the moment was a little extra reassurance.

He watched me as I walked once around the two beautiful, identical, tall, velvety-black dogs, and he moved aside, holding the leashes at arm's length to give me a better view.

"Jackie!" I said, trying the old trick that never worked. "Hey Jackie!" Two identical heads with identical expressions flicked around to look at me, four bright, identical, deep-yellow eyes stared into mine. There'd been a time when I fancied the eyes of one were a slightly darker yellow than those of the other. There'd also been a time when I thought I could recognize

Jackie because of a deeper brisket and a shade more muscle on the hindquarters. But it wasn't so.

"Come on," Claud said. He was hoping that today of all days I would make a bad guess.

"This one," I said. "This is Jackie."

"Which?"

"This one on the left."

"There!" he cried, his whole face suddenly beaming. "You're wrong again!"

"I don't think I'm wrong."

"You're about as wrong as you could possibly be. And now listen, Gordon, and I'll tell you something. All these last weeks, every morning while you've been trying to pick him out—you know what?"

"What?"

"I've been keeping count. And the result is you haven't been right even *one-half* the time! You'd have done better tossing a coin!"

What he meant was that if I (who saw them every day and side by side) couldn't do it, why the hell should we be frightened of Mr. Feasey. Claud knew Mr. Feasey was famous for spotting ringers, but he knew also that it could be very difficult to tell the difference between two dogs when there wasn't any.

He put the bowls of food on the floor, giving Jackie the one with the least meat because he was running today. When he stood back to watch them eat, the shadow of deep concern was back again on his face and the large pale eyes were staring at Jackie with the same rapt and melting look of love that up till recently had been reserved only for Clarice.

"You see, Gordon," he said. "It's just what I've always told you. For the last hundred years, there's been all manner of ringers, some good and some bad, but in the whole history of dog racing there's never been a ringer like this."

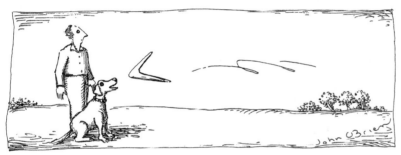

"Then what you buy him for?"

"Well," he had said, the big bovine face secret and cunning, "it occurred to me that maybe he might possibly look a little bit like Jackie. What d'you think?"

"I suppose he does a bit, now you come to mention it."

He had handed me the leash and I had taken the new dog inside to dry him off while Claud had gone round to the pen to fetch his beloved. And when he returned and we put the two of them together for the first time, I can remember him stepping back and saying, "Oh, Jesus!" and standing dead still in front of them like he was seeing a phantom. Then he became very quick and quiet. He got down on his knees and began comparing them carefully point by point, and it was almost like the room was getting warmer and warmer the way I could feel his excitement growing every second through this long silent examination in which even the toe nails and the dewclaws, eighteen on each dog, were matched alongside one another for color.

"Look," he had said at last, standing up. "Walk them up and down the room a few times, will you?" And then he had stayed there for quite five or six minutes leaning against the stove with his eyes half closed and his head on one side, watching them and frowning and chewing his lips. After that, as though he didn't believe what he had seen the first time, he had gone down

"I hope you're right," I said, and my mind began travelling back to that freezing afternoon just before Christmas, when Claud had asked to borrow the van, and had driven away in the direction of Aylesbury without saying where he was going. I had assumed he was off to see Clarice, but late in the afternoon he had returned bringing with him this dog he said he'd bought off a man for thirty-five shillings.

"Is he fast?" I had said. We were standing out by the pumps and Claud was holding the dog on a leash and looking at him, and a few snowflakes were falling and settling on the dog's back. The motor of the van was still running.

"Fast!" Claud had said. "He's just about the slowest dog you ever saw in your whole life!"

again on his knees to re-check everything once more; but suddenly, in the middle of it, he had jumped up and looked at me, his face fixed and tense, with a curious whiteness around the nostrils and the eyes. "All right," he had said, a little tremor in his voice. "You know what? We're home. We're rich."

And then the secret conferences between us in the kitchen, the detailed planning, the selection of the most suitable track, and finally every other Saturday, eight times in all, locking up my filling station (losing a whole afternoon's custom) and driving the ringer all the way up to Oxford to a scruffy little track out in the fields near Headingley where the big money was played but which was actually nothing except a line of old posts and cord to mark the course, an upturned bicycle for pulling the dummy hare, and at the far end, in

the distance, six traps and the starter. We had driven this ringer up there eight times over a period of sixteen weeks and entered him with Mr. Feasey and stood around on the edge of the crowd in the freezing raining cold, waiting for his name to go up on the blackboard in chalk. The Black Panther we called him. And when his time came, Claud would always lead him down to the traps and I would stand at the finish to catch him and keep him clear of the fighters, the gypsy dogs that the gypsies so often slipped in specially to tear another one to pieces at the end of a race.

But you know, there was something rather sad about taking this dog all the way up there so many times and letting him run and watching him and hoping and praying that whatever happened he would always come last. Of course, the praying wasn't necessary and we never really had

*"Leave it on."*

a moment's worry because the old fellow simply couldn't gallop and that's all there was to it. He ran exactly like a crab. The only time he didn't come last was when a big fawn dog by the name of Amber Plash put his foot in a hole and broke a hock and finished on three legs. But even then ours only just beat him. So this way we got him right down to bottom grade with the scrubbers, and the last time we were there all the bookies were laying him twenty or thirty to one and calling his name and begging people to back him.

Now at last, today, on this sunny day, it was Jackie's turn to go instead. Claud said we mustn't run the ringer any more or Mr. Feasey might begin to get tired of him and throw him out altogether, he was so slow. Claud said this was the exact psychological time to have it off, and that Jackie would win it anything between thirty and fifty lengths.

He had raised Jackie from a pup and the dog was only fifteen months now, but he was a good fast runner. He'd never raced yet, but we knew he was fast from clocking him round the little private schooling track at Uxbridge where Claud had taken him every Sunday since he was seven months old—except once when he was having some inoculations. Claud said he probably wasn't fast enough to win top grade at Mr. Feasey's, but where we'd got him now, in bottom grade with the scrubbers, he could fall over and get up again and still win it twenty—well, anyway ten or fifteen lengths.

So all I had to do this morning was go to the bank in the village and draw out fifty pounds for myself and fifty for Claud, which I would lend him as an advance against wages, and then at twelve o'clock lock up the filling station and hang the notice on one of the pumps saying "GONE FOR THE DAY." Claud would shut the ringer in the pen at the back and put Jackie in the van and off we'd

go. I won't say I was as excited about it as Claud, but there again, I didn't have all sorts of important things depending on it either, like buying a house and being able to get married. Nor was I almost *born* in a kennel with greyhounds like he was, walking about thinking of absolutely nothing else—except perhaps Clarice in the evenings. Personally, I had my own career as a filling-station owner to keep me busy, not to mention second-hand cars, but if Claud wanted to fool around with dogs that was all right with me, especially a thing like today—if it came off. As a matter of fact, I don't mind admitting that every time I thought about the money we were putting on and the money we might win, my stomach gave a little lurch.

The dogs had finished their breakfast now and Claud took them out for a short walk across the field opposite while I got dressed and fried the eggs. Afterward, I went to the bank and drew out the money (all in ones), and the rest of the morning seemed to go very quickly serving customers.

At twelve sharp, I locked up and hung the notice on the pump. Claud came around from the back leading Jackie and carrying a large suitcase made of reddish-brown cardboard.

"Suitcase?"

"For the money," Claud answered. "You said yourself no man can carry two thousand pound in his pockets."

Jackie looked wonderful, with two big hard muscles the size of melons bulging on his hindquarters, his coat glistening like black velvet. While Claud was putting the suitcase in the van, the dog did a little prancing jig on his toes to show how fit he was, then he looked up at me and grinned, just like he knew he was off to the races to win two thousand pounds and a heap of glory.

We got in the van and off we went. I was

doing the driving. Claud was beside me and Jackie was standing up on the straw in the rear looking over our shoulders through the windshield. Claud kept turning round and trying to make him lie down so he wouldn't get thrown whenever we went round the sharp corners, but the dog was too excited to do anything except grin back at him and wave his enormous tail.

"You got the money, Gordon?" Claud was chain-smoking cigarettes and quite unable to sit still.

"Yes."

"Mine as well?"

"I got a hundred and five altogether. Five for the winder like you said, so he won't stop the hare and make it a no race."

"Good," Claud said, rubbing his hands together hard as though he were freezing cold. "Good good good."

We drove through the little narrow High Street of Great Missenden and caught a glimpse of old Rummins going into the Nag's Head for his morning pint, then outside the village we turned left and climbed over the ridge of the Chilterns toward Princes Risbor-

ough, and from there it would only be twenty-odd miles to Oxford.

And now a silence and a kind of tension began to come over us both. We sat very quiet, not speaking at all, each nursing his own fears and excitements, containing his anxiety. And Claud kept smoking his cigarettes and throwing them half finished out the window. Usually, on these trips, he talked his head off all the way there and back, all the things he'd done with dogs in his life, the jobs he'd pulled, the places he'd been, the money he'd won; and all the things other people had done with dogs, the thievery, the cruelty, the unbelievable trickery and cunning of owners at the flapping tracks. But today I don't think he was trusting himself to speak very much. At this point, for that matter, nor was I. I was sitting there watching the road, and trying to keep my mind off the immediate future by thinking back on all that stuff Claud had told me about this curious greyhound-racing racket.

I swear there wasn't a man alive who knew more about it than Claud did, and ever since we'd got the ringer and decided to pull this job, he'd taken it upon himself to give me an education in the business. By now, in theory at any rate, I suppose I knew nearly as much as him.

It had started during the very first strategy conference we'd had in the kitchen. I can remember it was the day after the ringer arrived and we were sitting there watching for customers through the window, and Claud was explaining to me all about what we'd have to do, and I was trying to follow him as best I could until finally there came one question I had to ask him.

"What I don't see," I had said, "is why you use the ringer at all. Wouldn't it be safer if we use Jackie all the time and simply stop him the first half-dozen races so he come last? Then when

## PRIVATE WIRE

Among the pampered pets of the city is an elderly bull-dog who has his own telephone extension. He lives in an old-fashioned brownstone on the upper West Side with an old lady who clung for a long time to the wall-type instrument. The dog used to dash to the telephone every time it rang and worry the cord, with the result that the repairman had to be called in about once a month. When his mistress finally had a handset phone installed, she asked them to leave the old one on the wall. Now, whenever there is a call, the dog takes it on his own wire. Makes for peace of mind all around.    | 1938 |

we're good and ready, we can let him go. Same result in the end, wouldn't it be, if we do it right? And no danger of being caught."

Well, as I say, that did it. Claud looked up at me quickly and said, "Hey! None of that! I'd just like you to know stopping's something I never do. What's come over you, Gordon?" He seemed genuinely pained and shocked by what I had said.

"I don't see anything wrong with it."

"Now listen to me, Gordon. Stopping a good dog breaks his heart. A good dog knows he's fast, and seeing all the others out there in front and not being able to catch them—it breaks his heart, I tell you. And what's more, you wouldn't be making suggestions like that if you knew some of the tricks them fellers do to stop their dogs at the flapping tracks."

"Such as what, for example?" I had asked.

"Such as anything in the world almost, so long as it makes the dog go slower. And it takes a lot of stopping, a good greyhound does. Full of guts and so mad keen you can't even let them watch a race they'll tear the leash right out of your hand rearing to go. Many's the time I've seen one with a broken leg insisting on finishing the race."

He had paused then, looking at me thoughtfully with those large pale eyes, serious as hell and obviously thinking deep. "Maybe," he had said, "if we're going to do this job properly I'd better tell you a thing or two so's you'll know what we're up against."

"Go ahead and tell me," I had said. "I'd like to know."

For a moment he stared in silence out the window, and his face began slowly to assume the expression of a man who possesses dangerous secrets. "The main thing you got to remember," he had said, "is that all these fellers going to the flap-

ping tracks with dogs—they're artful. They're more artful than you could possibly imagine." Again he paused, marshalling his thoughts.

"Now take for example the different ways of stopping a dog. The first, the commonest, is strapping."

"Strapping?"

"Yes. Strapping 'em up. That's commonest. Pulling the muzzle strap tight around their necks so they can't hardly breathe, see. A clever man knows just which hole on the strap to use and just how many lengths it'll take off his dog in a race. Usually a couple of notches is good for five or six lengths. Do it up real tight and he'll come last. I've known plenty of dogs collapse and die from being strapped up tight on a hot day. Strangulated, absolutely strangulated, and a very nasty thing it was, too. Then again, some of 'em just tie two of the toes together with black cotton. Dog never runs well like that. Unbalances him."

"That doesn't sound too bad."

"Then there's others that put a piece of fresh-chewed gum up under their tails, right up close where the tail joins the body. And there's nothing funny about that," he had said, indignant. "The tail of a running dog goes up and down ever so slightly and the gum on the tail keeps sticking to the hairs on the backside, just where it's tenderest. No dog likes that, you know. Then there's sleeping pills. That's used a lot nowadays. They do it by weight, exactly like a doctor, and they measure the powder according to whether they want to slow him up five or ten or fifteen lengths. Those are just a few of the ordinary ways," he had said. "Actually, they're nothing. Absolutely nothing compared with some of the other things that's done to hold a dog back in a race, especially by the gypsies. There's things the gypsies do that are almost too disgusting to mention, such as when they're just putting the dog in the trap, things you wouldn't hardly do to your worst enemies."

And when he had told me about those—which were, indeed, terrible things because they had to do with physical injury, quickly, painfully inflicted—he had gone on to tell me what they did when they wanted the dog to win.

"There's just as terrible things done to make 'em go fast as to make 'em go slow," he had said softly, his face veiled and secret. "And perhaps commonest of all is wintergreen. Whenever you see a dog going around with no hair on his back or little bald patches all over him—that's wintergreen. Just before the race, they rub it hard into the skin. Sometimes it's Sloan's liniment, but mostly it's wintergreen. Stings terrible. Stings so bad that all the old dog wants to do is run run run as fast as he possibly can to get away from the pain.

"Then there's special drugs they give with the needle. Mind you, that's the modern method and most of the spivs at the track are too ignorant to use it. It's the fellers coming down from London in the big cars with stadium dogs they've borrowed for the day by bribing the trainer—they're the ones use the needle."

I could remember him sitting there at the

*"I guess cats just can't appreciate Frank Gehry."*

kitchen table with a cigarette dangling from his mouth and dropping his eyelids to keep out the smoke and looking at me through his wrinkled, nearly closed eyes, and saying, "What you've got to remember, Gordon, is this. There's nothing they won't do to make a dog win if they want him to. On the other hand, no dog can run faster than he's built, no matter what they do to him. So if we can get Jackie down into bottom grade, then we're home. No dog in bottom grade can get near him, not even with wintergreen and needles."

And so it had gone on. During each of the eight long trips we had subsequently made to the track with the ringer, I had heard more and more about this charming sport—more, especially, about the methods of stopping them and making them go (even the names of the drugs and the quantities to use). I heard about the "rat treatment" (for non-chasers, to make them chase the dummy hare), where a rat is placed in a can which is then tied around the dog's neck. There's a small hole in the lid of the can just large enough for the rat to poke its head out and nip the dog. But the dog can't get at the rat, and so naturally he goes half crazy running around and being bitten in the neck, and the more he shakes the can the more the rat bites him. Finally, someone releases the rat, and the dog, who up to then was a nice docile tail-wagging animal who wouldn't hurt a mouse, pounces on it in a rage and tears it to pieces. Do this a few times, Claud had said—"mind you, I don't hold with it myself"—and the dog becomes a real killer who will chase anything, even the dummy hare.

We were over the Chilterns now and running down out of the beechwoods into the flat elm and oak-tree country south of Oxford. Claud sat quietly beside me, nursing his nervousness and smoking cigarettes, and every two or three minutes he would turn round to see if Jackie was all right. The dog was at last lying down, and each time Claud turned round, he whispered something to him softly, and the dog acknowledged his words with a faint movement of the tail that made the straw rustle.

Soon we would be coming into Thame, the broad High Street where they penned the pigs and cows and sheep on market day, where the fair came once a year with the swings and roundabouts and bumping cars and gypsy caravans right there in the street in the middle of the town. Claud was born in Thame, and we'd never driven through it yet without him mentioning this fact.

"Well," he said as the first houses came into sight, "here's Thame. I was born and bred in Thame, you know, Gordon."

"You told me."

"Lots of funny things we used to do around here when we was nippers," he said, slightly nostalgic.

"I'm sure."

He paused, and I think more to relieve the tension building up inside him than anything else, he began talking about the years of his youth.

"There was a boy next door," he said. "Gilbert Gomm his name was. Little sharp ferrety face and one leg a bit shorter'n the other. Shocking things him and me used to do together. You know one thing we done, Gordon?"

"What?"

"We'd go into the kitchen Saturday nights when Mum and Dad were at the pub, and we'd disconnect the pipe from the gas ring and bubble the gas into a milk bottle full of water. Then we'd sit down and drink it out of teacups."

"Was that so good?"

"Good! It was disgusting! But we'd put lashings of sugar in and then it didn't taste so bad."

"Why did you drink it?"

Claud turned and looked at me, incredulous. "You mean you never drunk Snake's Water!"

"Can't say I have."

"I thought everyone done that when they was kids! It intoxicates you, just like wine only worse, depending on how long you let the gas bubble through. We used to get reeling drunk together there in the kitchen Saturday nights and it was marvellous. Until one night Dad comes home early and catches us. I'll never forget that night as long as I live. There was me holding the milk bottle, and the gas bubbling through it lovely, and Gilbert kneeling on the floor ready to turn off the tap the moment I give the word, and in walks Dad."

"What did he say?"

"Oh, Christ, Gordon, that was terrible. He didn't say one word, but he stands there by the door and he starts feeling for his belt, undoing the buckle very slow and pulling the belt slow out of his trousers, looking at me all the time. Great big feller he was, with great big hands like coal hammers and a black mustache and them little purple veins running all over his cheeks. Then he comes over quick and grabs me by the coat and lets me have it, hard as he can, using the end with the buckle on it and honest to God, Gordon, I thought he was going to kill me. But in the end he stops and then he puts on the belt again, slow and careful, buckling it up and tucking in the flap and belching with the beer he's drunk. And then he walks out again back to the pub, still without saying a word. Worst hiding I ever had in my life."

"How old were you then?"

"Round about eight, I should think," Claud said.

As we drew closer to Oxford, he became silent again. He kept twisting his neck to see if Jackie was all right, to touch him, to stroke his head, and once he turned around and knelt on the seat to gather more straw around the dog, murmuring something about a draft. We drove around the fringe of Oxford and into a network of narrow country roads, and after a while we turned in to a small bumpy lane and along this we began to overtake a thin stream of men and women all walking and cycling in the same direction. Some of the men were leading greyhounds. There was a large saloon car in front of us and through the rear window we could see a dog sitting on the back seat between two men.

"They come from all over," Claud said. "That one there's probably come up special from London. Probably slipped him out from one of the big stadium kennels just for the afternoon. That could be a Derby dog probably, for all we know."

"Hope he's not running against Jackie."

"Don't worry," Claud said. "All new dogs automatically go in top grade. That's one rule Mr. Feasey's very particular about."

There was an open gate leading into a field, and Mr. Feasey's wife came forward to take our admission money before we drove in.

"He'd have her winding the bloody pedals, too, if she had the strength," Claud said. "Old Feasey don't employ more people than he has to."

I drove across the field and parked at the end of a line of cars along the top hedge. We both got out and Claud went quickly round the back to fetch Jackie. I stood beside the van, waiting. It was a very large field with a steepish slope on it, and we were at the top of the slope, looking down. In the distance, I could see the six starting traps and the wooden posts marking the track which ran along the bottom of the field and turned sharp at right angles and came on up the hill toward the crowd, to the finish. Thirty yards beyond the finishing line stood the upturned bicycle for driving the hare. Because it is portable, this is

the standard machine for hare driving used at all flapping tracks. It comprises a flimsy wooden platform about eight feet high, supported on four poles knocked into the ground. On top of the platform, there is fixed, upside down with wheels in the air, an ordinary old bicycle. The rear wheel is to the front, facing down the track, and from it the tire has been removed, leaving a concave metal rim. One end of the cord that pulls the hare is attached to this rim, and the winder (or hare driver), by straddling the bicycle at the back and turning the pedals with his hands, revolves the wheel and winds in the cord around the rim. This pulls the dummy hare toward him at any speed he likes up to forty miles an hour. After each race, someone takes the dummy hare (with cord attached) all the way down to the starting traps again, thus unwinding the cord on the wheel, ready for a fresh start. From his high platform, the winder can watch the whole race and regulate the speed of the hare to keep it just ahead of the leading dog. He can also stop the hare any time he wants and make it a "no race" (if the wrong dog looks like winning) by suddenly turning the pedals backward and getting the cord tangled up in the hub of the wheel. The other way of doing it is to slow down the hare suddenly, for perhaps one second, and that makes the lead dog automatically check a little so that the others catch up with him. He is an important man, the winder.

I could see Mr. Feasey's winder already standing atop his platform, a powerful-looking man in a blue sweater, leaning on the bicycle and looking down at the crowd through the smoke of his cigarette.

There is a curious law in England which permits race meetings of this kind to be held only seven times a year over one piece of ground. That is why all Mr. Feasey's equipment was moveable; after the seventh meeting he would simply trans-

fer to the next field. The law didn't bother him at all.

There was already a good crowd, and the bookmakers were erecting their stands in a line over to the right. Claud had Jackie out of the van now and was leading him over to a group of people clustered around a small stocky man dressed in riding breeches—Mr. Feasey himself. Each person in the group had a dog on a leash and Mr. Feasey kept writing names in a notebook that he held in his left hand. I sauntered over to watch.

"Which you got there?" Mr. Feasey said, pencil poised above the notebook.

"Midnight," a man said who was holding a black dog. Mr. Feasey stepped back a pace and looked most carefully at the dog.

"Midnight. Right. I got him down."

"Jane," the next man said.

"Let me look. Jane . . . Jane . . . yes, all right."

"Soldier." This dog was led by a tall man with long teeth who wore a dark-blue, double-breasted lounge suit.

Mr. Feasey bent down to examine the dog. The other man looked up at the sky.

"Take him away," Mr. Feasey said.

The man looked down quick.

"Go on, take him away."

"Listen, Mr. Feasey," the man said, "now don't talk so bloody silly, *please*."

"Go on and beat it, Larry, and stop wasting my time. You know as well as I do the Soldier's got two white toes on his off fore."

"Now look, Mr. Feasey," the man said. "You ain't even seen Soldier for six months at least."

"Come on now, Larry, and beat it. I haven't got time arguing with you." Mr. Feasey didn't appear in the least angry. "Next," he said.

I saw Claud step forward leading Jackie. The large bovine face was fixed and wooden, the eyes staring at something about a yard above Mr.

Feasey's head, and he was holding the leash so tight his knuckles were like a row of little white onions.

Mr. Feasey suddenly started laughing. "Hey!" he cried. "Here's the Black Panther. Here's the champion."

"That's right, Mr. Feasey," Claud said.

"Well, I'll tell you," Mr. Feasey said, "you can take him right back home where he come from. I don't want him."

"But look here, Mr. Feasey—"

"Six or eight times at least I've run him for you now and that's enough. Look—why don't you shoot him and have done with it?"

"Now listen, Mr. Feasey, please. Just once more and I'll never ask you again."

"Not even once! I got more dogs than I can handle here today. There's no room for crabs like that."

I thought Claud was going to cry.

"Now honest, Mr. Feasey," he said, "I been up at six every morning this past two weeks giving him roadwork and massage and buying him beefsteaks, and believe me he's a different dog absolutely than what he was last time he run."

"Just the same, you can take him away. There's no sense running dogs as slow as him. Take him home now, will you please, and don't hold up the whole meeting."

I was watching Claud. Claud was watching Mr. Feasey. Mr. Feasey was looking round for the next dog to enter up. Under his brown tweedy jacket he wore a yellow pullover, and this streak of yellow on his breast and his thin gaitered legs and the way he jerked his head from side to side made him seem like some sort of a little perky bird—a goldfinch, perhaps.

Claud took a step forward. His face was beginning to purple slightly.

"I'll tell you what I'll do, Mr. Feasey. I'm so

absolutely sure this dog's improved I'll bet you a quid he don't finish last. There you are."

Mr. Feasey turned slowly round and looked at Claud. "You crackers?" he asked.

"I'll bet you a quid, there you are, just to prove what I'm saying."

It was a dangerous move, certain to cause suspicion, but Claud knew it was the only thing left to do. There was silence while Mr. Feasey bent down and examined the dog. I could see the way his eyes were moving slowly over the animal's whole body, part by part. There was something to admire in the man's thoroughness, and in his memory; something to fear also in this self-confident little rogue who held in his head the shape and color and markings of perhaps several hundred different but very similar dogs. He never needed more than one little clue— a small scar, a splay toe, a trifle in at the hocks, a less pronounced wheelback, a slightly darker brindle; Mr. Feasey always remembered.

So I watched him now as he bent down over Jackie. His face was pink and fleshy, the mouth small and tight as though it couldn't stretch enough to make a smile, and the eyes were like two little cameras focussed sharply on the dog.

"Well," he said, straightening up. "It's the same dog anyway."

"I should hope so, too!" Claud cried. "Just what sort of a feller you think I am, Mr. Feasey?"

"I think you're crackers, that's what I think. But it's a nice easy way to make a quid. I suppose you forgot how Amber Flash nearly beat him on three legs last meeting?"

"This one wasn't fit then," Claud said. "He hadn't had beefsteak and massage and roadwork like I've been giving him lately. But look, Mr. Feasey, you're not to go sticking him in top grade just to win the bet. This is a bottom-grade dog, Mr. Feasey. You know that."

Mr. Feasey laughed. The small button mouth opened into a tiny circle and he laughed and looked at the crowd who laughed with him. "Listen," he said, laying a hairy hand on Claud's shoulder, "I know my dogs. I don't have to do any fiddling around to win *this* quid. He goes in bottom."

"Right," Claud said. "That's a bet." He walked away with Jackie and I joined him.

"Jesus, Gordon, that was a near one!"

"Shook me."

"But we're in now," Claud said. He had that breathless look on his face again and he was walking about quick and funny, like the ground was burning his feet.

People were still coming through the gate into the field and there were easily three hundred of them now. Not a very nice crowd. Sharp-nosed men and women with dirty faces and bad teeth and quick, shifty eyes. The dregs of the big town. Oozing out like sewage from a cracked pipe and trickling along the road through the gate and making a smelly little pond of sewage at the top end of the field. They were all there—some with dogs, some without. Dogs led about on pieces of string, miserable dogs with hanging heads, thin mangy dogs with sores on their quarters (from sleeping on board), sad old dogs with gray muzzles, doped dogs, dogs stuffed with porridge to stop them winning, dogs walking stiff-legged—one especially, a white one. "Claud, why is that white one walking so stiff-legged?"

"Which one?"

"That one over there."

"Ah yes, I see. Very probably because he's been hung."

"Hung?"

"Yes, hung. Suspended in a harness for twenty-four hours with his legs dangling."

"Good God, but why?"

"To make him run slow, of course. Some people don't hold with dope or stuffing or strapping up. So they hang 'em."

"I see."

"Either that," Claud said, "or they sandpaper them. Rub their pads with rough sandpaper and take the skin off so it hurts when they run."

"Yes, I see."

And then the fitter, brighter-looking dogs, the better-fed ones who get horsemeat every day, not pig swill or rusk and cabbage water, their coats shinier, their tails moving, pulling at their leads, undoped, unstuffed, awaiting perhaps a more unpleasant fate, the muzzle strap to be tightened an extra four notches. *But make sure he can breathe now, Jock. Don't choke him completely. Don't let's have him collapse in the middle of the race. Just so he wheezes a bit, see. Go on tightening it up an extra notch at a time until you can hear him wheezing. You'll see his mouth open and he'll start breathing heavy. Then it's just right. But not if his eyeballs is bulging. Watch out for that, will you? O.K.?*

*O.K.*

"Let's get away from the crowd, Gordon. It don't do Jackie no good getting excited by all these other dogs."

We walked up the slope to where the cars were parked, then back and forth in front of the line of cars, keeping the dog on the move. Inside some of the cars I could see men sitting with their dogs, and the men scowled at us through the windows as we went by.

"Watch out now, Gordon. We don't want any trouble."

"No, all right."

These were the best dogs of all, the secret ones kept in the cars and taken out quick just to be entered up (under some invented name) and put back again quick and held there till the last min-

ute, then straight down to the traps and back again into the cars after the race so no nosy bastard gets too close a look. The trainer at the big stadium said so. *All right, he said. You can have him, but for Christsake don't let anybody recognize him. There's thousands of people know this dog, so you've got to be careful, see. And it'll cost you fifty pound.*

Very fast dogs these, but it doesn't much matter how fast they are, they probably get the needle anyway, just to make sure. One and a half cc.'s of ether, subcutaneous, done in the car, injected very slow. That'll put ten lengths on any dog. Or sometimes it's caffeine, caffeine in oil, or camphor. That makes them go, too. The men in the big cars know all about that. And some of them know about whiskey. But that's intravenous. Not so easy when it's intravenous. Might miss the vein. All you got to do is miss the vein and it don't work and where are you then? So it's ether, or it's caffeine, or it's camphor. *Don't give her too much of that stuff now, Jock. What does she weigh? Fifty-eight pounds. All right then, you know what the man told us. Wait a minute now. I got it written down on a piece of paper. Here it is. Point one of a cc, per ten pounds body weight equals five lengths over three hundred yards. Wait a minute now while I work it out. Oh, Christ, you better guess it. Just guess it, Jock. It'll be all right, you'll find. Shouldn't be any trouble anyway, because I picked the others in the race myself. Cost me a tenner to old Feasey. A bloody tenner I give him, and dear Mr. Feasey, I says, that's for your birthday and because I love you.*

*Thank you ever so much, Mr. Feasey says. Thank you, my good and trusted friend.*

And for stopping them, for the men in the big cars it's chlorbutal. That's a beauty, chlorbutal, because you can give it the night before, especially to someone else's dog. Or Pethidine. Pethidine and Hyoscine mixed, whatever that may be.

"Lot of fine old English sporting gentry here," Claud said.

"Certainly are."

"Watch your pockets, Gordon. You got that money hidden away?"

We walked around the back of the line of cars—between the cars and the hedge—and then I saw Jackie stiffen and begin to pull forward on the leash, advancing with a stiff crouching tread. About thirty yards away, there were two men. One was holding a large fawn greyhound, the dog stiff and tense like Jackie. The other was holding a sack in his hands.

"Watch," Claud whispered, "they're giving him a kill."

Out of the sack onto the grass tumbled a small white rabbit—fluffy white, young, tame. It righted itself and sat still, crouching in the hunched-up way rabbits crouch, its nose close to the ground. A frightened rabbit. Out of the sack so suddenly onto the grass with such a bump. Into the bright light. The dog was going mad with excitement now, jumping up against the leash, pawing the ground, throwing himself forward, whining. The rabbit saw the dog. It drew in its head and stayed still, paralyzed with fear. The man transferred his hold to the dog's collar, and the dog twisted and jumped and tried to get free. The other man pushed the rabbit with his foot, but it was too terrified to move. He pushed it again, flicking it forward with his toe like a football, and the rabbit rolled over several times, righted itself and began to hop over the grass away from the dog. The other man released the dog which pounced with one huge pounce upon the rabbit, and then came the squeals, not very loud but shrill and anguished and lasting rather a long time.

"There you are," Claud said. "That's a kill."

"Not sure I liked it very much."

"I told you before, Gordon. Most of 'em does it. Keens the dog up before a race."

"I still don't like it."

"Nor me. But they all do it. Even in the big stadiums, the trainers do it. Proper barbary I call it."

We strolled away, and below us on the slope of the hill the crowd was thickening and the bookies' stands with the names written on them in red and gold and blue were all erected now in a long line back of the crowd, each bookie already stationed on an upturned box beside his stand, a pack of numbered cards in one hand, a piece of chalk in the other, his clerk behind him with book and pencil. Then we saw Mr. Feasey walking over to a blackboard that was nailed to a post stuck in the ground.

"He's chalking up the first race," Claud said. "Come on, quick!"

We walked rapidly down the hill and joined the crowd. Mr. Feasey was writing the runners on the blackboard, copying names from his soft-covered notebook, and a little hush of suspense fell upon the crowd as they watched.

1. SALLY
2. THREE QUID
3. SNAILBOX LADY
4. BLACK PANTHER
5. WHISKEY
6. ROCKIT

"He's in it!" Claud whispered. "First race! Trap four! Now listen, Gordon! Give me a fiver quick to show the winder."

Claud could hardly speak from excitement. That patch of whiteness had returned around his nose and eyes, and when I handed him a five-pound note, his whole arm was shaking as he took it. The man who was going to wind the bicycle pedals was still standing on top of the wooden platform in his blue jersey, smoking. Claud went over and stood below him, looking up.

"See this fiver," he said, talking softly, holding it folded small in the palm of his hand.

The man glanced at it without moving his head.

"Just so long as you wind her true this race, see. No stopping and no slowing down, and run her fast. Right?"

The man didn't move but there was a slight, almost imperceptible lifting of the eyebrows. Claud turned away.

"Now look, Gordon. Get the money on gradual, all in little bits like I told you. Just keep going down the line putting on little bits so you don't kill the price, see. And I'll be walking Jackie down very slow, as slow as I dare, to give you plenty of time. Right?"

"Right."

"And don't forget to be standing ready to catch him at the end of the race. Get him clear away from all them others when they start fighting for the hare. Grab a hold of him tight and don't let go till I come running up with the collar and lead. That Whiskey's a gypsy dog and he'll tear the leg off anything as gets in his way."

"Right," I said. "Here we go."

I saw Claud lead Jackie over to the finishing post and collect a yellow jacket with "4" written on it large. Also a muzzle. The other five runners were there, too, the owners fussing around them, putting on their numbered jackets, adjusting their muzzles. Mr. Feasey was officiating, hopping

Overheard at the Metropolitan Museum, one young matron, to another. "In a way, it would be nice for the dogs to be reared with a sympathetic child."

| 1958 |

about in his tight riding breeches like an anxious perky bird, and once I saw him say something to Claud and laugh. Claud ignored him. Soon they would all start to lead the dogs down the track, the long walk down the hill and across to the far corner of the field to the starting traps. It would take them ten minutes to walk it. I've got at least ten minutes, I told myself, and then I began to push my way through the crowd standing six or seven deep in front of the line of bookies.

"Even money Whiskey! Even money Whiskey! Five to two Sally! Even money Whiskey! Four to one Snailbox! Come on now! Hurry up, hurry up! Which is it?"

On every board all down the line, the Black Panther was chalked up at twenty-five to one. I edged forward to the nearest book.

"Three pounds Black Panther," I said, holding out the money.

The man on the box had an inflamed magenta face and traces of some white substance around the corners of his mouth. He snatched the money and dropped it in his satchel. "Seventy-five pound to three Black Panther," he said. "Number forty-two." He handed me a ticket and his clerk recorded the bet.

I stepped back and wrote rapidly on the back of the ticket "75 to 3," then slipped it into the inside pocket of my jacket, with the money.

So long as I continued to spread the money out thin like this, it ought to be all right. And anyway, on Claud's instructions, I'd made a point of betting a few pounds on the ringer every time he'd run so as not to arouse any suspicion when the real day arrived. Therefore, with some confidence, I went all the way down the line staking three pounds with each book. I didn't hurry, but I didn't waste any time either, and after each bet I wrote the amount on the back of the ticket before slipping it into my pocket. There were seventeen bookies. I had seventeen tickets and had laid out fifty-one pounds without disturbing the price one point. Forty-nine pounds left to get on. I glanced quickly down the hill. One owner and his dog had already reached the traps. The others were only twenty or thirty yards away. Except for Claud. Claud and Jackie were only halfway there. I could see Claud in his old khaki greatcoat sauntering slowly along with Jackie pulling ahead keenly on the leash, and once I saw him stop completely and bend down, pretending to pick something up. When he went on again, he seemed to have developed a limp so as to go slower still. I hurried back to the other end of the line to start again.

"Three pounds Black Panther."

The bookmaker, the one with the magenta face and the white substance around the mouth, glanced up sharply, remembering the last time, and in one swift almost graceful movement of the arm he licked his fingers and wiped the figure twenty-five neatly off the board. His wet fingers left a small dark patch opposite Black Panther's name.

"All right, you got one more seventy-five to three," he said. "But that's the lot." Then he raised his voice and shouted, "Fifteen to one Black Panther! Fifteens the Panther!"

All down the line the twenty-fives were wiped out and it was fifteen to one the Panther now. I took it quick, but by the time I was through, the bookies had had enough and they weren't quoting him any more. They'd only taken six pounds each, but they stood to lose a hundred and fifty, and for them—small-time bookies at a little country flapping track—that was quite enough for one race, thank you very much. I felt pleased the way I'd managed it. Lots of tickets now. We stood to win something over two thou-

"It's always 'Sit,' 'Stay,' 'Heel'—never 'Think,' 'Innovate,' 'Be yourself.'"

sand pounds. Claud had said he'd win it thirty lengths. Where was Claud now?

Far away down the hill, I could see the khaki greatcoat standing by the traps and the big black dog alongside. All the other dogs were already in and the owners were beginning to walk away. Claud was bending down now, coaxing Jackie into No. 4, and then he was closing the door and turning away and beginning to run up the hill toward the crowd, the greatcoat flapping around him. He kept looking back over his shoulder as he ran.

Beside the traps, the starter stood, and his hand was up waving a handkerchief. At the other end of the track, beyond the winning post, quite close to where I stood, the man in the blue jersey was straddling the upturned bicycle on top of the wooden platform, and he saw the signal and waved back and began to turn the pedals with his hands. Then a tiny white dot in the distance—the artificial hare that was in reality a football with a piece of white rabbitskin tacked onto it—began to move away from the traps, accelerating fast. The traps went up and the dogs flew out. They flew out in a single dark lump, all together, as though it were one wide dog instead of six, and almost at once I saw Jackie drawing away from the field. I knew it was Jackie because of the color. There weren't any other black dogs in the race. It was Jackie all right. Don't move, I told myself. Don't move a muscle or an eyelid or a toe or a fingertip. Stand quite still and don't move. Watch him going. Come on Jackson, boy! No, don't shout. It's unlucky to shout. And don't move. Be all over in twenty seconds. Round the sharp bend now and coming up the hill and he must be fifteen or twenty lengths clear. Easy twenty lengths. Don't count the lengths, it's unlucky. And don't move. Don't move your head. Watch him out of your eye corners. Watch that Jackson go! He's

really laying down to it now up that hill. He's won it now! He can't lose it now . . .

When I got over to him, he was fighting the rabbitskin and trying to pick it up in his mouth, but his muzzle wouldn't allow it, and the other dogs were pounding up behind him and suddenly they were all on top of him grabbing for the rabbit, and I got hold of him round the neck and dragged him clear like Claud had said and knelt down on the grass and held him tight with both arms round his body. The other catchers were having a time all trying to grab their own dogs.

Then Claud was beside me, blowing heavily, unable to speak from blowing and excitement, removing Jackie's muzzle, putting on the collar and lead, and Mr. Feasey was there, too, standing with hands on hips, the button mouth pursed up tight like a mushroom, the two little cameras staring at Jackie all over again.

"So that's the game, is it?" he said.

Claud was bending over the dog and acting like he hadn't heard.

"I don't want you here no more after this, you understand that?"

Claud went on fiddling with Jackie's collar.

I heard someone behind us saying, "That flat-faced bastard with the frown swung it properly on old Feasey this time." Someone else laughed. Mr. Feasey walked away. Claud straightened up and went over with Jackie to the hare driver in the blue jersey who had dismounted from his platform.

"Cigarette," Claud said, offering the pack.

The man took one, also the five-pound note that was folded up small in Claud's fingers.

"Thanks," Claud said. "Thanks very much."

"Don't mention," the man said.

Then Claud turned to me. "You get it all on,

Gordon?" He was jumping up and down and rubbing his hands and patting Jackie, and his lips trembled as he spoke.

"Yes. Half at twenty-fives, half at fifteens."

"Oh, Christ, Gordon, that's marvellous. Wait here till I get the suitcase."

"You take Jackie," I said, "and go and sit in the car. I'll see you later."

There was nobody around the bookies now. I was the only one with anything to collect, and I walked slowly, with a sort of dancing stride and a wonderful bursting feeling in my chest, toward the first one in the line, the man with the magenta face and the white substance on his mouth. I stood in front of him and I took all the time I wanted going through my pack of tickets to find the two that were his. The name was Syd Pratchett. It was written up large across his board in gold letters on a scarlet field—"SYD PRATCH-ETT. THE BEST ODDS IN THE MIDLANDS. PROMPT SETTLEMENT."

I handed him the first ticket, and said, "Seventy-eight pounds to come." It sounded so good I said it again, making a delicious little chant of it. "Seventy-eight pounds to come on this one." I didn't mean to gloat over Mr. Pratch-ett. As a matter of fact, I was beginning to like him quite a lot. I even felt sorry for him having to fork out so much money. I hoped his wife and kids wouldn't suffer.

"Number forty-two," Mr. Pratchett said, turning to his clerk who held the big book. "Forty-two wants seventy-eight pound."

There was a pause while the clerk ran his finger down the column of recorded bets. He did this twice, then he looked up at the boss and began to shake his head.

"No," he said. "Don't pay. That ticket backed Snailbox Lady."

Mr. Pratchett, standing on his box, leaned over and peered down at the book. He seemed to be disturbed by what the clerk had said, and there was a look of genuine concern on the huge magenta face.

That clerk is a fool, I thought, and any moment now Mr. Pratchett's going to tell him so.

But when Mr. Pratchett turned back to me, the eyes had become narrow and hostile. "Now look, Charley," he said softly. "Don't let's have any of that. You know very well you bet Snailbox. What's the idea?"

"I bet Black Panther," I said. "Two separate bets of three pounds each at twenty-five to one. Here's the second ticket."

This time he didn't even bother to check it with the book. "You bet Snailbox, Charley," he said. "I remember you coming round." With that, he turned away from me and started wiping the names of the last-race runners off his board with a wet rag. Behind him, the clerk had closed the book and was lighting himself a cigarette. I stood watching them, and I could feel the sweat beginning to break through the skin all over my body.

"Let me see the book."

Mr. Pratchett blew his nose into the wet rag and dropped it to the ground. "Look," he said, "why don't you go away and stop annoying me?"

The point was this: a bookmaker's ticket, unlike a pari-mutuel ticket, never has anything written on it regarding the nature of your bet. This is normal practice, the same at every race track in the country, whether it's the Silver Ring at Newmarket, the Royal Enclosure at Ascot, or a tiny country flapping track near Oxford. All you receive is a card bearing the bookie's name and a serial number. The wager is (or should be) recorded by the bookie's clerk in his book, along-side the number of the ticket, but apart from that there is no evidence at all of how you betted.

"Go on," Mr. Pratchett was saying. "Hop it."

I stepped back a pace and glanced down the long line of bookmakers. None of them was looking my way. Each was standing motionless on his little wooden box beside his wooden placard, staring straight ahead into the crowd. I went up to the next one and presented a ticket.

"I had three pounds on Black Panther at twenty-five to one," I said firmly. "Seventy-eight pounds to come."

This man, who had a soft inflamed face, went through exactly the same routine as Mr. Pratchett, questioning his clerk, peering at the book, and giving me the same answers.

"Whatever's the matter with you?" he said quietly, speaking to me as though I were eight years old. "Trying such a silly thing as that."

This time I stepped well back. "You dirty thieving bastards!" I cried. "The whole lot of you!"

Automatically, as though they were puppets, all the heads down the line flicked round and looked at me. The expressions didn't alter. It was just the heads that moved, all seventeen of them, and seventeen pairs of cold, glassy eyes looked down at me. There was not the faintest flicker of interest in any of them.

"Somebody spoke," they seemed to be saying. "We didn't hear it. It's quite a nice day today."

The crowd, sensing excitement, was beginning to move in around me. I ran back to Mr. Pratchett, right up close to him, and poked him in the stomach with my finger. "You're a thief! A lousy rotten little thief!" I shouted.

The extraordinary thing was that Mr. Pratchett didn't seem to resent this at all.

"Well I never," he said. "*Look* who's talking!"

Then suddenly the big face broke into a wide, froglike grin, and he looked over at the crowd and shouted, "*Look* who's talking!"

All at once, everybody started to laugh. Down the line, the bookies were coming to life and turning to each other and laughing and pointing at me and shouting, "*Look* who's talking! *Look* who's talking!" The crowd began to take up the cry as well, and I stood there on the grass alongside Mr. Pratchett with this wad of tickets as thick as a pack of cards in my hand, listening to them and feeling slightly hysterical. Over the heads of the people, I could see Mr. Feasey beside his blackboard already chalking up the runners for the next race; and then beyond him, far away up the top of the field, I caught sight of Claud standing by the van, waiting for me with the suitcase in his hand.

It was time to go home.

| 1953 |

*"Scotch and toilet water?"*

UNDERDOGS

# THE DEPARTURE OF EMMA INCH

*Fiction*

## JAMES THURBER

Emma Inch looked no different from any other middle-aged, thin woman you might glance at in the subway or deal with across the counter of some small store in a country town, and then forget forever. Her hair was drab and unabundant, her face made no impression on you, her voice I don't remember—it was just a voice. She came to us with a letter of recommendation from some acquaintance who knew that we were going to Martha's Vineyard for the summer and wanted a cook. We took her because there was nobody else, and she seemed all right. She had arrived at our hotel in Forty-fifth Street the day before we were going to leave and we got her a room for the night, because she lived way uptown somewhere. She said she really ought to go back and give up her room, but I told her I'd fix that.

Emma Inch had a big scuffed brown suitcase with her, and a Boston bull terrier. His name was Feely. Feely was seventeen years old and he grumbled and growled and snuffled all the time, but we needed a cook and we agreed to take Feely along with Emma Inch, if she would take care of him and keep him out of the way. It turned out to be easy to keep Feely out of the way because he would be grousing anywhere Emma put him until she came and picked him up again. I never saw him walk. Emma had owned him, she said, since he was a pup. He was all she had in the world, she told us, with a mist in her eyes. I felt embarrassed but not touched. I didn't see how anybody could love Feely.

I didn't lose any sleep about Emma Inch and Feely the night of the day they arrived, but my wife did. She told me next morning that she had lain awake a long time thinking about the cook and her dog, because she felt kind of funny about them. She didn't know why. She just had a feeling that they were kind of funny. When we were all ready to leave—it was about three o'clock in the afternoon, for we had kept putting off the packing—I phoned Emma's room, but she didn't answer. It was getting late and we felt nervous—the Fall River boat would sail in about two hours. We couldn't understand why we hadn't heard anything from Emma and Feely. It wasn't until four o'clock that we did. There was a small rap on the door of our bedroom and I opened it and Emma and Feely were there, Feely in her arms, snuffing and snaffling, as if he had been swimming a long way.

My wife told Emma to get her bag packed, we were leaving in a little while. Emma said her bag *was* packed, except for her electric fan, and she couldn't get that in. "You won't need an electric fan at the Vineyard," my wife told her. "It's cool there, even during the day, and it's almost cold at night. Besides, there is no electricity in the cottage we are going to." Emma Inch seemed distressed. She studied my wife's face. "I'll have to think of something else then," she said. "Mebbe I could let the water run all night." We both sat down and looked at her. Feely's asthmatic noises were the only sounds in the room for a while. "Doesn't that dog ever stop that?" I asked, irritably. "Oh, he's just talking," said Emma. "He talks all the time, but I'll keep him in my room and he won't bother you none." "Doesn't he bother you?" I asked. "He *would* bother me," said Emma, "at night, but I put the electric fan on and keep the light burning. He don't make so much noise when it's light, because he don't snore. The fan

kind of keeps me from noticing him. I put a piece of cardboard, like, where the fan hits it and then I don't notice Feely so much. Mebbe I could let the water run in my room all night instead of the fan." I said "Hmmm" and got up and mixed a drink for my wife and me—we had decided not to have one till we got on the boat, but I thought we better have one now. My wife didn't tell Emma there would be no running water in her room at the Vineyard.

"We've been worried about you, Emma," I said. "I phoned your room but you didn't answer." "I never answer the phone," said Emma, "because I always get a shock. I wasn't there anyways. I couldn't sleep in that room. I went back to Mrs. McCoy's on Seventy-eighth Street." I lowered my glass. "You went back to Seventy-eighth Street last *night*?" I demanded. "Yes, sir," she said. "I had to tell Mrs. McCoy I was going away and wouldn't be there any more for a while—Mrs. McCoy's the landlady. Anyways, I never sleep in a hotel." She looked around the room. "They burn down," she told us.

It came out that Emma Inch had not only gone back to Seventy-eighth Street the night before but had walked all the way, carrying Feely. It had taken her an hour or two, because Feely didn't like to be carried very far at a time, so she had had to stop every block or so and put him down on the sidewalk for a while. It had taken her just as long to walk back to our hotel, too; Feely, it seems, never got up before afternoon—that's why she was so late. She was sorry. My wife and I finished our drinks, looking at each other, and at Feely.

Emma Inch didn't like the idea of riding to Pier 14 in a taxi, but after ten minutes of cajoling and pleading she finally got in. "Make it go slow," she said. We had enough time, so I asked the driver to take it easy. Emma kept getting to her feet and I kept pulling her back onto the seat. "I never been in an automobile before," she said. "It goes awful fast." Now and then she gave a little squeal of fright. The driver turned his head and grinned. "You're O.K. wit' me, lady," he said. Feely growled at him. Emma waited until he had turned away again, and then she leaned over to my wife and whispered. "They all take cocaine," she said. Feely began to make a new sound— a kind of high, agonized yelp. "He's singing," said Emma. She gave a strange little giggle, but the expression of her face didn't change. "I wish you had put the Scotch where we could get at it," said my wife.

If Emma Inch had been afraid of the taxicab, she was terrified by the Priscilla of the Fall River Line. "I don't think I can go," said Emma. "I don't think I could get on a boat. I didn't know they were so big." She stood rooted to the pier, clasping Feely. She must have squeezed him too hard, for he screamed—he screamed like a woman. We all jumped. "It's his ears," said Emma. "His ears hurt." We finally got her on the boat, and once aboard, in the salon, her terror abated somewhat. Then the three parting blasts of the boat whistle rocked lower Manhattan. Emma Inch leaped to her feet and began to run, letting go of her suitcase (which she had refused to give up to a porter) but holding onto Feely. I caught her just as she reached the gangplank. The ship was on its way when I let go of her arm.

It was a long time before I could get Emma to go to her stateroom, but she went at last. It was an inside stateroom, and she didn't seem to mind it. I think she was surprised to find that it was like a room, and had a bed and a chair and a washbowl. She put Feely down on the floor. "I think you'll have to do something about the dog," I said. "I think they put them somewhere and you get them when you get off." "No, they don't," said Emma. I guess, in this case, they didn't. I don't know. I shut the door on Emma Inch and Feely, and went away. My wife was drinking straight Scotch when I got to our stateroom.

"Other end, Mr. Pemberton."

The next morning, cold and early, we got Emma and Feely off the Priscilla at Fall River and over to New Bedford in a taxi and onto the little boat for Martha's Vineyard. Each move was as difficult as getting a combative drunken man out of the night club in which he fancies he has been insulted. Emma sat in a chair on the Vineyard boat, as far away from sight of the water as she could get, and closed her eyes and held onto Feely. She had thrown a coat over Feely, not only to keep him warm but to prevent any of the ship's officers from taking him away from her. I went in from the deck at intervals to see how she was. She was all right, or at least all right for her, until five minutes before the boat reached the dock at Woods Hole, the only stop between New Bedford and the Vineyard. Then Feely got sick. Or at any rate Emma said he was sick. He didn't seem to me any different from what he always was—his breathing was just as abnormal and irregular. But Emma said he was sick. There were tears in her eyes. "He's a very sick dog, Mr. Thurman," she said. "I'll have to take him home." I knew by the way she said "home" what she meant. She meant Seventy-eighth Street.

The boat tied up at Woods Hole and was motionless and we could hear the racket of the deckhands on the dock loading freight. "I'll get off here," said Emma, firmly, or with more firmness, anyway, than she had shown yet. I explained to her that we would be home in half an hour, that everything would be fine then, everything would be wonderful. I said Feely would be a new dog. I told her people sent sick dogs to Martha's Vineyard to be cured. But it was no good. "I'll have to take him off here," said Emma. "I always have to take him home when he is sick." I talked to her eloquently about the loveliness of Martha's Vineyard and the nice houses and the nice people and the wonderful accommodations for dogs. But I knew it was useless. I could tell by looking at her. She was going to get off the boat at Woods Hole.

"You really can't do this," I said, grimly, shaking her arm. Feely snarled weakly. "You haven't any money and you don't know where you are. You're a long way from New York. Nobody ever got from Woods Hole to New York alone." She didn't seem to hear me. She began walking toward the stairs leading to the gangplank, crooning to Feely. "You'll have to go all the way back on boats," I said, "or else take a train, and you haven't any money. If you are going to be so stupid and leave us now, I can't give you any money." "I don't want any money, Mr. Thurman," she said. "I haven't earned any money." I walked along in irritable silence for a moment; then I gave her some money. I made her take it. We got to the gangplank. Feely snaffled and gurgled. I saw now that his eyes were a little red and moist. I knew it would do no good to summon my wife—not when Feely's health was at stake. "How do you expect to get home from here?" I almost shouted at Emma Inch as she moved down the gangplank. "You're way out on the end of Massachusetts." She stopped and turned around. "We'll walk," she said. "We like to walk, Feely and me." I just stood still and watched her go.

When I went up on deck, the boat was clearing for the Vineyard. "How's everything?" asked my wife. I waved a hand in the direction of the dock. Emma Inch was standing there, her suitcase at her feet, her dog under one arm, waving goodbye to us with her free hand. I had never seen her smile before, but she was smiling now.

| 1935 |

# LOST DOG

## SUSAN ORLEAN

On August 6, 2003, Stephen Morris parked his car at the Atlanta History Center, expecting to spend half an hour or so edifying himself and his nephew on the particulars of the Civil War. It was the beginning of what would turn out to be a very bad day. At the time, though, everything seemed fine. Morris, a sinewy guy in his fifties with a scramble of light-brown hair and the deliberative air of a non-practicing academic, was at work on his doctoral dissertation—a biography of William Young, a seventeenth-century composer in the court of the Archduke of Innsbruck. Morris's teen-age nephew was visiting from British Columbia, and Morris had taken a break to show him the highlights of Atlanta. Morris's wife, Beth Bell, a compact, gray-haired, dry-witted epidemiologist whose specialty is hepatitis, was at her job at the Centers for Disease Control and Prevention, where she is a senior investigator; that day, she was knee-deep in a disease outbreak among attendees of jam-band concerts.

Morris found parking at the History Center easily enough—the open-air three-story garage is small but had plenty of available spaces. A sign above the entrance reads, "Help Us Keep Your Vehicle Safe While You Are Here. Please Remove All Valuables From Vehicle," but the History Center is in Buckhead, a prosperous, bosky section of the city where people and vehicles are generally out of harm's way. Morris and Bell's car—a dinged-up but serviceable 1999 Volvo station wagon—was not the sort to attract much attention anyway. The only noteworthy thing about the car was that Morris and Bell's dog,

Coby—a black Border collie with a false hip and a missing tooth—was in it, and so was a rather nice viola da gamba that Morris was looking after in his capacity as a rental-program director of the Viola da Gamba Society of America.

August 6th was a hot, soupy Wednesday in Atlanta. On Coby's behalf, Morris left the car in the History Center garage with its doors locked but with the engine running and the air-conditioner on—a bit of animal husbandry that is not unheard of in Southern climates if you leave your dog in a parked car and don't want to return to find him cooked. Uncooked dog notwithstanding, an unoccupied but idling car in a relatively empty parking garage might present to a certain kind of person an irresistible temptation. But if anyone saw such a person in the vicinity, he

didn't make an impression. Meanwhile, Morris and his nephew wandered through the cool, white halls of the museum, did a quick appraisal of the War Between the States, and then got ready to leave. At first, they thought they had misremembered where they'd parked the car, but after looking through the whole garage they came back to where they were sure they had left it. The Volvo, the viola da gamba, and the dog were gone. All that marked the spot was a glittering blue sprinkle of broken glass.

Around eighty cars are stolen in greater Atlanta every day—a steady but not exceptional amount, putting the city's number of disappearing cars a little behind Houston's and a little ahead of Seattle's. Most of the thefts reward the perpetrator with, in addition to a car, nothing more than a couple of cassette tapes, some

fast-food flotsam, and a clutch of exhausted air fresheners. Stephen Morris and Beth Bell's car, though, offered its unusual booty of dog and viola da gamba. The best guess is that the thief never even noticed; he was probably too excited about finding a car with a key in the ignition to take stock of its contents. Morris and Bell were upset about losing the viola da gamba—it was a fine reproduction of a fifteenth-century instrument and worth thousands of dollars—and they were not happy about losing their car, but those were trifling concerns compared with how they felt about losing their dog. In the report that Morris filed as soon as police arrived at the History Center, he didn't even mention the viola da gamba, but he brought up Coby's kidnapping a number of times.

Generally speaking, people love their dogs. Morris and Bell may be particularly devoted to Coby because they have nursed him through a variety of misadventures. They first spotted him at a sheepherding event nearly seven years ago when they were out bicycling in the Georgia countryside, but the breeder had promised the puppy to someone else, then decided that she wanted him for herself. Only after a day of negotiating did Coby end up with Morris and Bell. By the time he was two, he had full-blown dysplasia in his hips and needed a four-thousand-dollar surgery to replace one of them. At two and a half, he busted a tooth playing catch. Sometime later, he caught a stick wrong, and it jammed down his throat a few millimeters from his windpipe. Coby's vet likes to describe him as a dog with nine lives. In this life, anyway, Coby is a bushy-haired, prick-eared dog with tensed shoulders, an arresting stare, and an avid fetch-centric attitude. His dedication to retrieving bounceable rubber objects is so inexhaustible that it is exhausting. He has worn a deep, dusty path in Bell and Mor-

ris's yard between where they like to stand when they throw his Kong toy and where he likes to lie in wait for it. Morris has, thanks to Coby, developed a hot pitching arm and a firm way of saying, "That will do, Coby," when he runs out of steam.

So here was the problem: a dog on foot can travel at about five miles an hour, but a dog in a car can travel at sixty or seventy miles an hour. If Coby had jumped out of the car and walked away from the History Center, a perimeter of his possible whereabouts could have been plotted according to his likely pace. If he was still in the car—well, there was no way of knowing where he might be. Within an hour or two, he could have been in Alabama or South Carolina or Tennessee. Epidemiological science was of some help. That evening, a number of Bell's C.D.C. colleagues joined Morris, who had set out to search the thirty-three acres of the History Center and the surrounding area. "We were in the hypothesis-generation stage of the investigation," Bell said recently. "We first developed the hypothesis that Coby might still be at the History Center." Bell advanced the theory that the guy who had taken the car did not want a dog, and that it was likely that as soon as he noticed Coby he let him out. Her secondary theory was that as soon as the thief broke the window to get in, Coby had escaped. Both theories led to the Tullie Smith Farm—an antebellum homestead on the grounds of the History Center, where maidens in muslin churn butter and dip candles, and which, in the interest of total authenticity, also features a small herd of sheep. Border collies love sheep, so the crew of epidemiologists headed straight for the farm, and went there the next day, too. "We looked around and didn't see Coby, but we stopped everyone who passed us," one of the searchers told me. "We got some interesting responses. We approached one older woman and asked her if she had seen the dog, and she said no. Then she said that she had just lost her family and she asked us if we'd seen them." The search party hung some hastily made posters on light poles; they checked around trash cans and Dumpsters; they flagged down cars driving past on West Paces Ferry Road; they crisscrossed the History Center's Mary Howard Gilbert Memorial Quarry Garden and its Victorian Playhouse and its Swan Woods Trail. They searched until eleven on Wednesday, and most of the day Thursday, but there was no dog, and no sign of the dog.

In all sorts of circumstances, dogs go missing. They slip out the door with trick-or-treaters; they burrow under fences; they take off after unattainable squirrels and pigeons. Some dogs are repeat offenders. Recently, I heard the story of Huey and Dewey—Shetland-sheepdog siblings living in Massachusetts—who took exception to a visit to the veterinarian and ran off. Huey was recovered a quarter mile from the clinic by a dog-search volunteer after forty-three days, but Dewey was gone for good. A year and a half after that, Huey took exception to a visit to a kennel and was found eighty-nine days later a few feet from where she'd escaped. Sometimes a dog, presumed irretrievable, unexpectedly reappears: a certain Doberman pinscher from San Francisco, capable of standing on its head, vanished for three years; his owner finally located him when she overheard a waiter in a restaurant discussing his roommate's new dog, a Doberman with a knack for standing on its head. According to the American Pet Product Manufacturers Association, there are sixty-five million pet dogs in this country, and an estimated ten million of them go astray every year. About half of those are returned. Others end up in new homes under assumed names, or are killed by cars; most, though, disappear without a trace.

Dog-identification contraptions are a gigantic subset of the gigantic $34.3-billion-a-year pet-care industry. Aside from tags shaped like hearts and stars and hydrants in aluminum, gold, steel, and rhinestone, there is a brisk business in microchip tags—grain-size data-bearing devices that are implanted under the skin between an animal's shoulder blades. Microchips were introduced in the early eighties; AVID Identification Systems, of Norco, California, one of the largest microchip companies in the world, now has more than eleven million pets in its international database, and HomeAgain, another major microchip supplier, has chips in close to three million. And GPS Tracks, a Jericho, New York–based company, will soon introduce the world's first global-positioning system for dogs—a fist-size transmitter called a GlobalPetFinder, which will attach to the animal's collar and transmit its exact location every thirty seconds to a cell phone, computer, or a P.D.A. Before the device was even officially announced, the company had a waiting list of more than three thousand customers. "One night, it was pouring rain, my dogs had run away, the kids were hysterically crying, and I thought, This has to stop," Jennifer Durst, the founder and C.E.O. of GPS Tracks, said recently. "If they have Lo-Jack for cars, why can't there be a Lo-Dog for dogs?"

Coby, regrettably, had neither a microchip implant nor an early-release prototype of GlobalPetFinder. He wasn't even wearing his rabies tag, which is one more chance for an animal to be identified. Coby wears a nylon collar printed with his name and phone number and bearing his rabies tag, but Bell and Morris take it off every night so that Coby can sleep in the nude; that particular day, Morris hadn't put the collar on because he expected that the History Center trip would be brief and that Coby would be safely cosseted in the car. So the dog was now at large and anonymous, and everything that could identify him was at home, in a basket by the back door of Bell and Morris's sprawling split-level in Decatur, a suburb of Atlanta.

After Wednesday night's fruitless search, Bell decided that it was time to accelerate into an outbreak investigation—that is, to apply the same techniques she uses when analyzing, say, a wave of contagion among methamphetamine users in Wyoming. She and Morris blast-faxed Atlanta-area animal shelters, local rescue groups, and nearby veterinarian offices. They listed Coby on many of the almost countless Internet lost-pet

sites: PetFinder; Pets 911; Pets Missing in Action; FindFido; Petznjam; K9Finder; Dog Tracer; Lassie Come Home. They made hundreds of posters, and on Thursday hung them in high-volume, highly animal-sensitive areas like the parking lots of pet stores. They also hung them along Peachtree Road, which cuts diagonally through northeast Atlanta and is lined with the city's busiest restaurants and bars. Bell reasoned that it was one of the few places in Atlanta where people travel on foot—in other words, at a speed allowing for a close reading of a lost-dog poster.

They got responses immediately. A woman in northern Gwinnett County, about an hour's drive away, called to say that she had found a dog loosely fitting Coby's description; Bell and Morris drove up to take a look, but he turned out to be a Border collie someone else had lost. A woman called from Alabama, but the dog she had found was a small white poodle. The phone kept ringing—some of the calls reported dog-sightings, some offered advice, many were from people who had also lost dogs and just wanted to commiserate. Bell and Morris were also flooded with e-mails:

> Hi, This is Amy. . . . I'm so sorry to hear about this tragedy.

> Maybe the thieves put him out in Buckhead, but who knows? Wonder why the dog was left in a car on a HOT summer day??????

> I'm sorry your dog is missing, what a sad story.

On Thursday and Friday, they visited animal shelters around Atlanta to make sure that Coby wasn't waiting among the errant terriers and golden retrievers in the urban pounds, or the pit bulls and hounds languishing in shelters out of town. Bell realized that it was also time to start checking with the city employee who was assigned the unpleasant task of cataloguing each day's roadkill. "When you're searching for something, you never know what you're going to find," she said recently. "But you do have to ask the question."

One other question was whether to look for help elsewhere. The cohort of people with lost pets is large and constantly renewed, and forms a significant and often free-spending market to be served. In fact, one of the best-known lost-pet detectives in the country, Sherlock Bones, got into the business on a price-per-pound basis. Fed up with a job in the insurance industry, Bones, whose civilian name is John Keane, decided to start his own business but wasn't sure what to pursue until he noticed an ad for a lost Chihuahua. Keane said that the ad was an epiphany. "There was a thousand-dollar reward for that Chihuahua," he told me recently. "I thought to myself, That's five hundred dollars a pound." Keane, who started Sherlock Bones twenty-nine years ago and now operates out of Washougal, Washington, works on about five hundred cases a year. He used to do ground searches but now limits his involvement to consulting and to producing materials—primarily posters and mailers—for bereft owners. "Doing actual searches was very stressful," he said. At the time we spoke, he was out for a morning walk with his own dog, a French briard, and he was puffing lightly as he talked. "You're dealing with people in crisis. It's a serious business, since after eight hours it is unlikely someone will find their pet themselves, unless they're very lucky. They need help from someone who has the right information. You don't go to a rabbi to learn how to play baseball." He specializes in dogs and cats. "I don't deal with infrequent animals,"

he said. "Although I did make up a poster for a lost llama once, named Fernando Llama."

Bell and Morris decided to call Bones on Monday if they hadn't had any success; they also got in touch with a volunteer dog searcher named Debbie Hall, a member of a loose community of people across the country who trace lost pets for free. Hall helped them redesign their flyer, suggesting that they describe their car as well as the dog, and sent them extensive recommendations—eight long documents—on pet searches. Hall and her husband live in southeastern Massachusetts with a Yorkie-Chihuahua mix, a Yorkie-poodle mix, and three parakeets, two of which they got as a gift and a third that is probably someone's lost pet, because it just showed up in their yard one day. An entire room in the Halls' house is taken up by pet-detective appurtenances—a rack of camouflage clothes, a few Havahart traps, and half a dozen notebooks detailing her searches. Hall often stays out all night on cases. "It's a long-ass day," she explained, "but I love what I do. This is the one thing in my life that I'm good enough at to call my work." It has not been without its mishaps. She had a gun pulled on her while searching for a German shepherd in Virginia and once got trapped in her own six-foot Havahart trap. Worst of all, she has spent countless days mourning dogs that she found only after they had died. "It still hurts," she said, flipping to a page in her notebook about her first case—Tia, a runaway Border collie who eventually was found drowned. "But I am always optimistic that you will find your dog."

Late Saturday night, three days after Coby had disappeared, Bell and Morris got a break. A young guy walking down Peachtree had noticed one of their posters, and called to say that a few days earlier he had been playing rugby in a park downtown and had seen a dog that looked like

Coby. "He said a man had been walking around the park with the dog, saying someone had just dropped it off," Bell said.

First thing Sunday morning, Bell and Morris headed over to the park, a weary-looking plot of land in a hard-luck section of the city known as Old Fourth Ward. At the nearby Tabernacle Baptist Church and Mount Sinai Baptist Church, services were just ending, so Bell and Morris stopped and asked if anyone there had seen the dog, but no one had. They walked down Boulevard, the wide road on the western edge of Old Fourth Ward, past men playing dice in mini-mart parking lots and loitering in front of signs saying, "Private Property Do Not Sit On Wall." They passed out flyers and asked after Coby. "My brother has that dog," one of the men told Bell. "If you give me two dollars, I'll go get him." Someone else said he'd played catch with the dog. Bell and Morris handed out more flyers. A young man took one, walked away, and then turned on his heel and came back to talk to them. He said that his name was Chris Walker and that he didn't know anything about the dog, but he did know something about their car: he had seen it near the park over the last few days, and he recognized the driver because they'd been in police detention together a few months earlier.

"This guy Chris was a true scientist," Bell said, admiringly. "He said there were only three other people released from detention with him. One was Egyptian, one was elderly, and the third was the car thief, and that all we needed to do was get the detention records, eliminate those other two, and we would end up with this guy's name." Walker insisted that they call the police right away, so that they could check his story. He waited with them for almost an hour until a cruiser responded, and was disgusted that the police didn't have a computer in the car that could review detention records on the spot. Walker was so determined to have his tip substantiated that he accompanied Bell and Morris to a nearby precinct house to see if a police officer there would pull up the records. The officer wouldn't oblige them but he did believe that Walker was telling the truth, and he suggested that Morris and Bell contact Midtown Blue, an organization of police officers who do security work when they're off duty, which he thought might help them. Morris and Bell gave Walker reward money, but he seemed more interested in

N. Sloy

*"Once again I find myself in the rather awkward position of
having to ask one of you for a biscuit."*

making sure that they followed up on his tip. "It's a family curse," Walker's uncle Lee Harris told me when I visited him last summer. "We'll just bend over backward to help anyone in pain." Later that Sunday, after leaving Bell and Morris, Walker tangled with a police officer again and on Monday, when he called Bell to find out if she'd found her car, he was calling from jail.

As astonishing as Walker's story seemed, Bell and Morris came to believe that he had indeed seen their car, and that, from what the rugby player who had called them from Peachtree had told them, the thief had let the dog out in the park. On a shallow slope near the playing fields, they talked to the homeless people who sleep there under a small stand of oak trees, and they all remembered Coby. Some of those same people were still in the park this summer when I went to Atlanta. It was another blistering day, someone was listlessly banging tennis balls against a wall, and muffled cheers and hollers from a soccer game at the far end of the park rose up in the heavy air. Under a cement pavilion in a

sliver of shade, a man was sitting on a bench, plunking on a guitar held together with duct tape. He said that his name was Ben Macon, that he had lived in the park for ten years, and that he had spent several days during the previous summer with Coby, whom he described precisely, down to Coby's striking stare and predatory crouch while playing catch. "That dog was unbelievable," Macon said. "He was someone you could play with. He'd be your friend. You could tell he was a people dog." Macon strummed a little and then leaned on the guitar. "If I had a place of my own, I'd like a dog like that. But people with dogs, those are people who have good jobs." He paused for a moment and then added, "A dog like that gives you a warm feeling. I miss him."

By mid-afternoon that Sunday, Bell and Morris had spent hours searching in the park and going up and down Boulevard, so they took a break from handing out flyers and hanging posters and went home to shower and eat. Their phone rang. A woman on the line said that on

Saturday she and her partner had picked up a black male Border collie with no collar as he chased a tennis ball across Boulevard. They had had no luck finding his owner through rescue groups, and they were currently in their car with the dog on their way to the veterinarian because they had decided to keep him. But en route to the vet they had seen one of Bell and Morris's posters—they had probably hung it no more than an hour before. The woman, Danielle Ross, suggested that Bell and Morris meet them at the vet's. When she got off the phone, Ross, who also works at the C.D.C. but had never met Bell, decided to say the name of the dog on the poster to the dog in her car. First she pronounced it "Cobbie," and the dog, who looked reasonably healthy but was totally exhausted, didn't lift his head. Then she tried another pronunciation—"Cobee"—and he sat up. By the time she and her partner, Debbie Doyle, and the dog arrived at the Pets Are People, Too clinic, she knew the dog was going home.

When Bell and Morris pulled into the parking lot, they could see the dog through the front window of the clinic, and they knew it was Coby. As exhausted as he was, he raced to meet them at the door. Late that night, a police officer called Bell and Morris at home. There had been an automobile accident; the driver had fled; the car, which had been impounded, belonged to them. When Bell and Morris went to the police station the next day to claim it, they were first told that they were mistaken—that no car matching their car's identification numbers had been impounded. But then the officer checked the records again and determined that they did in fact have the car. It had been totalled.

Now, with both Coby and the car accounted for, Bell and Morris felt they might be on a streak. All they needed was to find the viola da gamba.

They decided to look in the phone book for pawn shops; there are nearly three hundred in the Atlanta area, so they concentrated on ones near the park where Coby had spent his time. One of them, Jerry's Pawn Shop, listed musical instruments among its specialties. It was a long shot—there are some ten thousand items pawned each month in downtown Atlanta alone, and it was just a guess that the car thief would have decided to cash in the instrument, that he would have chosen to do it at a pawn shop, and that he would have taken it to one near the park. Morris called Jerry's and asked after the viola da gamba. Yes, they had just got one from a fellow who had pawned it for twenty-five dollars. It was Morris's loaner. The man who pawned it? "Well, he didn't strike me as a viola da gamba player," Bill Hansel, who handled the transaction, recalled. According to Hansel, the man was youngish, in a hurry, and happy to sell the viola da gamba outright rather than pawn it. A Georgia law requires fingerprints and identification from anyone doing business with pawn shops. The police later traced the address that the non–viola da gamba player had provided; it turned out to be an empty house.

At this point, the police certainly knew the thief's name—it was on the pawn voucher and in the detention records from his previous lockup with Chris Walker, and there were fingerprints on the Volvo, the viola da gamba, the pawn voucher, and probably on Coby, but the man was still at large. Before the car was towed to a wrecking yard, Morris went through it one more time to see if there were any last belongings of his or Bell's still inside. There was nothing of theirs, but the thief had left behind some of his clothes, a bunch of computer parts, notes from his girlfriend, poetry he had written, and a stack of address labels bearing someone else's name.

| 2005 |

# TAPKA

*Fiction*

## DAVID BEZMOZGIS

Goldfinch was flapping clotheslines, a tenement delirious with striving. 6030 Bathurst: insomniac, scheming Odessa. Cedarcroft: reeking borscht in the hallways. My parents, Soviet refugees but Baltic aristocrats, took an apartment at 715 Finch, fronting a ravine and across from an elementary school—one respectable block away from the Russian swarm. We lived on the fifth floor, my cousin, aunt, and uncle directly below us on the fourth. Except for the Nahumovskys, a couple in their fifties, there were no other Russians in the building. For this privilege, my parents paid twenty extra dollars a month in rent.

In March of 1980, near the end of the school year but only three weeks after our arrival in Toronto, I was enrolled in Charles H. Best Elementary. Each morning, with our house key hanging from a brown shoelace around my neck, I kissed my parents goodbye and, along with my cousin Jana, tramped across the ravine—I to the first grade, she to the second. At three o'clock, bearing the germs of a new vocabulary, we tramped back home. Together, we then waited until six for our parents to return from George Brown City College, where they were taking an obligatory six-month course in English—a course that provided them with the rudiments of communication along with a modest government stipend.

In the evenings, we assembled and compiled our linguistic bounty.

293

Hello, havaryew?

Red, yellow, green, blue.

May I please go to the washroom?

Seventeen, eighteen, nineteen, twenny.

Joining us most nights were the Nahumovskys. They attended the same English classes and travelled with my parents on the same bus. Rita Nahumovsky was a beautician who wore layers of makeup, and Misha Nahumovsky was a tool-and-die maker. They came from Minsk and didn't know a soul in Canada. With abounding enthusiasm, they incorporated themselves into our family. My parents were glad to have them. Our life was tough, we had it hard—but the Nahumovskys had it harder. They were alone, they were older, they were stupefied by the demands of language. Being essentially helpless themselves, my parents found it gratifying to help the more helpless Nahumovskys.

After dinner, with everyone gathered on cheap stools around our table, my mother repeated the day's lessons for the benefit of the Nahumovskys and, to a slightly lesser degree, for the benefit of my father. My mother had always been an exceptional and dedicated student, and she extended this dedication to George Brown City College. My father and the Nahumovskys came to rely on her detailed notes and her understanding of the curriculum. For as long as they could, they listened attentively and groped desperately toward comprehension. When this became too frustrating, my father put on the kettle, Rita painted my mother's nails, and Misha told Soviet *anekdoti*.

In a first-grade classroom a teacher calls on her students and inquires after their nationalities. "Sasha," she says. Sasha says, "Russian." "Very good," says the teacher. "Arnan," she says. Arnan says, "Armenian." "Very

good," says the teacher. "Lyubka," she says. Lyubka says, "Ukrainian." "Very good," says the teacher. And then she asks Dima. Dima says, "Jewish." "What a shame," says the teacher. "So young and already a Jew."

The Nahumovskys had no children, only a white Lhasa Apso named Tapka. The dog had lived with them for years before they emigrated and then travelled with them from Minsk to Vienna, from Vienna to Rome, and from Rome to Toronto. During our first month in the building, Tapka was in quarantine, and I saw her only in photographs. Rita had dedicated an entire album to the dog, and, to dampen the pangs of separation, she consulted the album daily. There were shots of Tapka in the Nahumovskys' old Minsk apartment, seated on the cushions of faux–Louis XIV furniture; there was Tapka on the steps of a famous Viennese palace; Tapka at the Vatican, in front of the Colosseum, at the Sistine Chapel, and under the Leaning Tower of Pisa. My mother—despite having grown up with goats and chickens in her yard—didn't like animals and found it impossible to feign interest in Rita's dog. Shown a picture of Tapka, my mother wrinkled her nose and said, "Phoo." My father also couldn't be bothered. With no English, no money, no job, and only a murky conception of what the future held, he wasn't equipped to admire Tapka on the Italian Riviera. Only I cared. Through the photographs, I became attached to Tapka and projected upon her the ideal traits of the dog I did not have. Like Rita, I counted the days until Tapka's liberation.

The day Tapka was to be released from quarantine, Rita prepared an elaborate dinner. My family was invited to celebrate the dog's arrival. While Rita cooked, Misha was banished from their apartment. For distraction, he seated himself at our table with a deck of cards. As my mother reviewed sentence construction, Misha played hand after hand of *durak* with me.

"The woman loves this dog more than me. A taxi to the customs facility is going to cost us ten, maybe fifteen dollars. But what can I do? The dog is truly a sweet little dog."

When it came time to collect the dog, my mother went with Misha and Rita to act as their interpreter. With my nose to the window, I watched the taxi take them away. Every few minutes, I reapplied my nose to the window. Three hours later, the taxi pulled into our parking lot, and Rita emerged from the back seat cradling animated fur. She set the fur down on the pavement where it assumed the shape of a dog. The length of its coat concealed its legs, and, as it hovered around Rita's ankles, it appeared to have either a thousand tiny legs or none at all. My head ringing "Tapka, Tapka, Tapka," I raced into the hallway to meet the elevator.

That evening, Misha toasted the dog: "This last month, for the first time in years, I have enjoyed my wife's undivided attention. But I believe no man, not even one as perfect as me, can survive so much attention from his wife. So I say, with all my heart, thank God our Tapka is back home with us. Another day and I fear I may have requested a divorce."

Before he drank, Misha dipped his pinkie finger into his vodka glass and offered it to the dog. Obediently, Tapka gave Misha's finger a thorough licking. Impressed, my uncle declared her a good Russian

dog. He also gave her a lick of his vodka. I gave her a piece of my chicken. Jana rolled her a pellet of bread. Misha taught us how to dangle food just out of Tapka's reach and thereby induce her to perform a charming little dance. Rita also produced Clonchik, a red-and-yellow rag clown. She tossed Clonchik under the table, onto the couch, down the hallway, and into the kitchen; over and over, Rita called, "Tapka, get Clonchik," and, without fail, Tapka got Clonchik. Everyone delighted in Tapka's antics except my mother, who sat stiffly in her chair, her feet slightly off the floor, as though preparing herself for a mild electric shock.

After the dinner, when we returned home, my mother announced that she would no longer set foot in the Nahumovskys' apartment. She liked Rita, she liked Misha, but she couldn't sympathize with their attachment to the dog. She understood that the attachment was a consequence of their lack of sophistication and also their childlessness. They were simple people. Rita had never attended university. She could derive contentment from talking to a dog, brushing its coat, putting ribbons in its hair, and repeatedly

Shanahan

PRICE $5.99

THE

NEW YORKER

APRIL 30, 2012

throwing a rag clown across the apartment. And Misha, although very lively and a genius with his hands, was also not an intellectual. They were good people, but a dog ruled their lives.

Rita and Misha were sensitive to my mother's attitude toward Tapka. As a result, and to the detriment of her progress with English, Rita stopped visiting our apartment. Nightly, Misha would arrive alone while Rita attended to the dog. Tapka never set foot in our home. This meant that, in order to see her, I spent more and more time at the Nahumovskys'. Each evening, after I had finished my homework, I went to play with Tapka. My heart soared every time Rita opened the door and Tapka raced to greet me. The dog knew no hierarchy of affection. Her excitement was infectious. In Tapka's presence, I resonated with doglike glee.

Because of my devotion to the dog, and their lack of an alternative, Misha and Rita added their house key to the shoelace hanging around my neck. During our lunch break and again after school, Jana and I were charged with caring for Tapka. Our task was simple: put Tapka on her leash, walk her to the ravine, release her to chase Clonchik, and then bring her home.

Every day, sitting in my classroom, understanding little, effectively friendless, I counted down the minutes to lunchtime. When the bell rang, I met Jana on the playground and we sprinted across the grass toward our building. In the hall, our approaching footsteps elicited panting and scratching. When I inserted the key into the lock, I felt emanations of love through the door. And once the door was open Tapka hurled herself at us, her entire body consumed with the ecstasy of wagging. Jana and I took turns embracing her, petting her, covertly vying for her favor. Free of Rita's scrutiny, we also satisfied certain anatomical curiosities. We examined Tapka's ears, her paws, her teeth, the roots of her fur, and her doggy genitals. We poked and prodded her, we threw her up in the air, rolled her over and over, and swung her by her front legs. I felt such overwhelming love for Tapka that sometimes, when hugging her, I had to restrain myself from squeezing too hard and crushing her little bones.

It was April when we began to care for Tapka. Snow melted in the ravine; sometimes it rained. April became May. Grass absorbed the thaw, turned green; dandelions and wildflowers sprouted yellow and blue; birds and insects flew, crawled, and made their characteristic noises. Faithfully and reliably, Jana and I attended to Tapka. We walked her across the parking lot and down into the ravine. We threw Clonchik and said, "Tapka, get Clonchik." Tapka always got Clonchik. Everyone was proud of us. My mother and my aunt wiped tears from their eyes while talking about how responsible we were. Rita and Misha rewarded us with praise and chocolates. Jana was seven and I was six; much had been asked of us, but we had risen to the challenge.

Inspired by everyone's confidence, we grew confident. Whereas at first we made sure to walk thirty paces into the ravine before releasing Tapka, we gradually reduced that requirement to ten paces, then five paces, until finally we released her at the grassy border between the parking lot and the ravine. We did this not because of laziness or intentional recklessness but because we wanted proof of Tapka's love. That she came when we called was evidence of her love, that she didn't piss in the elevator was evidence of her love, that she offered up her belly for scratching was evidence of her love, that she licked our faces was evidence of her love. All of this was evidence, but it wasn't proof. Proof could come in only one form. We had intuited an elemental truth: love needs no leash.

That first spring, even though most of what was said around me remained a mystery, a thin rivulet of meaning trickled into my cerebral catch basin and collected into a little pool of knowledge. By the end of May, I could sing the ABC song. Television taught me to say "What's up, Doc?" and "super-duper." The playground introduced me to "shithead," "mental case," and "gaylord." I seized upon every opportunity to apply my new knowledge.

One afternoon, after spending nearly an hour in the ravine throwing Clonchik in a thousand different directions, Jana and I lolled in sunlit pollen. I called her shithead, mental case, and gaylord, and she responded by calling me gaylord, shithead, and mental case.

"Shithead."

"Gaylord."

"Mental case."

"Tapka, get Clonchik."

"Shithead."

"Gaylord."

"Come, Tapka-lapka."

"Mental case."

We went on like this, over and over, until Jana threw the clown and said, "Shithead, get Clonchik." Initially, I couldn't tell if she had said this on purpose or if it had merely been a blip in her rhythm. But when I looked at Jana her smile was triumphant.

"Mental case, get Clonchik."

For the first time, as I watched Tapka bounding happily after Clonchik, the profanity sounded profane.

"Don't say that to the dog."

"Why not?"

"It's not right."

"But she doesn't understand."

"You shouldn't say it."

"Don't be a baby. Come, shithead, come my dear one."

Her tail wagging with accomplishment, Tapka dropped Clonchik at my feet.

"You see, she likes it."

I held Clonchik as Tapka pawed frantically at my shins.

"Call her shithead. Throw the clown."

"I'm not calling her shithead."

"What are you afraid of, shithead?"

I aimed the clown at Jana's head and missed.

"Shithead, get Clonchik."

As the clown left my hand, Tapka, a white shining blur, oblivious to insult, was already cutting through the grass. I wanted to believe that I had intended the "shithead" exclusively for Jana, but I knew it wasn't true.

"I told you, gaylord, she doesn't care."

I couldn't help thinking, Poor Tapka. I felt moral residue and looked around for some sign of recrimination. The day, however, persisted in unimpeachable brilliance: sparrows winged overhead; bumblebees levitated above flowers; beside a lilac shrub, Tapka clamped down on Clonchik. I was amazed at the absence of consequences.

Jana said, "I'm going home."

As she started for home, I saw that she was still holding Tapka's leash. It swung insouciantly from her hand. I called after her just as, once again, Tapka deposited Clonchik at my feet.

"I need the leash."

"Why?"

"Don't be stupid. I need the leash."

"No, you don't. She comes when we call her. Even shithead. She won't run away."

Jana turned her back on me and proceeded toward our building. I called her again, but she refused to turn around. Her receding back was a blatant provocation. Guided more by anger than by logic, I decided that if Tapka was closer to Jana then the onus of responsibility would be on her. I picked up the doll and threw it as far as I could into the parking lot.

"Tapka, get Clonchik."

Clonchik tumbled through the air. I had put everything in my six-year-old arm behind the throw, which still meant that the doll wasn't going very far. Its trajectory promised a drop no more than twenty feet from the edge of the ravine. Running, her head arched to the sky, Tapka tracked the flying clown. As the doll reached its apex, it crossed paths with a sparrow. The bird veered off toward Finch Avenue, and the clown plummeted to the asphalt. When the doll hit the ground, Tapka raced past it after the bird.

A thousand times we had thrown Clonchik

and a thousand times Tapka had retrieved him. But who knows what passes for a thought in the mind of a dog? One moment a Clonchik is a Clonchik, and the next moment a sparrow is a Clonchik.

I shouted at Jana to catch Tapka and then watched in abject horror as the dog, her attention fixed on the sparrow, skirted past Jana and directly into traffic. From my vantage point on the slope of the ravine, I couldn't see what happened. I saw only that Jana broke into a sprint and I heard the caterwauling of tires, followed by Tapka's shrill fractured yip.

By the time I reached the street, a line of cars already stretched a block beyond Goldfinch. At the front of the line were a brown station wagon and a pale-blue sedan blistered with rust. As I neared, I noted the chrome letters on the back of the sedan: D-U-S-T-E-R. In front of the sedan, Jana kneeled in a tight semicircle with a pimply young man and an older woman with very large sunglasses. Tapka lay on her side at the center of their circle. She panted in quick shallow bursts. She stared impassively at me, at Jana. Except for a hind leg twitching at the sky at an impossible angle, she seemed completely unharmed. She looked much as she did when she rested on the rug at the Nahumovskys' apartment after a vigorous romp in the ravine.

Seeing her this way, barely mangled, I felt a sense of relief. I started to convince

*"Pray for it."*

myself that things weren't as bad as I had feared, and I tentatively edged forward to pet her. The woman in the sunglasses said something in a restrictive tone that I neither understood nor heeded. I placed my hand on Tapka's head, and she responded by opening her mouth and allowing a trickle of blood to escape onto the asphalt. This was the first time I had ever seen dog blood, and I was struck by the depth of its color. I hadn't expected it to be red, although I also hadn't expected it to be not-red. Set against the gray asphalt and her white coat, Tapka's blood was the red I envisioned when I closed my eyes and thought: red.

I sat with Tapka until several dozen car horns demanded that we clear the way. The woman with the large sunglasses ran to her station wagon, returned with a blanket, and scooped Tapka off the street. The pimply young man stammered a few sentences, of which I understood nothing except the word "sorry." Then we were in the back seat of the station wagon with Tapka in Jana's lap. The woman kept talking until she finally realized that we couldn't understand her at all. As we started to drive off, Jana remembered something. I motioned for the woman to stop the car and scrambled out. Above the atonal chorus of car horns, I heard: "Mark, get Clonchik."

I ran and got Clonchik.

For two hours, Jana and I sat in the reception area of a small veterinary clinic in an unfamiliar part of town. In another room, with a menagerie of afflicted creatures, Tapka lay in traction, connected to a blinking machine by a series of tubes. Jana and I had been allowed to see her once but were rushed out when we both burst into tears. Tapka's doctor, a woman wearing a white coat and furry slip-pers resembling bear paws, tried to calm us down. Again, we could neither explain ourselves nor understand what she was saying. We managed only to establish that Tapka was not our dog. The doctor gave us coloring books, stickers, and access to the phone. Every fifteen minutes, we called home. Between phone calls, we absently flipped pages and sniffled for Tapka and for ourselves. We had no idea what would happen to Tapka; all we knew was that she wasn't dead. As for ourselves, we already felt punished and knew only that more punishment was to come.

"Why did you throw Clonchik?"

"Why didn't you give me the leash?"

"You could have held on to her collar."

"You shouldn't have called her shithead."

At six-thirty, my mother picked up the phone. I could hear the agitation in her voice. The ten minutes she had spent at home not knowing where I was had taken their toll. For ten minutes, she had been the mother of a dead child. I explained to her about the dog and felt a twinge of resentment when she said, "So it's only the dog?" Behind her I heard other voices. It sounded as though everyone were speaking at once, pursuing personal agendas, translating the phone conversation from Russian to Russian until one anguished voice separated itself: "My God, what happened?" Rita.

After getting the address from the veterinarian, my mother hung up and ordered another expensive taxi. Within a half hour, my parents, my aunt, and Misha and Rita pulled up at the clinic. Jana and I waited for them on the sidewalk. As soon as the taxi doors opened, we began to sob uncontrollably, partly out of relief but mainly in the hope of engendering sympathy. I ran to my mother and caught sight of Rita's face. Her face made me regret that I also hadn't been hit by a car.

As we clung to our mothers, Rita descended upon us.

"Children, what, oh, what have you done?"

She pinched compulsively at the loose skin of her neck, raising a cluster of pink marks.

While Misha methodically counted individual bills for the taxi-driver, we swore on our lives that Tapka had simply got away from us. That we had minded her as always but, inexplicably, she had seen a bird and bolted from the ravine and into the road. We had done everything in our power to catch her, but she had surprised us, eluded us, been too fast.

Rita considered our story.

"You are liars. Liars!"

She uttered the words with such hatred that we again burst into sobs.

My father spoke in our defense.

"Rita Borisovna, how can you say this? They are children."

"They are liars. I know my Tapka. Tapka never chased birds. Tapka never ran from the ravine."

"Maybe today she did?"

"Liars."

Having delivered her verdict, she had nothing more to say. She waited anxiously for Misha to finish paying the driver.

"Misha, enough already. Count it a hundred times, it will still be the same."

Inside the clinic, there was no longer anyone at the reception desk. During our time there, Jana and I had watched a procession of dyspeptic cats and lethargic parakeets disappear into the back rooms for examination and diagnosis. One after another they had come and gone until, by the time of our parents' arrival, the waiting area was entirely empty and the clinic

## THE PROMOTION

I was a dog in my former life, a very good dog, and, thus, I was promoted to a human being. I liked being a dog. I worked for a poor farmer, guarding and herding his sheep. Wolves and coyotes tried to get past me almost every night, and not once did I lose a sheep. The farmer rewarded me with good food, food from his table. He may have been poor, but he ate well. And his children played with me, when they weren't in school or working in the field. I had all the love any dog could hope for. When I got old, they got a new dog, and I trained him in the tricks of the trade. He quickly learned, and the farmer brought me into the house to live with the family. I brought the farmer his slippers in the morning, as he was getting old, too. I was dying slowly, a little bit at a time. The farmer knew this and would bring the new dog in to visit me from time to time. The new dog would entertain me with his flips and flops and nuzzles. And then one morning I just didn't get up. They gave me a fine burial down by the stream under a shade tree. That was the end of my being a dog. Sometimes I miss it so I sit by the window and cry. I live in a high-rise that looks out at a bunch of other high-rises. At my job I work in a cubicle and barely speak to anyone all day. This is my reward for being a good dog. The human wolves don't even see me. They fear me not

—JAMES TATE  | 2002 |

officially closed. The only people remaining were a night nurse and the doctor in the bear-paw slippers, who had stayed expressly for our sake.

Looking desperately around the room, Rita screamed, "Doctor! Doctor!" But when the doctor appeared she was incapable of making herself understood. Haltingly, with my mother's help, it was communicated to the doctor that Rita wanted to see her dog. Pointing vigorously at herself, Rita asserted, "Tapka. Mine dog."

The doctor led Rita and Misha into the veterinary version of an intensive-care ward. Tapka lay on her little bed, Clonchik resting directly beside her. At the sight of Rita and Misha, Tapka weakly wagged her tail. Little more than an hour had elapsed since I had seen her last, but somehow over the course of that time Tapka had shrunk considerably. She had always been a small dog, but now she looked desiccated. She was the embodiment of defeat. Rita started to cry, grotesquely smearing her mascara. With trembling hands, and with sublime tenderness, she stroked Tapka's head.

"My God, my God, what has happened to you, my Tapkochka?"

Through my mother, and with the aid of pen and paper, the doctor provided the answer. Tapka required two operations. One for her leg. Another to stop internal bleeding. An organ had been damaged. For now, a machine was helping her, but without the machine she would die. On the paper, the doctor drew a picture of a scalpel, of a dog, of a leg, of an organ. She made an arrow pointing at the organ and drew a teardrop and colored it in to represent blood. She also wrote down a number preceded by a dollar sign. The number was fifteen hundred.

At the sight of the number, Rita let out a low animal moan and steadied herself against Tapka's little bed. My parents exchanged a glance. I looked at the floor. Misha said, "My dear God." The Nahumovskys and my parents each took in less than five hundred dollars a month. We had arrived in Canada with almost nothing, a few hundred dollars, which had all but disappeared on furniture. There were no savings. Fifteen hundred dollars. The doctor could just as well have written a million.

In the middle of the intensive-care ward, Rita slid down to the floor and wailed. Her head thrown back, she appealed to the fluorescent lights: "*Nu,* Tapkochka, what is going to become of us?"

I looked up from my feet and saw horror and bewilderment on the doctor's face. She tried to put a hand on Rita's shoulder, but Rita violently shrugged it off.

My father attempted to intercede.

*"I had my own blog for a while, but I decided to go back to just pointless, incessant barking."*

"Rita Borisovna, I understand that it is painful, but it is not the end of the world."

"And what do you know about it?"

"I know that it must be hard, but soon you will see. . . . Even tomorrow we could go and help you find a new one."

My father looked to my mother for approval, to insure that he had not promised too much. He needn't have worried.

"A new one? What do you mean, a new one? I don't want a new one. Why don't you get yourself a new son? A new little liar? How about that? New. Everything we have now is new. New everything."

On the linoleum floor, Rita keened, rocking back and forth. She hiccupped, as though hyperventilating. Pausing for a moment, she looked up at my mother and told her to translate for the doctor. To tell her that she would not let Tapka die.

"I will sit here on this floor forever. And if the police come to drag me out I will bite them."

"Ritochka, this is crazy."

"Why is it crazy? My Tapka's life is worth more than a thousand dollars. Because we don't have the money, she should die here? It's not her fault."

Seeking rationality, my mother turned to Misha—Misha who had said nothing all this time except "My dear God."

"Misha, do you want me to tell the doctor what Rita said?"

Misha shrugged philosophically.

"Tell her or don't tell her, you see my wife has made up her mind. The doctor will figure it out soon enough."

"And you think this is reasonable?"

"Sure. Why not? I'll sit on the floor, too. The police can take us both to jail. Besides Tapka, what else do we have?"

Misha sat on the floor beside his wife.

I watched as my mother struggled to explain to the doctor what was happening. With a mixture of words and gesticulations, she got the point across. The doctor, after considering her options, sat down on the floor beside Rita and Misha. Once again, she tried to put her hand on Rita's shoulder. This time, Rita, who was still rocking back and forth, allowed it. Misha rocked in time to his wife's rhythm. So did the doctor. The three of them sat in a line, swaying together, like campers at a campfire. Nobody said anything. We looked at each other. I watched Rita, Misha, and the doctor swaying and swaying. I became mesmerized by the swaying. I wanted to know what would happen to Tapka; the swaying answered me.

The swaying said: Listen, shithead, Tapka will live. The doctor will perform the operation. Either money will be found or money will not be necessary.

I said to the swaying: This is very good. I love Tapka. I meant her no harm. I want to be forgiven.

The swaying replied: There is reality and then there is truth. The reality is that Tapka will live. But, let's be honest, the truth is you killed Tapka. Look at Rita; look at Misha. You see, who are you kidding? You killed Tapka and you will never be forgiven.

| 2003 |

# PET SCAN

## JEROME GROOPMAN

E laine Ostrander, a geneticist at the Fred Hutchinson Cancer
Research Center, in Seattle, is awakened each morning around
seven by Tess, her purebred Border collie. When I spoke with
Ostrander not long ago, a steady cold rain was falling, but the weather
had not deterred her and Tess from their morning ritual in a park near
her house. Ostrander runs Tess hard for fifteen minutes, and then they
play for fifteen minutes, with Ostrander throwing a ball to the far end
of a field, and Tess fetching it. Border collies are herding dogs, bred for
alertness, focus, and determination. "They like to be kept busy," Ostrander says. "She needs to burn off her early-morning energy." They
return home, clean off the park mud, and go together to the Hutchinson Center. Ostrander's laboratory there has all the standard steel and
enamel fittings of molecular biology, including high-speed centri-
fuges, DNA sequencers, and P.C.R. machines. The only clue to her
particular specialty comes from the art on the laboratory walls: framed
prints and photographs of dogs. Tess nestles into her place on the floor
next to Ostrander's desk. When a visitor enters, Tess gets up and approaches. "She helps keep order in the laboratory," Ostrander says.
"She herds my students and postdocs."

A forty-year-old woman with straight brown hair and sharp green
eyes, Elaine Ostrander, along with a small network of colleagues and
collaborators, is mapping the dog genome. The DNA of dog and that
of man are sufficiently alike so that gene maps of inherited canine
diseases will help identify the genes for their human counterparts.
Moreover, the dog genome promises to help with the search for the

genetic basis of behavior. Purebred dogs have distinct temperaments, and with an accurate map the genes that determine their behavior can be identified—telling us what makes, say, Border collies like Tess so attentive, tenacious, and goal-driven. By contrast, cowering huskies and snappish spaniels may hold clues to treating psychiatric disorders in human beings. People and their pets, it turns out, may resemble each other even more than you'd think.

Dogs, as a species, were created by man. In the standard Darwinian model, natural forces in the wild would have selected for the perpetuation of those genes that favored survival and procreation. But dogs came into being through a process of artificial selection, when human beings, probably around a hundred thousand years ago, began to domesticate gray wolves into *Canis familiaris*. Man bred these animals to suit his work purposes and to be compatible with his social structures and his social behavior. Canines were trained to serve as hunters, trackers, herders, and sentinels, as well as playmates for children and companions for adults. The lives of man and dog became so closely integrated that we began to breed them for behaviors that were functional surrogates of our own. In the ancient Middle East, where grain was cultivated and livestock was husbanded, people bred dogs that had protective instincts. During the Middle Ages in Europe, many dogs were bred in monasteries, with preference given to traits seen as Christian, such as loyalty, cooperation, and affection. And over the past century man has shaped canine evolution even more systematically, by establishing breeds that meet kennel-club standards.

The way to select for prized physical and behavioral attributes—the ability to hunt foxes, say, or to guide the blind—is tight inbreeding. A chosen sire is often mated within a closed gene pool, and sometimes within its family: fathers may be paired with daughters, or brothers with sisters. But, although inbreeding of this sort preserves the desired trait, it also brings together dangerous recessive genes, which are normally diluted by mating outside the family. After several generations of inbreeding, valued lines of purebred show and performance dogs frequently develop serious physical ailments and behavioral disorders.

For a medical geneticist, these problems present an opportunity. Many of the hereditary canine illnesses have close human analogues. But they're vastly easier to find and study in dogs. Purebred dogs are far more genetically homogeneous than any human population, and that makes it easier to trace and identify recessive genes in them. You can amplify recessive traits by directed breeding, and, since dogs produce many more offspring than people do, it's easier to study how different disease-linked genes interact. And, of course, research into behavioral genetics has come to rely heavily upon separated-at-birth

siblings—a circumstance that is the norm with puppies but not with people.

Elaine Ostrander and Mark Neff, her collaborator at Berkeley, recently produced a map of the dog genome. It is being used to find the mutations responsible for a host of canine diseases: boxers with progressive weakness of the heart muscle, or cardiomyopathy; keeshonden with holes in the septum of the heart and a misshapen aorta, a condition called tetrology of Fallot; spaniels with spinal muscular atrophy, a degenerative neurological disease; Scottish terriers and chihuahuas with myasthenia gravis, an autoimmune disorder; and beagles and St. Bernards with epilepsy. Each of these dog disorders corresponds to a human one.

Greg Acland, a veterinary ophthalmologist and geneticist at Cornell, is using the map to investigate canine blindness. I recently watched Acland, an Australian with the blunt language, and girth, of an aging rugby player, as he examined one of his research subjects. The dog was mid-sized, with a rich mahogany coat, but I couldn't identify the breed. "The blindness gene we're studying originated in a line of Irish setters, and that accounts for the coloring," Acland told me. "We used beagles to crossbreed with the setters. Beagles have great personalities, are very fertile, and easily adapt to life in a colony. The gene turns up several generations later."

As Acland approached the dog from the side, there was no reaction. Only when he was directly

in front of the dog did it raise its head and move its snout to sniff. "The dog with retinal atrophy follows the same course as people with retinitis pigmentosa," Acland explained, referring to the most common cause of inherited human blindness, which currently affects perhaps a hundred thousand Americans. "First, there is loss of night vision, then loss of peripheral perception—that's called tunnel vision. Only very late is there complete blindness." Acland's dog was in the tunnel-vision stage. The kinds of dogs that are bred to serve as guide dogs for the blind are confident, flexible, and loyal, but some of them are also prone to retinal atrophy; sometimes such a dog will suffer the fate of its master. Since to breed and train such a dog costs between thirty and forty thousand dollars, the disorder has important economic ramifications. But the main impetus of Acland's work is to speed the search for blindness genes in man.

The first dog gene that will directly illuminate the pathology of a human disease may well be the one for narcolepsy. "We are close— it'll be a few months to a year," Dr. Emmanuel Mignot, a psychiatrist and the director of Stanford University's Narcolepsy Center, told me in ebullient, French-accented English. "The symptoms and signs of narcolepsy are so similar in dog and man it's scary."

Narcolepsy is a sleep disorder that affects about one in every two thousand Americans. It usually develops during adolescence, causing excessive daytime sleepiness, and it is frequently missed by physicians, who mistakenly ascribe the symptoms to teenage ennui, late-night parties, or covert drug use. In one study, the average time from the onset of symptoms to its diagnosis was fourteen years. Patients have abnormal REM sleep, and they suffer "hypnagogic," or dream-

"*You realize they won't know the difference.*"

like, auditory and visual hallucinations while they're dozing. The signature manifestation of narcolepsy is cataplexy—a sudden loss of muscular control which can last several seconds or several minutes. An episode is often triggered by pleasurable emotions: a narcoleptic might start laughing at a good joke and abruptly crumple to the floor.

Dr. Mignot oversees Stanford's colony of twenty-seven narcoleptic Doberman pinschers. As far as I could tell, his Dobermans looked like any others, with their fearsome visage, deep-brown eyes trained forward, sharp ears raised in surveillance. I observed a group of five Dobermans moving with typical tightly coiled grace, and then saw them fed—presented with the rare treat of beefsteak. After the first bite, the dogs dropped suddenly, their limbs sprawling, their heads lolling back. "We stimulate the Dobermans with an excellent cuisine," Dr. Mignot explained. "They experience the pleasure of the good food. And then they collapse." Those sleek, muscular creatures now looked like rag dolls tossed on the floor.

"It is a nightmare to look for a gene like this in humans," Dr. Mignot went on to say. "There are not enough families with several affected individuals." Once Mignot and his team at Stanford started using pedigree studies to study canine narcolepsy, they made the surprising discovery that canine narcolepsy seems to result from a single mutant gene.

"Our analysis of the region on the Doberman's chromosome and on the human chromosome shows them to be virtually identical," Dr. Mignot said. This means that once the dog gene is identified the human mutation will be easily pinpointed by the use of sequencing data from the Doberman study. The mystery of how a single gene can so alter cerebral function as to induce sleepiness, vivid hallucinations, and motor paralysis may soon be explained. Although finding a gene doesn't mean finding a treatment, it does mean that researchers can work back from the root cause. The mutant gene may be linked to a mutant protein, and a drug may be developed to correct for it.

Although narcolepsy appears to be caused by a single gene, the distinct personalities of purebred dogs are polygenic, which is to say that they are determined by many genes acting in concert. And "personalities" is surely the right term: the way dogs act can seem eerily similar to the way we act, as the result of both domestication and our propensity for projecting our emotions upon our pets. The desirable temperament of each breed in the American Kennel Club's *Complete Dog Book*, the bible of pedigrees, is elaborately anthropomorphic: boxers are meant to be "alert, dignified and self-assured," and, in the show ring, "should exhibit constrained animation"; rottweilers are "calm, confident and courageous," and exude "self-assured aloofness"; mastiffs display "grandeur and good nature . . . dignity rather than gaiety." The task of sorting out such polygenic traits isn't simple, but it helps to be able to study them in laboratory populations that can be inbred and crossbred.

While Ostrander is studying DNA sequences, Greg Acland, at Cornell, and Karen Overall, the director of the Behavior Clinic at the University of Pennsylvania Veterinary School, are working with groups of dogs in order to identify the genes that are responsible for several "neurotic" canine lines. Overall, a petite forty-three-year-old woman with waist-long blond hair, cool blue eyes, and glasses, is a veterinarian with expertise in both behavioral psychology and evolutionary biology, and she speaks with the sharp cadences of a rigorous experimentalist. Her work helped establish diagnostic criteria in animal behavior and led to the recent F.D.A. approval of Clomicalm, a psychotropic drug for dogs with separation anxiety—what headline writers dubbed "puppy Prozac."

Acland's and Overall's research has focussed on nervous pointers and shy Siberian huskies; doctors at the University of Pennsylvania are also studying bullterriers, fox terriers, and German shepherds, all of which exhibit obsessive-compulsive behavior—they may spend hours chasing their tails—and a line of English springer spaniels with poor impulse control: they react aggressively and capriciously to one another and to their handlers. "Breeders don't realize that when they select for refined forms of physical carriage those attributes are linked to behavioral genes," Karen Overall says. For example, the English springers bred for show promenade with their heads far forward, in an almost lunging posture. Several genes are believed to work together to produce such an appearance and gait, and they could include those which, in the species' evolutionary history, are linked to hunting and attacking. Hence the springer spaniels with impulsive aggression.

Among many huskies, such side effects of selection seem to have resulted in shyness. "The Siberian husky has a very special social structure,"

PRICE $5.99

THE NEW YORKER

JUNE 27, 2011

Acland says. "The Jack London myth—that in the Arctic you need a wolf dog, a primitive alpha male—is a lot of garbage. A good sled dog exhibits harmony. You need teamwork. The dog has to be rotated from the harness at the front of the sled, or it will become exhausted. There can't be fighting for position among the dogs, but deference." So the painful shyness could be an exaggerated expression of selected deference. Acland has bred a colony of husky crossbreeds in Pennsylvania, descendants of a Siberian husky named Earl. "He was a handsome, lovely dog, donated by a breeder who noticed that he was painfully shy," Acland says. The dog was comfortable with his owner; his extreme bashfulness emerged only when he encountered a stranger. "People like that trait," Acland notes. "It reinforces the feeling, 'This is *my* dog.'"

To study how the genes for shyness were inherited, the researchers mated Earl with a female beagle. The offspring included a female that was then mated with an unrelated male beagle. Among that dog's offspring were two very shy males. "This experiment shows, to a rough approximation, that shyness appears to be transmitted as a dominant trait," Acland says. But he emphasizes that the behavior is complex. There are different degrees of shyness in purebred huskies and in the offspring outbred with beagles, just as there are in people. "It's not binary," Acland says, "but a continuous, quantitative function of several genes."

If sled dogs are bred for team-spiritedness, pointers are bred to have a rigid posture and a tense focus, and the occasional appearance of "nervous" pointers seems to be a result. The pointers that Acland and Overall study are descended from a colony that was maintained at the University of Arkansas, in Fayetteville, in the early 1970s. "They were found by Pavlovian psy-

chiatrists looking for natural animal models of neurosis," Karen Overall says. "The doctors hoped they could condition against the avoidance response, but it didn't succeed in these pointers."

In a spacious state-of-the-art facility at the University of Pennsylvania, nervous pointers and their unaffected littermates are housed together. The mid-sized, brown-and-white dogs occupy large, comfortable metal-mesh cages, with special vinyl floors so their paws are not trapped or irritated. There are long, broad runs for regular exercise. The cages are cleaned two or three times a day, and a staff of seasoned handlers scrupulously attends to the animals, providing both grooming and affection.

When Greg Acland approached an affected pointer, the dog was startled, its wary eyes widening and its jaw tightening. He entered the dog's cage and extended a comforting hand, but the pointer froze in place, its wiry body rigid and statue-still. The prominent flank muscles trembled visibly. Acland affectionately stroked the dog's side, but the animal only became more distressed. As he gently patted the pointer's head, it panicked, and assumed a wide-splayed stance, its front feet extending forward and its back arching. During a four-minute encounter, the pointer was mute, emitting not a bark or a squeal. After Acland left the cage, the dog stayed frozen for a

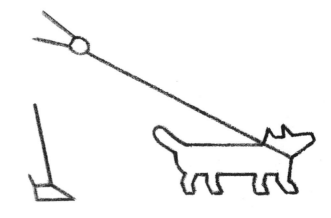

little while. Only with measured caution did it turn its head to confirm Acland's exit. Blood samples obtained immediately after such interactions show high levels of cortisol, an adrenal stress hormone, and the release of muscle enzymes from the uncontrolled muscle shaking.

The pointer's littermates, though they have been reared in the same environment, have a completely different response. After sniffing Acland's hand, they responded eagerly to his affectionate gestures, barking at the caresses and tousling of their fur. They followed him as he walked toward the cage's exit, seeking more play, and barking loudly to protest his departure.

The shy huskies, descendants of Earl and unaffected dogs, have different signs of anxiety from those of nervous pointers. As Greg Acland approached a shy female, the animal did not immediately freeze but skulked to the back of the cage—"like a wallflower at a party," he said. The husky turned her distinctive black-and-white lupine head away from Acland, while watching him out of the corner of her eye. As Acland extended his hand, the husky quickly lowered her head and retreated further, cowering behind her frisky littermates. The dog's limbs began to tremble, and saliva poured from her clenched mouth. Acland moved his hand closer and spoke in a friendly voice. The shy husky dodged the gesture, digging her white hind legs into the floor and

pressing her broad black flanks forcefully against the back wall of the cage.

"They are both anxious, but there are differences," Acland told me later. The shy husky, over time, has become comfortable with her daily handler. The nervous pointer has never done so, despite the best efforts of the regular caretakers. "It's hard to develop empathy with the affected pointers," Acland admitted. "They isolate themselves because of their anxiety and are never happy with anybody." He said that when he is directly in front of a dog and is trying to make eye contact "the pointer has a peculiar face, like an owl's—he stares right through you."

"We're always leery of making glib associations, but these responses in the nervous pointer and in the shy Siberian husky resemble forms of human anxiety disorders," Karen Overall said. In fact, when a measured amount of lactate, a harmless acidic solution, is given to the nervous pointers or the shy Siberian huskies, it triggers a state of uncontrolled anxiety—which is what the solution does in people with certain panic disorders. This suggests that a similar neurochemistry is at work in dogs and human beings.

"The genetic basis of these anxiety behaviors in dogs is complex," Overall told me, "and will not be solved as quickly as single-gene traits, like narcolepsy." But she believes that the dog research will be "priceless" for human psychiatry. She pointed out that primitive areas deep in the mammalian brain in canines and *Homo sapiens* are similar and have changed little in the course of evolution. "It is in these ancestral areas of the mammalian brain that studies of behavior in the dog will be most informative," she said. In human beings, a number of behavioral and affective disorders— panic attacks, outbursts of aggression, extreme anxiety—seem to involve various primitive sites, such as the caudate nucleus, the amygdala, and the hippocampus.

Whatever results come from Karen Overall's cages and Elaine Ostrander's DNA sequencers aren't likely to settle all our long-standing arguments about character and free will. And yet their genetic and biochemical findings will sharply focus these discussions. Though nearly everyone accepts the notion that the carriage and the personality of dogs arise from their breeding, there's no such consensus when it comes to our own propensities. We mostly prefer to imagine ourselves untethered by such twists of DNA. Still, Greg Acland, for one, seems to be reconciled to the idea. "Everyone who deals with dogs accepts our compatibility, accepts how owners resemble their breeds," he says. "Nobody wants to hear that when you grow up you turn into your father and mother. The older you get, though, the more you realize it's true."

| 1999 |

*"Is the homework fresh?"*

# THE DOG

*Fiction*

## RODDY DOYLE

S he'd been gone for a couple of hours, most of the afternoon—he wasn't sure—but she looked like she'd been in Spain. Or the Sahara. She'd been tied down and tortured, under a big round sun. She was suddenly tanned.

He watched her taking off her coat. He didn't know what color her hair was, the name for it. He sat still and said nothing.

It went back.

They hadn't coped well. He knew that.

His ear had been the start of it. Or a start. Years ago now. Mary had been kissing him. But she'd stopped and he'd heard something, trapped in her throat.

—What's wrong? he'd said.

—Nothing, she'd said. Your ear.

She'd stiffened beside him, but then he felt her kind of unfold, relax again.

—My ear?

—There's a hair on it.

—Hair? he said. There's hair in everyone's ear.

—On, she said.

—What?

—It's on your ear.

—On?

He saw her nod.

313

—I'll have to see this, he said, and got up.

But he couldn't see it. He put his face right up to the bathroom mirror. He turned his head, so his ear was nearly the only thing he could see. But he couldn't see a hair. He took off his glasses. And he saw it. All on its own. At the bottom, the lobe. Like a mustache hair. He put the glasses back on. The hair was gone. He took them off. And there it was.

He went back to the bedroom. He got into the bed. She was pretending to be asleep, breathing like a baby in an ad.

He dated it back to then. Five years, four years—he wasn't sure. When they stopped growing old together.

He'd shaved it off. He'd never had a mustache and he didn't want one now, growing on his ear. He'd taken his glasses off to do it—he'd had to. He needed the glasses, but sometimes he could see better without them. He took them off to read the paper. He had to put them on to find the fuckin' paper.

She was still taking her coat off. It looked new. He didn't think he'd seen it on her before. It was nice, soft-looking. He didn't know what to call the color of that, either. She was being careful. It must have been new. He said nothing.

Her knickers came after his ear. His revenge, he supposed, but he hadn't meant it that way. It had just happened. He'd been sitting up in the bed, reading. *Berlin: The Downfall, 1945* or *Stalingrad*—one of those big books he always liked, about a city getting hammered in the Second World War. He loved history. He could hear her locking the doors downstairs, and coming up the stairs, shoving the bedroom door open, coming in. It must have been the Stalingrad book, because he'd got to the bit about people eating the rats, and he'd looked away from the page. She was taking her jeans off, her back to him. She was kind of vague there, so he put his glasses back on, and saw them. Her knickers—her thong. New, and black. She was bending, to get her feet out of the jeans. Four decades of arse parked inside a piece of string.

He pretended he was going to vomit. He still regretted it.

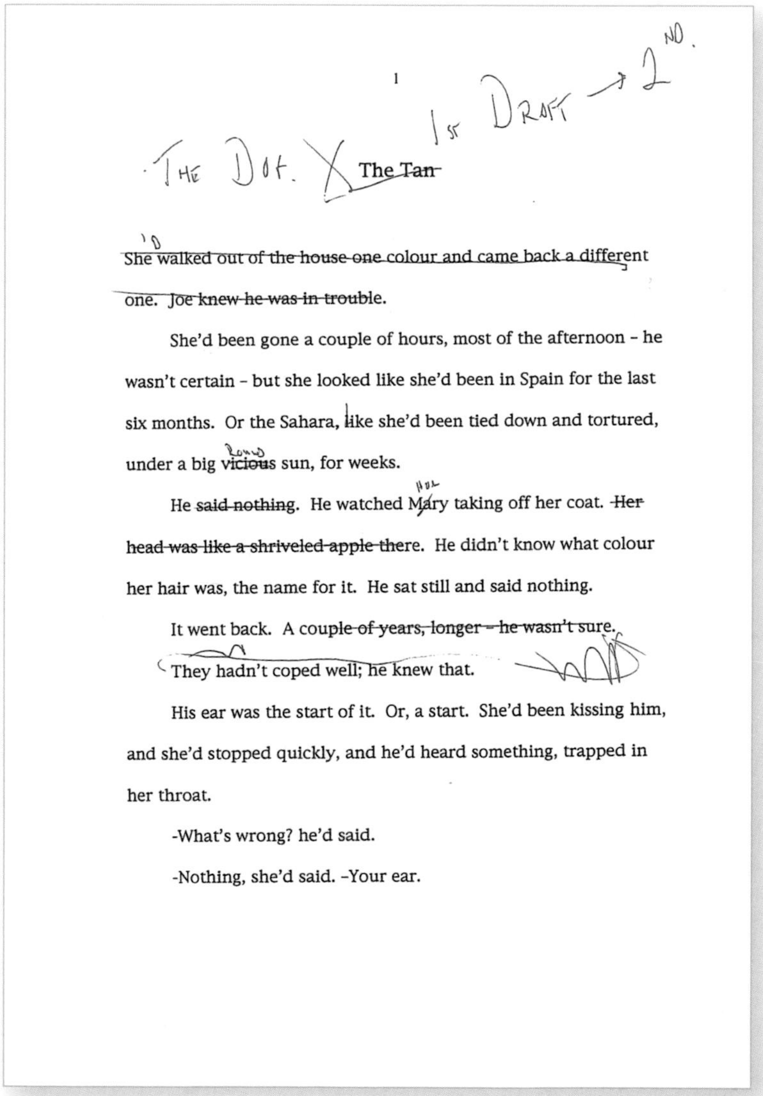

---

*[handwritten annotations: "THE DOT." and "1st DRAFT → 2ND."]*

**The Tan** ~~The Tan~~

1

~~She walked out of the house one colour and came back a different~~ ~~one. Joe knew he was in trouble.~~

She'd been gone a couple of hours, most of the afternoon – he wasn't certain – but she looked like she'd been in Spain for the last six months. Or the Sahara, like she'd been tied down and tortured, under a big ~~vicious~~ *long* sun, for weeks.

He ~~said nothing~~ *was*. He watched *his* Mary taking off her coat. ~~Her head was like a shriveled apple there.~~ He didn't know what colour her hair was, the name for it. He sat still and said nothing.

It went back. A coup~~le of years, longer~~ – he wasn't sure. ~~They hadn't coped well; he knew that.~~

His ear was the start of it. Or, a start. She'd been kissing him, and she'd stopped quickly, and he'd heard something, trapped in her throat.

-What's wrong? he'd said.

-Nothing, she'd said. –Your ear.

He made the gagging sound, and leaned over the side of the bed and let on he was emptying himself. He'd done it before, and she'd always laughed. Not this time.

He hadn't meant to hurt her. He'd thought he was just being funny. She'd said nothing about it.

He Googled menopause, but he soon gave up. Age of onset, cessation of menses; it was boring. Hot flushes—he had one of them every time he went up the stairs. But he kept an eye on her. He clucked sympathetically when he saw her sweating. He brought her a glass of water and put

it beside the bed. She stared at him before she thanked him.

The chest hair was next. His. He woke up sweating one morning. The room was bright. The sun was already pushing through the curtains. She was leaning right over him, looking straight down at his chest.

—Gray, she said.

—What?

There was something there, a pain—the memory. She'd done something to him while he was asleep.

1

2ⁿᵈ Draft → 3ʳᵈ.

The Dog

She'd been gone a couple of hours, most of the afternoon – he wasn't sure – but she looked like she'd been in Spain for the last six months. Or the Sahara. She'd been tied down and tortured, under a big round sun.

He watched her taking off her coat. He didn't know what colour her hair was, the name for it. He sat still and said nothing.

It went back.

They hadn't coped well; he knew that.

His ear was the start of it. Or, a start. Years ago now. She'd been kissing him, and she'd stopped quickly, and he'd heard something, trapped in her throat.

-What's wrong? he'd said.

-Nothing, she'd said. -Your ear.

She'd stiffened beside him, but he felt her kind of unfold, relax again.

-My ear?

1

3ʳᵈ Draft – 4.

The Dog

She'd been gone for a couple of hours, most of the afternoon – he wasn't sure – but she looked like she'd been in Spain. Or the Sahara. She'd been tied down and tortured, under a big round sun.

He watched her taking off her coat. He didn't know what colour her hair was, the name for it. He sat still and said nothing.

It went back.

They hadn't coped well. He knew that.

His ear was the start of it. Or, a start. Years ago now. She'd been kissing him, and she'd stopped quickly and he'd heard something, trapped in her throat.

-What's wrong? he'd said.

-Nothing, she'd said. -Your ear.

She'd stiffened beside him, but he felt her kind of unfold, relax again.

-My ear?

-There's a hair on it.

*"I've got the bowl, the bone, the big yard. I know I should be happy."*

—There's gray in your hair.

He was sure of it. She'd pulled the hair on his chest. She looked now like she was going to peck him, the way she was hanging there.

—Did you pull my hair? he said.

He could hear himself ask the question, almost like he wasn't the one talking. He wasn't sure he was awake.

She didn't answer.

—And white, she said.

—Did you?

—What?

—Pull my hair.

—What? Why would I do that?

She said it like she was miles away, or on the phone to someone else. Someone she didn't think much of.

He got up on one of his elbows. He looked down at his chest; he tried to see it properly. His eyes swam a bit. Her back was to him; she was getting up. She held her nightdress down as she climbed out of the bed.

—It's not really something you think about, is it? she said. What happens to you when you get older.

She was standing now, looking behind the curtain, out the window.

—It's a bit horrible, she said.

—It's only hair.

He'd had gray hair for a good while. It had started in his early thirties, on his head. A few at the side, just above his ears. She'd liked it; so she'd said. She'd said it made him look distinguished. A bit like Bill Clinton. You expected the hair on your head to change; you knew it was coming. But not the chest hair, or the pubic stuff. So she was right: it was a bit horrible.

He'd examined himself that morning. He'd looked no different. He took his glasses off so he could look at his face properly. He was still there, the same man. It was frightening, though, how little time you got. You became yourself when you were twenty-three or twenty-four. A few years later, you had an old man's chest hair. It wasn't worth it. He put his glasses back on.

He didn't decide to throw out the statue. One of the saints—he couldn't remember which one, a woman. A present from one of her aunts. He'd just picked it up, walking past it in the hall. Kept walking, into the kitchen, threw it in the bin. Tied the bag, brought it out to the wheelie, dropped it in. Went back to the kitchen and put a new biodegradable bag into the bin. The mark was there on the table, where the statue had been; the varnish was much darker, like a badge— "Something Used to Be Here." She'd never asked about it; she'd never said anything. He'd never felt guilty. She'd never tried to cover the mark; she'd never rearranged the crap on the table, and neither had he.

But she'd thrown out his medal. Not that he gave a fuck. But she had.

The statue first. They'd both laughed at it, when the aunt was in the taxi, going home, the night she'd given it to them. The big blue eyes, the snakes at the saint's plaster feet. He'd put it on the table in the hall; he'd made room for it. It was him who'd done it. He'd made a ceremony of it. This was the first Christmas they'd been in the house, two years after the wedding. They'd laughed, and she'd kissed him.

He just picked it up and threw it in the bin. He didn't know he was going to do it. He just did. He'd often hoped she'd ask him about it, because he could have told her. It could have been the beginning of something; they'd have talked. But she didn't, and he didn't.

The medal. It was the only one he'd ever won. The Community Games, Football—Under 10s. North Dublin. Runners-up. He remembered the final, losing three-nil, and not caring once he had the medal. And not caring much about the medal, either. His mother had put it away, in the glass cabinet in the front room. She'd given it to him when he'd moved into his own house, along with all his old school reports and his Inter and Leaving Certs and a few photographs: the team in their stripy jerseys, him at the front, smiling and freezing; him and his big sister on the back of a donkey-and-cart, both of them squinting; him in his first suit, the flared trousers, grinning and squinting, the day before his first real job. He could remember his father with the camera. "Smile, smile. Stop bloody squinting." He'd told his father to fuck off and walked straight out to the street. He could remember the noise of the trouser legs rubbing against each other.

She hadn't taken anything else. Just the medal. He hadn't been looking for it. He'd just noticed it, gone. He'd kept the stuff in the big envelope his mother had put it into, with "Joe" in her shaky writing on it. He'd kept it in a drawer in the bedroom, under socks and T-shirts. Over the years, the shape of the medal had been pressed into the paper of the envelope. Not the little footballer, or the "1969," or any of the other details. Just the circular shape. He'd been looking for a sock to match another one, and—he didn't know why—he'd put his finger on the circle and realized there was nothing under it. He took out the envelope and opened it. The medal was gone.

He searched the drawer. More than once. He took everything out. He shook all the socks. He slid the whole lot out of the envelope, and put it all back, one thing at a time. He tried the other drawers. He pulled the chest of drawers away from the wall and looked behind it. He took all the drawers out to see if the medal had slipped to the side, if it was standing on its edge on one of the plywood slats that held the drawers in place.

He put everything back.

He had no doubt at all: she'd done it.

But then the dog came into the house. They got a dog. She got the dog. A Jack Russell, a thoroughbred, papers and all. A mad little thing. It was there yapping at his heels when he got home from work.

—What's this? he said.

—What's it look like?

—A dog.

—There you go.

—Whose is it?

—Ours, she said. Mine.

—Serious?

—Yeah.

Price $3.00

THE
NEW YORKER

Feb. 1, 1999

MAIRA KALMAN

He looked down at it.

—Let go of me fuckin' trousers, he said.

But he'd liked it, immediately. He'd had dogs when he was a kid. There'd always been a dog. Dogs were all right.

She gave it the name. Emma. From a book she liked, and the film, by Jane Austen. But it still ran around the kitchen in circles and knocked its head against the rungs beneath the chairs. It never stopped. It was always charging around the gaff, or asleep, beside its mat at the back door. Never on the mat, always right beside it. It was a great dog. Didn't shed too much hair, was too small to jump onto the good furniture, learned to scratch at the door and yap when it wanted to get outside. Only shat in the kitchen now and again, and always looked apologetic. So it was grand. But he soon began to realize that they weren't living with the same animal. She talked to it; she had a special voice she used. She'd buy a bag of jelly babies and share them, one for her, one for the dog. There was a child in the house, before he really understood.

He got up one morning and she was down there before him, filling the kettle. The dog had taken a dump beside the mat.

—Emma had an accident, she said.

—As long as it wasn't you, he said.

She laughed and he bent down, got the dog by the scruff, and pushed its snout into the shite. He unlocked the back door with his free hand and threw the dog outside, lobbed it gently, so it would land on its feet.

And she exploded. She actually hit him. She smacked him on the back, a loud whack that didn't hurt but shocked him. She hit him again. More of a thump this time—his shoulder.

—What was that for?

—What d'you think you're doing?

The two of them breathing hard.

He didn't hit her back. He didn't even think about it, or lift his hand or anything.

He knew immediately what she meant, and why she was furious. Now that she was. He could see.

—That's how you train them, he said.

—No, it isn't.

—It is.

It was how they'd trained their dogs at home, when he was a kid. Nose in the dirt, out the door. It had always worked.

—What other way is there?

He never mentioned the fact that she'd hit him. He never brought it up again, that the only one who'd ever been violent was her.

She signed them up for training classes. One evening a week, for eight weeks. They brought the dog to a big barn of a place, an actual barn beside an abandoned farmhouse, at the back of the airport. It was a strange, flat landscape. There was the ruin of a castle on one side of the road and the airport runway on the other, just a couple of fields away. He could look straight up at the bellies of the planes. The dog trainers were lovely, three soft-spoken girls who loved the dogs and the racket and the smell. He enjoyed it. They both did. The dog was quick on the uptake, all the sits and the stays, and it was fine with the other dogs. He enjoyed getting there, and coming home. They had to drive through Ballymun and over the M50 motorway. They'd comment on the changes, all the old tower blocks knocked down, the new buildings going up. There was one time, on the road that ran right beside the runway, they saw something ahead—two things—getting clearer and sharper. It was two horses, pulling buggies, racing, on both sides of the road. He drove onto the hard shoulder, and they watched the horses trot past, and two Traveller kids in the buggies—they didn't even look at the car as they flew by.

—Jesus.

—That's disgraceful.

—Is it?

—It's dangerous.

—That's for sure.

He got out of the car—she did, too—and they watched the buggies till they were too far away, waiting to see if any other cars or trucks came at them. But the road was empty.

—I wonder who won, she said.

—Don't know, he said. A draw. I'd love to do it, myself.

—Yeah, she said. Not here, though.

—No.

They got back in and went on to the training center.

Another time, they drove past a family of Romanians, Gypsies, about seven of them, walking along the same road, beside the runway. It was like they'd just climbed over the perimeter fence and they were making a break for the city.

But, really, they were strolling along, and he'd no idea where to. He couldn't even imagine. There wasn't a shop or a house.

—Why would they want to be out here? she asked.

—Reminds them of home.

—Stop that.

—They're left alone out here, he said. That's my guess.

—You're probably right, she said. It's like a no man's land, isn't it?

—Yeah, he said. It's nowhere.

—It's sad, though. Isn't it?

—I suppose it is.

Driving back home, after the training, they saw the Romanians again, off the road this time, on the island in the center of the M50 round-about; there were kids going into the bushes. He realized it slowly, and so did she. The car was off the roundabout and going through Ballymun before she spoke.

—They live in there, she said.

—What?

—The Romanians, she said. They're living in the roundabout.

—It looked like it, all right.

—In the bushes.

—Yeah.

—Jesus.

—Yeah.

They brought the dog to the barn every Wednesday night, for the eight weeks. The dog could walk, stop, sit, stay, and shit, and there were no more rows or misunderstand-

"If you lie down with pugs, you wake up with pugs."

ings. She fed the dog. He picked the shit up off the grass in the back garden. And he brought the dog down to Dollymount Strand for a run, on the mornings when he didn't have an early start. And those mornings were the best thing about having the dog. He'd park the car and walk toward the wooden bridge, with the docks and the city behind it, and Dun Laoghaire to the left, across the bay, and the mountains. He saw herons one morning, two of them, standing still in the water. He'd never seen herons before; he hadn't even known that there were herons in Ireland. They didn't budge when the dog ran at them, until the last second. Then they were up together, and they flew off slowly, dragging their legs behind them, and they settled again, in the shallow water farther down the beach. It thrilled him to see that. He loved the whole thing. Even when it rained—when the rain came at him sideways, straight off the sea, and he was soaking before he'd really started—he loved it. But he'd never have done it on his own. He'd never have been comfortable by himself, walking along the empty beach in the morning. He'd have felt strange. What was he doing there, all by himself? But with the dog it was fine. He didn't have to explain anything, to himself or to anyone else. He was walking the dog. Throwing a ball. Both of them getting their exercise.

Then the dog went missing.

He came home, and Mary was already there. Her eyes were huge and angry and terrified.

—You left the gate open.

—I didn't, he said. What gate?

—The side gate.

—I didn't.

—It was open.

—I didn't touch it, he said. Oh fuck, the dog.

He'd forgotten about the dog.

—I went out, she said. I couldn't find her.

—She'll be grand, he said. Hang on.

He went out to his car and came back with the street atlas. He divided the neighborhood; he stayed calm. They'd get into their cars. She'd go right, he'd go left.

—She can't be gone too far.

He didn't believe that. He was already thinking about the next dog.

—D'you want a cup of tea before we go? he asked her.

He thought he was handling it well. She was crying. He wanted to hug her, but it was a long time since they'd done that. He knew she was angry. He'd look—he'd genuinely look for the dog. He'd stay out all night. He'd search everywhere. And he'd be delighted if he found it—he could feel it in his chest. But they'd been away all day. Nine hours. He'd left first—he remembered shouting "Seeyeh" up the stairs, just before he'd closed the front door. But he hadn't been outside, in the back garden. He'd let the dog out—he remembered that. He'd been first down to the kitchen. The dog had stood up and stretched. He'd gone straight over to the door, to let it out. He'd had his coffee and his banana, and he'd gone. But the gate. He hadn't opened it. The night before? No. He couldn't remember touching the gate. It hadn't happened.

They went out to the cars together.

—What if she comes back when we're gone?

—It's not likely, is it?

—I just thought—

—I know, but she's never been out on her own before.

—I know.

—Let's stick to Plan A, he said. What d'you think?

—O.K., she said.

He was looking at the side gate now, open.

—Would you prefer to stay here? he said. In case.

—No, she said. It's better if we both do it.

—Grand.

They didn't find the dog. He stayed out till after midnight. He drove past the house, twice, until he saw her car parked outside. Then he parked his own and went in.

—No luck?

—No, she said.

She didn't look at him. She was sitting at the kitchen table. Then she looked, and stopped.

—The bloody gate, she said.

—It wasn't me, he said. I don't think it was. It isn't bin day.

—Bin day?

—Yeah. Bin day. The day in the week when I put out the bin. When I open the side gate. Every fuckin' week for the last twenty fuckin' years. Sorry.

He sat. He stood up. She looked at him.

—I'm sorry, too, she said.

He sat.

—What'll we do?

—I don't know.

They went up to bed together and fell asleep, more or less, together. He was first out again in the morning. He didn't shout "Seeyeh" up the stairs. He couldn't.

He hadn't opened the gate.

He looked at it before be started the car. It was still open. He got out of the car and shut it.

It was open again when he got home.

—In case Emma comes back, she told him.

—Oh, he said. Fair enough.

They were out again that night, putting up little posters she'd designed and photocopied, in the shops and on lampposts. "Missing," and a photo of the dog, then "Emma—Beloved Pet." And their phone number and her mobile number. He went left, she went right. He was home first. He fell asleep on the couch. She was in bed when he went up. She wasn't asleep—he knew—but she didn't move or say anything.

They got a few calls.

—I seen your dog.

—How much is the reward?

—I ate Emma.

Kids mostly, messing. And a couple of weird ones. Three in the morning.

—Hello? Are you Emma's dad?

—Emma's a dog.

—Yes.

He was putting the phone down. He could hear the woman at the other end still talking. He put it back to his ear.

—She asked me to tell you she's fine. She's happy.

—She's a fuckin' dog.

—Yes.

He lay back on the bed and knew he'd be getting up in a minute. Sleep was gone.

—Was that someone about Emma? Mary asked.

—Yeah.

—Another nut?

—Maybe we should take the posters down.

—No.

—O.K. You're right. We'll keep at it.

Then there was the Web site. She showed it to him—www.missing-dogs.ie. She'd opened her own page. The same photo of the dog; the location last seen—a little map, their house filled in red. The dog's personality, "outgoing."

—Will people look at this? he asked.

—Yes, they will, she said. Dog-lovers will.

—Grand.

—And there are links to other sites, she said. All over the world.

Some prick in Hong Kong was staring at the picture of their dog.

He said nothing.

Nothing.

That was the way their life had drifted. They never recovered from the dog. They didn't get another one. He wasn't blaming the dog. Things had been heading that way before the dog. The dog had even saved them for a while, or slowed down the drift. They'd had something new in common for a couple of months, and the excursions to the land behind the airport.

He hadn't opened the gate. He hadn't left it open.

But he'd failed. He could have pretended. Cried a bit, let her console him, take over—he didn't know. It wasn't about the gate. It was about grief. She grieved. He didn't. Simple as that. He should have pretended. It would have been a different kind of honesty. He knew that now. He thought he did.

He'd said they should get a new one. She'd stared at him and walked away. It wasn't a house you could walk away in; she had to walk out. She came back. They had another row, and he walked out. It was his turn. He stayed away for hours. He went to the pictures. He came back.

The walking out stopped. The rows stopped. The talking, too; it was a wordless life. They'd drifted. But, actually, they hadn't drifted, and that was another problem. One of them should have gone. They should have looked at each other one night, over the dinner or something, and smiled, and known that enough was enough. But that wise moment had never happened. He hadn't let it. He'd wished for it, but he hadn't let it happen. He hadn't let his eyes sit on hers.

Now she was taking off her new coat.

He didn't know her. Didn't know her hair, didn't know why she'd have wanted a tan in January—didn't really know how it was done. Some sort of a lamp, or a bed. He didn't know.

—Your coat's nice, he said.

| 2007 |

*"And what do you think will happen if you _do_ get on the couch?"*

*Available Varitype* 5

Liebling—reporter

(set slug) April 28, 1949 ± 9 = B ± V ½/m SOON, NOT WINTER

(#3) A Reporter at Large    OCT 29 1949

(#6)  Line and Tree

A few
[5 ago]
~~Last~~ week I went to a coondog field trial in rural Conn-

ecticut as the guest of Mike Izzo, a neighborhood grocer in New

Haven who owns a dog named Indiana Trigger.  Mr. Izzo's dog

has a statewide fame among coondog-trial fans, and last year

(eight hundred dollars in prizes).
won about ~~$800~~ for his owner, which is a lot, considering the

kind of purses ~~they~~ run for in Connecticut.  The biggest and

richest coondog trials are held in the Midwest.  <u>Procyon lotor</u>,

the raccoon, is an omnivorous, courageous, and highly adaptable

arboreal mammal found in every part of the North American

to
continent, from Alaska ~~south into~~ Mexico (a man trapped one in

the fact that                    curtails his role in
the Bronx last summer) but he is completely nocturnal, coondog

which
trials, ~~————~~ are held by day, so that people can watch them. Real

Two hundred
Coonhunting is at least as old as the rifle (about ~~(200)~~ years),

ran Oct 29, 1949

# LINE AND TREE

## A. J. LIEBLING

Some time ago, I went to a coondog field trial in rural Connecticut as the guest of Mike Izzo, a neighborhood grocer in New Haven who owns a notable dog named Indiana Trigger. Mr. Izzo's dog has a statewide fame among coondog-trial fans, and last year won about five hundred dollars in prizes for his owner, which is a lot, considering the size of the purses run for in Connecticut. (The biggest and richest coondog trials are held in the Midwest.) *Procyon lotor*, the raccoon, is an omnivorous, courageous, and highly adaptable arboreal mammal found in every part of the North American continent, from Alaska to Mexico (a man trapped one in Brooklyn last spring), but the fact that he is almost completely nocturnal curtails his role in coondog trials, which are held by day, so that people can watch them. Coon-hunting is at least as old as the rifle (about two hundred years), but field trials, which are a combination of a drag hunt and a race, have been in favor only since around 1925. Their increasing popularity has brought about a bifurcation in the coondog business, much like the one that occurred, by slow stages, in the barber-surgeon's trade in the late Middle Ages, when practitioners who lacked fluency in conversation or a light hand at shaving turned to what seemed a less exacting specialty. "Night dogs," those used in the darkling pursuit of the wild raccoon, are often not much good at field trials. Many of the best field-trial dogs have never been hunted in the woods at night, and never will be, because they might there develop habits of ponderation that would unfit them for their purpose, which is the rapid pursuit of the obvious.

In a coondog trial, a sack filled with litter from a captive raccoon's kennel is dragged over a cross-country course a couple of miles long, ending at a tree in the upper branches of which a live raccoon in a cage has been placed. The dogs are usually let loose ten at a time at the starting line. A hundred and fifty feet from the tree with the raccoon in it, the course passes between a pair of flags, customarily nothing more than white rags tied to saplings, seventy-five feet apart. The first dog to pass between the flags is said to win "line," and the next dog "second line." Dogs that run outside the flags are disqualified. The first dog to spot the raccoon up the tree and bark at him as if he means it wins "tree." There are generally about a dozen qualifying heats in trials of the size that are run in Connecticut, and

after the last one the winners compete in a tree final, a line final, and a second-line final. The finals are run on other courses than the heats, so the dogs won't be aided by memory. The bag of litter is hauled over the track after each heat, so the scent will not go cold. Consequently, night-dog men say, a dog doesn't need much of a nose to follow it. In a real night hunt, a dog must sometimes follow a trail several hours old. On the other hand, a trial dog needs a lot more speed than a straight cooner. The publics for the two forms of the sport are separate but overlap. A man putting a dog in a trial pays an entry fee, usually three dollars, and all the prizes come out of the pooled fees. When a hundred dogs are entered, the finals for line and tree are worth about fifty dollars apiece.

Although an urban, non-arboreal, mammal myself, I got so interested in field trials after attending several last fall that I subscribed to a remarkable monthly called *Full Cry*, published in Sedalia, Missouri, which carries a schedule of trials as long as the list of books in the Fall Announcement number of *Publishers' Weekly*. It was from *Full Cry* that I learned about the field trial I attended with Mr. Izzo, at Southington, about twenty miles from New Haven. Mr. Izzo's acquaintance I made a year ago, at a trial near Baltic, a mill town not far from Norwich. (One of the minor advantages of following coondog trials is that you get to know geography in detail.) I arrived at Mr. Izzo's house, in New Haven, at five minutes to ten on a Sunday morning, and found him already in an aged two-door sedan, with three dogs loaded in a low trailer hitched on behind. Mr. Izzo is a stocky, sallow man in his late forties, who has a heavy, Roman-legionary jaw and wears steel-rimmed spectacles. The other human members of our party were Mrs. Izzo, a tiny, lively woman wearing slacks and high-heeled shoes; a coondog fancier named Jack Galligan, who works for the New Haven Bridge Department; and a twelve-year-old boy whom Izzo introduced as Mrs. Izzo's nephew, Junior Matrianno. Mr. Galligan, who looks like a ruddier, jowlier version of Al Smith, is one of those Irishmen who go in for mock solemnity, mock ferocity, and slow, reassuring winks. He has been a coondog man for nearly forty years, but he finds cooning at night a bit too rough for him now, and so sticks to trials. Last year, when I first met him, he had no trial dog, but he now informed me that he had acquired one, and that it was in the trailer with Indiana Trigger and another belonging to Izzo.

After we had all fitted ourselves into the car, we started out, the three dogs barking as if the sedan were a coon and they had hopes of catching it. "Trigger and Jiggs start barking as soon as they see the trailer," said Izzo, who was driving. Jiggs is his second-string dog, a youngster he got for nothing out of a dog pound a year and a half ago. (There is no such thing as a pure coonhound breed; any dog that will hunt coon or follow a trail with acumen and enthusiasm can be called a coonhound.) "My dog is the one with the beautiful voice on him," Galligan said. "He's a registered bluetick, but the man down in Tennessee that sold him to the fellow I bought him off of won't let go of the papers. The only thing I don't know is what will he do. He's never run in a trial before." A bluetick is predominantly white but flecked and mottled with a smoky blue. A setter with this marking is known, I believe, as a belton, and a horse as a blue roan.

There had been rain earlier in the morning, and the air was warm and moist. "The scent will be plain today," Galligan said. "No breeze to turn over the leaves." When the air is moist, the scent lies close to the ground and lasts longer. After we had gone about ten miles, Izzo drove into a large field by the side of a wood and we let the dogs out for a breather. Indiana Trigger, whom I had seen run twice before, is a small, compact black hound, with tan on face and breast. He hasn't the long, drooping ears of the classic black-and-tan type, but he is recognizably a hound dog. Galligan told me that Trigger had been whelped somewhere in the South and had been sold for ten dollars by the man who bred him, and then had passed through the hands of a dozen owners on his way North, each selling him at a profit.

When he got to Indiana, a man paid a hundred and twenty-five dollars for him and then sold him to Izzo for two hundred and fifty, after he had failed to win anything with the dog. "He's been running better for Mike than he ever did for anybody else," Galligan said. "He run maybe thirty times last year and was only beaten before the finals twice. That's the way with dogs. Sometimes they improve with a change of owners and sometimes they go sour." Galligan's Blue, the putative bluetick, also looked like a hound. But Jiggs, a long-legged dog with medium-length reddish hair, was simply and happily a cur. Junior Matrianno, speaking as a loyal friend of Jiggs', told me the dog was "shepherd and bull." Izzo said, more dispassionately, "He could be anything." The ability to follow a trail by scent is a hound characteristic, but dogs like Jiggs, with forthright native talent, keep coondog trials a highly democratic sport. After the dogs had taken their ease for a few minutes, Izzo called them. Jiggs and Trigger came lolloping back and hopped into the trailer. Blue was a bit hesitant.

Soon after we had passed through Cheshire, which is not far from Southington, we began to look for road signs that would indicate the way to the field trial. Trials are always held in thinly settled sections of townships, because the dogs need a lot of ground to run over. The routes leading to them are posted with cardboard signs bearing red arrows and the name of a dog-food company, which distributes them, on request, to field-trial sponsors. Sometimes the dog-food people give a free sack of food to every dog entered. We soon picked up the arrows, and after passing a couple of dairy farms that Galligan said belonged to famous coon-hunters we turned off the highway and onto a gravel road that led up the side of a long hill covered with spruce, hemlock, and hardwood trees. The top of the hill was a plateau, and ten or fifteen automobiles were already parked on it, most of them with dogs tethered to their bumpers. Other dogs were tied to trees, just out of reach of one another, and still others were being walked on leashes. Most of them howled in greeting as we arrived with our trailer, and Izzo, steering a course neatly among them, drove to a vacant spot near a tree, where we climbed out and disembarked our three dogs.

Galligan put a leash on Blue, and he and I took a walk around while Izzo moored Jiggs and Trigger. Blue stopped in front of a large, gaunt, anxious-looking, biscuit-colored middle-aged hound that was holding one forepaw off the ground. Galligan, carefully keeping Blue out of the old dog's reach, said to me, "There's a dog that win some of the biggest races in the East a couple of years ago, but he hurt his foot, and he's an adder now." "What's an adder?" I asked, as I was expected to, and Galligan said, "Puts down three and carries one." At that moment, the adder's owner, a very fat man in a green shirt, came up and shouted to Galligan, "Well, well, ain't seen you since what you done in Dalton, Mass.!" "What did he do in Dalton, Mass.?" I asked, since I was plainly supposed to play straight man. "Went into a strange church and passed the basket!" the fat man shouted, and immediately burst into loud laughter. "Never mind," said Galligan. "I never picked up no butts from the ground, like I seen you do." "I was just picking them up for you—get more flavor that way," his friend came back. Galligan laughed hard. "He's a witty fellow, that Warren," he said to me as we walked away. "Hell of a witty fellow."

Cars were arriving on the plateau in a steady stream now, and the majority of them were towing dog trailers. Most of the dogs looked like hounds, but usually like hounds with traces of sheep dog, bull terrier, or whippet. There was one coarse collie that showed no trace of anything else, and a number of sheep dogs and unclassifiable curs that might possibly have had a recessive dash of hound. The fastest pure-strain dogs—greyhounds and whippets—are no good for trials, because their instinct is to run with their heads high and their eyes on the quarry, making no effort to use their noses. These traits, the product of centuries of breeding, cannot be altered by any simple attempt at reeducation. Crosses between greyhounds or whippets and proved coonhounds—the result of one-generation attempts to combine a nose and speed—are seen at tracks, but they seldom work out; the dogs seem to be torn between conflicting inherited aptitudes. "I still think a hound with a good cat foot—a dog that stands high on his toes—is fast enough to beat any of them crosses," Galligan said. "The crosses run wide on the turns and have to wait for the dogs with noses to pick up the scent again. Look at the feet on Blue, now. I think he's got a future."

The Southington Sportsmen's Club, which owns the hillside over which the dogs were to run, is a member of the United Raccoon Hunters Field Trial and Protective Association of Connecticut. The Association makes up a regular schedule of trials, each of the member clubs holding one meet a year. A field trial gives the host club a chance to pick up a bit of cash for its treasury, the money coming from the sale of refreshments and a 30 percent cut of auction pools on the dogs, the standard form of betting on coondog trials. The members' wives in charge of the feeding arrangements remind one of the committeewomen at any church clambake; in fact, they *are* the women who run the church clambake when that event comes along. A field trial combines aspects of a church affair and of a very small race meeting, but it has an entirely individual sound accompaniment—the continual howls, barks, and snarls of the parliament of coon-dogs. Coondog men, incidentally, pay much attention to the noise their dogs make, and speak learnedly of "bawl-and-chops," "squall-and-chops," "long bawls," "short bawls," and "long bass bugles." Some dogs, known as silent trailers, steal up on a raccoon and give tongue only after they have treed him. They are deprecated by coonhunting aesthetes.

> For silent dogs don't give a thrill:
> With them it's two barks, then a kill,

a poet wrote in *Full Cry*. I attended a meet last year with a man who bought a dog on the spot for no other reason than that it had a beautiful baritone voice. It turned out that its gifts were exclusively vocal, so my friend sold it as a foxhound. "I didn't know but what he might be," he told me. "He certainly wasn't interested in coon."

The Southington clubhouse is a one-room structure, built of gray concrete blocks, on the slope of the hill just below the edge of the plateau. Under the downhill side of the clubhouse, there is an open basement, which serves as a restaurant, selling hamburgers, hot dogs, steamed clams, clam chowder, clam broth, raw onions, apples, pickles, coffee, birch beer, root beer, home-baked pies, a meat-loaf dinner for a dollar, and a number of other items that I forget. There was a beer bar outside. Hard liquor is sold at some trials, but none was evident at Southington, except in the gaits of a few of the sportsmen.

As it got on toward twelve o'clock, the members of the committee running the trial began to appeal to owners over a public-address system to get their entries in. The entry lists had been open since ten o'clock, the grounds were

packed with dogs, but only a few owners had paid their three dollars and put down their dogs' names. "Hanging back to see if they can get in a soft heat," Izzo said to me. "They want to wait until all the hot dogs are drawn." I asked him if he had entered Jiggs and Trigger yet, and he said he hadn't—he wanted to have a look at the lists first.

While the dog-owners were outwaiting one another, I stopped at the lunch counter for a moment to deal with a bottle of birch beer, a hamburger with raw onion, and a portion of steamed clams, and then went to look at the finish line of the course, in a field bounded by a low stone wall halfway down the hill. The starting line was about two miles away somewhere; the dogs in each heat would be taken to it in a pickup truck. A dog running through the flags of the finish line and continuing straight on could hardly fail, it would seem, to come right up against the coon tree, a tall walnut, alone amid low spruce. The

## LOST

There was hell to pay in the Gladstone Hotel the other morning. A lady guest who was in the throes of packing to check out reported that her Pekinese was lost. A squad of bellhops searched the premises for an hour or more before they found him. He had been packed.    | 1944 |

coon, in his cage, was already up in the crotch of a limb, about thirty feet above the ground, and the countryman who had put him there, probably a veteran bird's-nester, was already down. "I hope the boys get a lighter coon next time they hold a race," he said to me. "Nearly ruptured myself lugging him up there." As we talked, the track-layers, a couple of boys in their early teens, came into view, walking cater-cornered through the field, dragging the sack of coon litter behind them.

They were completing a sidehill scramble through briars and over fences, across pasture land and wood lots. On their way, they had marked their course by tying rags to trees, so that the sack could be hauled over the same trail after each heat. The boys walked across the line midway between the flags and then marched up to the tree in which the coon was perched. They smacked the bag vigorously against the trunk several times, then held it clear of the ground and walked over to us. They said they expected to go over the course a couple more times during the afternoon; other pairs of boys would spell them. "In some Western states, they allow you to drag a live coon along the trail in a wet bag," the tree-climber said, "but here the Humane Society won't let you. It doesn't make much difference, because even if you *had* a live coon, a good coondog could smell that there had been a man along there—man scent and coon scent all mixed together for two miles. He would know it wasn't on the level. You ask me, there are mighty few of these dogs that are fooled into thinking they're hunting a coon. They know it's just a race."

I climbed back up the hill and found that a set of dogs had at last been drawn for the first heat. Each dog is given a number when he is entered, and white clay marbles bearing corresponding numbers are put in a wire basket, from which ten at a time are rolled out to determine the starters in each heat. Galligan's Blue and Izzo's Jiggs had both been drawn for the first heat.

Dan Cole, a familiar figure at Connecticut field trials, was mounting a sort of stage near the clubhouse to run the first auction pool. Cole, an extremely fat man with a handsome, incongruously young face, was wearing a pale-gray sombrero and a flame-red cotton shirt. He lives in Shelton, not far from Southington, and spends every Sunday (and a good many Saturdays) auctioning pools at Connecticut meets. Once a year, he runs a trial of his own, near Shelton. He is a prosperous farmer and is said to own a number of highly talented gamecocks. He sometimes gets a fee from the clubs for whom he officiates as auctioneer, but often waives it when a trial doesn't draw well. Mostly, I suspect, he likes the authority he feels when he stands on the rostrum and wheedles the crowd into betting its money. His chief rival in this section is a fellow named Shorty Griffen, a railroad freight clerk from Poughkeepsie, whose style is modelled on that of the tobacco auctioneers on the radio. He chants more than Cole and wisecracks less.

The principle of an auction pool is simple: If you fancy a dog's chances, you try to "buy" him, and if there are others of the same opinion, they bid against you. The high bidder pays his money and gets a ticket. If there are ten dogs in a heat and they are bid in for a total of twenty dollars on tree, say, the holder of the ticket on the winning dog gets the pool (minus the sponsoring club's 30 percent cut), or fourteen dollars. Trial running isn't really a big-money sport, but since there are separate pools for tree, line, and second line in each heat, the home club may turn a profit of several hundred dollars during the afternoon if bidding is lively. The heaviest pools are those on the finals. In the preliminaries, the bidding sometimes starts at half a dollar, and not infrequently stops there. In such cases, it is always the owner who puts up the fifty cents. It is a point of honor to have four bits' worth of faith in your own dog. Favored dogs sometimes sell for seven or eight dollars but anything over five dollars is considered a stiff bid. In finals, dogs are occasionally bid in for as much as fifteen dollars.

Each time Cole called out the name and number of a dog, a man with a dog on leash would step out of the crowd and come up to the platform. Sometimes the dog would jump up on the platform (this usually indicates an experienced trial dog), and the man would stand beside it while Dan made his spiel. At other times, the owner would have to lift the dog onto the platform and sit with him, stroking him or clasping a fraternal arm about him to keep him calm. "Fred Clark's Rosie dog, one of the fastest track dogs in the East," Dan began. "Here's a dog that can really pour it on, gentlemen. Don't let her run in on you and then come around and say you weren't looking or that I didn't give you fair warning. Who'll start her at four dollars? Three I've got over there—three. Who'll say a half? . . ." The next dog was a tall, gangling newcomer, and Dan said, "Here's a good tree dog, gentlemen. I can see it. If he runs in, he can *look* into that cage. . . ." Later, confronted with a grizzled shepherd, plainly nine or ten years old, he began, *"Don't be influenced by the dog's appearance, friends. He's had *experience*. His owner lives just over the hill—had him over the course six times last night.

*"Schmooze!"*

The owner says half a dollar. Hello, Pete, you old chicken fighter [to a friend whom he sees studying the dog with a speculative expression], I want you to get back the money you lost on them chickens last week—say a dollar . . ."

A colored man named Yager, who lives in Poughkeepsie, turns up at almost all the Connecticut meets with a trailer full of dogs as well as with a whole bunch of sons and daughters—his dog-handlers. He is very serious about the business, and last year told me that he had just given up a good house in Poughkeepsie because it was too near the center of town for his dogs. He had moved to an isolated farm on a dirt road, where he could exercise them behind the family car every day without fear of having them run over. In "roading" dogs, a trainer keeps his car at about twenty miles an hour, occasionally speeding up to thirty or thirty-two for a short stretch. Yager had a bitch at Southington that Cole had never seen before, and when she was brought up to the platform, Dan asked, "Will she tree?" (Some young dogs who have learned enough to race for line think the event is over when they have crossed it.) "She have," Yager answered noncommittally. A coondog man named Ham Fish, a dairy farmer who keeps a big string of night dogs and trial dogs, next appeared, with a new dog that had a scarred head. "Will that dog fight?" Cole asked. "Might," said Fish, who looks like a robust version of Ernie Pyle. A fighting dog is, of course, a poor betting proposition, since he may stop racing and start fighting. Most fights, however, occur under the tree, and a man who knows he has a fighter sometimes lets him run only for line, and then rushes out and hauls him in before he can get into trouble. The best way to take a dog out of a fight, I am informed (I have no intention of trying it), is to grab him and press with your thumbs at the rear of his jaws, against his back teeth. A patient man named Porter, whom I have seen at several trials, once told me that he had lost nine thumbnails on one talented but pugnacious dog. "He couldn't help it," Porter said. "He had a bull cross."

When the last dog in the first heat had been auctioned, the crowd started down toward the coon tree and the finish line. There were almost as many women as men, most of them wearing slacks and shirts, and there seemed to be more children than adults, but this may have been an illusion caused by their greater mobility. A couple of boys were already engaged in retrieving abandoned beer bottles, which they would turn in for the two-cent deposit. They tacked about the grounds as if they, too, were trailing, and I half expected them to bawl and chop whenever they detected an empty Budweiser bottle under a bush. As the spectators trudged downhill, the voice of a club official came over the loudspeaker. "Al Rambeau," the voice said, "catch that big white hound of yours before he gets on the track. We can't run the heat while he is out there on the track." A maliciously delighted dog and an unhappy human figure raced each other through the field. While this was going on, the pickup truck, with the dogs and their owners in it, set out for the starting line, heading down the hill road to the main highway. By the time we had got to the finish line, we could see the truck well along the highway; then it turned off on another side road, leading uphill.

The course is customarily laid out so that while the dogs are making a wide-arced sweep across country, the truck can double back to the finish on a more direct line by road. As soon as the dogs have started, the men jump into the truck, which then takes off at a reckless clip to get to the finishing point before the dogs. The truck stops about a hundred feet back of the coon tree, and the men hop out. The dogs are usually in sight, or at least audible, by the time the truck arrives. The owners, leashes in hand, stand ready to grab their dogs as soon as the heat has been decided, but they are not allowed to crowd the tree, because a smart dog would then

run straight to his owner and bark, thus achieving a cheap victory.

At the starting point, the men lead their dogs up to the beginning of the track and let them nose around a bit. Then they unleash them, and each man hangs on to his dog by the collar or shoulder harness while the starter lines them up. Just before the start, some of the men cradle their dogs in their arms. At the whistle, these men throw their dogs forward on the trail (which can't really help them much in a two-mile race), while others hold their dogs back for an instant. These last are the owners of young dogs who, if they got in front, might miss the track. Such dogs simply trail the seniors until they are near the line, where, stimulated by the shouts of the crowd, they sometimes run in ahead of their preceptors.

The first trial on this particular day resulted in a dead heat, a term that in this sport means mass disqualification. We could hear the dogs and then see them coming toward the finish, but about fifty yards from the line the leaders swerved, and the others followed them outside the farther flag. They ran off into the brush and then straggled back toward the crowd singly or in twos, looking for their masters. "Rabbit!" a man next to me said disgustedly. "Cottontail must have run across the course, and those so-called coondogs took its trail." "Did not, either," another man said. "Too many people standing that side of the course. Fool dog ran toward the people and t'others followed him. They should get the people back of that line." Events indicated that he was probably right. In the later heats, the judges made the crowd stand back of the line, and only one or two dogs ran out during the rest of the day. Some of the owners of dogs in the first heat were wrathy, arguing that they ought to get their entry money back, inasmuch as the crowd should not have been there to distract their dogs. (In a dead heat, the auction-pool money goes to the club fund.) The official contention was that if the dogs had been following the trail by nose, as they were supposed to do, they wouldn't have allowed themselves to be distracted. Neither Jiggs nor Blue had been among the leading dogs, so Izzo and Galligan would have lost their entry money even if the heat had been a proper one.

Before the auction for the next heat, Izzo came over to me and said in a confidential tone that a dog named Dick, a black-and-white animal that looked more like a smooth collie than anything else, was a good bet, and that he would go halves with me if I bid him in for line and tree. "A great tree dog, a great line dog. Looka those legs!" Dan Cole began when Dick's owner, a red-faced man from Worcester, conducted him to the platform. "You know the boys didn't bring him all the way from Massachusetts just for the ride. Four dollars. Have I got four dollars for tree?" Nobody spoke until Dan asked for a dollar; then somebody bid, and the bidding rose by bold, one-dollar leaps until four was reached, when I said, "And a half." There was silence for a moment, and then Dan said, "Four and a half once, four and a half twice, and sold to the new convert for four and a half. Now how about line? This dog might lose tree once in a while—once in a *long* while—but when it comes to line, he can really fly!" I got Dick for line for five dollars.

This time, when the dogs came in sight of the finish, they were running true, headed straight for the midway point between the flags, but Dick was third as he crossed the line, with a red dog and a white one ahead of him. Having passed the line, the red dog began walking about rather aimlessly, as if he thought his work done. The white dog began investigating a small hemlock that even a fool should have realized wasn't big enough to hold a cage with a coon in it. I could see a couple of men with leashes jumping about in high excitement, and guessed that they were the owners of the first two dogs. In such circumstances, an owner can rely only on telepathy to tell his dog which tree the coon is in. Last fall, I saw a French-Canadian mill hand stand by in mute despair during a final while a dog of his scratched his back against the coon tree and then walked away. By raising his head and barking, the dog could have earned fifty dollars for his owner. Meanwhile, Dick came loping in, ran to the foot of the walnut, jumped as high as he could against the tree, and bayed. He stayed by the tree, making a noise—I don't know whether he was chopping or bawling—until the head tree judge blew a whistle. There are two line judges and three tree judges. Sometimes two dogs tree at almost the same time, and then a two-out-of-three vote decides. This time, however, there was no doubt. The red dog had won line and the white

dog second line, but Dick had got tree. Mike and I collected $14.35 for our $9.50. We felt that we had put across a sleeper.

Before the heat Indiana Trigger was to run in, Mike came to me and said that he never liked to bet on Trigger, because when he did, the dog lost. "There's only one in this heat I'm afraid of," he said. "He's a very fast line dog, but he isn't much on tree, and if Trigger is anywhere near him, Trigger will tree first." I bid in Trigger for tree, on my own account, and did not buy him for line. However, he fooled Mike. He was first across the line, but the second dog barked tree before he did. This contretemps cost me my winnings on Dick, plus $2.57½. The remaining heats were anticlimactic, since neither Mike nor Galligan had entries in any of them and advised no further investments. We had to stay, though, because Indiana Trigger had qualified for the line final. He had earned five dollars by winning line in his heat. Mike calculated that the prize for the final might be as much as seventy dollars.

The Izzos and Junior and I continued to walk up the hill after every heat and down the hill after every auction, but Galligan parked himself on a boulder near the finish line and remained there, talking to a couple of other sages. Blue was by this time back in the trailer, fast asleep. "He might be more of a woods dog, at that," Galligan said. "He throws up his head every now and then and sniffs around, as if he would take

*"I'll lay it out for you. We're cutting back,*
*and we no longer need a dog."*

an air scent. I think he might be a very good deerhound, or a fine dog after mountain lion. I think I'll put an ad in *Full Cry* or the *American Cooner* offering him on trial." On one of my up-hill trips, I bought a dog named King Cotton, a July hound, for tree. A July is a small white hound with tan ears, looking like a straight-legged beagle or a long-eared smooth fox terrier. "This dog has never been wrong on tree in his life," Dan said in auctioning him. King Cotton wasn't wrong this time, either. When he got to the tree, he barked right at it. The trouble was that five or six dogs had got there before him, and at least four of them had barked on arrival. After that, I decided that it was cheaper, as well as more restful, to sit with Galligan. The sky had cleared toward noon, and the early after-noon had been hot, with swarms of little flies and gnats settling on dogs and spectators alike, but as night drew on, the air grew cooler. By the finish of the tenth heat (two more to go), it was hard to tell the dogs apart, and it was evi-dent that the finals would have to be run in the dark.

Running trials in the dark is something that dog-owners, spectators, and particularly judges dislike, but it has come up at every meet I've been to. It is the subject of a long and pithy essay in an issue of the *American Cooner* of a few months back, by a man named Sam Hankins, a great owner of racing dogs and promoter of field trials at Hyde Park, New York. Mr. Hankins attri-butes the chronic lateness of dogmen at field tri-als principally to two causes—vice and virtue. There is one type of dogman, he says, who stays up late Saturday night drinking, always has a hangover Sunday morning, and doesn't begin to pull himself together until noontime, after which he loads his dogs and drives fifty or a hundred miles to a trial, stopping on the way to get some

breakfast and a few cans of beer. The other type likes to take his wife and children to church and then walk them home and have Sunday dinner with them. The outcome is the same, Mr. Han-kins says; both types arrive at the trial at about two in the afternoon, and then they stall around waiting for the fast dogs to be drawn before they make their entries. He does not indicate whether the fellows from church are more or less ethical about this last procrastination than the boys from the tavern. There are also, Mr. Hankins says, a couple of fellows at every meet who have real night dogs that are pretty good trial dogs, too; naturally, these men try to delay matters, figuring that their dogs will have an advantage after dark. They are happy to see the meet lag and the finals run under such conditions that no-body can see what is going on. Then, Mr. Han-kins continues, there are some fellows who will let their dogs go in the dark before the starting signal, meanwhile slapping their pants and whining like hounds to make the starter think they still have their dogs in hand. The most ex-asperating thing about late heats is that the judges are likely to call the wrong dog at the fin-ish line, since they cannot have any lights brighter than flashlights—car headlights, for instance, would frighten the dogs back into the woods. And dog-owners are afraid that their dogs will run into trees, get hung up in fences, or start down a wrong trail and wander off, to be stolen or run over before they can be found.

It was completely dark even before the start of the last heat, and Izzo said there would be no sense watching it; the thing for us to do was to load the dogs, get into the car, and drive down to the foot of the hill. It was so late that there were to be no auction pools on the finals. The line final was to be run across woods and pastures in the valley, ending at the highway. If we parked beside the highway, the truck going out to the start would have to pass us, and Mike could stop it and get on with Trigger. We did as he suggested, and when we had parked by the dark highway, Mike began to complain about late starts and said that he had half a mind to go home rather than risk his dog. I had once seen Trigger win a line final in the dark, so I knew Mike was not serious. He got out and took Trigger from the trailer on a leash, and we all stood in the road. I asked Junior if he had done his homework, and he said "Naw!" and walked as far from me as he could get. Pretty soon we could see the lights of the dog truck coming down the hill and hear the eleven dogs in it trying to fight with each other, and their owners cursing. Mike hailed the truck and climbed aboard with Trigger. Mrs.

---

## KNOTTY POINT

The kindly editor of a pet magazine has turned over to us (just before leaving for ten days in the Canadian woods) a letter from one of his subscribers that begins, "I am asking you to write me and tell me how to test if a cat or dog is dead or not."    | 1948 |

---

Izzo said that there was a black dog named Cinders in the line final that seemed to be in form, and that he was an awful fast dog. A couple of minutes after the truck had gone on, we all walked over into the pasture next to the road and stood as near the finish line as a state trooper and the local town constable would let us. We could see the white flags marking the finish in the dark, but people and trees, even those within a few feet of us, were only vague masses. We knew that the line judges, one at each flag, would turn their flashlights on the first dog they saw or heard going over the line. They would hear the dogs barking as they drew near. The danger was that if the leading dog was a

dark color and momentarily silent, he might sneak in on them. I stayed close by Mrs. Izzo as we stumbled through the dark. "I know Trigger's voice when I hear it," she said. "I'll be able to hear him coming." In what seemed a very short time, we heard the truck on its way back. It turned into the field and rolled in among the spectators. There were no casualties, or if there were, the victims died without a moan.

Then flashlights gleamed, and the dog-owners came rushing down off the truck. "Out with them lights!" the town constable yelled. "You want to scare them dogs back to the start?" The lights went out, and in another minute we heard the music of the dogs coming toward us in the dark. The owners were practically on the finish line this time. It didn't make any difference now, since the dogs couldn't see them. Someone yelled, "Here they be!" (In a lifetime of watching sporting events, I have never been the first spectator to see anything.) Then two thin beams of light shot out from the judges' flashlights, crossing on the form of a black dog traversing the line. It was Cinders. Two dogs followed close behind him, one of whom was Trigger.

"It was a good try anyway," Mike said after he had caught his dog. When we had got back in the car, Mrs. Izzo said, "I could tell from his bark he wasn't in front." Mike said, "Well, it wasn't such a bad day. I put in six dollars in entry fees, and the Trigger win five back in heat money, but I also won two-forty betting, so I made one-forty on the day." Junior said, "I bet Trigger will beat that Cinders by daylight." Jack Galligan said, "I met a man here today that says he knows where there is a wonderful dog. A great big hound with claws like a cat. I bet he would make a wonderful trial dog."

| 1949 |

# THE DOOR ON WEST TENTH STREET

*Fiction*

## MAEVE BRENNAN

Niobe the old black Labrador retriever is going to have a holiday from the city. She is going to Katonah, a distant suburb of New York, where she will have trees, grass, hedges, night-smells of earth, and, at a distance, a road to watch, and passing cars. She will have a house of her own, to guard. There is a field in Katonah where she can run as hard as she likes, and, not far away, a lake where she will swim, holding her head high, pouring herself through the water while her big, heavy old body feels light again and her legs stretch themselves. In the lake in Katonah, Niobe's short, thick, pow-

erful sea legs will stretch themselves until all the dull constriction of city sidewalks and city streets crumbles away from her webbed paws and from inside her muscles. Her legs will become sleek again and they will do what they like, sending her through the water at exquisite speed, so that the people watching her think, Why would anybody want to go faster than Niobe, and how can any-body bear to go more slowly than she goes when she swims?

Niobe is a changeling, anxious to please, but water is her element, and when she swims she becomes herself, a solitary reveller with a big, serious, courageous head and a store of indifference that make it seem sometimes that she might never come back to land. She always comes back, shaking herself so that the water springs off her and her fur stands up in spikes. And after shaking she stands for a minute, staring about her with the mad cousinly friendliness of her true cousin, the dolphin. She is ready for anything. At that moment, wet and rakish from her swim, Niobe seems to have travelled to earth from a far distance—from the bottom of the sea, twenty thousand fathoms down, where the Fish King has his court. The Fish King never speaks, not even to say "Now" or "At once." His words are made of thunder and they reverberate at his will. Great sounds issue from him—sounds of wrath, sounds of mirth, and sounds of hunger. But he never speaks. He sits in oceanic silence under an immense floating canopy that is really an upturned lake of fresh clear water, and in its blue depths and shallows small green flowers and silver goldfish play games with the sunlight that was trapped in the water on the day the lake was stolen—a Monday in Norway, centuries ago. Niobe has seen the Fish King and his canopy, and she knows his palace guard of dignified young whales, and the thousand sequined mermaids who are his dancing girls. She was at home with them, and she is at home with us. She has seen everything. It is written in her face, in her sad, bright eyes. There is hardly anything she does not know, except when to stop eating. Her true memories are ancestral—they haunt her sleep. In daily life, the compromise she makes is wholehearted, but there is nothing in it of acquiescence. Housebound, she remains herself. She is a dog.

But today Niobe is going to the country. She is going to Katonah, where her big, hungry nose will find something to smell besides concrete and stone and lampposts, and gutters that seem interesting but that always prove unresponsive in the end. Niobe does not know that her leash is going to be put away for a month. To her, this is an or-

dinary day, and it starts as usual in her Greenwich Village apartment. She rouses from her sleep on the bedroom floor, on a dark, flowery carpet that is thin and worn to pale string in spots—a length salvaged from the acres of carpeting that once covered the lobbies and stairs of one of those majestic old New York hotels that disappeared last year, or the year before, or the year before that. The carpet smells of Niobe's sleep and of the cats' sleep and of the vacuum cleaner, but that is all. There are no memories in it, no echoes of country grass and leaves and earth, no bits of sand, no woodsmoke, no pine needles, nothing of the house by the ocean in East Hampton, where Niobe lived for most of her life. This is an apartment carpet, anonymous, warm, comfortable, and dull. No field mice ever ran across it, flying for their lives from the cats; no field mice, no moles, no chipmunks, no baby rabbits. Once a regiment of tiny black city ants marched across it and disappeared into the wall. And once an enormous black water bug hurried out of the bathroom and across the carpet in the direction of the kitchen. And a soft, pale-green caterpillar, a visitor from nowhere, crawled timidly about in the dark foliage of the old carpet for a little while before he curled up to die. But that is all. It is a poor, boring carpet, and Niobe yawns when she wakes up, ignoring it. She stands and stretches and looks about her, showing she is ready for her walk.

Niobe's walk takes her around Washington Square, and as she passes the doorman of the big apartment house on the corner he grins and says, as he does every morning, "Hello, Old-Timer." Niobe is nearly eleven years old, and her young, original, shining black face is disguised by a dusty mask of grey hairs, grey eyebrows, grey muzzle, and long grey jaws. The mask makes her comical, and people smile when they see her and say, "Oh, my, that's an old dog." People walking behind her smile, too, because, although her thick, heavy tail is still coal black, her behind is grey and it waggles importantly as she goes along. But however she goes, trotting, cantering, plodding, or simply dawdling, she always looks what she is—a dog out of water, not at ease in the city but putting up with it very well. She is amiable, although not particularly obedient, and she accepts her leash and makes her way, leading with her strong, wide-set shoulders and getting all she can out of this strange world where she has to behave like a clockwork dog who can go only in squares, circles, and straight lines. And she searches. She keeps looking for a black door in a little white house on West Tenth Street. Twice on her walks she happened on that door and refused to pass it, struggling to get into the house and even barking once, but for weeks now, for months, she has not seen it.

The house belongs to a man who took Niobe to Montauk for six weeks last summer, and when she sees the door on West Tenth Street she knows what lies behind it—a cliff dropping into the Atlantic Ocean. Niobe loves that cliff, which gave her a wild dash to her morning swim and, on her way back, countless difficult crannies to dig and burrow into. The house on West Tenth Street looks like a real house, and no one passing it would dream that all of Montauk lies behind it—the cliff, the sand, and the ocean. Everything worthwhile is there behind that door, which Niobe knows is closed only to hide the sea from dogs who are not going there. She has not seen that door for a long time now, but she has not lost hope. She watches for it. She looks for it everywhere, on all the streets east and west of Fifth Avenue, and along Fifth Avenue, and along University Place, and on Fourth Avenue, and on Seventh Avenue, and on little Gay Street and on Cornelia Street and even on Bleecker Street, be-

hind the stalls of vegetables and fruit, but she is never confused into thinking that a strange door is the door she wants. There is only one door on West Tenth Street and she will know it when she sees it again.

Even in the city, Niobe had adventures. As she walked around Washington Square Park one morning, she came alongside a very, very old man sitting alone on one of the benches that line the paths around the grass. He was more than old, he was ancient, and although it was a glowing day, Indian summer, he was warmly dressed in an overcoat and a muffler and a crumpled grey hat, and he wore laced boots, and his hands were clasped together on his walking stick, and his eyes were closed. Niobe passed very close to him, and he may have heard her dramatic breathing as she pressed on in her pursuit of the Atlantic Ocean (hiding behind that door on West Tenth Street, so near, but where?), because he opened his eyes and saw her. He didn't smile, but he looked at her. "Hello, Snowball," he said, thoughtfully. "How are you doing, Snowball?" Then he closed his eyes again and went on sitting by himself in the warm sun.

Another time Niobe found a dead sparrow lying at a grass corner in the center of the Square, where the fountain is. (Where the fountain *was*. It has been dry for a long time.) The sparrow, no bigger than a withered leaf, lay on his side, with his wings folded and his legs close together. He was a very neat little dead body. A wild bird, his fate was strange anyway—to share a shabby city park with hungry, watchful pigeons, big fellows. How old had he been when he learned to dash in among them and grab his crumb? He must have been strong and clever to survive to his full size. His cleverness was finished now, and the story of his life was not even history—it was a big mystery that he had never known anything about, and that was wrapped about him now as he lay by the grass. He lay there, with the secret of his nature in open sight for anybody to look at; but only to look at, not to touch, not really to see, never to understand. He was a sparrow, whatever that is. Samuel Butler said life is more a matter of being frightened than of being hurt. And the sparrow might have replied, "But Mr. Butler, being frightened hurts."

Niobe looked at the sparrow, and then she sat down and began to contemplate him. There was nothing to smell, but the light breeze blowing from the south, from Sullivan Street, touched a loose feather and it stood up and waved, a tiny flag the color of dust. That was all. It was quite otherwise with the mighty pheasant, an emperor pheasant, Niobe found dead on the beach in East Hampton one autumn morning, her third autumn by the ocean, years ago. That was an unearthly morning— one mislaid at the beginning of the world and recovered in East Hampton under a high and massive sky of Mediterranean blue. An Italian sky, a young and delighted ocean, a blazing sun; and far away on the white sand something crimson that caught the wind. The wind was so new that it blew cold, in its first rush across the world, but the air was soft. The pheasant's head and body were almost buried in the powdery sand, but he had fallen with his wings wide open, and one of them slanted up to make a wedge of color in the air.

That autumn morning was early in November—the time of year when millions of small stones appeared in flattened wind formations at intervals along the lower part of the beach, where the sand is hard and flat near the water's edge. Some of the stones are as big as walnuts and some are as small as grains of rice, and they lie tightly packed, a harsh sea fabric, while their faint colors—ivory, green, silver, coral—are always vague, almost vanishing, always about to dissolve into the stone. Niobe used to race along the beach until she was almost out of sight, and at that distance, far away, she became a big black insect with four waving legs and a waving tail and wings that were either transparent or folded. Because it was impossible that a creature who skimmed so confidently and at such speed across the sand and in and out of the water and along the top of the dunes should not also be able to fly up and away and out to sea, with the seagulls.

*"All dogs go to Heaven, because we're not the ones who screwed up."*

The seagulls detested Niobe and flew off screeching with irritation whenever they saw her hurrying toward them. They stood in a long single line, staring at the water, and waited until she came close to them before they took flight. Their feet left a delicate tracery of pointed marks, a Chinese pattern, in the clean wet sand. Niobe's big paws made untidy holes in the sand, and sometimes troughs, and even when she did make a recognizable paw mark it was indistinct and awkward, not to be compared with the delicate seagull imprint. She had attacks of wanting to dig in the sand, and then she dug as frantically as a dervish looking for a place to whirl. She loved to chase her ball into the ocean. She had a succession of balls—red, green, blue, and white, and sometimes striped, but one by one they drifted out to sea while Niobe

stood at attention on the shore and watched them go. She knew the power of the big waves, and how they hurled themselves so far down into the sand that they were able to drag it out from around her legs.

After Christmas, when the storms began, the beach was whipped and beaten into bleak terraces—long ranges of sharp sand cliffs descending from the dunes to a struggling, lead-colored sea that foamed into mountains against the sad sky, while the seagulls screamed their warnings all day long. One day in January, Niobe received a present from the grocery shop of an enormous bone, a bone of prehistoric size and weight, a monumental thighbone with great bulging knobs at each end. She took hold of the bone at its narrowest place, in the middle, but

*"The cat's away—what would you like to hear?"*

even so she had to open her big jaws to their widest and her head was pulled forward by the bone's weight. She straightened up and carried the bone from the kitchen to the lawn in front of the house, where she placed it on the frozen grass and looked it over tenderly before she started to attack it. Two seagulls appeared out of the fog and circled about not far above her, watching for a chance at the bone, and the day was so strange that the seagulls seemed to speak as natural claimants for the fog that was taking possession of the house. It was a dark-white day under a lightless sky and the view was ghostly. The small grove of trees at the end of the driveway had become a dim outpost, and to the left of the house, toward the ocean, there was nothing to be seen except shapes formed by the fog. Outside the house only the two seagulls and Niobe with her bone had substance. The fog reached the windows as the afternoon wore on, and night came to find the house shrouded, lost, hidden, invisible, abandoned except by the ocean, which filled each room with the sound of eternity, great waves gathering themselves for the clash with earth and darkness. Niobe had been in and out of the house all day. About seven in the evening she cried to be let in, but when the door was opened to her she backed away from the light and was immediately lost except for her face, a thin grey mask with imploring eyes looking out of the fog. Her eyes were pleading, not for permission to come in but for permission to bring her bone into the house. She vanished and reappeared a minute later, a transparent dog face that held in its ghostly jaws the great bone, which glowed phosphorescent, while beyond it four round diamonds flamed suddenly—two of the cats returning from their usual night-watch. There was no moon that night; no moon, no stars, no clouds, no sky, no real world—only the little house settling slowly into its place in safest

memory, guarded by the silence that poured out of the voices of the waves.

The lawn in front of the house belonged to Niobe. In the summer she stretched herself out on it to bake, and in the winter when the snow was very deep she played boisterously in it, rocking and leaping and plunging, a dolphin again. The lawn was separated from the emerald acres of a famous golf course only by a thin line of trees, and from her place near the house Niobe could see the public road and the cars passing along there, going south to the beach or north to the village. Sometimes a car turned into her driveway and then she ran forward to welcome it. During her early days in the city she was surprised to find so many cars and all so close to her, parked along the sides of all the streets where she walked, and at first she thought they were all friends and she used to notice each car, and smell it, and look to see if there was a place in it for her. She soon discovered that in the city cars had no connection with her, and she stopped expecting anything from them, although it made her very restless to see a dog looking out of a car window, because she could not help hoping that somebody would offer her a ride, even a short ride, anywhere. Away from home, that is where Niobe dreamed of being, when she saw dogs in cars, and when she watched for the house on West Tenth Street. Away from home, that is where Niobe wanted to be.

One afternoon, just before the start of her holiday in Katonah, her walk took her a long way west, to Hudson Street and the walled garden of St. Luke's Chapel. It was a cool afternoon, with thin sunlight, and a complicated country fragrance drifted across the walls of the old garden and through the bars of the garden gate. Niobe put her nose to the gate and smelled.

She could see the big, old-fashioned garden, fading in autumn, and she smelled leaves, grass, and earth. Niobe smelled fresh earth. Somebody in the garden was digging.

In secret places in the neighborhood of her house in East Hampton Niobe used to bury her best bones. They were her treasures, and she knew they were still where she had left them, safely hidden, waiting for her. She smelled earth now, the same old earth, but she could not get into the garden because the gate was closed, and locked. There was a lady in the garden, walking near the gate, and Niobe wagged her tail, but the lady didn't see her, or didn't want to see her. Niobe stopped wagging, and two or three minutes later she turned from the gate and went around the corner onto Christopher Street. And there, as she walked west on Christopher Street, Niobe saw a vision. She saw the public road that cuts through the golf course in East Hampton, with the cars passing each other, going north and south, just as they always did. She was looking at the West Side Highway, which is cut out of the air around it just as the road in East Hampton is cut out of the green golf course. All she really saw was cars moving *in the distance*. It was months since Niobe had seen cars at a distance, and the distance between where she was on Christopher Street and the elevated highway was much the same as the distance between her old lawn in East Hampton and her old view of the golf course. Everything was happening at once. Her head was still full of the smell of new earth, and she was seeing her view again, and now she smelled, very close to her, the Hudson River. The river did not smell like the Atlantic Ocean, but Niobe knew she was walking toward water, big water. Perhaps she was going to have a swim. Her ears went up and she began to hurry, pulling on her leash. But then she turned another corner and found herself back in the same old concrete quadrangle, walking her geometrical city-dog walk, with only miserable lampposts to tease her starving nose. In her disappointment Niobe lost her temper and charged furiously across the sidewalk to threaten a five-pound nuisance, a miniature white poodle who yapped rudely at her, and who stood like a hero on his four tiny paws and glared up at her until she was dragged away, seventy pounds of raging disgrace.

Poor Niobe. She is being made foolish in her old age. She would like to go swimming, show them all what she can do. She would like to go swimming, show them all what she really is. She would like to dig up a bone. She would like to go for a ride in a car. She would like to find that door on West Tenth Street. Most of all, she would like to get away from Home. Yes, she would very much like to get away from Home, who now marches along behind her, holding her leash.

Home speaks: "Good Niobe. Good Dog. Nice Walk. Good Niobe."

Home's voice is consoling, but Niobe can't be bothered to listen. Niobe is sick of Home, who holds her on a leash and won't let her go anywhere or do any of the things she wants to do.

"Good Niobe," Home says.

Niobe begins to go faster and now it is Home's turn to be dragged along, hanging on to the leash. Home protests angrily.

"Stop it, Niobe," Home says. "Bad Niobe. Bad Dog. *Bad.*"

Niobe doesn't care. She begins to speed.

Home shouts, *"Bad, bad!"*

Niobe is pulling so hard that her chain collar hurts her throat but she only goes faster and faster. Disappointment and boredom have turned her into a fiend, and all she wants is to get as far as she can from Home.

But that was several days ago. Today, Niobe is going to Katonah for a holiday in the country. The car comes at twelve, as it promised to do. Niobe is led out of her apartment house on her leash, just as though she was going for her ordinary walk. But then the car door is opened and Niobe leaps into the back seat. She is mad with joy. She tumbles over herself and tries to tumble into the front seat, but as soon as the car starts off she quiets down and sits looking out through the window at the streets she is leaving. She is trembling with happiness. She makes no sound, but her eyes are shining with adoration for everything she sees—for the streets, and for the car she is in, and for the driver of the car, and for Home, who sits beside her in the back seat. Yes, Niobe is going away from Home, and Home is going with her. Niobe turns her head from the window and looks at Home, who is smoking a cigarette and smiling. "Good Niobe," Home says, and Niobe stretches herself out on the seat and puts her head in Home's lap. "Good Niobe," Home says. Niobe sighs and half closes her eyes. Her tongue comes out and she licks her lips. She settles herself for a long ride. The wheels of the car go round and round and they sound as though they might keep going forever and ever.

| 1967 |

## RED DOG

We bought you for our son. Half-grown,
already your bag of skin sagged everywhere,
you fell to sleep like the dark in corners,
predictably where we wouldn't look: under
wash piled and waiting, in closets, the moan and
wheeze of your easy breathing pointed
with pips and starts of other sounds, cries
rising, a chain of woof-woof-woofs soon to
decline like cars down the hill's far glide
of night where we said he might never go.
Of course he went, as with him went also you.

You dragged, then lost a bright steel chain: two tags
hung like my dad's world war loudly declared
"Red Dog," your name, our place, and that year's
shots, identities you'd shake off to wander
the possible world. I'd hear you, coming back,
my son still out looking, afraid you'd got
worse than traveller's bite on your mopy flanks.
His shoes puffed up dirt like spurts of time. You
mostly don't expect to find the lost—and yet
fearful, I'd shout, then sleep, then shout. Gone.
You'd wait. You'd creep like sun across the lawn,
then, with him, leap up everywhere, dying splits

of rockets in the roses, crushing mulched shoots
faithfully planted year after year, and roots
whose volunteers you watered brown. When we knew
he'd leave, you'd chase God knows what twitch
of spoor, still, we took your balls. You slowed. Dirt
bedded you till you smelled. Your bones fouled floors.
Squirrels reclaimed their nuts. The awful spew
of what spoiled in you, lying by our fire,
comes back to me as the vet says you've worn
out the heart that banged to sleep beside my son.

What does it sound like, I ask? The vet listens.
Once you climbed a six-foot fence, barking, one leap,
a storm of breath we loved. Now you only eat,
ninety wheezing pounds, a processor of meat.
Like my dad, you face me, hesitate, then piss
blankets and floor. Deaf, eyes blank, the chain
slipped again, you're lost. You don't miss a boy's
games, nothing swells your interest, even the moon's
rattling tags I've hung above old yard rakes.
The vet claims it's time; he'd put you down.
Calling at last, I say "Son. It's Red. Come home."

—DAVE SMITH  | 1999 |

# OBEDIENCE

## JOAN ACOCELLA

The other day, we accompanied our favorite dog, Louis, to his class at the Port Chester Obedience Training Club. Louis is a two-year-old German shepherd, and he is not what you would call a natural student. At the end of his first semester in obedience training, he got left back. But all that is forgotten now. He has passed Basic I and Basic II and is currently in Novice. In the car on the way to the class, Louis's owner, Diane, told us she hopes that he will eventually get his C.D. (Companion Dog) title, or even a C.D.X. (Companion Dog Excellent). Louis looked skeptical.

We get to school early. Basic I, the occasion of Louis's early humiliation, is going through its paces. There is a Siberian husky, a German shepherd, a huge, hairy brown poodle named Saki (after the writer), and a tiny, refined cocker spaniel named Zach. Presiding over the dogs is their teacher, Mary Ann O'Grady, who is wearing bluejeans and a shirt with a ceramic dog pin on the collar. Under Mary Ann's direction, the owners are putting the dogs through their sits, stands, heels, pivots, and stops, for which they are rewarded with dog cookies. "Remember to randomize your treats!" Mary Ann urges the owners. If a dog gets a treat for every deed well done, he or she will soon get full or complacent, with predictable consequences for obedience motivation. The dogs do not get the point of this rule, and neither do some of the owners. We observe several treats being quietly distributed on an unrandomized basis.

Now Mary Ann is explaining to the owners another principle: they must start giving their dogs hand signals at the same time that they issue vocal commands. "Dogs get deaf as they get older," she says. "If they only know vocal commands, they'll stop obeying."

To show what she wants, she brings out her own dog, Cora, a Border collie. Cora is so obedient that she gets to do television commercials. "Here, Cora," Mary Ann says, and that is the last thing she says to Cora. From then on, Mary Ann performs a mime routine worthy of a Japanese temple dancer—hand up, hand down, hand scooping the air, hand sweeping the air, hand with fingers open, hand with fingers closed—all of which clearly means something, for Cora, in response, walks, heels, turns, jumps, stays, sits, puts up her paw, and, as her finale, lies down on the floor like an odalisque. The other dogs finish their lesson while Cora, still reclining, looks on, impassive.

Mary Ann dismisses Basic I. "Next week, we talk about grooming," she says.

"Good. We could use it," says the owner of Saki. If Tiny Tim were a dog, he would look like Saki.

Once Basic I has cleared out, the Novice class moves into the teaching area. There are two Welsh corgis, a Great Dane, a boxer, a golden retriever, a Portuguese water dog named Clyde, and two German shepherds, Lucas and Louis. Diane and the other owners have given us the lowdown on each of them. Lucas is being trained by one of the school's senior instructors, Margie English. He is as large as she is, and when she pats him on the chest it makes a big, hollow *thwonk*, as if it were a wine barrel. Katie, the Great Dane, is going to be a show dog. Hope, the golden retriever, has a sort of saintly status in the class. She has been chosen to be a brood bitch for Guiding Eyes for the Blind, an organization that breeds and trains guide dogs. Her puppies will lead the blind. As for Louis, Diane confesses, he has a tendency to walk out of the class when he gets tired of it.

The Novice dogs are way beyond the simple sits and stops of Basic I. They don't just do steps; they do combinations. They also undergo psychological trials, which test whether they can go on sitting and staying while faced with dire temptations to do oth-

erwise. They all sit down in a row on one side of the room, their owners next to them, and Mary Ann, now wearing a Mephistophelian expression, weaves in and out among them, squeaking a squeak toy and bouncing a tennis ball. Necks become rigid, breathing becomes short, eyes gaze upon owners in an agony of indecision, but all the dogs stay put. Then Mary Ann *throws* the ball. This is too much for Ivory, the boxer. She races after the ball and has to be brought back into line. "We didn't see that," Mary Ann says. Then she ups the ante further, bringing out Cora and playing fetch with her. All the dogs hold their places. They saw what happened to Ivory. Now Mary Ann asks the owners to go to the other side of the room, so that the dogs can try the exercise without them.

Diane is not even halfway across when Louis walks out of the class. Diane goes to retrieve him. "He did it perfectly on the first day," she says. "I don't know what's the matter."

Now the dogs get to do their jumps. Mary Ann erects an eight-inch hurdle in the middle of the room, and the dogs take turns charging over it. For the small dogs, this is an inspiriting challenge, and they go at it like Olympians. To observe Marvin the corgi, his stubby legs drawn up, his little tubelike frame quivering with joy as he sails through the air like a kielbasa shot from a bow, is to see a creature rising to what for him is one of life's great occasions. For the large dogs, however, an eight-inch hurdle is nothing to write home about. Katie and Lucas step over it nonchalantly. Louis leaves the class.

Finally, the session is over, and Louis

leaves for good, with Diane in tow, while we stay to put some questions to Mary Ann. In addition to teaching obedience class, Mary Ann operates a private service, Cara Na Madra Dog Training, out of Greenwich, Connecticut. "*Cara na madra* means 'friend of the dog' in Irish—I'm Irish—and when I say 'friend of the dog' I mean it," she explains. "By the time I'm called in, it's almost always a matter of saving the dog from euthanasia or from getting dumped in the pound. When people dispose of dogs, it's usually for one of two reasons—barking or no housebreaking. Housebreaking isn't really a problem. Mostly, you have to train the people, not the dog. They have to take the dog out more often.

"With barking, too, you have to train the owners. They stick the dog out in the yard for four hours, and he gets bored. Or he gets anxious. 'Hey, I'm out here. I don't know what to do. I'm scared.' So he barks. And they won't let him inside because he barks. You have to get the owners to praise the dog when he's quiet, not just scold him when he barks. That's why I say, 'Accentuate the positive, eliminate the negative.' I have that on my business card."

"Do dogs have humanlike feelings?" we ask. "Do they feel proud? Do they feel guilty?"

"They certainly feel proud," Mary Ann says. "You can see it when they know they've done something good. They stick up their ears. Their whole body says 'Look at me!' As for guilty, I don't know. If they do, it's not for long."

We go out to the parking lot to rejoin Louis and Diane. Louis is now happy as a clam. He scratches himself, he chews on his leash, he smells the grass tufts sticking through the sidewalk. Life stretches before him. Obedience class is behind him, at least for this week.

| 1992 |

## DOG ON A CHAIN

So that's how it's going to be,
A cold day smelling of snow.
Step around the bare oak tree
And see how quickly you get
Yourself entangled for good.
Your bad luck was being friendly
With people who love their new couch
More than they love you.

Fred, you poor mutt, the night
Is falling. The children playing
Across the road were cold,
So they ran in. Watch the smoke
Swirl out of their chimney
In the windy sky as long as you can.
Soon, no one will see you there.
You'll have to bark even if
There's no moon, bark and growl
To keep yourself company.

—CHARLES SIMIC    | 2000 |

# REACH FOR THE SKY

*Fiction*

## JIM SHEPARD

Guy comes into the shelter this last Thursday, a kid, really, maybe doing it for his dad, with a female golden/Labrador cross, two or three years old. He's embarrassed, not ready for forms and questions, but we get dogs like this all the time, and I'm not letting him off the hook, not letting him out of here before I know he knows that we have to kill a lot of these dogs, dogs like his. Her name is Rita and he says, "Rita, sit!," like being here is part of her ongoing training. Rita sits halfway and then stands again, and looks at him in that tuned-in way goldens have.

"So . . ." The kid looks at the forms I've got on the counter, like no one told him this was part of the deal. He looks up at the sampler that the sister of the regional boss did for our office: "A Man Knows Only as Much as He's Suffered—St. Francis of Assisi." He has no answers whatsoever for the form. She's two, he thinks. Housebroken. Some shots. His dad handled all that stuff. She's spayed. Reason for Surrender: she plays too rough.

She smashed this huge lamp, the kid says. Of one of those mariners with the pipe and the yellow bad-weather outfit. His dad made it in a ceramics class.

Rita looks over at me with bright interest. The kid adds, "And she's got this thing with her back legs, she limps pretty bad. The vet said she wouldn't get any better."

"What vet?" I ask. I'm not supposed to push too hard, it's no better if they abandon them on highways, but we get sixty dogs a day here,

349

and if I can talk any of them back into their houses, great. "The vet couldn't do anything?"

"We don't have the money," the kid says.

I ask to see Rita's limp. The kid's vague, and Rita refuses to demonstrate. Her tail thumps the floor twice.

I explain the bottom of the form to the kid: when he signs it, he's giving us permission to have the dog put down if it comes to that.

## SUMMARY

A young lady whose first name is Geraldine lost her dog under what she considered to be suspicious circumstances, so she went around to her precinct police station to report the matter. There she was introduced to a plain-clothes man, a keen-eyed Dashiell Hammett character, who asked for her name and address and questioned her at length about the missing dog. She was pretty much impressed by the whole business and thought that the dog was as good as found—until, as she was leaving the room, she got a glimpse of the detective's notes on the case, written in a firm, official hand on a desk pad: "Geraldine. Dog."    | 1936 |

"She's a good dog," he says helpfully. "She'll probably get someone to like her."

So I do the animal-shelter Joe Friday, which never works: "Maybe. But we get ten goldens per week. And everybody wants puppies."

"O.K., well, good luck," the kid says. He signs something on the line that looks like "Fleen." Rita looks at him. He takes the leash with him, wrapping it around his forearm. At the door he says, "You be a good girl, now." Rita pants a little with a neutral expression, processing the information.

It used to be you would get owners all the time who were teary and broken up: they needed to know their dog was going to get a good home, you had to guarantee it, they needed to make

their problem yours, so that they could say, Hey, when *I* left the dog it was fine.

Their dog would always make a great pet for somebody, their dog was always great with kids, their dog always needed A Good Home and Plenty of Room to Run. Their dog, they were pretty sure, would always be the one we'd have no trouble placing in a nice family. And when they got to the part about signing the release form for euthanasia, only once did someone, a little girl, suggest that if it came to that they should be called back, and they'd retrieve the dog. Her mother had asked me if I had any ideas, and the girl suggested that. Her mother said, "I asked *him* if *he* had any ideas."

Now you get kids; the parents don't even bring the dogs in. Behind the kid with the golden/Lab mix there's a girl who's maybe seventeen or eighteen. Benetton top, Benetton skirt, straw-blond hair, tennis tan, she's got a Doberman puppy. Bizarre dog for a girl like that. Chews everything, she says. She holds the puppy like a baby. As if to cooperate, the dog twists and squirms around in her arms trying to get at the penholder to show what it can do.

Puppies chew things, I tell her, and she rolls her eyes like she knows *that*. I tell her how many dogs come in every day. I lie. I say we've had four Doberman puppies for weeks now. She says, "There're forms or something, or I just leave him?" She slides him on his back gently across the counter. His paws are in the air and he looks a little bewildered.

"If I showed you how to make him stop chewing things, would you take him back?" I ask her. The Doberman has sprawled around and got to his feet, taller now than we are, nails clicking tentatively on the counter.

"No," she says. She signs the form, annoyed

by a sweep of hair that keeps falling forward. "We're moving, anyhow." She pats the dog on the muzzle as a goodbye and he nips at her, his feet slipping and sliding like a skater's. "God," she says. She's mad at me now, too, the way people get mad at those pictures that come in the mail of dogs and cats looking at you with their noses through the chain-link fences: *Help Skipper, who lived on leather for three weeks.*

When I come back from taking the Doberman downstairs there's a middle-aged guy at the counter in a wheelchair. An Irish setter circles back and forth around the chair, winding and unwinding the black nylon leash across the guy's chest. Somebody's put some time into grooming this dog, and when the sun hits that red coat just right he looks like a million dollars.

I'm not used to wheelchair people. The guy says, "I gotta get rid of the dog."

What do you say to a guy like that: Can't you take care of him? Too much trouble? The setter's got to be eight years old.

"Is he healthy?" I ask.

"She," he says. "She's in good shape."

"Landlord problem?" I say. The guy says nothing.

"What's her name?" I ask.

"We gotta have a discussion?" the guy says. I think, This is what wheelchair people are like. The setter whines and stands her front paws on the arm of the guy's chair.

"We got forms," I say. I put them on the counter, not so close that he doesn't have to reach. He starts to sit up higher and then leans back.

"What's it say?" he says.

"Sex," I say.

"Female," he says.

Breed? Irish setter. Age? Eleven.

Eleven! I can feel this dog on the back of my neck. On my forehead. I can just see myself sell-

ing this eleven-year-old dog to the families that come in looking. And how long has she been with him?

I walk back and forth behind the counter, hoist myself up, flex my legs.

The guy goes, like he hasn't noticed any of that, "She does tricks."

"Tricks?" I say.

"Ellie," he says. He mimes a gun with his forefinger and thumb and points it at her. "Ellie. Reach for the sky."

Ellie is all attention. Ellie sits, and then rears up, lifting her front paws as high as a dog can lift them, edging forward in little hops from the exertion.

"Reach for the sky, Ellie," he says.

Ellie holds it for a second longer, like those old poodles on *The Ed Sullivan Show*, and then falls back down and wags her tail at having pulled it off.

"I need a Reason for Surrender," I say. "That's what we call it."

"Well, you're not going to get one," the guy says. He edges a wheel of his chair back and forth, turning it a little this way and that.

"Then I can't take the dog," I say.

"Then I'll just let her go when I get out the door," the guy says.

"If I were you I'd keep that dog," I say.

"If you were me you would've wheeled this thing off a bridge eleven years ago," the guy says. "If you were me you wouldn't be such an asshole. If you were me you would've taken this dog, no questions asked."

We're at an impasse, this guy and me.

He's let go of Ellie's leash, and Ellie's covering all the corners of the office, sniffing. There's a woman in the waiting area behind him with a bull-terrier puppy on her lap and the puppy's keeping a close eye on Ellie.

"Do you have any relatives or whatever who could take the dog?" I ask him.

The guy looks at me. "Do I sign something?" he says.

I can't help it, when I'm showing him where to sign I can't keep the words back, I keep thinking of Ellie reaching for the sky: "It's better this way. We'll try and find her a home with someone who's equipped to handle her."

The guy doesn't come back at me. He signs the thing and hands me my pen, and says, "Hey Ellie, hey kid," and Ellie comes right over. He picks up her trailing leash and flops the end onto the counter where I can grab it, and then hugs her around the neck until she twists a little and pulls away.

"She doesn't know what's going on," I say.

He looks up at me and I point, as if to say, "Her."

The guy wheels the chair around and heads for the door. The woman with the bull terrier watches him go by with big eyes. I can't see his face, but it must be something. Ellie barks. There's no way to fix this.

I've got A.S.P.C.A. pamphlets unboxed and all over the counter. I've got impound forms to finish by today.

"Nobody's gonna want this dog," I call after him. I can't help it.

It's just me now, at the counter. The woman stands up, holding the bull terrier against her chest, and stops, like she's not going to turn him over, like whatever her reasons are, they may not be good enough.

| 1987 |

IT'S TIME TO TREAT YOUR DOG TO

*Le Bon Chien.*

THE FIRST HAMBURGER-FLAVORED LIQUEUR <u>FOR</u> CANINES <u>ONLY</u>!

Try serving Le Bon Chien in any of these delightful ways:

"Fido."
Fill bowl with ice cubes. Pour 3 oz. Le Bon Chien over ice. Serve.

"Lassie in Reruns"
Mix 2 cups water with ¼ cup Le Bon Chien in bowl. Serve.

"101 Dalmatians"
Pour 12 oz. club soda into bowl. Add 3 oz. Le Bon Chien. Float slice of bologna on top. Serve.

R. Chst

# SHAGGY-DOG STORY

## KATE JULIAN

The thinking used to be that a dog would provide security, not require it. But this was before Paris Hilton's Chihuahua, Tinkerbell, went missing, in 2004. ("They'll hold it for ransom," Hilton said at the time. "Everyone knows I'm rich, so they'll want millions.") It was before Trouble, Leona Helmsley's white Maltese, inherited, in quick succession, twelve million dollars, a series of death threats, and a six-figure bodyguard detail. It was before the former *Post* publisher Ken Chandler and his wife responded to the disappearance of their blond dachshund, Gus, by hiring a publicist and a private detective. And it was before the subject of the Secret Service's future canine charge became a national fixation.

There are no reliable statistics about dog thefts, either citywide or nationwide, but a couple of years ago Lisa Peterson, of the American Kennel Club, took it upon herself to begin monitoring what she saw as a disturbing trend. Her list of the disappeared includes not only Samantha, a Maltese from Brooklyn; Misha, a bichon frise from Flushing; and Enzo, a Yorkie from Chappaqua (later returned to his owner, former Miss America Vanessa Williams), but also LeeLoo, a poodle from Sugar Land, Texas; Bean, a pit bull from Durham, North Carolina; Pixie, a pug from Bolingbrook, Illinois; and more than two hundred others in twenty-four states.

And then, several weeks ago, dog-napping terror hit the Upper West Side. E-mails began circulating (one subject line: "DOGNAPPING attempts in NYC with RAZOR and RANSOM—get dogs ON LEASHES—happening on West Side"), and flyers were posted at dog runs and veterinary offices and pet stores ("COMMUNITY ALERT: DOGNAPPING attempts on the West Side"). Dog owners, particularly women with small dogs—said to be the prime target—began to panic.

A survey of Upper West Side dog runs and pet stores turned up various versions of the same story. "There's a two-man team, with one in a gray hoodie on a bicycle who comes by and slices the leash with a razor, then goes away with the dog. The other guy calls you up later on and says, 'Hey, I found your dog! What's it worth to you?'" said Charlie Allen, the owner of Gotham Pups pet services, who was glumly watching two of his charges (Beezus, a mutt, and Delta, a yellow Labrador) romp across the dog run on West Eighty-first Street the other day. "It's completely unpleasant."

Most people were saying that the dognappers made their ransom demands by calling the number on a stolen dog's tags. Either that or they waited for a reward sign to be posted. "I think maybe in this neighborhood there would be more purebreds and more people who would pay a ransom," Jason Frix (Billy Bob, bullmastiff) said. "Crime increases in tough times." People said there'd been dognappings in other nice neighborhoods. "I heard Chelsea," someone said. "Also Battery Park City."

Marilyn Pasekoff (Hogan, German shepherd), who was walking in Riverside Park, said that the dognappers might be supplying research labs. "My vet gave me a book on what a burgeoning industry that is—collecting dogs and giving them to laboratories for experiments." And Allison Rowey (Billy, Pomeranian) had heard that the dogs were being stolen for illegal dogfights. "They've been getting smaller dogs to practice the big dogs on," she said.

The police hadn't received a single dognapping report. "It's been two weeks now, and no one's come in," Officer Clark Tiger, of the Twentieth Precinct, said. "Nothing like that's ever happened in this neighborhood before." But, still, local residents were focussing on preventive measures. Emily Emmett (Dahlia, Border terrier) said she'd heard people say, "Don't leave your dog outside Starbucks. And don't use leashes that people can slice through." Emmett said that she hadn't seen a dog left unattended anywhere on the Upper West Side in at least two weeks. She had bought a thick leather leash to replace her dog's lightweight nylon one.

"I'm paranoid," Becca Yuré (Hudson, mutt) said as she left the Pet Health Store on Amsterdam, having just picked out a heavy new leash. "I almost bought two, so that if they cut one he'll still be on one." The store was selling lots of leashes. Meanwhile, back in Riverside Park, Penny Mandel (Becky and Polly, cockapoos) said, "I am aware when someone comes by on a bike—I keep an eye on them, and pull the leash tight."

Taking pet dogs hostage is not a new idea. As the social reformer Henry Mayhew wrote, in 1861, it was a popular racket in Victorian London. Nappers used a piece of liver or a bitch in heat to lure dogs from their owners, whereupon financial negotiations would begin. "They steal fancy dogs ladies are fond of—spaniels, poodles, and terriers," Mayhew wrote. Among them was Elizabeth Barrett Browning's cocker spaniel, Flush, who was snatched and ransomed no fewer than three times. Each time, Browning dutifully paid up.

But why, in the absence of a single documented case, had a whole neighborhood in contemporary Manhattan collectively fixated on dog thievery? Corey Robin, a political-science professor at Brooklyn College and the author of *Fear: The History of a Political Idea*, blamed the financial crisis. He suggested that the scare reflected "the displacement of economic anxiety." "The class that's been hit the hardest is the financial sector. And if it's small dogs that are well cared for that are the targets—well, they're a sort of boutiquey item," he said. "A small dog creates a tremendous amount of emotional attachment, but at the same time it is a luxury item—and that's being taken away."

| 2009 |

*"Of course, all the good ones are fixed."*

# DEATHS OF DISTANT FRIENDS

*Fiction*

## JOHN UPDIKE

Though I was between marriages for several years, in a disarray that preoccupied me completely, other people continued to live and die. Len, an old golf partner, overnight in the hospital for what they said was a routine examination, dropped dead in the lavatory, having just placed a telephone call to his hardware store saying he would be back behind the counter in the morning. He owned the store and could take sunny afternoons off on short notice. His swing was too quick, and he kept his weight back on his right foot, and the ball often squirted off to the left without getting into the air at all, but he sank some gorgeous putts in his day, and he always dressed with a nattiness that seemed to betoken high hopes for his game. In buttercup-yellow slacks, sky-blue turtleneck, and tangerine cashmere cardigan he would wave from the practice green as, having driven out from Boston through clouds of grief and sleeplessness and moral confusion, I would drag my cart across the asphalt parking lot, my cleats scraping, like a monster's claws, at every step.

Though Len had known and liked Julia, the wife I had left, he never spoke of my personal condition or of the fact that I drove an hour out from Boston to meet him instead of, as formerly, ten minutes down the road. Golf in that interim was a great haven; as soon as I stepped off the first tee in pursuit of my drive, I felt enclosed in a luminous wide bubble, safe from women, stricken children, solemn lawyers, disapproving old acquaintances—the entire offended social order. Golf had its own order, and its own love, as the three or four of us staggered and shouted our way toward each hole, laughing at misfortune and applauding the rare strokes of relative brilliance. Sometimes the summer sky would darken and a storm arise, and we would cluster in an abandoned equipment shed or beneath a tree that seemed less tall than its brothers. Our natural nervousness and our impatience at having the excitements of golf interrupted would in this space of shelter focus into an almost amorous heat—the breaths and sweats of middle aged men packed together in the pattering rain like cattle in a boxcar. Len's face bore a number of spots of actinic keratosis; he was going to have them surgically removed before they turned into skin cancer. Who would have thought the lightning bolt of a coronary would fall across his plans and clean remove him from my tangled life? Never again (no two snowflakes or fingerprints, no two heartbeats traced on the oscilloscope, and no two golf swings are exactly alike) would I exultantly see his so hopefully addressed drive ("Hello dere, ball," he would joke, going into his waggle and squat) squirt off low to the left in that unique way of his, and hear him exclaim in angry frustration (he was a born-again Baptist, and had developed a personal language of avoided curses), "Ya dirty ricka-fric!"

I drove out to Len's funeral and tried to tell his son, "Your father was a great guy," but the words fell flat in that cold bare Baptist church. Len's gaudy colors, his Christian effervescence, his game and futile swing, our crowing back and forth, our fellowship within the artificial universe composed of variously resistant lengths and types of grass were tints of life too delicate to capture, and had flown.

A time later, I read in the paper that Miss Amy Merrymount, 91, had at last passed away, as a dry leaf passes into leaf mold. She had always seemed ancient; she was one of those New Englanders, one of the last, who spoke of Henry James as if he had just left the room. She possessed letters, folded and unfolded almost into pieces, from James to her parents, in which she was mentioned, not only as a little girl but as a young lady "coming into her 'own,' into a liveliness fully rounded." She lived in a few rooms, crowded with antiques, of a great inherited country house of which she was constrained to rent out the larger portion. Why she had never married was a mystery that sat upon her lightly in old age; the slender smooth beauty that sepia photographs remembered, the breeding and intelligence and, in a spiritual sense, ardor she still possessed must have intimidated as many suitors as they attracted and given her, in her own eyes, in an age when the word "inviolate" still had force and renunciation a certain prestige, a value whose winged moment of squandering never quite arose. Also, she had a sardonic dryness to her voice and something restless and dismissive in her manner. She was a keen self-educator; she kept up with new developments in art and science, took up organic foods and political outrage when they became fashionable, and liked to have young people about her. When Julia and I moved to town with our babies and fresh faces, we became part of her tea circle, and in an atmosphere of tepid but mutual enchantment maintained acquaintance for twenty years.

Perhaps not so tepid: now I think Miss Merrymount loved us, or at least loved Julia, who always took on a courteous brightness, a soft daughterly shine, in those chill window-lit rooms crowded with spindly, feathery heirlooms once spread through the four floors of a Back Bay town house. In memory the glow of my former wife's firm chin and exposed throat and shoulders merges with the ghostly smoothness of those old framed studio photos of the Merrymount sisters—three of whom two died sadly young, as if bequeathing their allotment of years to the third, the survivor sitting with us in her gold-brocaded wing chair. Her face had become unforeseeably brown with age, and totally wrinkled, like an Indian's, with something in her dark eyes of glittering Indian cruelty. "I found her rather disappointing," she might say of an absent mutual acquaintance, or, of one who had been quite dropped from her circle, "She wasn't absolutely first-rate."

The search for the first-rate had been a pastime of her generation. I cannot think, now, of whom she utterly approved, except Father Daniel Berrigan and Sir Kenneth Clark. She saw them both on television. Her eyes with their opaque glitter were failing, and for her cherished afternoons of reading while the light died outside her windows and a little fire of birch logs in the brass-skirted fireplace warmed her ankles were substituted scheduled hours tuned in to educational radio and television. In those last years, Julia would go and read to her—Austen, *Middlemarch*, Joan Didion, some Proust and Mauriac in French, when Miss Merrymount decided that Julia's accent passed muster. Julia would practice a little on me, and, watching her lips push forward and go small and tense around the French sounds like the lips of an African mask of ivory, I almost fell in love with her again. Affection between women is a touching, painful, exciting thing for a man, and in my vision of it—tea yielding to sherry in those cluttered rooms where twilight thickened until the pages being slowly turned and the patient melody of Julia's voice were the sole signs of life—love was what was happening between this gradually dying old lady and my wife, who had gradually become middle-aged, our children grown into absent adults, her voice nowhere else harkened to as it was here. No doubt there were confidences, too, between the pages. Julia always returned from Miss Merrymount's, to make my late dinner, looking younger and even blithe, somehow emboldened.

In that awkward post-marital phase when old friends still feel obliged to extend invitations and one doesn't yet have the wit or courage to decline, I found myself at a large gathering at which Miss Merrymount was present. She was now quite blind and invariably accompanied by a young person, a round-faced girl hired as companion and guide. The fragile old lady, displayed like peacock feathers under a glass bell, had been established in a chair in a corner of the room beyond the punch bowl. At my approach, she sensed a body coming near and held out her withered hand, but when she heard my voice her hand dropped. "You have done a

IT'S ALWAYS 'GOOD DOG'—NEVER 'GREAT DOG.'

GREGORY

dreadful thing," she said, all on one long intake of breath, like a draft rippling a piece of crinkly cellophane. Her face turned away, showing her hawk-nosed profile, as though I had offended her sight. The face of her young companion, round as a radar dish, registered slight shock; but I smiled, in truth not displeased. There is a relief at judgment, even adverse. It is good to know that somewhere a seismograph records our quakes and slippages. I imagine Miss Merrymount's death, not too many months

*"Well, your nose feels cold."*

after this, as a final serenely flat line on the hospital monitor attached to her. Something sardonic in that flat line, too—of unviolated rectitude, of magnificent patience with a world that for over ninety years failed to prove itself other than disappointing. By this time, Julia and I were at last divorced.

Everything of the abandoned home is lost, of course—the paintings on the walls, the way shadows and light contended in this or that corner, the gracious warmth from the radiators. The pets. Canute was a male golden retriever we had acquired as a puppy when the children were still a tumbling, pre-teen pack. Endlessly amiable, as his breed tends to be, he suffered all, including castration, as if life were a steady hail of blessings. Curiously, not long before he died, my youngest child, who sings in a female punk group that has just started up, brought Canute to the house where now I live with Jenny as my wife. He sniffed around politely and expressed with only a worried angle of his ears the wonder of his old master reconstituted in this strange-smelling home; then he collapsed with a heavy sigh onto

the kitchen floor. He looked fat and seemed lethargic. My daughter, whose hair is cut short and dyed mauve in patches, said that the dog roamed at night and got into the neighbors' garbage, and even into one neighbor's horse feed. This sounded like mismanagement to me; Julia's new boyfriend is a middle-aged former Dartmouth quarterback, a golf and tennis and backpack freak, and she is hardly ever home, so busy is she keeping up with him and trying to learn new games. The house and lawn are neglected; the children drift in and out with their friends and once in a while clean out the rotten food in the refrigerator. Jenny, sensing my suppressed emotions, said something tactful and bent down to scratch Canute behind one ear. Since the ear was infected and sensitive, he feebly snapped at her, then thumped the kitchen floor with his tail in apology.

Like me when snubbed by Miss Merrymount, my wife seemed more pleased than not, encountering a touch of resistance, her position in the world as it were confirmed. She discussed dog antibiotics with my daughter, and at a glance one could not have been sure who was the older, though it was clear who had the odder hair. It is true, as the cliché runs, that Jenny is young enough to be my daughter. But now that I am fifty everybody under thirty-five is young enough to be my daughter. Most of the people in the world are young enough to be my daughter.

A few days after his visit, Canute disappeared, and a few days later he was found far out on the marshes near my old house, his body bloated. The dog officer's diagnosis was a heart attack. Can that happen, I wondered, to four-footed creatures? The thunderbolt had hit my former pet by moonlight, his heart full of marshy joy and his stomach fat with garbage, and he had lain for days with ruffling fur while the tides went in and out. The image makes me happy, like the sight of a sail popping full of wind and tugging its boat swiftly out from shore. In truth—how terrible to acknowledge—all three of these deaths make me happy, in a way. Witnesses to my disgrace are being removed. The world is growing lighter. Eventually there will be none to remember me as I was in those embarrassing, disarrayed years while I scuttled without a shell, between houses and wives, a snake between skins, a monster of selfishness, my grotesque needs naked and pink, my social presence beggarly and vulnerable. The deaths of others carry us off bit by bit, until there will be nothing left; and this too will be, in a way, a mercy.

| 1982 |

## "DAS MITBRINGEN VON HUNDEN

## IST POLIZEILICH VERBOTEN"

(Sign at the Entrance to a
Beer Garden on the Rhine)

Alas, poor canines! Out of bounds
Forever are these cheerful grounds.
In vain on eager evening rounds,
Attracted by the cheerful sounds,
You seek admission. Man astounds
The world of dogs by building pounds
And even monumental mounds
For canines strayed or dead, yet founds
No canine tavern—which redounds
To man's discredit among hounds.
This is too much. It irks me. Zounds!
The world in kindly dogs abounds:
Why be so mean to friendly hounds?

Dog damn the tyrant who propounds
This law policely banning hounds!

—DAVID DAICHES    | 1952 |

# V.I.P. TREATMENT

BEN McGRATH

Bruno the Brussels griffon, age one, commutes to lower Manhattan from his home in Jackson Heights. He rides the E train in a blue bag slung over the shoulder of either Jeff Simmons, a former adviser to the mayoral candidate Bill Thompson, or Alfonso Quiroz, a Con Edison spokesman, and spends his mornings and afternoons at Spot, a doggy-day-care facility on Murray Street, where he has a reputation for being rambunctious, happy-go-lucky, and a bit of a "ladies' man," as Simmons puts it. Bruno has light-brown fur, a block face, plaintive eyes that remind Quiroz of the young boy in the 1948 Italian movie *The Bicycle Thief,* and more than five hundred Facebook friends. His brief disappearance the other day prompted Yetta Kurland, an attorney in the West Village, to e-mail some twenty thousand people in search of help. One wrote back, "Dear Yetta, I am living in Paris, France, for the moment." Most of the other e-mail recipients were Manhattanites, neighborhood activists and journalists whom Kurland had courted during her failed run for City Council, last fall. "But we all know somebody who has an aunt or an uncle in Queens," she explained recently, and added, "I ran on a humane platform, of awareness to animal issues."

Bruno's escape came on a day when Simmons and Quiroz had chosen to leave him behind in their apartment, with a dog-walker. "We found a friend of a friend who takes care of a blind cat," Quiroz said. "You would think if there's anybody who's good with animals it's someone who takes care of a blind and elderly cat." Evidently not: within ten minutes of the dog-walker's arrival Bruno bolted into the street. The dog-walker then hailed a cab to give chase—and ended up leaving Bruno's collar and leash in the back seat. Thus began Operation Save Bruno, a P.R. campaign run with an efficiency rarely observed in municipal politics, Quiroz, a one-time loser for City Council in the Twenty-fifth District, commissioned a series of robo-calls to in-form neighbors in the 11372 Zip Code of a dog on the loose. Mike DenDekker, a Queens assemblyman, and Helen Sears, a former City Council member, volunteered to canvass Jackson Heights, while, over on the Upper East Side, Gayle Horwitz, a former deputy comptroller, visited a local shelter, in case Bruno had hopped on the subway, attempting the commute solo. Simmons, who years ago had worked for the cable channel NY1, successfully planted a report on the next morning's news, and the doggy-day-care owners at Spot drove out to Queens to assist in placing flyers on car windshields and telephone poles along Northern Boulevard. "After we got forty blocks away from their house, there were some very scary neighborhoods," one of them recalled. "If I was fearing for our safety, then Bruno was definitely fearing for his."

As it turned out, Bruno had long since found safety, in College Point, in the home of Juan Arroyave, a Colombian window installer, who spotted a small dog dodging trucks on Roosevelt Avenue and scooped him up. "He was going to keep the dog," Quiroz said. "But just by happenstance he went out shopping on Northern Boulevard the next day and saw the posters." About thirty hours had passed. Simmons and Quiroz welcomed Bruno home with ten liver treats. (He threw up.) By then, Bruno had become such a neighborhood celebrity that Quiroz felt compelled to bring him to a nearby park, for a meet-and-greet. "There was an e-waste recycling event going on," Quiroz said. "Everybody was crying, and they were giving him kisses." Quiroz made a five-minute YouTube video of the occasion, complete with swelling music and a clip from *The Bicycle Thief*, which Yetta Kurland then e-mailed to her original list of twenty thousand. "I just wanted to let you all know that, thanks to your help, against all odds, Bruno was reunited with his family," she wrote. Bill Thompson, who has a couple of pet lizards, but no dogs, e-mailed Simmons a note of congratulations.

So Bruno may be "the most well-known dog in Jackson Heights," according to Quiroz, but on Murray Street last week he cut a fairly ordinary profile, stopping to pee on a planter across from the Borough of Manhattan Community College and at one point squaring off against a pit bull, who looked unimpressed. "We as humans should try to emulate dogs more," one of the owners of Spot said. "Bruno's going to have no memory of what he's gone through. But we will, forever."

| 2010 |

# THE AMERICAN DOG IN CRISIS

## CALVIN TOMKINS

Not so long ago, the great majority of American dogs were reasonably secure. Dog and man both knew where they stood—with each other and with their own kind. This was, to be sure, before the advent of dog psychiatrists, and it is possible that some dogs were going around even then with anxieties they simply didn't know they had. But it can no longer be denied that today, after the cataclysms and upheavals of the last two decades, the dog's basic concept of himself has been seriously undermined, his fundamental ethos threatened. Let us face facts: The American dog has clearly lost his way.

Evidence of the breakdown is all around us. Since 1940, mental illness in dogs has increased 31 percent across the country (47 percent in California). Young dogs and puppies, victims of an overly permissive environment, are flunking out of obedience schools in fantastic numbers. Among mature dogs, there is a marked tendency to revert to such infantile symptoms as slipper-chewing, tail-biting, and the persistent door-scratching that typifies the indoor-outdoor syndrome. Confused and uncertain, seeking firm standards in a world of collapsing social values, the American dog looks for guidance to the natural leaders of his race, but usually he looks in vain. Popular entertainment often provides a key to socio-economic changes, and we have only to turn on television to see the dog's problem in miniature.

Consider, for example, the dilemma recently faced by Lassie, the great dog star, in her television series.[1] The death, a year or two ago, of a supporting player (human) and the growing up of the actor playing Lassie's young master, Jeff, made production changes in the show imperative. The producers' solution was to have Jeff go away to school, after first giving Lassie to a new family. Followers of traditional dog dramaturgy knew what searing scenes they could expect from this farewell. Everything pointed to two harrowing half-hour episodes in which Lassie, spurning the comfort and affection of her new home, would chew the rope that held her, and strike out into the night. Pelted by sleet and snow, reviled by farmers, pursued by yelling street gangs and dogcatchers, she would pause only to capture an escaped convict and save a child from drowning before she arrived, bedraggled but happy, in time to dissuade Jeff from accepting a gambler's bribe to throw the hockey game with Groton. Jeff would then return to the farm, but would share Lassie with the new little boy (who would, of course, be on crutches).

Those who watch the program know this is not what happened at all. Jeff and his mother went away, Lassie waved goodbye, and that was that. The only hint of the emotional cost involved has been a tendency, probably unnoticed by younger viewers, for Lassie to scratch herself behind the ear when she thinks the camera is pointed elsewhere. (A nervous tic?) We may well ask what has happened to the ancient code of canine loyalty when Lassie can change masters without a whimper of protest. Dr. Ernst Engel-

brecht, of Leopoldville, whose *Dogs in Transition: 1900–1950* is the classic study in this field (unhappily, out of print at the moment), has recently devoted a series of lectures to this very problem. "Lassie's decision," writes Dr. Engelbrecht, "must either be rejected or assimilated by every dog over three years of age. It cannot be ignored."

Fears of incipient disloyalty, however rationalized, are probably at the root of most canine neuroses. As the old individualistic standards of conduct disappear and the ancient virtues of speed, agility, and resourcefulness give way to the modern suburban dog's obsession with security and "acceptance," a vicious circle of tensions is built up. The dog who doubts his own dogness pretends not to see his master throw the tennis ball—and then suffers unimaginable pangs when the master withholds love in return. One watchdog in Lake Forest developed such anxieties about his supposed inability to bark at intruders that he took to barking at his own master and succeeded, finally, in driving him away from the house for good. Evidence exists that these tragic confusions are not confined to American dogs. What, for example, are we to make of Laika, the Soviet rocket dog, who was so clearly willing to sacrifice her own life *for the wrong side*?

Adding to the dog's basic insecurity is the gnawing question of status. Where do dogs stand in our society today? If we must ask the question ourselves, we may be sure the dogs have been asking it for some time. And it is difficult to escape the conclusion that in several important respects the American dog has been slipping badly.

---

[1] Lassie is, of course, a female *impersonator* whom we refer to as "she" merely to avoid confusion. This kind of transvestitism has long been fairly common in the theatre, dating back to pre-Elizabethan times, and we must not give it undue stress.

Modern dogs seem to shrink from the demands of high public office. Consider, for example, President Eisenhower's Weimaraner. Passing over the fact that a non-American dog must almost certainly suffer tensions in such a very American milieu, it remains to be said that the dog has left no imprint whatever on the White House. He does not travel with the President, nor does he sit at Ike's feet during telecasts. His personal habits, his food preferences, even his name and age, are unknown. In the past, the electorate could watch Fala taking an active part in the day-to-day life of President Roosevelt, but today we are in some doubt as to whether Mr. Eisenhower's Weimaraner is even admitted to meetings of the National Security Council. Similarly, one wonders about Checkers. The Vice-President's cocker sprang to fame in a dramatic broadcast some years ago, but since then he has sunk into limbo. Mr. Nixon himself took a commanding role in last autumn's election campaign, when his name appeared almost daily on the front pages of all the newspapers, but if Checkers gave him any assistance, or even stood loyally by in case of need, we are unaware of it. Surely this indicates a serious failure of leadership on the part of our top dogs, at a time when this can least be afforded.

It is in the home, though, that we find the most alarming symptoms of canine withdrawal. Few can deny that the dog's home life is fraught with new anxieties. The trend to multi-dog families, far from encouraging individual initiative, as some sociologists had hoped, has had precisely the opposite effect. Conformity on the surface, fierce competition when the family is out—this seems to be the pattern. "The family hearth," writes Engelbrecht, "has supplanted the dog pound as a source of canine traumatization."

In determining a dog's status at home, the question of breed has now assumed overwhelming (and highly destructive) importance. It used to be that the more popular breeds stayed in vogue for years at a time, and this led to the establishment of a relatively stable hierarchy, in which each dog could formulate his self-respect within certain agreed limits. During the reign of the Airedale, for example, there was some intermittent friction between Scotties (No. 4) and wire-haired fox terriers (No. 5), but none at all

## COMPLAINT

Mr. John Conroy has started heckling the Pennsylvania Railroad because Felix, his dachshund, can't get through the automatic doors in the Pennsylvania Station. Felix is so short that he doesn't break the beam of light that controls the mechanism, and if he tries to sneak in behind somebody else, he gets caught. Mr. Conroy wrote the stationmaster a letter, describing the situation and asking what about it. This is the reply he got: "I have your letter of recent date in regard to the difficulty your dog Felix has in operating our automatic doors, and have referred your letter to our officials for their attention. Yours truly, W. H. Egan." This is a very temperate reply indeed, we think, considering that our own impulse would be to ask Mr. Conroy why he didn't get a wolfhound or patronize the Grand Central. Mr. Conroy says he isn't going to let matters rest the way this letter leaves them; but we have an idea that the Pennsylvania Railroad *is*, if you know what we mean.   | 1935 |

between collies (No. 2) and Lhasa Apsos (No. 47). Now, however, the wild and chaotic fluctuations in popular taste have caused great anguish up and down the line. As the No. 1 position passed from cocker to boxer to beagle, all semblance of class distinction crumbled. Matters have now reached a point where dachshunds and bulldogs scarcely know from one week to the next where they stand in relation to each other. The sporting breeds dread taking the field, for fear they will lose out in the frenzied behind-the-scenes maneuvering in the big kennel clubs. Their fears are not groundless. Last year, a well-connected English setter, a fine hunting dog who was also considered a leading candidate for Best in Show at the next Westminster Kennel Club show, returned from field trials in Maryland to find that all his papers had somehow been "lost." This breed has since declined in the over-all standings. Today, rumors spread unchecked, and as more owners adopt the deplorable practice of changing breeds each year, the climate of insecurity grows steadily worse. The upshot of all this is clearly predictable: American dogs, in despair over their personal status, are beginning to lose all sense of *self*. Pomeranians try to jump like Dobermans, and have heart attacks. Whippets refuse to run, in the forlorn hope that they will be mistaken for basset hounds. And surely there is no sadder sound in nature than the sound of a once proud cocker baying the moon in a cracked, tone-deaf, but unmistakable imitation of a beagle.

In some extreme cases, the deranged animal, dimly aware that being a dog is no longer *enough*, goes over the brink and impersonates human reactions. How else are we to account for the fate of Rex, the Coast Guard's celebrated lifesaving Labrador, who is said to have gone down in calm water off Newport while trying to swim the breast stroke? Poodles, of course, have always looked upon themselves as a "bridge species," somewhere between men and dogs, and it is no coincidence that this is the breed most frequently in need of analysis. But perhaps the most disturbing example of this sort of tragic confusion was the case of Lalique, the lovely Afghan bitch who shot and killed Mendelsen Beatty III last winter.

Controversy still rages over the circumstances of this disagreeable incident. Beatty, the millionaire sportsman, had taken Lalique everywhere for six years. She shared his stateroom on countless Atlantic crossings, welcomed the guests to his famous little dinner parties, and made her exquisite manners a byword from Montevideo to Biarritz. When Beatty announced his engagement to a tin-plate heiress in Buenos Aires, Lalique was prostrated. The gossip columns of three continents reported the details of the poor creature's struggles to displace her rival—from her abject delivery of small gifts at the feet of her heartless master to a pathetic and patently insincere attempt at a relationship with Beatty's best friend. It was all considered funny, but, alas, it was not. The night before the wedding, Beatty was cleaning his Mannlicher .30–06. The houseboy heard a shot, rushed upstairs, and found Beatty already dead, and Lalique, whimpering piteously, trying to extricate her slender paw from the trigger guard. Significantly, no action has ever been taken against the dog.

It must be clear to all that there is cause for concern in the modern dog's rudderless, uprooted circumstances. But the prospects are by no means wholly discouraging. For the first time, American dogs are beginning to understand their problems and to face them squarely—a most encouraging sign. Any thinking dog knows there can be no return to the simple certainties of the past. But if the dog is to reach out for a new way of life and a new concept of himself *qua* dog, it is apparent that he cannot do it alone. Nor does he pretend he can. These days, when a dog jumps up on the couch, the chances are he isn't looking for affection at all. He is trying to tell us that he needs help.

| 1959 |

# AVA'S APARTMENT

*Fiction*

## JONATHAN LETHEM

Perkus Tooth, the wall-eyed former rock critic, awoke the morning after the party he vowed would be his last, the night after the worst blizzard of the winter, asleep on a staircase, already in the grip of a terrific cluster headache. He suffered these regularly, knew the drill, felt himself hunkering into the blinding, energy sapping migraine by ancient instinct. Nobody greeted him, his hosts asleep themselves, or gone out, so he made his way downstairs, groped to locate his coat in their closet, and then found his way outdoors.

Perkus's shoes were, of course, inadequate for the depth of freshly fallen snow. He'd have walked the eight blocks home in any event—the migraine nausea would have made a cab ride unbearable—but there wasn't any choice. The streets were free of cabs and any other traffic. Some of the larger, better-managed buildings had had their sidewalks laboriously cleared and salted, the snow pushed into mounds covering hydrants and newspaper boxes, but elsewhere Perkus had to climb through drifts that had barely been traversed, fitting his shoes into boot prints that had been punched knee-deep. His pants were quickly soaked, and his sleeves as well, since between semi-blindness and poor footing he stumbled to his hands and knees several times before he even got to Second Avenue. Under other circumstances he'd have been pitied, perhaps offered aid, or possibly arrested for public drunkenness, but on streets the January blizzard had remade there was no one to observe him, apart from a cross-country skier who stared merci-

*"This isn't really about the beagles, is it."*

lessly from behind solar goggles, and a few dads here and there dragging kids on sleds. If they noticed him at all they probably thought he was out playing, too. There was no reason for someone to be making his way along impassable streets so early the day after. Not a single shop was open, all the entrances buried in drift.

When he met the barricade at the corner of Eighty-fourth, he at first tried to bluster his way past, thinking the cop had misunderstood. But no. His building was one of three the snowstorm had undermined, the weight of the snow threatening the soundness of its foundation. He talked with neighbors he hadn't spoken to in fifteen years of dwelling on the same floor, though gripped in the vise of his cluster headache he barely heard a word they said, and he couldn't have made too good an impression. *You need to find someplace to sleep tonight*—that was a frag-

ment that got through to him. *They might let you in for your stuff later, but not now. You can call this number* . . . but the number he missed. Then, as Perkus teetered away: *Get yourself indoors, young man.* And: *Pity about that one.*

Perkus Tooth had already been at a watershed, wishing to find an exit from himself, from his life and his friends, his tatter of a career—to shed it all like a snakeskin. The city in its twenty-first-century incarnation had no place for him, but it couldn't fire him—he'd quit instead. For so many years he'd lived in his biosphere of an apartment as if it were still 1978 outside, as if placing the occasional review in the *Village Voice* or *New York Rocker* gave him credentials as a citizen of the city, but the long joke of his existence had reached its punch line. The truth was that he'd never thought of himself as a critic to begin with, more a curator. His apartment—bursting with vinyl LPs, forgotten books, binders full of zines, VHS cassettes of black-and-white films taped from PBS and *Million Dollar Movie*—was a cultural cache shored against time's indifference, and Perkus had merely been its caretaker, his sporadic writings the equivalent of a catalogue listing items decidedly *not* for sale.

And his friends? Those among whom he wasted his days—the retired actor, now a fixture on the Upper East Side social scene; the former radical turned cynical mayor's operative; the once aspiring investigative journalist turned hack ghostwriter—had all used up their integrity, accommodated themselves to the simulacrum that Manhattan had become. Perkus had come to an end with them, too. He needed a new life. Now, incredibly, the storm had called his bluff. This was thrilling and terrifying at once: who would he be without his apartment, without that assembly of brunching mediocrities?

There was only one haven. Perkus had one friend who was unlike the others: Biller. (Perkus had never heard a last name. Biller was just Biller.) Homeless in a Manhattan that no longer coddled the homeless, Biller was crafty, a squatter and a survivor, an underground man. Now, as if in a merciful desert vision, the information that Biller had once jotted on a scrap of receipt on Perkus's kitchen table appeared before him: Biller's latest digs, in the Friendreth Apartments, on Sixty-fifth near York. Perkus couldn't remember the numerical address, but he didn't need that; from Biller's descriptions of the odd building and its inhabitants he'd surely be able to find it.

Yes, Biller was the one he needed now. Trudging sickened through the snowdrifts like a Napoleonic soldier in retreat from Moscow, Perkus was adequately convinced. He had got complacent in his Eighty-fourth Street apartment. Time to go off the grid. Biller knew how to do this, even in a place like Manhattan, which was nothing *but* grid. Biller was the essential man. They could compare notes and pool resources, Perkus preferring to think of himself as not yet completely without resources. Perkus laughed at himself now: in his thinking, Biller was becoming like Old Sneelock, in Dr. Seuss's *If I Ran the Circus,* the one who'd single-handedly raise the tents, sell the pink lemonade, shovel the elephants' shit, and also do the high-wire aerialist

act. In this manner, dismal yet self-amused, Perkus propelled his body to Sixty-fifth Street, despite the headache's dislodging him from himself, working with the only body he had—a shivering, frost-fingered, half-blind stumbler in sweat- and salt-stained party clothes.

He trailed a dog and its walker into the lobby, catching the swinging door before it clicked shut, one last act of mastery of the mechanics of outward existence, and then passed out in a melting pool on the tile just inside. Biller would later explain to Perkus that another dog walker had sought Biller out, knowing that the tall black man in the spotted fur hat functioned as ambassador for the vagabond entities sometimes seen lurking in the building, and that this tatterdemalion in the entranceway was nothing if not one of those. Biller gathered Perkus up and installed him in what he would come to know as Ava's apartment. It was there that Perkus, nursed through the first hours by Biller's methodical and unquestioning attentions, his clothes changed, his brow mopped, his sapped body nourished with a simple cup of ramen and beef broth, felt his new life begin.

Perkus Tooth had twenty-four hours alone in the apartment before Ava arrived. Biller kept close tabs on all the vacancies in the building and assured him that this was the best way, the intended result being that Ava would take him for granted, detect his traces on the floors and walls and in the bed and then unquestioningly settle in as a roommate. So Perkus spent the first night by himself on the surprisingly soft bed, half-awake in the dark, and then was up to pace the rooms at first light. He dwelled in the space alone just long enough to posit some conjunction between his new self—shorn of so many of its defining accoutrements, dressed in an ill-fitting, lumpish blue-and-orange sports sweatshirt with an iron-on decal name, presumably of some star player, his right temple throbbing with cluster, a really monstrous attack, ebbing in its fashion but still obnoxious, yet his brain also, somehow, seemed to have awoken from a long-fogging dream, a blind spot in sight, yes, but peripheral vision around the occlusion's edges widened, refreshed—between this self and the apartment in which he'd strangely landed, the apartment that had been fitted, like his body, with hand-me-downs, furnishings that would have been rejected even by a thrift shop. The presump-

## CANINE CUSTODY

We fell in with a taxi-driver last week who told us that he was sitting pretty because he has a steady contract one day a week. "What I do," he said, "is go up to Seventieth and Park every other Thursday and pick up a big poodle from a lady. Then I take the poodle down to a man on Gramercy Park, who pays me. On the Thursdays in between, I go to Gramercy Park and pick up the poodle from the man and take it back to Seventieth and Park. Then the lady pays me. The poodle is a very nice passenger. It's all because this lady and her husband are divorced, and this is how they settled what to do about the pooch."    | 1958 |

tion was that if he puzzled at the weird decrepit prints hung over the decaying living-room set, the framed *Streamers* poster, or the Blue Period Picasso guitarist sun-faded to yellow over the nonworking stove in the dummy kitchen, he should be able to divine what sort of person he'd become since the last time his inquiries had turned inward. Who he was seemed actually to have slipped his mind.

Yet no. The rooms weren't going to tell him who he was. They weren't his. This was Ava's apartment, only she hadn't come yet.

Perkus hadn't encountered another soul in the hours he'd been installed in the Friendreth, had only gazed through immovable paint-sealed windows at minute human forms picking through drifts on the Sixty-fifth Street sidewalk seven stories below, the city a distant stilled terrarium. This corner of Sixty-fifth, where the street abutted the scraps of parkland at the edge of Rockefeller University, formed an utter no man's land in the winterscape. He listened at the walls, and through the sound of spasmodic barking imagined he heard a scrape of furniture or a groan or a sigh that could be human, but no voices to give proof, until the morning, when the volunteers began to arrive. Perkus sought to parse Biller's words, a clustery confusion from the night before, working to grasp what form his new roommate might take, even as he heard the volunteers at individual doors, calling each apartment's resident by name, murmuring "good boy" or "good girl" as they headed out to use the snowdrifts as a potty.

Even those voicings were faint, the stolid prewar building's heavy lath and plaster making fine insulation, and Perkus could feel confident that he would remain undetected if he wished to be. When clunking footsteps and scrabbling paws led to his threshold, his apartment's unlocked door opened to allow a dog and its walker through. Perkus hid like a killer in the tub, slumping down behind the shower curtain to sit within the porcelain's cool shape. He heard Ava's name spoken then, by a woman who, before leaving, set out a bowl of kibble and another of water on the kitchen floor, and cooed a few more of the sweet doggish nothings a canine lover coos when fingering behind an ear or under a whiskery chin. Biller's words now retroactively assumed a coherent, four-footed shape. Perkus had never lived with a dog. But much had changed just lately, and he was open to new things. He couldn't think of

*"And only __you__ can hear this whistle?"*

a breed to wish for but had an approximate size in mind, some scruffy mutt with the proportions of, say, a lunch pail. The door shut, and the volunteer's footsteps quickly receded in the corridor. Perkus had done no more than rustle at the plastic curtain, preparing to hoist himself from the tub, when the divider was nudged aside by a white grinning face—slavering rubbery pink lips and dinosaur teeth hinged to a squarish ridged skull nearly the size of his own, this craned forward by a neck and shoulders of pulsing and twitching muscle. One sharp, white, pink-nailed paw curled on the tub's edge as a tongue slapped forth and began brutalizing Perkus's helpless lips and nostrils. Ava the pit bull greeted her roommate with grunts and slobber, her expression demonic, her green-brown eyes, rimmed in pink, showing piggish intellect and gusto, yet helpless to command her smacking, cavernous jaws. From the first instant, before he even grasped his instinctive fear, Perkus understood that Ava did her thinking with her mouth.

The next moment, falling back against the porcelain under her demonstrative assault, watching her struggle and slip as she tried, and failed, to hurtle into the tub after him, as she braced and arched on her two back legs, he saw that the one front paw with which she scrabbled was all she

had for scrabbling: Ava was a three-legged dog. This fact would regularly, as it did now, give Perkus a crucial opening—his only physical edge on her, really. Ava slid awkwardly and fell on her side with a thump. Perkus managed to stand. By the time he got himself out of the tub she was on her three legs again, flinging herself upward, forcing that boxy skull, with its smooth, loose-bunching carpet of flesh, into his hands to be adored. Ava was primally terrifying, but she soon persuaded Perkus she didn't mean to turn him into kibble. If Ava killed him it would be accidental, in seeking to stanch her emotional hungers.

Biller had bragged of the high living available at the Friendreth, an apartment building that had been reconfigured into a residence for masterless dogs, an act of charity by a private foundation of blue hairs. Perkus's homeless friend had explained to him that though it was preferable that Perkus keep himself invisible, he had only to call himself a "volunteer" if anyone asked. The real volunteers had come to a tacit understanding with those, like Perkus now, who occasionally slipped into the Friendreth Canine Apartments to stealthily reside alongside the legitimate occupants. Faced head on with the ethical allegory of homeless persons sneaking into human-shaped spaces in a building reserved for abandoned dogs, the pet-rescue workers could be relied upon to defy the Friendreth Society's mandate and let silence cover what they witnessed. Snow and cold made their sympathy that much more certain. Biller further informed Perkus that he shared the building with three other human squatters among the thirty-odd dogs, though none were on his floor or immediately above or below him. Perkus felt no eagerness to renew contact with his own species.

Those first days were all sensual intimacy, a feast of familiarization, an orgy of pair-bonding, as Perkus learned how Ava negotiated the world—or at least the apartment—and how he was to negotiate the boisterous, insatiable dog, who became a kind of new world to him. Ava's surgery scar was clean and pink, an eight- or ten-inch seam from one shoulder blade to a point just short of where he could detect her heartbeat, at a crest of fur beneath her breast. Some veterinary surgeon had done a superlative job of sealing the joint so that she seemed like a muscular furry torpedo, missing nothing. Perkus couldn't tell how fresh the scar was or whether Ava's occasional stumbles indicated that she was still learning to walk on three legs—mostly she made it look natural, and never once did she wince or cringe or otherwise indicate pain, but seemed cheerfully to accept tripod status as her fate. When she exhausted herself trailing him from room to room, she'd sometimes sag against a wall or a chair. More often she leaned against Perkus, or plopped her muzzle across his thigh if he sat. Her mouth would close then, and Perkus could admire the pale brown of her liverish lips, the pinker brown of her nose, and the raw pale pink beneath her scant, stiff whiskers—the same color as her eyelids and the interior of her ears and her scar and the flesh beneath the transparent pistachio shells of her nails. The rest was albino white, save a saucer-size chocolate oval just above her tail to prove, with her hazel eyes, she was no albino. At other times, that mouth was transfixingly open. Even after he'd convinced himself that she'd never intentionally damage him with that massive trap full of erratic, sharklike teeth, Perkus found it impossible not to gaze inside and marvel

at the map of pink and white and brown on her upper palate, the wild permanent grin of her throat. And when he let her win the prize she most sought—to clean his ears or neck with her tongue—he'd have a close-up view, more than he could really endure. Easier to endure was her ticklish tongue bath of his toes anytime he shed the ugly Nikes that Biller had given him, though she sometimes nipped between them with a fang in her eagerness to root out the sour traces.

Ava was a listener, not a barker. As they sat together on the sofa, Ava pawing at Perkus occasionally to keep his hands moving on her, scratching her jowls or the base of her ears or the cocoa spot above her tail, she'd also cock her head and meet his eyes and show that she, too, was monitoring the Friendreth Canine Apartments' other dwellers and the volunteers who moved through the halls. (As Perkus studied the building's patterns, he understood that the most certain evidence of human visitors, or other squatters, was the occasional flushing of a toilet.) Ava listened to the periodic fits of barking that possessed the building, yet felt no need to reply. Perkus thought this trait likely extended from the authority inherent in the fantastic power of her own shape, even reduced by the missing limb. He guessed she'd never met another body she couldn't dominate, so why bark? She also liked to gaze out the window whenever he moved a chair to a place where she could make a sentry's perch. Her vigilance was absolutely placid, yet she seemed to find some purpose in it, and could watch the street below for an hour without nodding. This was her favorite sport, apart from love.

Ava let him know they were to sleep in the bed together that first night, joining him there and, then, when he tried to cede it to her, clambering atop him on the narrow sofa to which he'd retreated, spilling her sixty or seventy writhing pounds across his body and flipping her head up under his jaw in a crass seduction. That wasn't going to be very restful for either of them, so it was back to the twin-size mattress, where she could fit herself against his length and curl her snout around his hip bone. By the end of the second night, he had grown accustomed to her presence. If he didn't shift his position too much in his sleep she'd still be there when dawn crept around the heavy curtains to rouse him. Often then he'd keep from stirring, ignoring the growing pressure in his bladder, balancing the comfort in Ava's warm weight against the exhausting prospect of her grunting excitement at his waking—she was at her keenest first thing, and he suspected that, like him, she pretended to be asleep until he showed some sign. So they'd lie together both pretending. If he lasted long enough, the volunteer would come and open the door and Ava would jounce up for a walk at the call of her name (and he'd lie still until the echoes of "O.K., Ava, down, girl, down, down, *down*, that's good, no, down, *down*, yes, I love you, too, down, down, *down* . . ." had trickled away along the corridor).

Though the gas was disabled, the Friendreth's electricity flowed, thankfully, just as its plumbing worked. Biller provided Perkus with a hot plate on which he could boil water for coffee, and he'd have a cup in his hand by the time Ava returned from her walk. He imagined the volunteer could smell it when she opened the door. Coffee was the only constant between Perkus's old daily routine and his new one, a kind of lens through which he contemplated his transformations. For there was no mistaking that the command had come, as in Rilke's line: You must change your life. The physical absolutes of coexistence with the three-legged pit bull stood as the outward emblem of a new doctrine: Recover

bodily prerogatives, journey into the real. The night of the blizzard and the loss of his apartment and the books and papers inside it had catapulted him into this phase. He held off interpretation for now. Until the stupendous cluster headache vanished, until he learned what Ava needed from him and how to give it, until he became self-sufficient within the Friendreth and stopped requiring Biller's care packages of sandwiches and pints of Tropicana, interpretation could wait.

The final step between Perkus and the dog came when he assumed responsibility for Ava's twice-daily walks. (He'd already several times scooped more kibble into her bowl, when she emptied it, having discovered the supply in the cabinet under the sink.) On the fifth day, Perkus woke refreshed and amazed, alert before his coffee, with his migraine completely vanished. He clambered out of bed and dressed in a kind of exultation that matched the dog's own, for once. He felt sure that Ava was hoping he'd walk her. And he was tired of hiding. So he introduced himself to the volunteer at the door, and said simply that if she'd leave him the leash he'd walk Ava now and in the future. The woman, perhaps fifty, in a lumpy cloth coat, her frizzy hair bunched under a woollen cap, now fishing in a Ziploc of dog treats for one to offer to Ava, having certainly already discerned his presence from any number of clues, showed less surprise than fascination that he'd spoken to her directly. Then she stopped.

"Something wrong with your eye?"

He'd gone unseen by all but Biller for so long that her scrutiny disarmed him. Likely his unhinged eyeball signified differently now that he was out of his suits and dressed instead in homeless-man garb, featuring a two-week beard. To this kindly dog custodian it implied that Ava's spectral cohabitant was not only poor but dissolute or deranged. A firm gaze, like a firm handshake, might be a minimum.

"From birth," Perkus said. He tried to smile as he said it.

"It's cold out."

"I've got a coat and boots." Biller had loaded both into the apartment's closet, for when he'd need them.

"You can control her?"

Perkus refrained from any fancy remarks. "Yes."

*"Since we're both being honest, I should tell you I have fleas."*

On the street, fighting for balance on the icy sidewalks, Perkus discovered what Ava's massiveness and strength could do besides bound upward to pulse in his arms. Even on three legs, she rode and patrolled the universe within the scope of her senses, chastening poodles, pugs, Jack Russells, even causing noble rescued racetrack greyhounds to bolt, along with any cats and squirrels foolish enough to scurry through her zone. Ava had only to grin and grunt, to strain her leash one front-paw hop in their direction, and every creature bristled in fear or bogus hostility, sensing her imperial lethal force. On the street she was another dog, with little regard for Perkus except as the rudder to her sails, their affair suspended until they returned indoors. That first morning out, the glare of daylight stunned Perkus but also fed an appetite he had no idea he'd been starving. The walks became a regular highlight, twice a day, then three times, because why not? Only a minority of female dogs, he learned, bothered with marking behaviors, those scent-leavings typical of all males. Ava was in the exceptional category, hoarding her urine to squirt parsimoniously in ten or twenty different spots. Biller brought

Perkus some gloves to shelter his exposed knuckles but also to protect against the chafing of Ava's heavy woven leash, that ship's rigging, on his landlubber palms. Perkus learned to invert a plastic baggie on his splayed fingers and deftly inside-out a curl of her waste to deposit an instant later in the nearest garbage can. Then inside, to the ceremonial hail of barking from the Friendreth's other inhabitants, who seemed to grasp Ava's preferential arrangement through their doors and ceilings.

It was a life of bodily immediacy. Perkus didn't look past the next meal, the next walk, the next bowel movement (with Ava these were like a clock's measure), the next furry, sighing caress into mutual sleep. Ava's volunteer—her name revealed to be Sadie Zapping—poked her head in a couple of times to inquire, and once pointedly intersected with Perkus and Ava during one of their walks, startling Perkus from reverie, and making him feel, briefly, spied upon. But she seemed to take confidence enough from what she witnessed, and Perkus felt he'd been granted full stewardship.

Now the two gradually enlarged their walking orbit, steering the compass of Ava's sniffing curiosity, around the Rockefeller campus and the Weill Cornell Medical Center, onto a bridge over the Drive, to gaze across at the permanent non sequitur of Roosevelt Island, defined for Perkus by its abandoned t.b. hospital, to which no one ever referred, certainly not the population living there and serviced by its goofy tram, as if commuting by ski lift. "No dogs allowed," he reminded Ava every time she seemed to be contemplating that false haven. Or down First Avenue, into the lower Sixties along Second, a nefariously vague zone whose residents seemed to Perkus like zombies, beyond help.

Perkus learned to which patches of snow-scraped earth Ava craved return, a neighborhood map of invisible importances not so different, he decided, from his old paces uptown: from the magazine stand where he preferred to snag the *Times,* to H&H Bagels or the Jackson Hole burger mecca. Perkus never veered in the direction of Eighty-fourth Street, though, and Ava never happened to drag him there. His old life might have rearranged itself around his absence, his building reopened, his paces waiting for him to re-inhabit them—but he doubted it. Occasionally he missed a particular book, felt himself almost reaching in the Friendreth toward some blank wall as though he could pull down an oft-browsed volume and find consolation in its familiar lines. Nothing worse than this; he didn't miss the old life in and of itself. The notion that he should cling to a mere apartment he found both pathetic and specious. Apartments came and went, that was their nature, and he'd kept that one too long, so long that he had trouble recalling himself before it. Good riddance. There was mold in the grout of the tiles around the tub which he'd never have got clean in a million years. If Ava could thrive with one forelimb gone,

the seam of its removal nearly erased in her elastic hide, he could negotiate minus one apartment, and could live with the phantom limb of human interdependency that had seemingly been excised from his life at last.

Biller wasn't a hanger-outer. He had his street scrounger's circuit to follow, and his altruistic one, too, which included checking in with Perkus and, most days, dropping off donated items of food or clothing that he thought might fit. Otherwise, he left Perkus and Ava alone. When Perkus was drawn unexpectedly a step or two back into the human realm, it was Sadie Zapping who drew him. Sadie had other dogs in the building and still looked in from time to time, always with a treat in her palm for Ava to snort up. This day she also had a steaming to-go coffee and a grilled halved corn muffin in a grease-spotted white bag which she offered to Perkus, who accepted it, this being not a time in life of charity refused or even questioned. She asked him his name again and he said it through a mouthful of coffee-soaked crumbs.

"I thought so," Sadie Zapping said. She plucked off her knit cap and shook loose her wild gray curls. "It took me a little while to put it together. Me and my band used to read your stuff all the time. I read you in the *Voice.*"

Ah. Existence confirmed, always when you least expected it. He asked the name of her band, understanding that it was the polite response to the leading remark.

"Zeroville," she said. "Like the opposite of Alphaville, get it? You probably saw our graffiti around, even if you never heard us. Our bassist was a guy named Ed Constantine—I mean, he renamed himself that, and he used to scribble our name on every blank square inch in a ten-block radius around CBGB's, even though we only ever played there a couple of times. We did open for Chthonic Youth once." She plopped herself down now, on a chair in Ava's kitchen which Perkus had never pulled out from under the table. He still used the apartment as minimally as possible, as if he were to be judged afterward on how little he'd displaced. Ava gaily smashed her square jowly head across Sadie's lap, into her cradling hands and scrubbing fingers. "Gawd, we used to pore over those crazy posters of yours, or broadsides, if you like. You're a lot younger-looking than I figured. We thought you were like some punk elder statesman, like the missing link to the era of Lester Bangs or Legs McNeil or what have you. It's not like we were holding our breath waiting for you to *review* us or anything, but it sure was nice knowing you were out there, somebody who would have gotten our jokes if he'd had the chance. Crap, that's another time and place, though. Look at us now."

Sadie had begun to uncover an endearing blabbermouthedness (even when not addressing Perkus she'd give forth with a constant stream of *Good girl, there you go, girl, aw, do you have an itchy ear? There you go, that's a girl, yes, yessss, good dog, Ava, whaaata good girl you are!*) but another elegist for Ye Olde Lower East Side was perhaps not precisely what the doctor ordered just now. Perkus, who didn't really want to believe that when his audience made itself visible again it would resemble somebody's lesbian aunt, sensed himself ready to split hairs—*not so much Lester Bangs as Seymour Krim, actually*—but then thought better of it. He was somewhat at a loss for diversions. He couldn't properly claim that he had elsewhere to be.

Sadie, sensing resistance, provided her own non sequitur. "You play cribbage?"

"Sorry?"

"The card game? I'm always looking for someone with the patience and intelligence to give me a good game. Cribbage is a real winter sport, and this is a hell of a winter, don't you think?"

With his consent, the following day Sadie Zapping arrived at the same hour, having completed her walks, and unloaded onto the kitchen table two well-worn decks of cards, a wooden cribbage board with plastic pegs, and two packets of powdered Swiss Miss. Perkus, who hated hot chocolate, said nothing and, when she served it, drained his mug. The game Sadie taught him was perfectly poised between dull and involving, as well as between skill and luck. Perkus steadily lost the first few days, then got the feel of it. Sadie sharpened, too, her best play not aroused until she felt him pushing back. They kept their talk in the arena of the local and mundane: the state of the building; the state of the streets, which had borne another two-inch snowfall, a treacherous slush carpet laid over the now seemingly permanent irregularities of black ice wherever the blizzard had been shoved aside; the ever-improving state of Perkus's cribbage; above all, the state of Ava, who thrived on Sadie's visits and seemed to revel in being discussed. Perkus could, as a result, tell himself that he tolerated the visits on the dog's account. It was nearly the end of February before Sadie told him the tragedy of Ava's fourth limb.

"I thought you knew," she said, a defensive near-apology.

He didn't want to appear sarcastic—did Sadie think Ava had told him?—so said nothing, and let her come out with the tale, which Sadie had spied in Ava's paperwork upon the dog's transfer to the canine dorm. Three-year-old Ava was a citizen of the Bronx, it turned out. She'd lived in the Sack Wern Houses, a public development in the drug dealers' war zone of Soundview, and had been unlucky enough to rush through an

"*He may be a fine veterinarian, but we're going to get some funny looks.*"

ajar door and into the corridor during a police raid on the apartment next door. The policeman who'd emptied his pistol in her direction, one of three cops on the scene, misdirected all but one bullet in his panic, exploding her shank. Another cop, a dog fancier who'd cried out but failed to halt the barrage, had tended the fallen dog, who, even greeted with this injury, wanted only to beseech for love with her tongue and snout. Her owner, a Dominican who may or may not have considered his pit bull ruined for some grim atavistic purpose, balked at the expense and bother of veterinary treatment, so Ava's fate was thrown to the kindly cop's whims. The cop found her the best, a surgeon who knew that she'd be happier spared cycling the useless shoulder limb as it groped for a footing it could never attain, and so excised everything to the breastbone. It was the

love-smitten cop who'd named her, ironically, after his daughter, whose terrified mom forbade their adopting the drooling sharky creature. So Ava came into the Friendreth Society's care.

"She's got hiccups," Sadie pointed out another day, a cold one, but then they were all cold ones. "She" was forever Ava, no need to specify. The dog was their occasion and rationale, a vessel for all else unnameable that Perkus Tooth and Sadie Zapping had in common. Which was, finally, Perkus had to admit, not much. Sadie's blunt remarks and frank unattractiveness seemed to permit, if not invite, unabashed inspection, and Perkus sometimes caught himself puzzling backward, attempting to visualize a woman onstage behind a drum kit at the Mudd Club. But that had been, as Sadie had pointed out, another time and place. For all her resonance with his lost

*"The quick brown dog jumps over the lazy fox."*

world, she might as well have been some dusty LP from his apartment, one that he rarely, if ever, played anymore. If Perkus wanted to reenter his human life, Sadie wasn't the ticket. Anyway, this was Ava's apartment. They were only guests.

"Yeah, on and off for a couple of days now." The dog had been hiccing and gulping between breaths as she fell asleep in Perkus's arms or as she strained her leash toward the next street corner. Sometimes she had to pause in her snorting consumption of the pounds of kibble that kept her sinewy machine running, and once she'd had to cough back a gobbet of bagel and lox that Perkus had tossed her. That instance had seemed to puzzle the pit bull, but otherwise she shrugged off a bout of hiccups as joyfully as she did her calamitous asymmetry.

"Other day I noticed you guys crossing Seventy-ninth Street," Sadie said. On the table between them she scored with a pair of queens. "Thought you never went that far uptown. Weren't there some people you didn't want to run into?"

He regarded her squarely, playing an ace and advancing his peg before shrugging in reply to her question. "We go where she drags us," he said. "Lately, uptown." This left out only the entire truth: that at the instant of his foolish pronouncement a week ago, enunciating the wish to avoid those friends who'd defined the period of his life just previous, he'd felt himself silently but unmistakably reverse the decision. He found himself suddenly curious about his old apartment; he missed his treasure, his time machine assembled from text and grooved vinyl and magnetic tape. He even, if he admitted it, pined for his friends. Without Perkus choosing it, at first without his noticing, the dog had been making him ready for the world again.

So he'd been piloting Ava, rudder driving sails for once, uptown along First Avenue to have a look in the window of the diner called Gracie Mews. He was searching for his friend the retired actor, regular breakfast companion of Perkus's previous existence, the one with whom he'd sorted through the morning paper—Perkus even missed the *Times*, he was appalled to admit—and marvelled at the manifold shames of the twenty-first century. Of all his friends, the actor was the most forgivable, the least culpable in Manhattan's selling out. He was an actor, after all, a player in scripts that he didn't write himself. As was Perkus, if he was honest.

The hiccupping dog could tell soon enough that they were on a mission, and pushed her nose to the Mews's window, too, looking for she knew not what, leaving nose doodles, like slug trails, that frosted in the cold. It turned out that it was possible to wish to become a dog only exactly up to that point where it became completely impossible. Ironically, he was embarrassed to admit to Sadie Zapping, who was a human being, that he wished to be human again. With Ava, he felt no shame. That was her permanent beauty.

| 2009 |

★ Feb. 29, 1936 Price 15 cents

# THE NEW YORKER

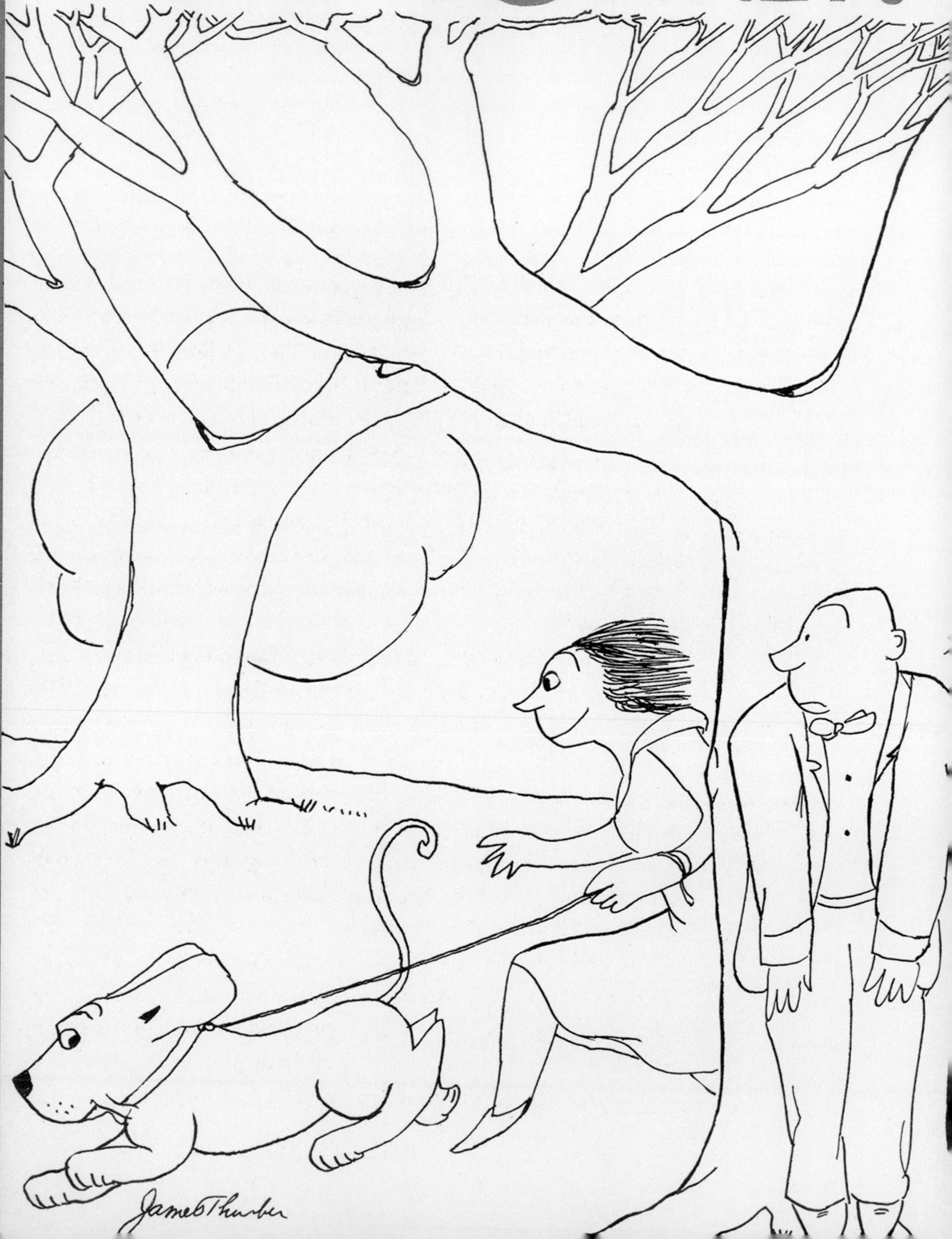

# A NOTE ON THURBER'S DOGS

## ADAM GOPNIK

The Zen Buddhists, it's said, ask one question to indicate another: "Why did Bodhidharma leave for the east?" really means something like "What is the essence of Buddhism?" or just "What is the way?" (Bodhidharma was a Buddhist sage who ran out of India and headed for China.) Those of us who care about dogs—and *The New Yorker*—ask a similar straightforward-seeming question that also provokes several trick turns. For us, the question "Why did James Thurber always draw dogs?" really means something like "Why do dogs matter for writers?" or even "What draws writers to *any* of their strange obsessive subjects?" (Which is another way of asking, "What is the way?")

For Thurber doesn't just draw dogs. He writes dogs, sings dogs, *owns* dogs as Liebling owns Frenchmen, or Charles Addams mansard roofs. On the cover of this book, in so many pages inside the cover, it is Thurber who is the first man of the dog. There is even a charming work of concert music called "Thurber's Dogs"—by Peter Schickele, of P.D.Q. Bach fame—and there probably have been more dogs called Thurber than have ever been named after any other American writer. There is even *the* Thurber dog: that melancholic, dubious bloodhound that he loved to draw, over and over.

So why dogs? The answer is simple: for Thurber, the dog chimed with, represented, the American man in his natural state—a state that, as Thurber saw it, was largely scared out of him by the American woman. When Thurber was writing about dogs, he was writing about men. The virtues that seemed inherent in dogs—dignity, peaceful-

*Postcard from Thurber to Harold Ross*

ness, courage, and stoical indifference to circumstance—were ones that he felt had been lost by their owners. The American man had the permanent jumps, and the American dog did not. The dog was man set free from family obligations, Monastic Man. Dogs "would in all probability have averted the Depression, for they can go through lots tougher things than we and still think it's boom time. They demand very little of their heyday; a kind word is more to them than fame, a soup bone than gold; they are perfectly contented with a warm fire and a good book to chew (preferably an autographed first edition lent by a friend); wine and song they can completely forgo; and they can almost completely forgo women." For Thurber, the dog is not man's best friend so much as man's sole

dodgy ally in his struggle with man's strangest necessity, woman.

It's a language, and a way of talking, that seems a little alien to us now. But it's central to what Thurber is up to, and why he's up to it. The war between men and women is his subject, and the Thurber dog is, so to speak, the third body in a three-body problem that fills his work. There's the Thurber wife and the Thurber husband, and between them is the Thurber dog. The Thurber wife is certain, sighing, exasperated, and idiosyncratically knowing; it's the wife who knows that the only good diners on the highways are the ones "not at an angle to the road." The Thurber husband is daydreaming, frightened, and neurotic. The Thurber dog is between them: steadfast, melancholic, in every sense dogged, but complete in himself. When I write about food I write about hunger, M.F.K. Fisher said. When I write about dogs, I write about dignity, Thurber could have said, because dogs still have it and men do not.

We know now that the Thurber wife became the Thurber wife because of her confinement; her exasperation at the Thurber husband rises from her frustration at being only a wife. She became the Thurber wife because she could not become, as she can now, the Thurber boss; her bossiness is an expression of her being precluded from being an actual leader. The Thurber triangle is altered now. But that doesn't reduce the intensity with which it was realized, or make less moving its third angle, that of dog and man. What gets to Thurber is not so much the dog's eagerness, or the loyalty, or the bravery, or any other would-be virtue so much as the dog's inherent and ordinary dignity.

Within the world of the Thurber dog there are many different specimens and varieties. Thurber dogs worth thinking about include the Boston bull terrier Feely, whom Emma Inch, the part-time cleaning lady, carries with her in her arms wherever she goes, and the poodle who threw up in Thurber's car on her way to a dog show. Then there are the memorable dogs who filled up the cellar at 921 South Champion Avenue, only to emerge one night in "a snarling, barking yelping swirl of yellow and white, black and tan, gray and brindle as the dogs tumbled into the kitchen, skidded on the linoleum, sent the food flying from the plate, and backed Aunt Mary into a corner." But the Alpha and the Omega, the two poles of Thurber's dog lore, are dogs from his Columbus boyhood: Muggs the Airedale, portrayed in "The Dog That Bit People," and Rex the bull terrier, memorialized in one of the *New Yorker* pieces collected in this book, "Snapshot of a Dog." (Rex is actually what we now call a pit bull.) Muggs is the stubborn, stolid, unpleasant side of the nature that man and dog share, though with man now it must be kept under wraps. He bites. Rex is the noble, stoical side of that same nature. He fetches. (He fights, too, but the fighting is somehow more ritual than rage.)

Muggs, though irredeemably bad-tempered, is still an essentially benevolent presence, since it is his essence to do what he likes: "He was sorry immediately, Mother said. He was always sorry, she said, after he bit someone, but we could not understand how she figured this out. He didn't act sorry." This perfect sequence of observations marks the Thurber sound: simple to the point of bareness, they're funny because they make no effort to bridge the man/dog gap, and because they leave no simpler way with which to say what must be said. (A lesser writer might have written, "You never sensed in his behavior any regret," instead of "He didn't

act sorry.") Resolutely unsentimentalized, Muggs makes a pass at everyone, even his mother—Muggs has the simple dignity of the unpersuadable. He may be difficult, but he isn't absurd. Rex is the other side, as dumb as a post, but as resolute as one, too: "There was a nobility about him. He was big and muscular and beautifully made. He never lost his dignity even when trying to accomplish the ex-

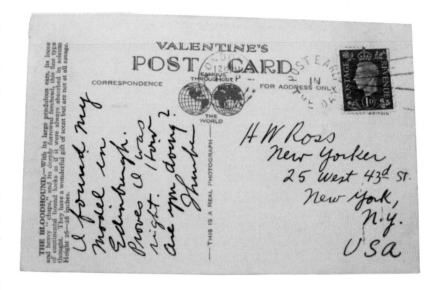

travagant tasks my brother and myself used to set for him." His readiness to do anything he's asked is what makes Rex matter:

That reminds me of the night, way after midnight, when he went a-roving in the light of the moon and brought back a small chest of drawers that he found somewhere— how far from the house nobody ever knew; since it was Rex, it could easily have been half a mile. There were no drawers in the chest when he got it home, and it wasn't a good one—he hadn't taken it out of anybody's house; it was just an old cheap piece that somebody had abandoned on a trash heap. Still, it was something he wanted, probably because it presented a nice problem in transportation. It tested his mettle. We first knew about his achievement when, deep in the night, we heard him trying to get the chest up onto the porch. It sounded as if two or three people were trying to tear the house down. We came downstairs and turned on the porch light. Rex was on the top step trying to pull the thing up, but it had caught somehow and he was just holding his own. I suppose he would have held his own till dawn if we hadn't helped him. The next day we carted the chest miles away and threw it out. If we had thrown it out in a nearby alley, he would have brought it home again, as a small token of his integrity in such matters.

Rex's story ends with one of the most moving (because so quietly done) elegiac set pieces in American writing:

Even death couldn't beat him down. He died, it is true, but only, as one of his admirers said, after "straight-arming the death angel" for more than an hour. Late one afternoon he wandered home, too slowly and uncertainly to be the Rex that had trotted briskly homeward up our avenue for ten years. I think we all knew when he came through the gate that he was dying. He had apparently taken a terrible beating, probably from the owner of some dog that he had got into a fight with. His head and body were scarred. His heavy collar with the teeth marks of many a battle on it was awry; some of the big brass studs in it were sprung loose from the leather. He licked at our hands and, staggering, fell, but got up again. We could see that he was looking for someone. One of his three masters was not home. He did not get home for an hour. During that hour the bull terrier fought against death as he had fought against the cold, strong current of Alum Creek, as he had fought to climb twelve-foot walls. When the person he was waiting for did come through the gate, whistling, ceasing to whistle, Rex walked a few wabbly paces toward him, touched his hand with his muzzle, and fell down again. This time he didn't get up.

Integrity, even grouchy growling integrity, in a world that doesn't value it; nobility in a time that doesn't want it—what Thurber's dogs do is absurd or even pernicious (they bite people, or drag junk furniture for miles) but demonstrates the necessary triumph of the superfluous. Which is what dogs are all about; it is the canine way. Nothing is less necessary than a pet dog, or more needed. Thurber's theme is that a dog's life is spent, as a man's life should be, doing pointless things that have the dignity of inner purpose.

And perhaps this is why the most memorable images of the dog that Thurber left us are contained within his wonderful, mysterious series called "The Bloodhound and the Bug." The bloodhound tracks the bug, finds the bug's hideout in a mouse hole, and then leaves the bug alone. It's not that the pleasure is in the pursuit so much that the wisdom lies in the knowing when it doesn't matter. "The best way to get along with his kind of people," Huck Finn writes about his crazy ranting father, in one of the best and wisest proto-Thurber sentences in American writing, "is to let them have their own way." The deep wisdom of permanent inaction is one Thurber's men take from their dogs. By legend, the best answer to the question of why Bodhidharma left India is a lovely non sequitur: "That cypress tree in the corner." The best answer to the question "Why did Thurber draw dogs?" may be "That fly left unmolested, over there."

# ACKNOWLEDGMENTS

This book has truly been a collective endeavor—we've depended upon the varied skills and judgment of those who point, flush, retrieve, terrier, herd, guard, or rescue. But special thanks go to Roger Angell, Michael Boland, Noah Eaker, Hannah Elnan, Adam Gopnik, Malcolm Gladwell, Whitney Johnson, Susan Kamil, Rachel Lee, Robert Mankoff, Pam McCarthy, Caitlin McKenna, Jon Michaud, Wyatt Mitchell, Françoise Mouly, Lynn Oberlander, Beth Pearson, Paolo Pepe, David Remnick, Suzanne Shaheen, Eric Simonoff, and Susan Turner. Very special thanks go to Giles Harvey, who—in addition to performing all of the foregoing functions with an unflagging nose for humor, literary excellence, and visual zest—raced over the snowy peaks of our archives with a small wooden keg of brandy around his neck. And to Henry Finder, because someone must call "*Mush!*"

# CONTRIBUTORS

JOAN ACOCELLA has written for *The New Yorker* since 1992 and became the magazine's dance critic in 1998. Her books include *Mark Morris, Willa Cather and the Politics of Criticism,* and *Twenty-eight Artists and Two Saints.*

ROGER ANGELL has been a contributor to *The New Yorker* since 1944. He became a fiction editor in 1956 and is now a senior editor and staff writer at the magazine. His books include *The Summer Game, Season Ticket,* and *Let Me Finish.*

DONALD BARTHELME (1931–1989) published 128 stories in *The New Yorker* over twenty-six years. His collection *Sixty Stories* was a PEN/Faulkner Award finalist in 1982.

VIRGINIA WOODS BELLAMY (1890–1976) contributed poems to *The New Yorker* in the 1930s and 1940s. Her books include *And the Evening and the Morning . . .*

DAVID BEZMOZGIS is the author of the collection *Natasha* and a novel, *The Free World.*

BURKHARD BILGER has been a staff writer at *The New Yorker* since 2001. He is the author of *Noodling for Flatheads,* which was a finalist for the PEN/Martha Albrand Award.

T. CORAGHESSAN BOYLE has published nine short-story collections and thirteen novels, including *Talk Talk, The Women,* and *When the Killing's Done.*

MAEVE BRENNAN (1917–1993) joined the staff of *The New Yorker* in 1949 and for many years wrote the column "The Long-Winded Lady" for the Talk of the Town. She published two volumes of short stories, most of which appeared originally in *The New Yorker.*

JOHN CHEEVER (1912–1982) sold his first story to *The New Yorker* in 1935 and was a regular contributor of fiction to the magazine until his death. His books include *The Wapshot Chronicle, The Wapshot Scandal, Bullet Park,* and *Falconer.*

RICHARD COHEN is a contributing editor at *Rolling Stone* and *Vanity Fair.* His books include *Tough Jews, Sweet and Low,* and *The Fish That Ate the Whale.*

LAUREN COLLINS has worked at *The New Yorker* since 2003 and is currently a staff writer based in England. Her subjects have included Michelle Obama, the graffiti artist Banksy, and Donatella Versace.

ROALD DAHL (1916–1990) was a novelist, short-story writer, and poet and one of the world's best-selling children's authors. His books include *James and the Giant Peach, Charlie and the Chocolate Factory, Fantastic Mr. Fox,* and *The Twits.*

DAVID DAICHES (1912–2005) was a Scottish literary critic, scholar, and poet. His books include *The Novel and the Modern World, Some Late Victorian Attitudes,* and *A Weekly Scotsman and Other Poems.*

RODDY DOYLE is an Irish novelist, dramatist, and screenwriter. His novel *The Commitments* was made into a successful film of the same name. He won the Booker Prize in 1993 for *Paddy Clarke Ha Ha Ha.*

STEPHEN DUNN won a 2001 Pulitzer Prize for poetry for *Different Hours.* His other books of poems include *Everything Else in the World, Here and Now,* and *What Goes On: Selected and New Poems 1995–2009.*

IAN FRAZIER has written humor and reported pieces for *The New Yorker* since 1974, when he published his first piece in The Talk of the Town. His books include *Dating Your Mom, Great Plains, On the Rez,* and *Travels in Siberia.*

ALEXANDRA FULLER is the author of four books of nonfiction, including *Don't Let's Go to the Dogs Tonight,* which won the Winifred Holtby Memorial Prize, and *Cocktail Hour Under the Tree of Forgetfulness.*

MARJORIE GARBER is a professor of English and Visual and Environmental Studies at Harvard University and the author of numerous books, including *Vested Interests, Dog Love, Shakespeare After All,* and *Patronizing the Arts.*

ANGELICA GIBBS (1908–1955) was a staff writer at *The New Yorker* for many years. Her short story "The Test," which originally appeared in the magazine, has been widely anthologized.

MALCOLM GLADWELL joined *The New Yorker* as a staff writer in 1996. He is the author of four bestselling books: *The Tipping Point, Blink, Outliers,* and *What the Dog Saw.*

ADAM GOPNIK has written for *The New Yorker* since 1986. He is the recipient of three National Magazine Awards and a George Polk Award for magazine reporting. His books include *Paris to the Moon, Through the Children's Gate,* and *The Table Comes First.*

JEROME GROOPMAN, a staff writer at *The New Yorker* since 1997, is the Recanati Professor of Medicine at Harvard. His books include *How Doctors Think* and *Your Medical Mind,* coauthored with Dr. Pamela Hartzband.

DONALD HALL was the United States poet laureate in 2006–2007. His books include *Without, White Apples and the Taste of Stone,* and *The Back Chamber.*

KATE JULIAN is a former managing editor of *The New Yorker* and is currently a senior editor at *The Atlantic.*

E. J. KAHN, JR. (1916–1994), began to write for *The New Yorker* in 1937 and was one of *The New Yorker*'s most prolific contributors. His subjects ranged from Coca-Cola and the world's foodstuffs to Frank Sinatra and Eleanor Roosevelt.

ERIC KONIGSBERG is the author of the book *Blood Relation*. He has contributed Talk of the Town pieces to *The New Yorker* since 1994 and began writing feature stories for the magazine in 2001.

JONATHAN LETHEM is the author of almost twenty books of fiction and nonfiction, including *The Ecstasy of Influence*, *The Fortress of Solitude*, *Chronic City*, and *Motherless Brooklyn*, which won the National Book Critics Circle Award for fiction.

A. J. LIEBLING (1904–1963) joined the staff of *The New Yorker* in 1935. During World War II he was a correspondent in Europe and Africa. After the war he wrote the magazine's "Wayward Press" column for many years. His other subjects included boxing, food, and horse racing.

ELIZABETH MACKLIN is the author of two poetry collections, *A Woman Kneeling in the Big City* and *You've Just Been Told*, and is the translator of the Basque writer Kirmen Uribe's *Meanwhile Take My Hand*.

BEN MCGRATH has been a staff writer at *The New Yorker* since 2003. He writes frequently for The Talk of the Town and also writes about sports for the magazine.

REBECCA MEAD joined *The New Yorker* as a staff writer in 1997. She has written articles on a wide range of topics, including legalized prostitution,

the spring-break business, and God-based diet programs. She is the author of *One Perfect Day*.

ARTHUR MILLER (1915–2005) was one of the most celebrated American playwrights of the twentieth century. His works include *All My Sons*, *The Crucible*, and *Death of a Salesman*, which won a Pulitzer Prize.

OGDEN NASH (1902–1971) published his first poem in *The New Yorker* in 1930, and they continued to appear in the magazine for the rest of his life. His books include *I'm a Stranger Here Myself*, *Bed Riddance*, and *Good Intentions*.

SUSAN ORLEAN began contributing articles and Talk of the Town pieces to *The New Yorker* in 1987 and became a staff writer in 1992. She is the author of *The Orchid Thief*, *The Bullfighter Checks Her Makeup*, *My Kind of Place*, and *Rin Tin Tin*.

CATHLEEN SCHINE is the author of several novels, including *Rameau's Niece*, *The Love Letter*, *She Is Me*, *The New Yorkers*, and *The Three Weissmanns of Westport*.

ANNE SEXTON (1928–1974) was an American poet. Her books include *To Bedlam and Part Way Back*, *The Awful Rowing Toward God*, and *Live or Die*, which won a Pulitzer Prize.

JIM SHEPARD is a novelist and short story writer. His collection *Like You'd Understand, Anyway* won the Story Prize and was nominated for the National Book Award. His other books include *Project X* and *You Think That's Bad*.

CHARLES SIMIC is a poet, essayist, and translator and served as the United States poet laureate in 2007–2008. His books include *My Noiseless En-*

*tourage, That Little Something,* and *Master of Disguises.*

DAVE SMITH is an American poet, novelist, and critic whose books include *Hunting Men, The Wick of Memory, Hawks on Wires,* and *Little Boats, Unsalvaged.* He is the co-editor of *Afield: American Writers on Bird Dogs.*

RUTH STONE (1915–2011) was the author of many books of poetry, including *In the Dark, Ordinary Words,* and *What Love Comes To.*

MARK STRAND was the United States poet laureate in 1990–1991. His books include *Blizzard of One, Man and Camel,* and *Almost Invisible.*

WISLAWA SZYMBORSKA (1923–2012) was a Polish poet and the winner of the 1996 Nobel Prize in Literature. Her books include *Here, People on a Bridge,* and *View with a Grain of Sand.*

DOROTHEA TANNING (1910–2012) was an American artist and writer. Her books include *Between Lives, A Table of Content,* and *Coming to That.*

JAMES TATE is an American poet. His collection *Worshipful Company of Fletchers* won a National Book Award and his *Selected Poems* won a Pulitzer Prize.

JAMES THURBER (1894–1961) joined *The New Yorker* in 1927 as an editor and writer; his idiosyncratic cartoons began to appear there four years later. His books include two children's classics—*The 13 Clocks* and *The Wonderful O*—and an autobiography, *My Life and Hard Times.*

CALVIN TOMKINS has been a staff writer for *The New Yorker* since 1960. His books include *The Bride and the Bachelors, Living Well Is the Best Revenge,* and *Lives of the Artists.*

JEFFREY TOOBIN has been a staff writer for *The New Yorker* since 1993. His books include *The Oath, The Nine, A Vast Conspiracy, The Run of His Life,* and *Too Close to Call.*

GEORGE W. S. TROW (1943–2006) first wrote for *The New Yorker* in 1966 and co-founded *National Lampoon* in 1970. He is the author of a novel, *The City in the Mist,* and a collection of satirical short stories, *Bullies.*

JOHN UPDIKE (1932–2009) contributed fiction, poetry, essays, and criticism to *The New Yorker* for half a century. He published twenty-three novels, including the Pulitzer Prize–winning *Rabbit Is Rich* and *Rabbit at Rest,* seventeen books of short stories, eight collections of poetry, five children's books, a memoir, and a play.

MONA VAN DUYN (1921–2004) was an American poet. Her books include *To See, to Take,* which won a National Book Award, and *Near Changes,* which won a Pulitzer Prize. She was the United States poet laureate in 1992–1993.

STEPHANIE VAUGHN is the author of the short-story collection *Sweet Talk.* She teaches creative writing at Cornell University.

E. B. WHITE (1899–1985) joined the staff of *The New Yorker* in 1927. He wrote the children's classics *Stuart Little, Charlotte's Web,* and *The Trumpet of the Swan.* He received the Presidential Medal of Freedom in 1963 and was awarded an honorary Pulitzer Prize in 1978 for his work as a whole.

CALLAN WINK received his MFA from the University of Wyoming and is completing a novel, *Beartooth*.

ALEXANDER WOOLLCOTT (1887–1943) joined *The New York Times* in 1909 and was a feared and famous drama critic there from 1914 to 1922. A central figure at the Algonquin Round Table in the 1920s, he was one of the first contributors to *The New Yorker*.

KEVIN YOUNG is the author of several books of poetry, including *Most Way Home, For the Confederate Dead*, and *Ardency*.

*"It's very gratifying, but there's a lot of responsibility that goes along with it."*

# ILLUSTRATION CREDITS

94–95: Martin Schoeller

103: Landon Nordeman

108: John Sann

118: Jules Feiffer

125: Mark Ulriksen

138: Typescript drafts of "Tennis Ball" by Donald Hall reproduced courtesy of the author and the Milne Special Collections, University of New Hampshire Library.

142: Typescript of "Chablis" by Donald Barthelme, Donald Barthelme Literary Papers, Special Collections, University of Houston Libraries. Copyright © 1983 by Donald Barthelme (The Wylie Agency LLC).

145: Hermina Selz

149: Helene E. Hokinson

161: Ana Juan

162–63: Valerie Shaff

164: James Thurber

168: Getty Images, Inc.

173: Getty Images, Inc.

187: Peter Arno

188: Splash News

197: Mark Ulriksen

206: Constantin Alajalov

210: Elliott Erwitt/Magnum Photos

219: Manuscript and typescript drafts of "The Unruly Thoughts of the Dog Trainer's Lover" by Elizabeth Macklin reproduced courtesy of the author.

222: Ward Schumaker

224: Typescript of "Monologue of a Dog Ensnared in History" by Wislawa Szymborska reproduced courtesy of the the Wislawa Szymborska Foundation.

229: William Wegman, *Ray Cat* (1978)

233: Galley page of "Dogology" by T. Coraghessan Boyle

236: Eric Drooker

248: Mark Ulriksen

254–55: Manuscript page from "Dog Race" by Roald Dahl © RDNL. Courtesy of The Roald Dahl Museum and Story Centre.

265: Barry Blitt

278: Illustration by James Thurber of "The Departure of Emma Inch" from *The Middle-Aged Man on the Flying Trapeze*. Copyright © 1935 by Rosemary A. Thurber. Reprinted by arrangement with Rosemary A. Thurber and The Barbara Hogenson Agency. All rights reserved.

284: Landon Nordeman

289: William Steig

292: Photograph by Jacques Henri Lartigue © Ministère de la Culture—France/A.A.J.H.L.

296: Peter de Sève

309: John Cuneo

314: Typescript pages from "The Dog" by Roddy Doyle reprinted courtesy of the author and the National Library of Ireland.

318: Maira Kalman

324: Typescript of "Line and Tree" by A. J. Liebling reproduced courtesy of the Estate of A. J. Liebling and the Division of Rare and Manuscript Collections, Cornell University Library. Copyright © 1949 by A. J. Liebling (The Wylie Agency LLC).

337: Peter Arno

380: James Thurber

382, 383: James Thurber postcard to Harold Ross reproduced courtesy of Rosemary A. Thurber and New Yorker Records, Manuscripts and Archives Division, The New York Public Library, Astor, Lenox and Tilden Foundations.

Cartoons by Charles Addams (20, 247, 287), Peter Arno (377), Charles Barsotti (52, 70, 143, 323, 341, 371), Harry Bliss (121, 244), George Booth (viii, 72, 126, 371), David Borchart (195), Roz Chast (115, 352), Tom Cheney (177), Leo Cullum (122, 158, 192, 202, 275, 359), Chon Day (299), Robert Day (30), Edward Frascino (39), Alex Gregory (98, 302, 358), J. B. Handelsman (306), Pete Holmes (174), Bruce Eric Kaplan (130, 205, 374), Anatol Kovarsky (56), Arnie Levin (17, 214), Eric Lewis (262), Lee Lorenz (241, 342), Robert Mankoff (378), Michael Maslin (290), Warren Miller (276), Paul Noth (368), John O'Brien (257), Mischa Richter (391), Victoria Roberts (320), Al Ross (213), Danny Shanahan (44, 104, 150, 258, 295, 306, 312, 355), Bernard Schoenbaum (332), David Sipress (331), Otto Soglow (23), Saul Steinberg (14, 160), Peter Steiner (135, 272), Mick Stevens (xi), James Thurber (78, 167, 281), Tom Toro (307), Mike Twohy (155, 316), Robert Weber (10–11, 334), Bill Woodman (269), Jack Ziegler (191, 266)

Spot art by Tom Bachtell, Charles Barsotti, Abe Birnbaum, George Booth, Devera Ehrenberg, Ian Falconer, Lee Lorenz, Daniel Maja, Mariscal, Eugene Mihaesco, Emmanuel Pierre, Ronald Searle, Otto Soglow, Ralph Steadman, James Thurber, Philippe Weisbecker.